Palgrave Studies in Citizenship Transitions

Series editors

Michele Michiletti is Lars Hierta Chair of Political Science at Stockholm University, Sweden. **Ludvig Beckman** is Professor of Political Science, Stockholm University, Sweden. **David Owen** is Professor of Social and Political Philosophy, University of Southampton, UK.

The Editorial Board: **Keith Banting** (Queen's University, Canada), **Rainer Baubock** (European University Institute, Italy), **Russell Dalton** (University of California at Irving, USA), **Avigail Eisenberg** (University of Victoria, Canada), **Nancy Fraser** (The New School for Social Research, USA), **David Jacobson** (University of South Florida, USA) and **Ariadne Vromen** (The University of Sydney, Australia).

This series focuses on citizenship transitions encompassing contemporary transformations of citizenship as institution, status, and practice as well as normative and explanatory analysis of these transformations and their cultural, social, economic, and political implications. The series bridges theoretical and empirical debates on democracy, transnationalism, and citizenship that have been too insulated from each other. It takes citizenship transitions as its starting point and studies the status, role, and function of citizenship within contemporary democratic systems and multi-layered governance structures beyond the state. It aims to add a broader array of critical, conceptual, normative, and empirical perspectives on the borders, territories, and political agents of citizenship. It scrutinizes the possibilities and challenges of citizenship in light of present broad processes of political fragmentation and pluralization and the ways emerging ideals and expectations of citizenship are inspired by new social, political, and environmental movements. Its cross-disciplinary approach intends to capture the transitions of citizenship from an apparently simple relation between the state and its citizens into a cluster of complex responsibility claims and practices that raise questions concerning citizenship borders and obligations, the public-private scope of citizenship, and even how political actors attempt to and in fact avoid citizenship.

Titles in the series include:

Palgrave Studies In Citizenship Transitions series
Series Standing Order ISBN 978–1–137–33137–3

You can receive future titles in this series as they are published by placing a standing order. Please contact your bookseller or, in case of difficulty, write to us at the address below with your name and address, the title of the series and the ISBNs quoted above.

Customer Services Department, Macmillan Distribution Ltd, Houndmills, Basingstoke, Hampshire RG21 6XS, England

Citizenship after Orientalism

Transforming Political Theory

Edited by
Engin Isin

palgrave
macmillan

First published 2015 by
PALGRAVE MACMILLAN

Palgrave Macmillan in the UK is an imprint of Macmillan Publishers Limited,
registered in England, company number 785998, of Houndmills, Basingstoke,
Hampshire RG21 6XS.

Palgrave Macmillan in the US is a division of St Martin's Press LLC,
175 Fifth Avenue, New York, NY 10010.

Palgrave Macmillan is the global academic imprint of the above companies and has
companies and representatives throughout the world.

Palgrave® and Macmillan® are registered trademarks in the United States,
the United Kingdom, Europe and other countries.

ISBN: 978–1–137–47949–5

This book is printed on paper suitable for recycling and made from fully
managed and sustained forest sources. Logging, pulping and manufacturing
processes are expected to conform to the environmental regulations of the
country of origin.

A catalogue record for this book is available from the British Library.

A catalog record for this book is available from the Library of Congress.

Contents

Preface and Acknowledgements

There is a strong sense today that the world we have come to inhabit is on the cusp of profound transformations. Using one of Michel Foucault's favourite phrases, at least in English translation, 'societies like ours' – by which he meant Western and Christian societies, based as they are on the sovereignty of the nation-state and its inventions of liberty, solidarity, and equality, if not citizenship and democracy – are contested both from within and outside their borders. If we refer to these 'societies' more specifically as 'Euro-American', we can understand why the talk of the rise of China, India, and other societies is so unsettling. In this world of sovereign states, divided into seemingly discrete societies such as 'ours' and 'theirs', we may wonder how it has come to be that 'our' societies see themselves as somehow independent of 'theirs'. How is it that struggles in Israel and Palestine, Syria, Egypt, Libya, Sudan, Yemen, not to mention in Afghanistan and Iraq or Venezuela, Argentina, or Brazil are seen as isolated, unrelated, and far from our societies? How can we imagine that the societies of Euro-America developed independently when the scramble for colonies – a phrase from the late nineteenth century when European powers such as Belgium, France, Germany, Italy, Portugal, Spain, and Great Britain sought expansion – is now joined by a new scramble to protect and secure the borders of Western and Christian societies?

We do not as yet and we may never have a dominant narrative about these transformations. However we interpret them, our narratives will reflect the grounds from which we speak – meaning, we speak from both a geographic location but also a social, cultural, and economic position. To put it another way, there is no singular or comprehensive *perspective* from which we can see these transformations. The world is experienced very differently from Beijing, Caracas, Kiev, London, Paris, or Ramallah. That is perhaps why Foucault was always concerned with designating the scope of his studies as 'societies such as ours' or 'Western and Christian societies'. Foucault's caution was well intended yet inevitably misfired. Foucault would have or should have known that delimiting 'ours' was simultaneously and inescapably creating a relation to 'theirs'. *It was all very well to focus on societies such as ours, but what if societies such as ours were made out of 'societies such as theirs'?* The place of societies such as ours in the world without relations to societies such as theirs can no longer be simply put as a matter of delimiting the scope of our analysis. Rather, rethinking them together in their relations has become an urgent scholarly task.

Arguably, this scholarly task was begun with Edward Said's *Orientalism* (1978) and continued apace with the development of postcolonial studies. We have now a rigorous literature on orientalism, colonialism, and imperialism, and the ways in which societies like ours have been implicated in societies like theirs. Of course, I am aware that I am now using 'ours' and 'theirs' only playfully since the studies of interwoven trajectories and lineages of societies have demonstrated that these are performative statements rather than constative descriptions. In other words, we are now in a situation where as critical scholars we can no longer assume that we can study liberty, solidarity, and equality if not citizenship and democracy as though they developed independently in societies such as ours with no relations of domination and oppression to societies such as theirs.

Yet, and curiously, although various concepts of political theory such as democracy, the state, liberty, and even fraternity have been subjected to postcolonial critique, citizenship has not received the same attention. To put it differently, political theories of citizenship proceed either with the assumption that societies like theirs did not develop citizenship or that societies like ours were the first to develop it. This book is an invitation to think differently about this assumption and attend to the interwoven trajectories and lineages out of which citizenship has been constructed as a living political concept and as political subjectivity.

Between January 2010 and April 2015, six postdoctoral researchers, two visiting postdoctoral fellows, and three PhD students have conducted research on the vexed relationship between citizenship and orientalism at the Open University as part of the Citizenship after Orientalism (Oecumene) project. They explored ways of rearticulating or reimagining this relationship. Drawing upon this research, these chapters present a critique of citizenship as exclusively and even originally a European institution. These chapters document research that provides a glimpse of how we might (and must) *begin* to think differently about citizenship as political subjectivity. They engage this task from different but intersecting vantage points. One vantage point is, of course, critique. Some chapters demonstrate how our dominant political imaginary masks or conceals that there are different political subjectivities and that these differences cannot be merely placed on a spectrum of relative superiority and inferiority. Another vantage point is to illustrate what these differences are and bring them into our political imaginary. Finally, another vantage point is to cultivate a different political imaginary with which these differences are understood.

Citizenship after Orientalism: Transforming Political Theory explores these vantage points not with reference to the dominant figure of the citizen and its orientalizing perspective but as a challenge to them. The project's name, 'Oecumene', plays on the unstable etymology of the word, which originally meant the inhabited world, separating it from 'another' world in ancient Greece. It then acquired a meaning that included other 'worlds', finally standing for the 'whole' world. Its adoption is a playful resignification of this ambiguity concerning what exactly 'oecumene' refers to.

The thread that binds these diverse chapters is precisely performing political theory in a world without Europe at its centre. But it is not a world without Europe as such. It is impossible to speak from nowhere (that is without a perspective), and we, the members of this project, are 'located' in Europe. But we are speaking from Europe through a political theory against frontiers, if you like: that is, without creating boundaries as a series of presences and absences of political subjectivity between Europe and its others or 'societies such as ours' and 'societies such as theirs'. Instead, we are investigating citizenship as political subjectivity, the ways in which people make themselves political subjects.

A project such as this, including the present book, accumulates debts that go beyond accounting but some of which it is possible to name. I am truly grateful to my research fellows and research students not only for skilfully undertaking research under principles that I originally set out but also for creatively resignifying these principles and giving variously different and genuinely imaginative inflections on what it might mean to explore citizenship after orientalism. Although their names grace the book as chapter authors, I would like to name them here all together: Tara Atluri, Iker Barbero, Deena Dajani, Jack Harrington, Aya Ikegame, Alessandra Marino, Andrea Mura, Zaki Nahaboo, Lisa Pilgram, Leticia Sabsay, and Dana Rubin.

Five people played very special roles during the project. Anne Paynter and Radha Ray were project secretaries. Their commitment and dedication to the project, the humanity with which they handled the many problems that such a project inevitably occasions, and the great humour that they brought into play were truly gifts to the project. Lisa Pilgram was not only a researcher as a PhD student but also took on the massive task of managing the project. Her professionalism and efficiency were matched only by her sensible, reflexive, and flexible manner. Niccolò Milanese played a significant role in liaising with the European Commission and its various institutions, skilfully embedding research results in its cultures of communication. Amandine Scherrer translated many of our activities into legible narratives that made sense to people outside the project.

I would like to thank Michael Saward as the head of the Department of Politics and International Studies (POLIS) and Jef Huysmans as the director of the Centre for Citizenship, Identities, and Governance (CCIG) at the Open University for their support throughout the project. And, more broadly speaking, the Open University was an exceptionally organized and embracing host for the project.

I am grateful to the advisory board members Vikki Bell, John Clarke, Roberto Dainotto, Rada Ivekovic, Fuat Keyman, Sumi Madhok, Sandro Mezzadra, Parvati Nair, Nalini Persram, Raia Prokhovnik, Ranabir Samaddar, Michael Saward, Sanjay Seth, Yasemin Soysal, Kath Woodward, and Meyda Yeğenoğlu, who in various stages of the project provided critical commentaries on our collective research by participating in different events we organized. The visiting research fellows Sarah Bracke, Mubi Brighenti, Iain Chambers, Jacob Copeman, Lidia Curti, Agnes Czajka, Elsa Dorlin, Nacira Guénif, Jordi Moreras,

Elena Ostanel, Teresa Pullano, Enrica Rigo, and Edward Ziter made a major contribution to the project by bringing their knowledge and expertise of areas beyond our competence to bear critically on the research we undertook. I would also like to thank Zahra Albarazi, Raghda Butros, Brendan Donegan, Tidita Fshazi, Ashraf Milad, Cynthia Morel, and Laura van Waas, who brought activist perspectives to bear on our collective research. I would like to sincerely thank especially Rosi Braidotti, Melissa Butcher, Ranabir Samaddar, and Vron Ware, who joined our workshops and engaged with our theoretical and political questions with lectures and seminars.

I would like to thank the hundreds of delegates, participants, commentators, discussants, and inquirers who graced the many events that we organized and provided their critical insights on many aspects of our research; their contributions served to challenge, if not wholly destabilize, our assumptions. I would like to especially extend my thanks to the keynote speakers Judith Butler, Costas Douzinas, Paul Gilroy, David Harvey, Saba Mahmood, and Walter Mignolo, who continued to engage with our research not only during the events in which they participated but also long after.

I would also like to thank our collaborators on two research trips to Guangzhou and Rome. At Sun Yat-Sen University, Zhonghua Guo, Taihui Guo, and Xia Ying were exceptional hosts who entered into dialogue with the project with huge enthusiasm and engagement. At Teatro Valle, Dario Gentili, Chiara Belingardi, Ilenia Caleo, Federica Giardini, and Isabella Pinto were formidable intellectual inquisitors, whose activities were equally inspiring. Andrea Mura was a tireless and creative intellectual organizer of our research trip to Rome.

I am especially grateful to Jack Harrington, who played various roles during this project. He joined the project with a remit to organize its relations with groups outside the university, quickly moved to develop a research programme on imperial citizenship that has had a significant influence on the project as a whole, and eventually became a de facto co-editor of the present book.

I would like to extend special thanks to the editors of *Palgrave Studies in Citizenship Transitions*, Michele Micheletti, Ludvig Beckman, and especially David Owen, who proposed the idea, for their excellent editorial guidance and counsel. I am grateful to Eleanor Davey Corrigan and Hannah Kašpar at Palgrave both for their editorial judgement and for making working together a genuine pleasure.

I acknowledge that the research leading to this book was supported by funding from the European Research Council (ERC) Advanced Research Grant 249379 entitled Citizenship After Orientalism (Oecumene).

This project would not have come into being if not for the unconditional gift of Evelyn Ruppert, who subsequently provided the impetus I needed to summon up, conspire, and conjure with to pursue it – all without indebtedness.

List of Contributors

Tara Atluri's postdoctoral research was funded by the Social Sciences and Humanities Research Council of Canada (SSHRC).

Iker Barbero is a lecturer in the Department of Administrative and Constitutional Law and Philosophy of Law in the Faculty of Law of the University of the Basque Country.

Deena Dajani is based in London and works as a consultant on education-related projects.

Jack Harrington is based in the Research Division of the London School of Economics and Political Science, UK.

Aya Ikegame is an associate professor at the Institute for Advanced Studies on Asia, the University of Tokyo, Japan.

Engin Isin is Professor of Politics in the Department of Politics and International Studies (POLIS) at The Open University, UK.

Alessandra Marino is a researcher based at The Open University, UK.

Andrea Mura is Lecturer in Middle East Politics and Political Thought at the Institute of Arab and Islamic Studies at the University of Exeter, UK.

Zaki Nahaboo is Lecturer in Society and Culture at INTO City University, UK.

Lisa Pilgram is Senior Project Manager in the Research Office and a PhD student in the Department of Politics and International Studies (POLIS) at The Open University, UK.

Dana Rubin is a PhD student in the Department of Politics and International Studies (POLIS) at The Open University, UK.

Leticia Sabsay is an assistant professor of Gender and Contemporary Culture at the LSE Gender Institute, London School of Economics and Political Science, UK.

1
Transforming Political Theory

Engin F. Isin

Abstract

This chapter lays out a perspective on the research project that produced the 12 chapters presented in this book. How to perform political theory after the postcolonial critique, and in doing so contribute to the decentring of Euro-American political theory, is a question that troubles many scholars today. This chapter argues that a performative political theory must not only attend to the origins but also the workings of institutions by studying how both political theorists and political theories are embedded in them. The book is a response to the question of how to perform political theory by taking one essential institution – citizenship – and focusing on its workings.

Introduction

This book presents critical perspectives on citizenship and its uses in political theory. 'Citizenship' is amongst the most important concepts of political theory. This is partly because both as a legal status and social practice citizenship has been an essential aspect of political modernity at least since the American and French revolutions.[1] The word 'citizen' evokes a particular legacy that is inexorably associated with 'European' values that are seen to define Euro-American states especially. These include secularism, democracy, law, and rights.[2] However, since 1945, these very values have been increasingly placed under question from various perspectives, so much so that to call them solely European values or to assert that Europe has fulfilled their promise is to encounter scepticism. The influence of works by J. M. Blaut, Jack Goody, and Patrick Chabal among others has steadily contributed to this scepticism.[3]

  This scepticism is part of a broader shift that concerns the place of Europe in the world. For centuries, Europe has asserted its place at the centre of the world – both geographically (as represented by cartography) and historically (as principally represented by historiography). Arguably, and as Walter Mignolo has shown, this has been the case since that period which is called the 'renaissance' or rebirth, or at least since the modern experiences of colonization and imperialism, which were certainly a part of the renaissance, or

1

perhaps its dark side. Europe, and later its expanded image 'the West', has come to dominate how the world is seen if not made. It has been argued that despite all the resistance or protest against it, Europe placed itself in the centre of the world in more ways than one. And now there is a strong sense that it can no longer do so – or be able to do so – at least without stronger and more persistent resistance against such placement. Europe (and the West) may no longer remain at the centre of the world. As both Dipesh Chakrabarty and Walter Mignolo have illustrated, the consequences of this displacement, provincializing, and decentring are profound.[4] Their work and that of the first generation of scholars on postcolonial theory have signalled that an era is passing – that of Euro-American empire. The so-called turn to empire or the imperial turn – meaning the resurgence of critical studies on imperialism and colonialism – is yet another signal. So are attempts to reassert the vitality or superiority of Euro-America.[5] Yet, far more palpably than in the last decade, we are now living through the consequences of the decentring or provincializing of Euro-America.

One of the consequences of postcolonial critique and its project of decentring Euro-America has been the need to question political theory that aims to grasp (and shape) norms, laws, and practices through which power is exercised. If 'political theory', with its primary concepts such as power, state, law, justice, and citizenship, is not only performed by canonical thinkers such as Niccolò Machiavelli or John Rawls but also by those who have political lives, we must ask what kind of activity is political theory. A distinction suggested by Michael Freeden is useful to broaden the remit of political theory.[6] For Freeden, the study of political thinking or thought involves two dimensions. First, it involves investigating political thinking in actually existing practices, situations, and institutions. The focus here is to investigate how thought is deployed in concrete instances geared toward achieving specific objectives (and exercising power), whether these are consciously articulated (and articulable) or not. Second, it also involves studying thinking about politics embedded in ideational configurations. The focus here is thought that is geared toward achieving policies, programmes, visions, arrangements, rules, and entities that function as contested and contestable ideational or ideological configurations. For Freeden, thinking politically is different from thinking about politics. Often the latter is considered as the proper domain of political theory, and if the former comes into view it functions as rarely more than a 'background' or 'context'. Yet, the two dimensions of studying political thought are interrelated and complement each other for a critical and reflective political theory. The important aspect of this distinction is to recognize that while *all* subjects engage in political thinking, thinking about politics is open to *only* those subjects whose authority (status and position) allow them to engage in production of language broadly defined as all aural, visual, or textual speech acts concerning politics. These are ideological configurations not in the sense of distorted representations of realities but in the sense of being constitutive elements of the making of realities. So not only is political theory something that canonical political thinkers perform but their performance of political theory is embedded in practical settings and arrangements of politics.[7]

This broadened understanding of political theory is crucial if we are to appreciate the radical intervention by postcolonial theory in demonstrating how colonialism and imperialism operated in both dimensions of political theory. Classic if not clichéd illustrations are that John Locke was not only the author of *Two Treatises of Government* (1680) but also a helping hand in drafting a colonial constitution and that John Stuart Mill was not only the author of *Considerations on Representative Government* (1861) but an officer of the East India Company.[8] The point is that political theory is a speech act proper: it does not merely describe the world, it is also in it and by saying something about that world brings it into being.[9] The contributions to this book are animated by a performative understanding of political theory. They aim to shift attention from a political theory that features canonical authors (from Aristotle to Žižek) to a political theory embedded in how people perform politics in and by saying things political.

Once we shift our focus from canonical political theory to performative political theory, we recognize that Europe not only stamped its authority on how and by whom political theory was performed since the renaissance but also made political theory perform Europe, or the West, as centred, that is, placed at the geographic and historical centre of the world. It is not an exaggerated claim that political theory was amongst the most powerful mechanisms by which Europe has sustained its centrality. One of the major contributions of postcolonial theory, which took European political theory and its assumptions, approaches, and concepts to task, was precisely this point.[10] And, postcolonial theory would have been unthinkable without Edward Said's intervention with *Orientalism* (1978). Said highlighted that one of the strategies by which political theory – again performatively understood since Said's primary focus was art – centred Europe was by distinguishing itself from other 'cultures' through a series of presences and absences. Europe was the space of presence of such things as capitalism, law, science, medicine, and labour and of concepts or processes such as rationality, the state, secularism, and bureaucracy. When Said critically intervened in the debate over how a divide was opened between ostensibly independently existing civilizations or cultures – between the West and the East (or the Occident and the Orient) – his specific concern was with representations of the Orient in Western art, especially literature. This was neither surprising nor a problem, Said being, in his own words, '… by training and practice a teacher of the mainly European and American humanities, a specialist in modern comparative literature'.[11] Orientalism in governmental, legal, sociological, and political discourses was not Said's main concern. True, he remarks that orientalism functioned as a 'type' – an analytical device in the social sciences – and that by using orientalism as a type, 'Weber's studies of Protestantism, Judaism, and Buddhism blew him (perhaps unwittingly) into the very territory originally charted and claimed by the Orientalists'.[12] But Said never explained what he meant by Weber being blown into a territory originally charted by orientalists except further remarking that Weber '... found encouragement amongst all those nineteenth-century thinkers who believed that there was a sort of ontological difference between Eastern and Western economic (as well as religious) "mentalities"'.[13] Said then referred the reader to Maxime Rodinson's *Islam and Capitalism* 'for a sustained proof of Weber's total inaccuracy'.[14] Said appears to have held a view of orientalism in which the role of the social sciences in general and political theory in particular in constructing the Orient seems derivative. When Said broadened his critique in *Culture and Imperialism* (1994) and located orientalism as part of imperialism, his focus still remained broadly 'culture'.[15]

It is only recently that the debate on orientalism began challenging this derivative view of orientalism in political theory and documented how political thought was in the forefront of the emergence and development of orientalism in colonial and imperial discourse.[16] As a result, the orientalist workings of such political concepts as the state, democracy, rule of law, and citizenship came under renewed postcolonial critique. This book is a contribution to our understanding of the orientalist workings of citizenship as a political concept emerging out of colonial and imperial experience.

In Euro-American political theory, a significant presence and absence that came to be associated exclusively with Europe was the concept of 'citizenship'. European colonial and imperial projects proceeded with assumptions that understood colonial subjects as not only without history but also without political subjectivity.[17] In other words, the ways in which people occupy political positions by claiming a right, if not *the* right, to have rights were seen to be inimical to the supposedly limited political capacities of subject peoples. This was the most poignant observation made by pioneering critics such as Aimé Césaire, Frantz Fanon, and Albert Memmi.[18]

Yet, despite the enourmous influence of postcolonial theory on studies concerning decolonization, colonialism, and imperialism, in citizenship studies there has been scarcely any sustained analysis or debate on the orientalist, colonialist, and imperial prefiguration of citizenship; how a transformed political theory would refigure it; what sources it would draw from; and what methods it would deploy. With the exception of notable but very recent studies on the prefiguration and figuration of citizenship outside Euro-America, in political theory this work has barely begun.[19]

This book contributes to the task of decolonizing citizenship in political theory. It clearly comes out of and contributes to a conversation concerning the postcolonial condition in general and the question of politics of citizenship in a world where Euro-America is no longer the epicentre of political and social thought. From this vantage point, it speaks to Hui Wang's *The Politics of Imagining Asia* and Walter Mignolo's *The Darker Side of Western Modernity*.[20] It also speaks to concerns about the legacies of empire such as Pankaj Mishra's *From the Ruins of Empire*.[21] It engages new literature on orientalism such as Daniel Vukovich's *China and Orientalism*.[22] It also participates in the debate over legal and imperial orientalism in works such as Teemu Ruskola's *Legal Orientalism,* Turan Kayaoğlu's *Legal Imperialism,* and Laura Benton's *A Search for Sovereignty.*[23] It also speaks to Nalini Persram's *Postcolonialism and Political Theory* and É. Balibar's *We, the People of Europe?.*[24] It also enters into conversation with emerging non-Western studies of citizenship such as Niraja Gopal Jayal's *Citizenship and Its Discontents,* Sukanya Banerjee's *Becoming Imperial Citizens,* and Joshua Folge and Peter Zarrow's *Imagining the People.*[25]

To avoid misunderstanding, it seems necessary to emphasize that this book is not merely about non-European or non-Western conceptions and practices of citizenship. It is a critique of how Euro-American workings of citizenship perform political theory by dividing practices – creating divisions or binaries between normal and abnormal, man and woman, white and black, West and East, and so on. While critical studies are beginning to change our understanding of political theory and its performativity, critique of citizenship in Euro-American democracies over the last two decades has demonstrated that the abstract and ostensibly universal and secular figure of the citizen was in fact a projection of a male, propertied, white, heterosexual, able-bodied, generally Christian figure.[26] More significantly, this critique raised doubts about the strategy of progressively including subaltern figures such as women, blacks, queers, Muslims, and eventually non-Westerners into that figure through sexual citizenship, multicultural citizenship, or indigenous citizenship. Although it provided openings, such representation has also meant that subaltern figures could appear only in terms of the qualities of the dominant figure of the citizen. It has also meant that the logic of citizenship as a dividing practice remained intact – there would always be new social groups defined by their supposed ineligibility to be considered citizens in the societies in which they lived. Thus, subaltern figures appeared only insofar as they become subjects of integration, security, and border regimes. In other words, alternatives to orientalist and imperialist conceptions of citizenship proved much harder to develop than anticipated.

Citizenship after Orientalism: Transforming Political Theory contributes to this task by exploring acts and practices of those who constitute themselves as political subjects not in terms of the dominant figure of the citizen and its orientalizing perspective but as a challenge to them. The chapters presented here draw on a project that conducted research between 2010 and 2015 that explored ways of rearticulating or reimagining the relationship between citizenship, orientalism, colonialism, and imperialism. The chapters present critical perspectives on citizenship as an exclusive European value by considering how we might (and must) begin to think differently about citizenship as political subjectivity. They engage this task from different but intersecting perspectives, which can usefully be grouped under the categories 'undoing', 'uncovering', and 'refiguring' citizenship, and these three types of approach have been a major innovation of the project.

The chapters in Part I, 'undoing citizenship', aim to take apart the assumptions that hold together the contemporary figure of citizenship by asking comparative but unorthodox questions. Leticia Sabsay, for example, asks how the conditions of freedom (rather than being universal) vary with choices that subjects are invited to make. She illustrates how political agency is denied to those who make undesirable choices and how this logic is implicit in orientalism. Sabsay's intervention demonstrates how performing autonomy reinforces or generates dividing practices. Andrea Mura illustrates how an economy of anxiety that has been originally introduced in emerging economies is now being mobilized in Euro-American economies. For the subjects of government in Europe, the regulation of desire shifts from an injunction of pleasure to the restraint of excess. But this regime of austerity induces a peculiar crisis in European values reconfiguring Europe's relationship to other peoples. Jack Harrington shows that the imperial idea of citizenship had an indelible impact on the very idea of citizenship in Europe, so much so that they cannot be considered separately. He does this by focusing on the period between the 1830s and 1940s, comparing the imperial subject that emerged under British policies in India with French imperial policies for conferring and withholding the rights of the citizen to Muslim, Jewish, and 'secular' Christian subjects in Algeria. Dana Rubin illustrates the fragile threads of the project of creating a modern Israeli state and how this project is both supported yet endangered by those whose identities don't quite fit with the Zionist image of the modern state and its homogenous citizenship. What the chapters in Part I accomplish is not an intentional dismantling of citizenship that 'undoing' might imply. Rather, these chapters illustrate the fragile if not shaky foundations on which citizenship is grounded and how citizenship in 'Western' political theory already contains the seeds of its own undoing.

The chapters in Part II are more attuned to revealing incipient but also enduring practices through which subjects make themselves into political beings that otherwise would not have been legible from orientalist perspectives of understanding political subjectivities. Aya Ikegame, for example, illustrates how gurus perform sovereign practices that generate possibilities for people to bring themselves into public spaces as political subjects. By illustrating alternative legal practices of guru-sovereigns and the kinds of citizenship that they give rise to, Ikegame brings to our attention practices that would have been seen as merely 'religious'. Iker Barbero focuses on a relatively unknown episode in Barcelona when Pakistani and Indian migrants were detained for their alleged involvement in terrorism. What Barbero illustrates is how this episode then brought women, youth, and children to forge and claim political subjectivities that were hardly legible not only before but also since then. The episode, as recounted by Barbero, reveals how orientalism effectively works as a strategy in contemporary Europe to suppress and delegitimize Muslim migrants. Zaki Nahaboo identifies how practices of defining and defending multicultural society have resulted in orientalist expressions of citizenship.

Nahaboo uncovers this through a party political campaign, a contemporary TV show and an anti-war protest. They each prescribe routes for contesting racial hierarchies that paradoxically enable orientalism and 'the multicultural' to function as a linchpin for state racism. By demonstrating this, Nahaboo argues that we need to be more attentive to how citizens' deployment of anti-essentialist discourse can revitalise and legitimate contemporary state racism. Lisa Pilgram also focuses on the seemingly everyday practices of Muslim citizens in the UK in negotiating their family affairs, whether it is marriage, divorce, or inheritance. Pilgram argues that such everyday practices give rise to a market for legal services in family law and produce what she calls a hybrid Muslim and British family law. This field of practice enables certain subjects to take up positions where they think of themselves as entitled to make choices and claim certain rights. Pilgram says that we don't yet know the consequences of this incipient field and the subjects it produces, but we should not mislead ourselves to think that because they are mundane they must be insignificant.

The focus of Part III shifts from undoing and uncovering citizenship to refiguring it – or, rather, practices that outline new forms of citizenship, indicate new subjects that are coming into being, and new performative acts that bring them into being. Through the use of speech-act theory, Alessandra Marino gives an account of the less well-known practices of two rather well-known Indian woman writers, Arundhati Roy and Mahasweta Devi. She illustrates that both authors perform a kind of citizenship through acts of writing. Or, rather, writing for these women became an act through which they have articulated not simply 'their own' rights but the rights of others whose claims to political subjectivity they take seriously. Writing is an act not simply because it performs politics but also performs it differently. Their writing, brimming with exuberant political subjects, not only articulates and expresses these subjects or their subjectivity but also literally brings them into being. It is in this sense that these acts of writing are performative rather than descriptive. Tara Atluri draws our attention to Āzādi, an emerging figure of the citizen in India. She traces the emergence of this figure to the protests against the gang rape of a woman in December 2012 and the practices these protests initiated. But she also traces the archetypal Indian women from colonial legal discourse to the streets of contemporary urban India, where she embodies the new incarnation of Āzādi. She finds new political vocabularies are slowly but surely articulating this figure, and these vocabularies are present in various sites of struggle in contemporary India. Deena Dajani traces a rather surprising figure as the source of thinking about citizenship as political subjectivity. The figure of the fool might be thought of as the opposite of reason, a presumed precondition of citizenship – but let's not be fooled by that image, she says. Instead, she traces the subversive and witty renaissance court-fool and compares this European 'wise-folly' with the Islamic tradition of sane madmen. An act in itself, Dajani's genealogy of the fool moves freely across the supposed intellectual boundaries between

'East' and 'West' and notices uncanny similarities in this paradoxical social position of the fool. She wonders if this history of the fool might provide a different figure of the citizen whose unconscious is structured as a folly.

It will be readily seen that these three perspectives – undoing, uncovering, refiguring – are not mutually exclusive but overlapping ways of developing alternative conceptions of citizenship as political subjectivity. In each it is a question of emphasis, but the aim is to work through political subjectivity with the rich panorama of sources that it requires. These perspectives developed in *Citizenship after Orientalism* strongly resonate with a call James Tully made when he said 'we in the West have yet to enter into the difficult kind of dialogue with the others of the world that brings this horizon of persisting languages and practices into the space of questions and opens the interlocutors to a non-imperial relationship of dialogue and mutual understanding.'[27] Tully was speaking about how political theory might find alternative forms of thought to the imperialism that permeates it. Such a dialogue for Tully 'would be the beginning of an alternative to imperialism'.[28] *Citizenship after Orientalism* is one attempt to initiate such a dialogue over citizenship.

These three parts are enveloped by the two chapters that I offer as my contribution to the book both as its editor and the principal investigator of the project from which the chapters are drawn. Thus, these two chapters are not merely an introduction and conclusion to the book but to the broader project going back more than a decade. In the present chapter I attempted to lay out developments in two fields – postcolonial studies and citizenship studies – that I mentioned above and illustrate how bringing together both provides new perspectives on citizenship but also exposes their limits. The conclusion, 'citizenship's empire', is my statement on where I now stand on the prospects and promises of theorizing citizenship as political subjectivity in political theory as an alternative to orientalism and imperialism. But the chapter is not a theoretical exercise. Rather, it traces genealogies of citizenship in two 'postcolonial' sites – the Ottoman Empire and Chinese Empire – at the moment of their disintegration and the invention of citizenship as a strategy of government. I understand this moment as a condition of transforming political theory of citizenship as we inherit it.

Notes

1   By 'political modernity' I mean modernity of political institutions and arrangements such as liberal democracy, rule of law, representative government, and regime of rights and responsibilities. D. B. Heater, *Citizenship: The Civic Ideal in World History, Politics, and Education* (London: Longman Group, 1990); R. Bellamy, *Citizenship: A Very Short Introduction* (Oxford: Oxford University Press, 2008).

2   J. Habermas, *The Philosophical Discourse of Modernity: Twelve Lectures* (Cambridge, MA: MIT Press, 1985).

3   J.M. Blaut, *The Colonizer's Model of the World: Geographical Diffusionism and Eurocentric History* (New York: Guilford Press, 1993); J. Goody, *The Theft of History*

(Cambridge: Cambridge University Press, 2007); P. Chabal, *The End of Conceit: Western Rationality after Postcolonialism* (London: Zed, 2012).

4 D. Chakrabarty, *Provincializing Europe* (Princeton, NJ: Princeton University Press, 2000); W. Mignolo, *The Darker Side of the Renaissance: Literacy, Territoriality, and Colonization*, 2nd ed. (Ann Arbor, MI: The University of Michigan Press, 2003).

5 The genre in establishing or reasserting European values and demonstrating their triumph or superiority has produced a vast literature. But Francis Fukuyama, Samuel Huntington, and Niall Ferguson, despite their differences, belong to this genre as oft-cited examples. S.P. Huntington, *The Clash of Civilizations and the Remaking of World Order* (New York: Simon & Schuster, 1996); N. Ferguson, *Civilization: The West and the Rest* (London: Allen Lane, 2011); F. Fukuyama, *The End of History and the Last Man* (New York: Free Press, 1992). The trope of post-orientalism has become a civilizational discourse. See H. Dabashi, *Post-Orientalism* (New Brunswick, NJ: Transaction Publishers, 2009).

6 M. Freeden, "Thinking Politically and Thinking About Politics: Language, Interpretation, and Ideology," in *Political Theory: Methods and Approaches*, ed. D. Leopold and M. Stears (Oxford: Oxford University Press, 2008).

7 The imperial entanglements of sociology and anthropology as disciplines in both senses of the term as organized knowledge and controlling conduct have now been studied rather extensively. For recent examples see G. Steinmetz, ed., *Sociology & Empire: The Imperial Entanglements of a Discipline* (2013); G.R. Trumbull, *An Empire of Facts: Colonial Power, Cultural Knowledge, and Islam in Algeria, 1870–1914* (Cambridge: Cambridge University Press, 2009).

8 D. Armitage, "John Locke, Carolina, and the Two Treatises of Government," *Political Theory* 32 (2004); L. Zastoupil, *John Stuart Mill and India* (Stanford, CA: Stanford University Press, 1994).

9 In identifying political theory as speech act proper, I am using J.L. Austin's original formulation and following Judith Butler's influential use of it to articulate a politics of the performative. J. L. Austin, *How to Do Things with Words* (Oxford: Oxford University Press, 1962); J. Butler, *Excitable Speech: A Politics of the Performative* (London: Routledge, 1997).

10 G. Prakash, *After Colonialism: Imperial Histories and Postcolonial Displacements* (Princeton, N.J.: Princeton University Press, 1994); N. Persram, *Postcolonialism and Political Theory* (Lanham: Lexington Books, 2007).

11 E.W. Said, *Orientalism*, 2nd ed. (New York: Vintage, 2003), xii.

12 Ibid., 259.

13 Ibid.

14 Ibid., 376.

15 E.W. Said, *Culture and Imperialism* (New York: Vintage, 1994).

16 M. Salama, *Islam, Orientalism and Intellectual History: Modernity and the Politics of Exclusion since Ibn Khaldun* (London: I. B. Tauris, 2011); D. F. Vukovich, *China and Orientalism: Western Knowledge Production and the P. R. C.* (London: Routledge, 2011); T. Ruskola, *Legal Orientalism: China, the United States, and Modern Law* (Cambridge, MA: Harvard University Press, 2013).

17 I began the project 'citizenship after orientalism' originally in Canada. It is now continuing in Europe as an international collaborative project. The project has focused on citizenship in political theory after orientalism and connected critiques of citizenship in both postcolonial studies and citizenship studies. See E.F. Isin, "Citizenship after Orientalism: Genealogical Investigations," in *Comparative Political Thought: Theorizing Practices*, eds. M. Freeden and A. Vincent

(London: Routledge, 2013); E.F. Isin, "Citizenship after Orientalism: An Unfinished Project," *Citizenship Studies* 16, 5–6 (2012); E. F. Isin, "Ottoman Waqfs as Acts of Citizenship," in *Held in Trust: Waqf in the Muslim World*, ed. P. Ghazaleh (Cairo: American University in Cairo Press, 2011); E. F. Isin, "Beneficence and Difference: Ottoman Awqaf and 'Other' Subjects," in *The Other Global City*, ed. S. Mayaram (London: Routledge, 2009); E.F. Isin and E. Üstündağ, "Wills, Deeds, Acts: Women's Civic Gift-Giving in Ottoman Istanbul," *Gender, Place and Culture* 15, 5 (2008); E. F. Isin, "Ottoman Awqaf, Turkish Modernization, and Citizenship," in *Remaking Turkey: Globalization, Alternative Modernities, and Democracy*, ed. E. F. Keyman (Lanham, MD: Lexington Books, 2007); E. F. Isin, "Citizenship after Orientalism: Ottoman Citizenship," in *Citizenship in a Globalizing World: European Questions and Turkish Experiences*, eds. F. Keyman and A. Içduygu (London: Routledge, 2005).

18   A. Césaire, *Discourse on Colonialism*, trans. J. Pinkham (New York: Monthly Review Press, 2000); F. Fanon, *The Wretched of the Earth* (New York: Grove Press, 1963); A. Memmi, *The Colonizer and the Colonized*, trans. H. Greenfeld, 3rd ed. (London: Earthscan, 2003).

19   N. G. Jayal, *Citizenship and Its Discontents: An Indian History* (Cambridge, MA: Harvard University Press, 2013); B. Manby, *Struggles for Citizenship in Africa* (London: Zed Books, 2009); J. A. Fogel and P. G. Zarrow, eds., *Imagining the People: Chinese Intellectuals and the Concept of Citizenship, 1890–1920* (Armonk, NY: M. E. Sharpe, 1997).

20   H. Wang, *The Politics of Imagining Asia*, trans. T. Huters (Cambridge, MA: Harvard University Press, 2011); W. Mignolo, *The Darker Side of Western Modernity: Global Futures, Decolonial Options* (Durham, NC: Duke University Press, 2011).

21   P. Mishra, *From the Ruins of Empire: The Revolt against the West and the Remaking of Asia* (London: Allen Lane, 2012).

22   Vukovich, *China and Orientalism: Western Knowledge Production and the P. R. C.*

23   Ruskola, *Legal Orientalism: China, the United States, and Modern Law*; T. Kayaoğlu, *Legal Imperialism: Sovereignty and Extraterritoriality in Japan, the Ottoman Empire, and China* (Cambridge, UK: Cambridge University Press, 2010); L. A. Benton, *A Search for Sovereignty: Law and Geography in European Empires, 1400–1900* (Cambridge, UK: Cambridge University Press, 2010).

24   Persram, *Postcolonialism and Political Theory*; É. Balibar, *We, the People of Europe?: Reflections on Transnational Citizenship* (Princeton, NJ: Princeton University Press, 2004); E.L. Santner, *The Royal Remains: The People's Two Bodies and the Endgames of Sovereignty* (Chicago: University of Chicago Press, 2011).

25   Jayal, *Citizenship and Its Discontents*; S. Banerjee, *Becoming Imperial Citizens: Indians in the Late-Victorian Empire* (Durham, NC: Duke University Press, 2010).

26   The literature on differentiated citizenship ranges from feminist and queer critiques to civil rights critiques. I. M. Young, "Polity and Group Difference: A Critique of the Ideal of Universal Citizenship," *Ethics* 99 January (1989); I. M. Young, *Justice and the Politics of Difference* (Princeton, NJ: Princeton University Press, 1990); R. Lister, *Citizenship: Feminist Perspectives* (New York: New York University Press, 1997); D. T. Evans, *Sexual Citizenship: The Material Construction of Sexualities* (London: Routledge, 1993); S. Phelan, *Sexual Strangers: Gays, Lesbians, and Dilemmas of Citizenship* (Philadelphia: Temple University Press, 2001); L. Sabsay, "The Emergence of the Other Sexual Citizen: Orientalism and the Modernisation of Sexuality," *Citizenship Studies* 16 (2012).

27 J. Tully, *Public Philosophy in a New Key: Imperialism and Civic Freedom* (Cambridge, UK: Cambridge University Press, 2008), 164–5.
28 Ibid., 165.

References Cited

Armitage, David. "John Locke, Carolina, and the Two Treatises of Government," *Political Theory* 32 (2004): 602–27.

Austin, J. L. *How to Do Things with Words* (Oxford: Oxford University Press, 1962).

Balibar, Étienne. *We, the People of Europe?: Reflections on Transnational Citizenship* (Princeton, NJ: Princeton University Press, 2004).

Banerjee, Sukanya. *Becoming Imperial Citizens: Indians in the Late-Victorian Empire* (Durham, NC: Duke University Press, 2010).

Bellamy, Richard. *Citizenship: A Very Short Introduction* (Oxford: Oxford University Press, 2008).

Benton, Lauren A. *A Search for Sovereignty: Law and Geography in European Empires, 1400–1900* (Cambridge: Cambridge University Press, 2010).

Blaut, J. M. *The Colonizer's Model of the World: Geographical Diffusionism and Eurocentric History* (New York: Guilford Press, 1993).

Butler, Judith. *Excitable Speech: A Politics of the Performative* (London: Routledge, 1997).

Césaire, Aimé. *Discourse on Colonialism* (1972), trans. Joan Pinkham (New York: Monthly Review Press, 2000).

Chabal, Patrick. *The End of Conceit: Western Rationality after Postcolonialism* (London: Zed, 2012).

Chakrabarty, Dipesh. *Provincializing Europe* (Princeton, NJ: Princeton University Press, 2000).

Dabashi, Hamid. *Post-Orientalism* (New Brunswick, NJ: Transaction Publishers, 2009).

Evans, David T. *Sexual Citizenship: The Material Construction of Sexualities* (London: Routledge, 1993).

Fanon, Frantz. *The Wretched of the Earth* (New York: Grove Press, 1963).

Ferguson, Niall. *Civilization: The West and the Rest* (London: Allen Lane, 2011).

Fogel, Joshua A., and Peter Gue Zarrow, eds., *Imagining the People: Chinese Intellectuals and the Concept of Citizenship, 1890–1920* (Armonk, NY: M.E. Sharpe, 1997).

Freeden, Michael. "Thinking Politically and Thinking About Politics: Language, Interpretation, and Ideology," in *Political Theory: Methods and Approaches*, eds. David Leopold and Marc Stears (Oxford: Oxford University Press, 2008), 196–215.

Fukuyama, Francis. *The End of History and the Last Man* (New York: Free Press, 1992).

Goody, Jack. *The Theft of History* (Cambridge, UK: Cambridge University Press, 2007).

Habermas, Jürgen. *The Philosophical Discourse of Modernity: Twelve Lectures* (Cambridge, MA: MIT Press, 1985).

Heater, Derek Benjamin. *Citizenship: The Civic Ideal in World History, Politics, and Education* (London: Longman Group, 1990).

Huntington, Samuel P. *The Clash of Civilizations and the Remaking of World Order* (New York: Simon & Schuster, 1996).

Isin, Engin F. "Citizenship after Orientalism: Ottoman Citizenship," in *Citizenship in a Globalizing World: European Questions and Turkish Experiences*, eds. Fuat Keyman and Ahmet İçduygu (London: Routledge, 2005), 31–51.

Isin, Engin F. "Ottoman Awqaf, Turkish Modernization, and Citizenship," in *Remaking Turkey: Globalization, Alternative Modernities, and Democracy*, ed. Emin Fuat Keyman (Lanham, MD: Lexington Books, 2007), 3–15.

Isin, Engin F. "Beneficence and Difference: Ottoman Awqaf and 'Other' Subjects," in *The Other Global City*, ed. Shail Mayaram (London: Routledge, 2009).

Isin, Engin F. "Citizenship after Orientalism: An Unfinished Project," *Citizenship Studies* 16, 5–6 (2012): 563–72.

Isin, Engin F. "Citizenship after Orientalism: Genealogical Investigations," in *Comparative Political Thought: Theorizing Practices*, eds. Michael Freeden and Andrew Vincent (London: Routledge, 2013).

Isin, Engin F. "Ottoman Waqfs as Acts of Citizenship," in *Held in Trust: Waqf in the Muslim World*, ed. Pascale Ghazaleh (Cairo: American University in Cairo Press, 2011), 209–29.

Isin, Engin F., and Ebru Üstündağ. "Wills, Deeds, Acts: Women's Civic Gift-Giving in Ottoman Istanbul," *Gender, Place and Culture* 15, 5 (2008): 519–32.

Jayal, Niraja Gopal. *Citizenship and Its Discontents: An Indian History* (Cambridge, MA: Harvard University Press, 2013).

Kayaoğlu, Turan. *Legal Imperialism: Sovereignty and Extraterritoriality in Japan, the Ottoman Empire, and China* (Cambridge, UK: Cambridge University Press, 2010).

Lister, Ruth. *Citizenship: Feminist Perspectives* (New York: New York University Press, 1997).

Manby, Bronwen. *Struggles for Citizenship in Africa* (London: Zed Books, 2009).

Memmi, Albert. *The Colonizer and the Colonized*, trans. Howard Greenfeld, 3rd ed. (London: Earthscan, 2003).

Mignolo, Walter. *The Darker Side of the Renaissance: Literacy, Territoriality, and Colonization*, 2nd ed. (Ann Arbor, MI: The University of Michigan Press, 2003).

Mignolo, Walter. *The Darker Side of Western Modernity: Global Futures, Decolonial Options* (Durham, NC: Duke University Press, 2011).

Mishra, Pankaj. *From the Ruins of Empire: The Revolt against the West and the Remaking of Asia* (London: Allen Lane, 2012).

Persram, Nalini. *Postcolonialism and Political Theory* (Lanham, MD: Lexington Books, 2007).

Phelan, Shane. *Sexual Strangers: Gays, Lesbians, and Dilemmas of Citizenship* (Philadelphia: Temple University Press, 2001).

Prakash, Gyan. *After Colonialism: Imperial Histories and Postcolonial Displacements* (Princeton, NJ: Princeton University Press, 1994).

Ruskola, Teemu. *Legal Orientalism: China, the United States, and Modern Law* (Cambridge, MA: Harvard University Press, 2013).

Sabsay, Leticia. "The Emergence of the Other Sexual Citizen: Orientalism and the Modernisation of Sexuality," *Citizenship Studies* 16 (2012): 605–23.

Said, Edward W. *Culture and Imperialism* (New York: Vintage, 1994).

Said, Edward W. *Orientalism* (1978), 2nd ed. (New York: Vintage, 2003).

Salama, Mohammad. *Islam, Orientalism and Intellectual History: Modernity and the Politics of Exclusion since Ibn Khaldun* (London: I. B. Tauris, 2011).

Santner, Eric L. *The Royal Remains: The People's Two Bodies and the Endgames of Sovereignty* (Chicago: University of Chicago Press, 2011).

Steinmetz, George, ed., *Sociology and Empire: The Imperial Entanglements of a Discipline* (Durham: Duke University Press, 2013).

Trumbull, George R. *An Empire of Facts: Colonial Power, Cultural Knowledge, and Islam in Algeria, 1870–1914* (Cambridge: Cambridge University Press, 2009).

Tully, James. *Public Philosophy in a New Key: Imperialism and Civic Freedom* (Cambridge: Cambridge University Press, 2008).

Vukovich, Daniel F. *China and Orientalism: Western Knowledge Production and the P.R.C.* (London: Routledge, 2011).

Wang, Hui. *The Politics of Imagining Asia*, trans. Theodore Huters (Cambridge, MA: Harvard University Press, 2011).

Young, Iris Marion. *Justice and the Politics of Difference* (Princeton, N.J.: Princeton University Press, 1990).

Young, Iris Marion. "Polity and Group Difference: A Critique of the Ideal of Universal Citizenship," *Ethics* 99 January (1989): 250–74.

Zastoupil, Lynn. *John Stuart Mill and India* (Stanford, CA: Stanford University Press, 1994).

Part I
Undoing Citizenship

2
Abject Choices? Orientalism, Citizenship, and Autonomy

Leticia Sabsay

Abstract

What are the conditions under which the promise of citizenship after orientalism could be fulfilled? This rather ambitious question, which has haunted our work together for some years in myriad manners and continues breathing through this volume, is the point of departure of this chapter. Of course, such a question cannot be answered in all its dimensions. In fact, this is an open question whose value rests less in the definite answers it could deliver than in the orientation that it proposes, one that indicates the need to question basic assumptions inherited from Western political thought. As an entry point to this question, then, here I focus on the need to rethink the entanglement between the imaginaries of autonomy and citizenship. This entanglement becomes perhaps most apparent when we look at it along the lines of gender.

Introduction

From a normative point of view, individual autonomy functions as a central precondition to be considered a potential citizen. In other words, the entitlement to potentially become part of a political community relies on the presumption that the subjects of such community are inherently autonomous. However, not all subjects are considered to count on this condition conceived as a capacity to be constituted as such. For instance, within the borders of post-enlightenment Europe, women were deemed to be lacking such an attribute. In our contemporary postcolonial condition, it is at the intersection of gender and culture where we may see how the imagined link between autonomy and citizenship works differentially. If, as I argue in this chapter, autonomy is underpinned by, and rearticulates orientalist views by which citizenship has always already been compromised by its constitutive cultural exclusions, it does so in gendered ways. Hence, there is a necessity to reconsider the conditions of gendered

17

citizenship in a way that does not reiterate its orientalist legacy. At this point, I propose that a politics of critical cultural translation may offer a way to challenge this inheritance.

As a long tradition of feminist scholarship has amply argued, contrary to the normative notion of individual autonomy embedded in the liberal tradition, the experience and the meanings of autonomy are differentiated and not universal and abstract.[1] The traits of liberal individuality would be free and reasoned judgement, non-conditioned free will, and ownership of one's own body. This set of faculties, which, in turn, shape moral autonomy as constitutive of the self, rely on the assumption that the subject of rights exercising autonomy is an undifferentiated subject. But this assumption does not account for the epistemological and material conditions that point to a differential distribution of such faculties,[2] nor the fact that this conception of the self corresponds to the particular cultural tradition of Western modernity.[3] Notwithstanding the extensive critique that this conception of autonomy has received, normative ideas of moral autonomy continue to be deeply engrained in dominant theories of democracy within the field of political theory. Furthermore, autonomy has assumed a renewed impulse through the lens of choice (reducing freedom qua free will as the freedom to choose) in our neoliberal times.[4] It is in this context that, among a number of frameworks contesting these assumptions, I engaged the basic tenets of this project, taking as a point of departure the idea that political subjects enact political citizenship in the very act of claiming rights, regardless of whether or not they are entitled to do so (Isin in this volume); in particular, renegotiating the terms by which autonomy has been hegemonically configured as an exclusionary construct. At the intersection of certain interpretations of gender and cultural background, the neoliberal idea of autonomy as free and unconditioned choice serves the purpose of disavowing these enactments of citizenship. In what follows, I explore how autonomy qua choice does precisely this, functioning as a most powerful political rhetorical device, one that nonetheless may be challenged and renegotiated.

Consider the following two scenes: 1) the campaigns against sex trafficking where governmental actors and some feminist groups alike criminalize sex workers while portraying migrant sex workers as victims of this crime, and 2) attacks against wearing a veil in public in different sites of Europe, as in Denmark, Germany, France, the Netherlands, and Spain. What is common in these scenes? To put it simply, when women make 'wrong' choices they face the force of law. On the one hand, women are urged to make personal choices as an expression of their freedom and to consider themselves as subjects of rights. On the other hand, when women make 'wrong' choices they are denied the autonomy and the rights that they are promised: one cannot decide to be a sex worker or to wear a veil in public. What must these women do to qualify for freedom? The answer, it seems, is that until they make the 'right' choices they cannot be free.

To be an autonomous subject that can claim rights on the basis of one's own capacity to make decisions and choose is an ineluctable requisite to be considered as a potential citizen. But this requirement, together with the figure of the abstract, disembodied, and rational individual, who is at the core of the Western notion of citizenship, depends on orientalist logic insofar as this figure of 'the ideal citizen' is constructed against a constitutive cultural other that does not qualify for it. In this chapter, I argue that one particular mechanism of the orientalist logic of citizenship is to deny political agency to those who make wrong choices. But how does this logic of denial, which is central to modern (European and Western) conceptions of citizenship, work? I address this question by focusing on gendered and sexual forms of political subjectivity, and I argue that one particular way in which this occurs is by defining wrong choices as those that do not express the autonomy of the person who chooses, and therefore as non-choices. Within the orientalist logic, sex workers portrayed as victims of international sex trafficking networks and women wearing a veil in public not only embody the 'wrongness' of their choice; also, and more crucially, by those very same choices, these women are said to express their lack of autonomy, hence their incapacity to choose.

At this point it seems necessary to highlight that the question of choice is clearly much more complicated than what the binary choice/non-choice can possibly capture, as 'choices' are never purely free but rather always already traversed and even formed by the conditions in which they can be made and the options available according to them. Here is where the notion of agency offers a far more nuanced and complex understanding of autonomy (reduced to free will and/or choice), as feminists have extensively demonstrated.[5] It is not the question of whether or not there is agency on the part of those women who are targeted as lacking the capacity to make decisions on their own that I want to discuss in this chapter. In fact, my point of departure is that there is agency in their claims. Rather, what I want to underscore here is how those arguments that point to the victimization of women mobilize autonomy – understood as a crucial political rhetorical device – as the condition of citizenship and that they do so in orientalist ways.

Usually, women's freedoms are hijacked in the name of liberal democracy, but then, the illiberal logic that lies at the core of this deprivation of autonomy needs to be disavowed. Otherwise, the contradictory principle, which denies freedom in the name of freedom, would be exposed. One of the ways in which this disavowal works is by displacing the question of choice onto a 'bad other' that allegedly precludes women's right to choose. The logic of victimhood, which is central to this mechanism of denial of autonomy, not only produces a subaltern subject that 'cannot speak' insofar as being a victim both deprives her of agency and prevents her from speaking as a self-owned individual; it also does so through the constitution of a victimizer.[6] This victimizer will embody the inversion of all those democratic values that the West is supposed to stand for, and it is then against this 'bad other' that such women 'without autonomy' (and Western values alike) will need to be 'rescued'. It is by defining these women outside the field of autonomy – that is, characterizing women precisely as those who lack autonomy – that they can appear as 'good others' worthy of rescue after all.

Trafficking Sex Paradigms

The persecution of sex work has heightened over the last decade, particularly in Europe but also globally. Over the last two years, we have witnessed overt campaigns against sex work, with ample media coverage of police successfully persecuting the sex industry, subsuming it into the prosecution of international sex work trafficking networks. Raids in London increased throughout 2012 and 2013, culminating in December 2013 in Soho with the closure of at least 18 independent safe sex work places. Two days after the raids, *The Evening Standard*, a London newspaper, informed us of the following:

> Hundreds of police officers launched a massive Soho swoop on premises allegedly linked to rape, sex trafficking and muggings... After the raids last night a dozen women, mostly from eastern Europe, working in squalid rooms, were taken to safe locations where they will be questioned. Police believe that some were trafficked into the country and forced into prostitution... Inquiries have shown that Soho's vice industry has been taken over by eastern European gangs in recent years.[7]

This parallels media coverage of systematic raids carried out in France more recently.[8] The Soho raids followed the killing of Mariana Popa in October 2013 in East London, a consequence of the added danger to sex workers from such police clamp-downs. To avoid the police, sex workers have been forced to work in more isolated places and apart from their peers.[9] Such actions also followed the frenzy about the increase of 'trafficking for sexual exploitation' on the occasion of the 2012 London Olympics, which, according to the leader of the Greater London Authority Conservatives, Andrew Boff, included an extra £500m secured by the Metropolitan Police Force or 'Met' as it is often known.[10] Certainly, the situation intensified, with European Union campaigning for a legal reform on sex work following the Swedish model that criminalizes clients at that time – a conservative move that was facilitated in great part by the hegemony gained by the reframing of the battle against the sex industry within the trafficking paradigm in the last years.[11] Thus, it comes as no surprise that the demands of sex workers' organizations for the decriminalization of commercial sex both at local and international levels have become invisible as a political issue and remain unheard.

It is against this background that the debates over sex work bring to the attention two of the aspects of the orientalization of gendered and sexual political subjectivity that this chapter addresses: the denial of autonomy when certain wrong choices are made and the orientalization of such choices as non-choices. On the one hand, both the contempt towards sex work and abolitionist feminist arguments alike are based in an imaginary opposition between sexual desire and economic trade.[12] Selling sexual services cannot be, according to this discourse, the expression of free choice. When sex workers argue that it has been their choice to do so, they are accused of false consciousness, of being victims of brainwashing or some version of the Stockholm syndrome. Using these arguments, abolitionists refuse to recognize the decisions and liberties of those they pretend to speak for. In the name of freedom, freedom is denied. These arguments are epitomized by the figure of the victim of sex trafficking. Undeniably, the victim of sex trafficking has not made a choice. The question here is not about the reality of these networks but the purposes served by this anti-trafficking discourse and the way it operates.

As many sex workers' organizations have repeatedly indicated, the anti-trafficking umbrella does not have much impact on the effective disarticulation of operative trafficking networks, nor does it serve the aim of saving victims of trafficking. Instead, it works as an anti-migration policy, targeting migrant sex workers and fuelling racial profiling.[13] In this respect, Niki Adams, from the English Collective of Prostitutes, cautioned in an article published by *The Guardian* on 26 January 2014: 'Ms Popa was Romanian. The 2012 police raids in Mayfair targeted Thai and Romanian women, the swoops in Harrow Roma Brothels.' As for the Soho raids, she added, '[U]nder the guise of freeing trafficking victims, [they] dragged handcuffed Eastern European mothers in their underwear on to the streets.'[14] In a similar spirit, the Sex Workers' Open University responded in a press release:

> On the 4th December police raided 25 premises in Soho and evicted, detained and harassed sex workers. They kicked down doors, closed working flats, took money and personal items, and manhandled women in the street... The media presence included Sky news, BBC and the Evening Standard. It would seem that 'victims' of sex work need to be publicly humiliated and shamed in the media in order to be properly saved from their work. The raids were supposedly undertaken in order to locate 'stolen goods' and to tackle 'prostitution' (despite the fact that selling sex is not actually a crime) and to 'tackle' human trafficking. A number of migrant sex workers, many of whom have lived in the UK for years, have – devastatingly – been conveyed to the UKBA detention centre at Heathrow; this, despite having reassured police that they had not been trafficked into the country, and were working voluntarily.[15]

The Soho raids were part of Operation Demontere, which, after 18 months of intelligence work, resulted in not one case of trafficking being identified. Likewise, according to Boff's report, the Met identified only four cases of trafficking in 2011 and just another four in 2012.[16] And yet, the discourse of sex trafficking does its work. And it does so, in my view, not only because it provides a productive alibi for moral crusades and heightened border patrols but also because it imaginarily locates the question of the sex industry somehow outside the 'advanced West'. The rhetoric propounded by the sex trafficking paradigm actually provides another figure for reinforcing the borders between the West and its other, this time delineating a neat distinction between the 'sources' that mark the provenance of sex workers and traffickers and the causes for joining the sex industry (poverty, marginalization) 'there', in the direction of the East and the South, and its final end 'here', where privileged consumers live. The foreign character of the criminalized actors amounts to the foreignness of this 'underground economy' that the West supposedly wants to be rid of.[17] Along the same lines as the *Evening Standard* quoted above, the Scottish *Sunday Record* stated in its headlines:

> From eastern Europe to slavery: Nearly half of sex workers come from the east and trafficked girls are left terrified when they don't earn enough to satisfy their foreign paymasters.

Noticeable in this regard is the particular targeting by the police and media of Eastern European migration to the UK. After the accession to the European Union of the Czech Republic, Estonia, Hungary, Latvia, Lithuania, Poland, Slovakia, and Slovenia in 2004, followed by that of Bulgaria and Romania in 2007, A8 and A2 citizens (meaning nationals from these two sets of member states) have been using their newly acquired mobility rights to migrate to UK, leading to increased media attention, often verging on panic.[18] In supposedly countering these 'bad' Eastern European networks, the state deprives migrant sex workers of agency altogether, either turning them into mere victims or criminalizing their choices and doing so by denying that they could or would make these choices freely at all. What this scene illustrates, amongst other things, is that while women are denied autonomy for making a choice to become sex workers, their constitution as victims displaces the burden on migrants as guilty subjects.

Veiling Choices

Exercising autonomy, understood in terms of personal choice, functions as a requirement for becoming a subject of rights. Yet, as we have just seen, this conception of autonomy reveals its limits when certain choices appear as if they were not choices at all. How do these limits play out when translated to postcolonial communities? The debates over the use of the veil in public in Europe provide us with another vantage point to explore the tension between the current imaginary of autonomy as exercised over one's own body and the colonial-orientalist presumptions at work in this idea of autonomy. What are the conditions that a subject has to comply with in order to count as a political agent? How does the relationship between subjectivity, embodiment, and agency function within these grammars of choice?

The ways in which the rescue narrative concerning 'Muslim women' was mobilized in the aftermath of the so-called War on Terror have been extensively documented.[19] As many critical feminists have highlighted, both politicians and liberal feminists explicitly linked the invasion of Afghanistan and the impulse to save the 'Muslim woman' from the Taliban, extending it afterwards to the invasion of Iraq and leading to a widespread Islamophobic wave, where gender equality and sexual freedom took centre stage.[20] The current discourse on the 'clash of civilizations' between the West and Islam – which, in fact, dates back to well before the last decade – proposes an opposition between secular universal democratic values on the one hand and the primacy of religion and culture on the other.[21] In Europe, this dynamic has been particularly central to anti-migration campaigns and policies, with the prominence gained by the movement *Ni Putes ni Soumises* ('Neither Whores nor Submissives') founded by Adela Amara in France since 2003, the assassination of Theo Van Gogh in the Netherlands in 2004, and the scandal of the Danish cartoons in Denmark in 2005 figuring as central landmarks. Women's rights (and also sexual minorities' rights) became, in this context, both the pivot signifier defining the West and the marker of the presumptive incompatibility of Islamic values with it; and the hijab has been a privileged symbol in catalysing all of this.[22]

It is not the status of women in different countries in the Middle East, or in other Muslim regions, that is at stake here. I do not propose to revisit the complexities of this debate either, which has been amply studied by feminists. Rather, I am interested in the role that the debates on the use of hijab mainly in educational institutions in Europe can tell us about the orientalist logics that ground Western notions of universal citizenship, in particular with regards to the question of women's autonomy and their freedom as expressed by their right to choose. Insofar as the campaigns in favour of banning the hijab in certain public spaces confined it to a representation of women's oppression, the question of choice as the expression of women's freedom has remained central to this debate. Why do Muslim women choose to wear a hijab? Are women really choosing to cover themselves? How could it be that they choose to be subordinated? Is this an authentic choice? Anyone who has paid any attention to this debate would have seen in myriad TV and radio public debates, endless interviews, and Internet blogs that Muslim women have been asked to explain over and over again to Western audiences their reasons for such a choice and defend themselves from the accusation that they were not really choosing, or, if they were, this was because they were blinded to their own oppression, subdued to a false consciousness that made them believe they were choosing when in truth they were not.

The responses of these women seem inaudible to the Western hegemonic ear.[23] Different Muslim women give a wide range of disparate reasons for using a hijab, positioning themselves as agentic political subjects assuming different positionalities, either identifying themselves as feminists or not, holding diverse political and religious views, carrying different cultural backgrounds and diasporic histories. It could be their will to present themselves in public as Muslims, and show their adherence to Islam to both Muslim and non-Muslim audiences, as Aminah Assilmi, once director of the International Union of Muslim Women, has repeatedly insisted. It could be a way of enacting their virtue and piety. It could be the desire to observe God's command, which then might lead to the conclusion that the question of choice is irrelevant insofar as the use of hijab is a religious obligation, as Zara Faris argues.[24] Or it could be the *will* to practise a personal connection to God, in which case, the way to cast this connection (either wearing a hijab or not) frames it as a matter of personal choice as it often appears among younger generations, or at least as a matter subject to deliberation, as it is posited by the Muslim Debate Initiative among others.[25] Wearing the veil has also been related to fashion and social markers rather than an enactment of the right to cultural difference in Europe.[26] Wearing the veil in public could be understood as a political act of citizenship itself. Indeed, its use has been largely defended as a manifestation of Muslim women in Europe exercising their freedom of expression and their religious liberties; in other words, precisely as exercising a right to choose.

This heterogeneity exposes the error of both homogenizing 'the Muslim world' and supposing that there is only one meaning that could be attached to the hijab. Not least, it shows that it is utterly mistaken to take the hijab as a synonym of oppression. Further, as highlighted above, in many cases the arguments expose an already syncretic mixture of Western Liberal and Muslim principles, where Muslim women in Europe are negotiating their conditions of life.[27] As Sarah Joseph asserted in a CNN debate with Mona El-Tahawy in April 2011 about the French government of Nicolas Sarkozy's ban of the hijab in public places:

> This politics is illiberal... It is not about whether she likes it (referring to the hijab) or I like it. What it is about is whether the State has a right to dictate what women wear. Now, whether that happens on the streets of Teheran, which says you shall wear a chador, or on the streets of Paris, which says you shall not wear this because we, the State, are supreme and we believe in dictating what you wear. Women's right to choose is whether to wear that or not to wear it... Muslims will respond, as they are

responding: You are always talking to us about freedom; you are always talking to us about your liberal values; you are always telling us how we have to accept Danish cartoons in the name of freedom, but at the end of the day, when we try to express what we want to do... we cannot do what we want. Your freedom is false; it is a lie.[28]

This is what Islamophobic discourse cannot bear: a challenge to Islam's incompatibility with Western (European) values. This reluctance to hear Muslim women as political subjects, to move beyond orientalist assumptions about how citizenship rights should be exercised, became apparent in recent campaigns against the 'Islamization' of the world organized by FEMEN, the worldwide sextremist feminist network. As part of this program, on 2 March 2013, FEMEN activists made a demonstration in Stockholm against the hijab in Sweden, with the slogan 'No to hijab'. On this occasion, the lead performer proclaimed: 'Hijab is not my choice... No to Hijab... No to the Islamic Republic of Iran... No to Sharia Law'.[29] Likewise, FEMEN declared an 'International Topless Jihad Day' on 4 April 2013. On this day, the group stated on its website:

> FEMEN insists on toppling regimes that arose after the Arab spring, which brought Islamist clouds over the Arab region. FEMEN decries the deteriorating situation of women in the region and insists on the need for a new Arab women's revolution to liberate women from the medieval traditions that are controlling their lives. Freedom for women![30]

FEMEN, in common with any liberal feminists, conservatives, and progressives who also subscribe to Islamophobic views, present Muslim women with only two positions. Either they are enlightened by Western values and brought back to the present, which can only be Western, and they decide to make 'the journey from the darkness of "medieval traditions" to the light of the true inheritors of the Enlightenment', as Fatima el Tayeb has put it, or they remain victims.[31] Under this logic, the price these women pay for not assimilating is the confirmation that they are destitute political subjects, lacking agency and incapable of making right choices (the first one being the reluctance to integrate into Western modernity on its own terms).[32] Again, the figure of the victim becomes crucial here as well, epitomizing the false character of the choice, redefined as a 'non-choice'.

This movement displaces 'the wrong choice' to the figure of the victimizer, who, in turn, figures as the representative of the (hegemonic masculinities belonging to) patriarchal culture that characterizes the orientalized other. The third voice that shows the hybridity, or the compatibility of Islam with democracy and feminism, is erased in this view. In terms of the argument deployed by FEMEN in the quote above, it is worth noting how this argument is transplanted to whole peoples and regimes. I will address this latter issue in the next section, but firstly I would like to bring attention to some of the counter-voices provoked by this campaign. In response to FEMEN, a network of Muslim Women Against FEMEN was organized. In their Facebook page, the network states that they are 'Muslim women who want to expose FEMEN for the Islamophobes/Imperialists that they are. We are making our voices heard and reclaiming our agency!' Their cover photo includes a banner affirming: 'Nudity DOES NOT liberate me, and I DO NOT need saving'.[33] They organized a counter-campaign, the Muslimah Pride Day.

I do not intend to suggest that this response is representative of Muslim feminists or that it is the more authentic or proper challenge. Of course, there are quite different positions among Muslim feminists as well as among Muslim women who do not identify themselves as feminists, as much as among their non-Muslim peers. What interests me about this response is its straightforward challenge to the 'rescue paradigm' and the Western presumptions about the lack of agency of hijab users that goes with it. Reclaiming agency in its own terms, while questioning the liberating connotations of nudity, this response questions which relations to our bodies might express autonomy and which ones do not. This debate also opens up further questions, touching on key assumptions about choice and freedom. Saba Mahmood, for instance, shows that piety should be valued in its own terms and not as a limitation to autonomy.[34] What happens when autonomy understood in these specific terms is not the most valued goal to achieve in order to have a good life? And what is at stake when trying to determine what might count as an authentic choice or not? These questions cannot have an answer in advance but rather seem to be indispensable to a move toward practices of genuine cultural translation leading to redefinitions of citizenship without orientalism.

Inclusion as Misrecognition

If, according to Edward Said, the orientalist logic affirms that a) the others are not like us, and b) they do not appreciate our values, one can easily see that while not being like us still leaves space for the 'good other' (who wants to be alike or arrive at our stage of development, maybe subject to minoritization), the lack of appreciation of our values opens the path to the 'bad other', who subsequently becomes inassimilable and an object of hatred.[35] It is the 'bad other' whose choices antagonize Western values and cannot be integrated; it is the 'good other' whose choices either point to the appropriation of Western values – allowing for narratives of univocal progress towards a Western present – or appear to express a particular version of a Western value. This can happen in different ways. As we have seen in the two cases developed, it could work by orientalizing certain choices, such as whether to work in the sex industry, redefining it as trafficking and locating it outside the idealized image of a civilized and advanced West. Equally it could work by orientalizing a population according to the choices they make, as in the case of the uses of the hijab, interpreted as a signifier of the resistance to assimilate. In either case, at least in their gendered form, key to this othering logic is the rejection of these choices as an expression of autonomy, which in turn is a requirement to be recognized as a potential subject of rights. When autonomy expresses choices that contradict the terms in which a Western idea of citizenship has been predefined, and thus become too proximate to the 'bad other' with which Western ideas of freedom antagonize, its status crumbles.

Arguably, those 'brown men from whom brown women should be saved' to whom Gayatri Spivak drew our attention more than 25 years ago, figure as a constitutive 'bad other', that is, as the ineluctable condition under which any 'good other' can emerge.[36] As Nacira Guénif-Souliamas has pointed out in relation to French nationalism, the systematic vilification of masculinities of men and boys from Arab and North-African descent contrasts with the victimization of women of the same descent.[37] Arguably, these vilified masculinities form the foil that allows these women to appear as 'good others' – indeed, one could speculate that these women are visualized as potentially susceptible to integration precisely to the extent that their acts can be read as non-autonomous.

The 'good others' who are either lost in their victimhood, or willing to assimilate to Western values, or to offer 'acceptable' diverse versions of themselves, depend on this 'bad other' to become recognizable. If this is the case, the 'bad other' is constitutive of both hegemonic Western anti-difference and pro-recognition inclusive discourses. That is a severe limitation of the paradigm of recognition and inclusion for expanding citizenship to 'others'. Not only does the version of the 'good other' reconfirm the hegemony of Western values, this very same inclusive logic also depends on the demonization of its bad counterpart.

This split of the other into a good and a bad one parallels the distinction that Dipesh Chakrabarty makes between 'minority histories' and 'subaltern pasts'.[38] According to the author, 'minority histories' relate to the 'democratic project of including all groups and peoples within mainstream history', that is, including the other within the canon of Western historiographic hegemony.[39] In contrast, 'subaltern pasts' refer to 'moments or points... that resist historization' and thus cannot be assimilated into the narrative of progress of modernity.[40] If one takes into account that such histories amount to the history of a *polis*, this parallel helps us to notice the limits of citizenship (as a claim to belong to the polis), when restricted to a politics of inclusion that relies on predetermined conditions, which in turn define in advance the terms in which rights claims can be articulated. Chakrabarty states:

> [G]ood minority history is about expanding the scope of social justice and representative democracy, but the talk about the 'limits of history',

on the other hand, is about struggling, or even groping, for non-statist forms of democracy that we cannot yet either completely understand or envisage.[41]

Both good histories and others depend on constitutive exclusions, 'bad others' and outside inarticulate histories are the exterior that the universalizing logic of citizenship demands. In other words, set in hegemonic Western terms, the imaginary ideal citizen is always already constituted against a constitutive exterior, which is embodied by a bad orientalized other, and that is why the politics of recognition cannot satisfy the ideal of universal inclusion it presumes to achieve.

This is evident in the international LGBT approach to the universality of (homo)sexuality to solve the problem of difference in terms of diversity, namely by universalizing (homo)sexuality as including all the different ways in which one can be gay or homosexual.[42] Equally, it is observable in the extension of the denial of autonomy to whole peoples when 'they make the wrong choice'. As FEMEN's declarations made clear, 'no to hijab' was at the same time, by metonymic extension, 'no to the Islamic Republic of Iran'.[43] This is not an exception. On the contrary, maybe due to its racist naiveté, FEMEN expresses overtly what remains implicit in the accusations against Eastern European networks of trafficking, or in the passage from Western widespread celebration of the overthrow of Mubarak in 2011 to a muted response to the overthrow of a democratically elected president from the Muslim Brotherhood, Mohamed Morsi.

In effect, the logic of conditional freedom I have described above is also applied to people in societies or communities considered as non-Western, be they either within or without the West. If 'non-Western' people are willing to part ways with those actions, practices, and markers of identity that appear antagonistic to desired freedoms that are already available in Western societies, then they are considered to be making the right choices. If not, they face the wrath of orientalism (or other forms of minoritization under the guise of coloniality, as has been pointed out by Dipesh Chakrabarty in relation to historical narratives).[44] This logic constitutes the core of a hegemonic politics of citizenship, which divides those who deserve it by virtue of having made the right choices and those who don't by virtue of having chosen a wrong path.

When forms of political agency only recognizable as Western are translated to other peoples, they assume different shapes and produce different consequences, enabling the development of other strategies for governing others. This process of direct translation produces new versions of the original model, hence its creative and productive sides. But at the same time, this logic of direct translation replicates the power relations between the West and the rest. Finally, it also reproduces the orientalist logic of othering that is already there in the very paradigm of direct and unidirectional translation itself. The difficulties of this form of translation and the obstacles to its implementation normally give rise to orientalist discourses and condemnations of those peoples who are to experience this translation to the Western model.

In light of these scenes, to challenge the power of Western political paradigms, it would be necessary to attend to those moments of critical translation (those subaltern pasts, in the words of Chakrabarty)[45] when the claim or the choice at stake demands that translation goes both ways. In other words, a process of critical translation would be one in which, for instance, the presumptions of what autonomy is and how it might be expressed are not defined in advance. Rather, these presumptions should be the object of open agonistic renegotiation. After all, if freedom depends on a notion of autonomy that proves to be exclusionary, and pivotal to state violence and the logic of othering, it would be worth rethinking the terms in which both freedom and autonomy, as the conditions and goals of citizenship, are described.

This project directs us to an expansion of the debate beyond the question of the inclusion of others (first within, and later without) and the politics of recognition associated with it. Within the paradigm of direct translation, inclusion will only happen insofar as the others at stake conform to the values already established by the original paradigm. By contrast, a process of critical translation would not just point to expanding or diversifying a particular field by the extension of preconceived women's political agency, sexual human rights, or liberal democracy to those configured as cultural others. Rather, it would demand us to rearticulate those categories that structure the field at stake. This project of critical translation would have to give an account of the fact that the logic of othering is already present in the categories that shape the political body or, in other words, in the way we have organized the political order, and account for the fact that if we do not take critical translations seriously, what is conceived as political will remain already delineated by an orientalist logic, and the promise of citizenship after orientalism will never be fulfilled.

Notes

1 For a review of the feminist critique of the abstract and universal conceptions of autonomy and freedom, see A. Phillips, *Engendering democracy* (London: Polity, 1991); J.W. Scott, *Only Paradoxes to Offer: French Feminists and the Rights of Man* (Cambridge, MA: Harvard University Press, 1996); L. Zerilli, *Feminism and the Abyss of Freedom* (Chicago, Ill: University of Chicago Press, 2005).

2 See M. Davies, "Queer Property, Queer Persons: Self-Ownership and Beyond," *Social & Legal Studies* 8, 3 (1999); and J. Butler and A. Athanasiou, *Dispossession: The Performative in the Political* (Cambridge, CA: Polity Press, 2013).

3 For a feminist critique of the self as the locus of undetermined moral autonomy, see W. Brown, *Regulating Aversion: Tolerance in the Age of Identity and Empire* (Princeton, NJ: Princeton University Press, 2006); J.W. Scott, *The politics of the veil*

(New Jersey, NJ: Princeton University Press, 2007); A. Allen, *The Politics of Our Selves: Power, Autonomy, and Gender in Contemporary Critical Theory* (New York, NY: Columbia University Press, 2008).

4 The neoliberal reformulation of freedom as freedom to choose has been exten-sively analysed within studies on postfeminism. See A. McRobbie, *The Aftermath of Feminism: Gender, Culture and Social Change* (London: Sage, 2009); and Y. Tasker and D. Negra, eds., *Interrogating Postfeminism: Gender and Politics of Popular Culture* (Durham, NC: Duke University Press, 2007).

5 See A. Phillips, "Feminism and Liberalism Revisited: Has Martha Nussbaum Got It Right?," *Constellations* 8, 2 (2001); S. Madhok, "Autonomy, Gender Subordina-tion and Transcultural Dialogue," *Journal of Global Ethics* 3, 3 (2007); S. Madhok, *Rethinking Agency: Developmentalism, Gender and Rights* (London: Routledge, 2013); A. Phillips, S. Madhok and K. Wilson, eds., *Gender, Agency and Coercion: Thinking Gender in Transnational Times* (London: Palgrave, 2013).

6 G. Spivak, "Can the Subaltern Speak?," in *Marxism and the Interpretation of Culture*, eds. C. Nelson and L. Grossberg (Urbana: University of Illinois Press, 1988).

7 http://www.standard.co.uk/news/crime/22-arrested-as-met-swoops-on-soho -venues-allegedly-linked-to-sex-trafficking-and-rapes-8984378.html (accessed 28 December 2013).

8 http://www.sexworkeropenuniversity.com/2/post/2013/12/press-release-swou -responds-to-the-soho-raids.html (accessed 28 December 2013).

9 http://www.theguardian.com/society/2014/jan/19/woman-killed-prostitute -police-blame/print (accessed 20 January 2014).

10 A. Boff, *Shadow City: Exposing Human Trafficking in Everyday London*, GLA Conserv-atives Report 2013, http://glaconservatives.co.uk/wp-content/uploads/2013/10/ Shadow-City.pdf (accessed 20 January 2014).

11 See L.M. Agustín, *Sex at the Margins. Migration, Labour Markets and the Rescue Indus-try* (London: Zed Books, 2007); and R. Andrijasevic, *Migration, Agency and Citizen-ship in Sex Trafficking* (London: Palgrave, 2010).

12 See L. Agustín, *Sex at the Margins*.

13 Global Network of Sex Workers Projects, "Sex Work is not Trafficking," Briefing Paper 3.

14 http://www.theguardian.com/theobserver/2014/jan/26/letters-criminalisation -prostitution-women-at-risk/print (accessed 10 February 2014).

15 http://www.sexworkeropenuniversity.com/2/post/2013/12/press-release-swou -responds-to-the-soho-raids.html (accessed 10 February 2014).

16 See FN 4 and 5.

17 http://www.theguardian.com/commentisfree/2013/dec/12/europe-prostitution -sex-trafficking-nordic-model (accessed 12 January 2014).

18 http://www.migrationobservatory.ox.ac.uk/briefings/migration-flows-a8-and -other-eu-migrants-and-uk (accessed 1 December 2014). The website of Migration Watch UK, a think-tank 'concerned about the present scale of immigration into the UK', offers an overview of media news on migration flows to UK, particularly from Eastern Europe and Middle East. http://www.migrationwatchuk.com/media -reports (accessed 1 December 2014).

19 See L. Abu Lughod, "Do Muslim Women Really Need Saving? Anthropological Reflections on Cultural Relativism and Its Others," *American Anthropologist*, New Series 104, 3 (2002); C. Hirschkind and S. Mahmood, "Feminism, the Taliban, and Politics of Counter-Insurgency," *Anthropological Quarterly* 75, 2 (2002); J. Puar, *Ter-rorist Assemblages: Homonationalism in Queer Times* (Durham, NC: Duke University Press, 2007); F. El-Tayeb, *European Others. Queering Ethnicity in Postnational Europe* (Minneapolis, MN: University of Minnesota Press, 2011); and S. Bracke, "From

'Saving Women' to 'Saving Gays': Rescue Narratives and Their Dis/continuities," *European Journal of Women's Studies* 19, 2 (2012).

20 L. Sabsay, "The Emergence of the Other Sexual Citizen: Orientalism and the Modernisation of Sexuality," Citizenship Studies 16, 5–6 (2012).

21 See W. Brown, *Regulating Aversion*; T. Asad et al., *Is Critique Secular?: Blasphemy, Injury, and Free Speech* (Berkeley, CA: University of California Press, 2009); and S. Bano, *Muslim Women and Shari'ah Councils* (London: Palgrave, 2012).

22 F. El-Tayeb, *European Others*.

23 On the incapacity of Western feminists to recognize Muslim-women agency and their choice for the hijab in France, see J. Scott (Op. Cit., 2007).

24 http://zarafaris.com/2013/04/14/hijab-to-veil-or-not-to-veil/ (accessed 3 January 2014).

25 In relation to those who advocate the use of the veil as personal choice, Riyedis-lam's video 'Judged', a Bangladeshi-based art initiative, is a case in point. The video 'Judged' can be seen at http://www.youtube.com/watch?v=lfqoddK_FJw&list =TLv0rWryBEoHAhDj-ME5aLctqfViGH2S-i

26 See the Muslim Debate Initiative at http://www.muslimdebate.org/ Also, the blog 'Hijab is my fashion and my beauty', works along these lines, opening up a dis-cussion rather than prescribing an exclusive position: http://hijabismyfashionand myduty.blogspot.co.uk/ (all accessed 12 January 2014).

27 On British-Muslim family law as a hybrid field, see L. Pilgram, "British-Muslim Family Law and Citizenship," *Citizenship Studies* 16, 5–6 (2012).

28 http://www.youtube.com/watch?v=5IK0U5GWVJ4 (accessed 12 January 2014).

29 According to FEMEN, this action was jointly organized with an Iranian young activist from the communist party, whose name is not provided. http://femen .org/en/gallery/id/148#post-content (accessed 12 January 2014). In this post, FEMEN also reminds us that: 'on the 20th of December 2012 famous Egyptian activist Alia Al Mahdi, together with FEMEN made an antiislamist protest next to the Egyptian embassy in Stockholm. The aim of the protest was to draw the world's attention to the threat of islamization of Egyptian constitution and the introduction of Morsi's Shariah Law.'

30 http://femen.org/gallery/id/178#post-content (accessed 12 January 2014).

31 F. El-Tayeb, *European Others*.

32 On the process of othering as a twofold displacement that involves a spatial dimension that imaginarily locates European Muslims as not belonging to Europe, and a temporal dimension that imaginarily locates Islam in the past, see J. Butler, "Sexual Politics, Torture and Secular Time," *The British Journal of Sociology* 59, 1 (2008), and El-Tayeb, *European Others*.

33 https://www.facebook.com/MuslimWomenAgainstFemen (accessed 12 January 2014).

34 S. Mahmood, "Feminist Theory, Embodiment, and the Docile Agent: Some Reflec-tions on the Egyptian Revival," *Cultural Anthropology* 16, 2 (2001).

35 E. Said, *Orientalism* (New York, NY: Vintage Books, 1979).

36 G. Spivak, "Can the Subaltern Speak?"

37 N. Guénif-Souilamas, "Straight Migrants Queering the European Man," in *What's Queer about Europe: Productive Encounters and Re-Enchanting Paradigms,* eds. M. Rosello and S. Dasgupta (New York, NY: Fordham University Press, 2014).

38 D. Chakrabarty, "Minority Histories, Subaltern Pasts," *Economic and Political Weekly*, 28 February 1998.

39 Ibid., 477.

40 Ibid., 475.

41 Ibid., 477.

42   L. Sabsay, "The Emergence of the Other Sexual Citizen."
43   http://femen.org/en/gallery/id/148#post-content (accessed 12 January 2014).
44   D. Chakrabarty, "Minority Histories, Subaltern Pasts."
45   Ibid.

References Cited

Abu Lughod, Lila. "Do Muslim Women Really Need Saving? Anthropological Reflections on Cultural Relativism and Its Others," *American Anthropologist*, New Series 104, 3 (2002): 783–90.

Agustín, Laura María. *Sex at the Margins. Migration, Labour Markets and the Rescue Industry* (London: Zed Books, 2007).

Allen, Amy. The *Politics of Our Selves: Power, Autonomy, and Gender in Contemporary Critical Theory* (New York: Columbia University Press, 2008).

Andrijasevic, Rutvitca. *Migration, Agency and Citizenship in Sex Trafficking* (London: Palgrave, 2010).

Asad, Talal, Wendy Brown, Judith Butler, and Saba Mahmood. *Is Critique Secular?: Blasphemy, Injury, and Free Speech* (Berkeley, CA: University of California Press, 2009).

Bano, Samia. *Muslim Women and Shari'ah Councils* (London: Palgrave, 2012).

Bracke, Sarah. "From 'Saving Women" to "Saving Gays': Rescue Narratives and Their Dis/continuities," *European Journal of Women's Studies* 19, 2 (2012): 237–52.

Brown, Wendy. *Regulating Aversion. Tolerance in the Age of Identity and Empire* (Princeton, NJ: Princeton University Press, 2006).

Butler, Judith. "Sexual Politics, Torture and Secular Time," *The British Journal of Sociology* 59, 1 (2008): 1–23.

Butler, Judith and Athena Athanasiou. *Dispossession. The Performative in the Political* (Cambridge, CA: Polity Press, 2013).

Chakrabarty, Dipesh. "Minority Histories, Subaltern Pasts," *Economic and Political Weekly*, 28 February 1998: 473–80.

Davies, Margaret. "Queer Property, Queer Persons: Self-Ownership and Beyond," *Social & Legal Studies* 8, 3 (1999): 327–52.

El-Tayeb, Fatima. *European Others. Queering Ethnicity in Postnational Europe* (Minneapolis, MN: University of Minnesota Press, 2011).

Global Network of Sex Workers Projects, "Sex Work Is Not Trafficking," Briefing Paper 3.

Guénif-Souilamas, Nacira. "Straight Migrants Queering the European Man," in *What's Queer about Europe: Productive Encounters and Re-Enchanting Paradigms*, eds. Mireille Rosello and Sudeep Dasgupta (New York: Fordham University Press, 2014).

Hirschkind, Charles and Saba Mahmood. "Feminism, the Taliban, and Politics of Counter-Insurgency," *Anthropological Quarterly* 75, 2 (2002): 339–54.

Madhok, Sumi. "Autonomy, Gender Subordination and Transcultural Dialogue," *Journal of Global Ethics* 3, 3 (2007): 335–57.

Madhok, Sumi. *Rethinking Agency: Developmentalism, Gender and Rights* (London: Routledge, 2013).

Mahmood, Saba. "Feminist Theory, Embodiment, and the Docile Agent: Some Reflections on the Egyptian Revival," *Cultural Anthropology* 16, 2 (2001): 202–36.

McRobbie, Angela. *The Aftermath of Feminism: Gender, Culture and Social Change* (London: Sage, 2009).

Phillips, Anne. *Engendering democracy* (London: Polity, 1991).

Phillips, Anne. "Feminism and Liberalism Revisited: Has Martha Nussbaum Got It Right?," *Constellations* 8, 2 (2001): 250–66.

Phillips, Anne, Sumi Madhok, and Kalpana Wilson, eds. *Gender, Agency and Coercion: Thinking Gender in Transnational Times* (London: Palgrave, 2013).

Pilgram, Lisa. "British-Muslim Family Law and Citizenship," *Citizenship Studies* 16, 5–6 (2012): 769–82.

Puar, Jasbir. *Terrorist Assemblages: Homonationalism in Queer Times* (Durham, NC: Duke University Press, 2007).

Sabsay, Leticia. "The Emergence of the Other Sexual Citizen: Orientalism and the Modernisation of Sexuality," *Citizenship Studies* 16, 5–6 (2012): 605–23.

Said, Edward. *Orientalism* (New York: Vintage Books, 1979).

Scott, Joan. *Only Paradoxes to Offer: French Feminists and the Rights of Man* (Cambridge, MA: Harvard University Press: 1996).

Scott, Joan. *The politics of the veil* (Princeton, NJ: Princeton University Press, 2007).

Spivak, Gayatri Chakravorty. "Can the Subaltern Speak?," in *Marxism and the Interpretation of Culture*, eds. C. Nelson and L. Grossberg (Urbana, IL: University of Illinois Press, 1988).

Tasker, Yvonne and Diane Negra, eds. *Interrogating Postfeminism: Gender and Politics of Popular Culture* (Durham, NC: Duke University Press, 2007).

Zerilli, Linda. *Feminism and the Abyss of Freedom* (Chicago: University of Chicago Press, 2005).

3
Disorienting Austerity: The Indebted Citizen as the New Soul of Europe

Andrea Mura

Abstract

This chapter examines the relation between citizenship and orientalism under the new conditions of indebtedness resulting from austerity. By broadly drawing on Lacanian psychoanalysis, the chapter argues that austerity has enacted a new economy of anxiety predicated upon the 'intensification' of certain affects (sacrifice, pain, restraint) and disavowal of others (indulgence, gratification, pleasure), contributing to reconfigure European political subjectivities. Taking its departure from this new economy, the crisis of Europe is described as the anxiety produced by a reversal of those paradigms that have sustained the image of Europe so far. This reversal coincides with a return in Europe of that which for a long time was ejected outside in order for Europe itself to be constituted as a unified symbolic reality. The chapter illustrates how this new economy has exposed a certain 'disorienting' effect of austerity, contributing to rekindling the ambiguities of Europe and therefore reconfiguring the image of the European self against its others. It concludes that this reconfiguration forms the background against which a new relationship between citizenship and orientalism in contemporary Europe should be examined.

Introduction

In a famous elaboration of the concept of crisis in the *Prison Notebooks*, Antonio Gramsci pointed to that particular context in which 'the ruling class has lost its consensus' and the masses 'have become detached from their traditional ideologies'. The crisis, he added, 'consists precisely in the fact that the old is dying and the new cannot be born; in this interregnum a great variety of morbid symptoms appear'.[1] Zygmunt Bauman has recently emphasized how Gramsci's understanding of crisis had resignified the traditional idea of interregnum, detaching it 'from its habitual association with the interlude of (routine) transmission of hereditary or electable power'.[2] By allowing for new productive uses of this category, which stressed the transition to a new institutional and ideological system, Gramsci could thus relate his notion of crisis to the extraordinary situations in which 'the extant legal frame of social order loses its grip and can hold no longer, whereas a new frame, made to the measure of newly emerged conditions responsible for making the old frame useless, is still at the designing stage, has not yet been fully assembled, or is not strong enough to be put in its place'.[3] In light of such a resignification, the present-day planetary condition would constitute for Bauman an inter-regnum, signalling the dying of the 'old' triune principle of territory, state, and nation as 'the key to the planetary distribution of sovereignty' in the face of a 'new' context in which sovereignty is 'so to speak, unanchored and free-floating'. New forces emerge, including multinational financial, industrial, and trade companies. 'Times of interregnum are thus times of uncertainty.'[4]

When actualizing Bauman's proposition, accounting for what is perhaps not yet a fully assembled 'new frame' in Europe, we might ask whether: 'Times of interregnum are thus times of austerity'. It is in fact since the beginning of 2010 that a number of signifiers have begun to resurface and float in the European public space, assuming primary symbolic relevance. For many years, they had been either repressed or deferred (*ejected*) to 'alien' contexts – in Europe but in other 'times' or in the same times but in other 'places'. Signifiers such as 'austerity', 'sacrifice', and 'indebtedness' began to appear in the headings of official documents and policy measures devised to counter the disastrous effect of the 2008 financial crisis as well as in the headlines of world leading newspapers commenting on those same policies. Titles like 'No age of austerity for the rich'[5] or 'Europe embraces the cult of austerity – but at what cost?'[6] accounted for the reactivation of 'austerity' as the term – full of historical connotations – that could best reflect the kind of vision informing the massive cuts on public spending that European governments were just about to put in place. Indeed, in spring 2010, massive public sector cuts were announced across Europe. The UK Chancellor of the Exchequer, George Osborne, delivered what he termed an 'unavoidable budget', a £40bn package of emergency tax increases and welfare cuts. German Chancellor Angela Merkel's 'unprecedented' austerity package involved initial spending cuts of 11.2 billion euros.[7]

In this play of resignification, old statements acquired new meaning, assuming deep symbolic value, as we shall see shortly. A phrase pronounced by Merkel during a meeting with the Christian Democrat party in December 2008 in the southwest German region of Swabia, 'hub of the Protestant work ethic', became a new universal trope, able to capture the kind of linguistic play that discourses on austerity would instantiate henceforth with their intertwining of economic (pragmatic) assertions and moral connotations.[8] 'One should,' she declared, 'simply have asked a Swabian housewife, she would have told us her worldly wisdom: in the long run, you can't live beyond your means.'[9] Besides the reassuring figure of the good 'austere' housewife who knows how to keep a sensible family budget free from excessive and 'inessential' pleasure – times of austerity in Europe have indeed come to be associated very often with female prime ministers (read Margaret Thatcher in the United Kingdom and Merkel in Germany) – this sentence stirred a sense of fear and anxiety with regard to the political plan it was about to sustain. Fears now surrounded the very idea of Europe. The possibility emerged that those features that up to that point had been seen as its fundamental assets could be compromised or *reversed* altogether (i.e., stability, wealth). 'By undermining social cohesion, this strategy also weakens public support for the entire European project on which past economic success has been built. The deficit hawks must not prevail.'[10]

In the wake of the Greek debt crisis from late 2009 onwards, the economies of some European Union members became bound ever more tightly to financial markets, credit rating agencies, and international institutions such as the International Monetary Fund. Pressure was put on Germany to use its financial weight to sustain a bailout package and realize the possibility of a different economic governance in the euro zone. This pressure, however, was soon accompanied by new internal tensions in Europe, vividly highlighting the symbolic instability of European self-representation as an assumed unified cultural reality. If 'a reluctant Berlin' was thus accused of being 'irresponsible, selfish and even un-European', Merkel's statement about the Swabian housewife was used not simply as a general and systemic assertion (*we*, citizens of Europe, have all enjoyed far too much, beyond *our* means). It was quickly *turned* against Germany's neighbours in the EU, assuming immediate cultural nuances. As the *New York Times* was quick to observe, 'if France wants Germany to be more European, Germany wants Europe to be more Swabian'.[11] Needless to say, following the sovereign-debt crisis in South Europe, Merkel's statement performed a major metaphorical role, embodying strong moral hints when referred to – or perceived by – the henceforth-labelled category of PIGS (Portugal, Italy, Greece, and Spain). The message becomes: If European indulgence was naïve, yours was deceitful and guilty, the recurrent sign of your time-honoured corruption, the mark of an abusive inclusion in the club of the Europeans for which you were culturally inadequate.

It is precisely these kinds of turns and detours in regard to the recent financial 'crisis' and politics of austerity that are examined in this chapter. As canonical tradition has never stopped reminding us, the concept of *crisis* entails not just the phase of deterioration of a medical condition but the turning point in a disease.[12] The temporal and spatial dimension in which a *separation* is enacted between two planes (from Greek *krei* 'to distinguish, to separate') and a *decision* (*krinein* 'to judge') has therefore to be assumed in regards to the direction to be taken. Because of its fundamental function as a 'limit' in its own etymology, this turning point does not appear without its tensions. Rather than figuring as a 'rupture' at its purest, or the linear and progressive unfolding of a movement towards a necessary direction (e.g., the degeneration of a disease), this 'turn' stands as a para-doxical moment of suspension (*interregnum*) inhabited by reversals, shifts, rotations, detours, and transgressions between continuity and discontinu-ity. It is in this sense that Antonio Gramsci, in his continuous reworking of the notion of crisis while addressing the 'catastrophic' effects of the 1929 Wall Street Crash, warned against the temptation to conceive the crisis as an 'event' rather than a 'complex process' or an unfolding (*svolgimento*): 'the cri-sis is nothing but the quantitative intensification of certain elements (which are neither new nor original) – but especially the intensification of certain phenomena – while others, which previously appeared and worked together with them, have been immunized, becoming either inoperative or disap-pearing altogether'.[13]

Our interest in this chapter is to explore the discursive dimension of this austere 'complex' interregnum, highlighting the type of resignification that these detours have entailed, and accounting for the destabilizing 'morbid symptoms', as Gramsci put it, that have appeared at the level of European political subjectivities. While more generally maintaining that Europe func-tions, constitutively, as a *concept of crisis* – with the idea of Europe standing as a critical process of constant separation and decision over what constitutes the field of the European (self, citizen, other) – this chapter accounts for some of the major turns that austerity discourses have triggered in the *debt crisis*, with a play of 'intensification' and *reactivation* of certain phenomena to the detriment of others that have become 'immunized', or simply (tem-porarily) 'inoperative'. This has enacted what can be called an *economy of anxiety*, contributing to reconfigure the image of the European and the rela-tion with its others.

The Il-liberal Turn[14]

In his recent inquiry into the socio-political predicament of the (European) financial crisis, Maurizio Lazzarato highlighted the biopolitical effects pro-duced by the creditor and debtor relationship.[15] According to Lazzarato, the *working poor* stand out as the new subjective figure of a system in which debt and shareholding are proposed as the only alternatives to the increas-ing impoverishment that the reduction of salary and the elimination of social provisions have produced in the last decades. With declining wages and pensions mostly postponed to later age, access to credit and personal share portfolios have been proposed as a tool, a form of *investment* in the self, able to compensate for changed social and economic conditions. Cru-cially, the *right* to higher education, housing, forms of social protection, and social services has been reformulated in the form of *benefit*, while its very possibility of enjoyment is conditional upon the adoption of housing and mortgage credit, student loans, and private insurance. According to Laz-zarato, the ultimate nexus between private debt and sovereign debt that the crisis has exposed in Europe would finally reflect the function of debt 'as a "capture", "predation" and "extraction" machine on the whole of society', and a 'mechanism for the production and "government" of collective and individual subjectivities'.[16]

The new discursive emphasis on 'scarcity' and 'indebtedness' in Europe triggered by austerity has furthermore been accompanied in recent years by a critical convergence of *budget deficit* and *democratic deficit*. To intervene on budget deficit has very often required bypassing democratic procedures. This includes the following: the routinization of constitutional tools originally thought of to deal with cases of particular 'necessity and urgency' in places such as Italy and Greece; the increasing use of confidence votes effectively curbing parliamentary debate; the growing dispossession of parliaments' legislative and oversight prerogatives; and the attempts, in specific cases, to halt popular consultation through votes, elections, or referenda in countries such as Italy, Cyprus, or Greece. This overall picture problematizes well-established accounts of neoliberal discourse, whose distinct 'ideological' traits have long been associated with rhetorics of prosperity, unlimited consumption, and the celebration of a 'post-ideological' world promising a cosmopolitan future of harmony and enjoyment, where social tensions are said to be accommodated by way of consensus-seeking procedures which render social conflict unnecessary, ideological divisions obsolete, and all material needs satisfied.[17] In psychoanalytic terms, advanced capitalist societies have long been related to an obscene context modelled around the neoliberal injunction to enjoy, which transforms social bonds into objectified and consumerist relations, demanding the production of increased quotas of surplus enjoyment (*plus-de-juir*).[18]

But what happens when the object of satisfaction is no longer available? When austerity programmes emerge that impose new limits on consumption and seem to go against the neoliberal and capitalist injunction to enjoy? For Lazzarato, this denotes the beginning of a 'new phase' marked by an 'authoritarian turn'.[19] With this formula, he refers to the final abandonment of the 'European social model' and the attempt by the state to organize the passage from the neoliberal policies of credit of the 1980s and the 1990s 'to the new authoritarian and repressive forms of the repayment of debt and the figure of the indebted men'.[20] In contrast to what seems to be Lazzarato's connotation of this 'turn' as a moment of change and rupture, however, we would like to stress the level of structural complexity informing this term, highlighting its link to that Gramscian idea of crisis as a complex unfolding mentioned above. From this standpoint, the il-liberal turn points to a shift in the rhetoric of freedom, with a downplaying of its usual play on liberal attitudes, success, prosperity, and credit in favour of other elements that were once thrust aside (or 'outside' the cultural borders of Europe) and that are now intensified – namely, illiberal practices, failure, poverty, and debt. These two sides constitute what we call the *il-liberal nexus*, with the dash in this term emphasizing the structural contiguity of credit and debt, 'liberal' and 'illiberal' tendencies (the latter, thus, being just an internal component of it). At this point, a Lacanian perspective can be introduced to expose the level of complexity at stake.

According to French psychoanalyst Charles Melman, the psycho-social paradigm organizing advanced capitalist societies could be described in terms of a 'generalized perversion'.[21] Roughly, in Lacanian psychoanalysis 'perversion' denotes a structural position in which the subject veils the symbolic experience of castration through *disavowal* ('I know it happened, but I carry on *as if* it hasn't').[22] It denotes the subject's attempt to pursue *'jouissance* as far as possible', moving beyond the pleasure principle, the Freudian homeostatic limit imposed on bodily pleasure in order for it to be bearable to the subject.[23] The expression 'generalized perversion' denotes, therefore, the tendency of what Lacan once called 'the discourse of the capitalist' to promote a certain *excess* of pleasure, transgressing the limits and the norms that sustain the pleasure principle.[24] Melman's reference to perversion, in this regard, fully adapts to an old context dominated by the neoliberal celebration of credit and prosperity. We believe, however, that this clinical figure can also help understand the kind of libidinal economy that the debt economy instantiates, revealing the way in which anxiety interacts with lack, *jouissance,* and castration in times of austerity.

In Freudian psychoanalysis, while anxiety was initially seen as the effect of an inadequate discharge of 'physical sexual tension' arising out of libido,[25] it became, in later theories, an 'affective state' situated at the level of the ego and resulting from the perception of a threat.[26] Besides linking the nature of this threat to the possibility of organic injury, however, Freud also connected it to the overwhelming dimension of the event, to what Lacan would later define in terms of the real. With this term, Lacan referred to the excessive character of the event, pointing to the impossibility to fully symbolize and codify empirical reality. In this respect, anxiety emerges in association with a situation that is or can be traumatic and *uncodable* – such as the loss of the mother ('separation anxiety'), loss of love, object-loss, and so on. It is an effect – or the anticipation of an effect – of an encounter with the uncoded, an experience of trauma and castration that cannot be symbolized.

In addition, Lacan also considers anxiety as a condition emerging when lack itself fails to appear, when 'the lack happens to be lacking'.[27] If translated into the Oedipal scene, anxiety here would not result from loss and separation but would be an effect of the very proximity with the incestuous object. In this context, anxiety results from a full access to *jouissance*, which would obstruct or veil the emergence of lack. This means that the subject would experience the condition that occurs when lack happens to be lacking, a condition of absence of norms, prohibitions, and limits to *jouissance*, a deadly proximity to the object of satisfaction that would 'consummate' the subject when the object is 'consumed':

I'll simply point out to you that a good many things may arise in the sense of anomalies, but that's not what provokes anxiety in us. But should all the norms, that is, that which makes for anomaly just as much as that which makes for lack, happen all of a sudden not to be lacking, that's when the anxiety starts.[28]

It is precisely because of the complex dynamics of anxiety, as an effect of both separation and loss on the one hand, and proximity and lack of limits on the other, that Lacan can state that: 'anxiety is very precisely the meeting point where all my previous discourse awaits you'.[29] It is here that we can trace the perverse character of neoliberal discourse, where the saturation of lack produced by the proliferation of libidinal objects makes the very anxiety of the subject vibrate, an anxiety that consummates the subject at the very moment it consumes its object of satisfaction.

This consummation, however, is itself an object of consumption. The consummation of the other is an effect of the instrumental character of *jouissance* in the discourse of the capitalist. The ability of a system marked by the neoliberal discourse to rouse the anxiety of the subject can also be seen, in fact, in terms of the instrumental logic informing perverse desire. In subcategories of perversion such as sadism and masochism, for instance, the subject becomes the *powerful* 'instrument of the Other's *jouissance*'.[30] By assuming the position of the object-instrument of the 'will-to-enjoy', a perverse position finds its possibility of *jouissance* reliant on the *jouissance* of the other, working and directing its activity to achieve this objective. In allowing the other a certain access to *jouissance*, however, the power to provoke the experience of anxiety is also constituted. While the very proximity to *jouissance* by the other remains somehow an excessive experience, this proximity is irremediably dependent on the whims of the pervert who acts as its means and who might, in fact, tend to enact a play of presence and absence of this access, offer, and subtraction of *jouissance*, support for its access, and blackmail as soon as this access is realized. What we have is then an ultimate transferral of the very experience of castration to the field of the other. As Lacan put it: 'the anxiety of the other, his essential existence as a subject in relation to this anxiety, this is precisely the string that sadistic desire means to pluck'.[31] By stirring the anxiety of the other through an encounter with *jouissance*, hence consummating the other through a transposal of castration, a certain consumption of libidinal economy is also secured for the pervert and ultimately realized.

A fundamental link between *jouissance* and anxiety, excitement and blackmail, consumption and consummation characterizes, therefore, the perverse framework here delineated. Renata Salecl has examined the dangerous allure that the pervert exerts over the other, accounting for the destabilizing encounter of pleasure (for instance, sexual pleasures, freedom of choice, and consuming the object of satisfaction, etc.) and fear (AIDS, Anthrax attacks in the 1990s, 'guilt' when the very possibility to enjoy is prevented) across several 'ages of anxiety' intensifying in the period between the 1990s and the recent War on Terror.[32] We believe that this link finds expression, more recently, in those elements of corruption and generalized blackmail that Lazzarato, for instance, considers to be 'consubstantial to the neoliberal model', but which appear also as the structural effects of that very regime of freedom that Foucault himself detected.[33] It is within this perverse scenario that, for instance, we interpret the anti-social function of the so-called precariat.[34] This stands as a new form of proletariat trapped in the pervasive logic of blackmail *qua* condition for excitement: hence, neoliberal labour policies murmuring, from a perverse standpoint, 'if you wish to work, to *enjoy* the benefits of work, then you need to accept your exposure to uncertainty, precarity and lack of rights, even at the cost of exploitation'. While the economic convenience of the recent proliferation of temporary jobs, mini-jobs, precarious jobs in Europe is questionable (minor labour costs are often accompanied by minor productivity in terms of motivation and qualification of the *working poor*), the disciplinary effects are clear, contributing to enhance the level of uncertainty and blackmailing of society as a whole.[35]

It is, again, within this framework that we read the incredible rhetorical force of those gauges that in the last years have measured the level of threat and danger, and whose use, however, has functioned to increase uncertainty and anxiety. We think, for instance, about the way in which national terrorist alert scales were devised during the 'War on Terror', using the colours of the traffic light to signal the level of imminent danger, with the result, of course, that colours changed so quickly and unreasonably, even several times per day, that paralysis was produced as a result, with people ultimately unable to rate their condition of safety and inclined, in conditions of anxiety, to accept heavy restrictions on civil rights. As Jackson put it, 'the language of threat and danger was not inevitable or simply a neutral or objective evaluation of the threat. Rather, it was the deliberative and systematic construction of a social climate of fear'.[36]

It is in this complex context of *jouissance* and anxiety, excitement and blackmail, that the logic of credit and the logic of debit disclose their structural contiguity, manifesting the contradictory nature of capital as an unrelenting producer of codes. Capitalism reveals here its axiomatic nature, dominated by 'abundance' in conjunction with 'scarcity', as Deleuze put it in his lessons preceding the publication of the *Anti-Oedipus*: 'an axiomatic with a limit that cannot be saturated' so that when it encounters something new which it does not recognize, 'it is always ready to add one more axiom to restore its functioning'.[37] It is here that the logic of an abundance of capital intersects with the logic of scarcity and austerity in a terrain where 'semiotics of guilt' and 'semiotics of innocence' overlap.[38] Hence, the impersonal voice of a fluctuating 'market' emerges whispering: 'you should enjoy and live in harmony with your credit. But if you do, be ready for the failing effects of this enjoyment, your condition of indebtedness!' Or, conversely: 'you should abstain from enjoyment in times of austerity, yet, shame on you if you do abstain, as you are not helping your economy!' In this respect, the il-liberal nexus sustaining the phantasm of freedom of neoliberal discourse appears to be marking not so much the erupting emergence of a debt economy opening a new authoritarian phase but the critical and complex *processuality* of an economy of anxiety in a context where old and new codes coexist, guilt and innocence overlap, liberal and illiberal practices coalesce, and the subject is suspended in the uncodable terrain of a contradictory circularity between success and failure, satisfaction and emptiness, limitless credit and limitless debt. In the face of this uncodable terrain where conflicting codes overlay, where the neoliberal emphasis on self-entrepreneurship and success is contrasted with the inability to properly manage the all-pervasive dimension of indebtedness, anxiety emerges as the inevitable condition of a real encounter with the uncoded.

The Disorienting Function of Austerity: European Detours

It is against this background that crucial questions arise in the wake of the 2014 elections to the European Parliament, which juxtaposed pro-European against anti-European factions, challenging, as never before, the validity and the meaning of the European project, its ability to provide a shared political, cultural, and imaginary horizon for millions of citizens within the European borders. What has been the impact of this overall debate on the idea of Europe? What are the effects of an economy of anxiety on current rearticulations of orientalist narratives and possible reconfigurations of European subjectivities?

Returning to our definition of Europe as a concept of *crisis*, we believe that the conceptualization of limits, the ability to draw and 'decide' lines of 'separation' between planes, spaces, phases, whether in the form of political borders or cultural boundaries, is a good starting point for attempting to answer this set of questions. When considering, for instance, the construction of the nation-state discourse in Europe, and the progressive affirmation of the very idea of Europe as the cultural and political horizon of those nations, a 'paranoid' principle of integrity can be said to have played a major constitutive role. By this we mean it has allowed for the adoption of rigid and clear-cut lines of separation, for example between the inside and the outside of the nation or the idea of Europe as a whole vis-à-vis a savage, oriental outside. In broad psychoanalytic terms, this required reverting a fundamental logic informing the fantasy of the subject, its relation to that something (*object petit a,* as Lacan termed it) that should be excluded, mediated, and kept at a distance in order for the subject to have normal access to reality. In the clinical figure of paranoia, this primordial movement of reversion is realized by *ejecting* this inassimilable something outside, *projecting* it into the other who, precisely because of its superimposed association with this something, will figure henceforth as a threatening and persecutory presence. It is, however, this ejection that allows a certain field (the field of the subject, whether the national or the European subject) to be constituted as an image of pure unity and integrity. A paranoid regime of separation, when linked to concepts of rectitude and innocence, has been crucial to sustain the ideal of moral supremacy of European nations, enacting an intimate link between national narratives and logocentric orientalist motifs. Since Said's groundbreaking work, *Orientalism*,[39] wide attention has been given to the negative dialectic informing the cultural imaginary of European nations, with colonial subjects becoming the object of pervasive forms of power-knowledge through which they were perceived as 'other' and defined in terms not simply of *difference* but of *radical opposition*. As Hardt and Negri pointed out, 'What first appeared as a simple logic of exclusion, then, turns out to be a negative dialectic of recognition. The colonizer does produce the colonized as negation, but, through a dialectical twist, that negative colonized identity is negated in turn to found the positive colonizer Self'.[40] Hence, the long series of dichotomies defining a colonizable and orientalized other as uncivilized, emotional, undemocratic, and allowing for the dialectical construction of a new civilized, rational, and liberal European citizen. This logic, therefore, informs the orientalist gesture of Europe at an embryonic level, allowing that something that cannot be symbolized of its own history and politics, its own 'impurity', to be ejected in the figure of the stranger: its oriental and *orienting* other. It is because of the construction of this oriental excessive other, in fact, that Europe could 'orient' itself at the level of the constitution of the Self along a principle of integrity.

An early example of this dynamic can be found in the range of discourses on Asiatic despotism that began to circulate in Europe in the seventeenth and eighteenth centuries. In his *The Sultan's Court*, Alain Grosrichard links Asiatic despotism to an ongoing tension between democratic and absolutist instances at the time of the emergence of European nations. This resulted in the re-elaboration of the classic concept of 'tyranny', which was so central to the philosophical and political debate in ancient Greece.[41] Tyrannical tendencies were extracted from the image of Europe and distorted, located, and ejected in the figure of the oriental despot, which came to epitomize the 'nature' of Asiatic societies, allowing, at the same time, for the reorganization of European subjectivities along the unitary, liberal, and 'integral' character of the 'people'. This entailed distancing national identity historically, from both feudal and absolutist modes of power, and culturally, by moving towards geo-political settings against which the new national Self could play its specificity. It is precisely the paranoid mechanism described above that permits tracing the internal logic of this movement whereby the image of a deviant and intrusive otherness marked by historical obsolescence and cultural anomie (e.g., Asiatic patrimonial and personalistic modes of power based on bodily pleasure and license) was functional to the self-representation of a new Europe. In place of the contemporaneous figure of the oriental despot (as a locus of infinite and perverse *jouissance*), the rational and liberal traits of emerging European nations could then be forged and mobilized externally, in colonial settings, and internally, as a disciplinary paradigm, reflecting the fundamental paranoid logic of reversion described here through a phantasmatic relation between external *aggression* and internal *subversion*.

In recent decades, a sharp contrast between 'capitalist authoritarian states' and 'liberal-democratic counterparts' or, more succinctly, between 'Western' and 'authoritarian' capitalism has denoted a similar mechanism in motion. New capitalist developments in countries such as China, Russia, and some East Asian economies (Singapore, Taiwan, etc.) have been said to retain forms of direct coercion that characterize precapitalist economic systems, with politically unorganized labour deprived of those forms of social protection that distinguished class-formed 'Western' capitalism in its crucial association with democratic political systems.[42] While a key achievement of the latter has long been located in the 'expansion of social citizenship associated with the welfare state', such achievement assumes full significance when juxtaposed with 'Asiatic societies', where the supposed lack of customary and social rights and state control and the absence of forms of social articulation qualifies the deviant authoritarian trait of these economic systems.[43] This juxtaposition, as we have seen, is not a new one. Besides old-fashioned discourses about Asiatic despotism, Marx's writings on the economic modes of production in India deployed a similar mechanism, using analyses of precapitalist Europe to describe economic developments in the 'Orient'. This mechanism of reversion was certainly strengthened by the hegemonic affirmation of modernist theories, whereby a number of stages were posed in the evolutionary process from 'traditional' to modern 'mature' societies, with emphasis put on the process of industrialization as being productive of socioeconomic transformations (such as an increasing institutional differentiation) and distinct cultural paradigms (scientific rationality, democratization, the belief in progress).

The limits of this approach – whether with theories of the origin of capitalism or modernist analyses of traditional societies – have been largely discussed, exposing the distortions that analyses using Western experience to inquire into non-Western contexts produce.[44] The aspect that we would like to highlight, however, concerns the way that such accounts are retrospectively used to recount and validate European theories themselves and the self-representation of Europe. Again, a logic of reversion is at stake here, one that fully mobilizes the *orienting* function of the Orient to account for Europe's past, present, and future. It is not surprising that even when caution is displayed against orientalist tropes, such an orienting function is retained: 'Modern-day China is not an oriental-despotic distortion of capitalism, but rather the repetition of capitalism's development in Europe itself'.[45] In the European transition from 'welfare state to the new global economy', authoritarian capitalism stands not as 'merely a remainder of our past but a portent of our future'. This statement by Žižek, with its limits and merits, was enounced in the context preceding the 2008 financial crisis.

But what happens when this transition to the new global economy seems to have reached its final stage? What happens when the debt economy brings about the ultimate dismantling of European welfare states, and those same features that had been ejected to the East are now reinstated to discipline European societies? What happens when budget deficit and democracy deficit become more and more the concrete reality of Europe itself, and austerity discourses emerge that assume the enfeeblement of social and labour rights as a necessary remedy against the challenges of the present, if not a marker of progress, a way to keep abreast of the times? To put it another way, what happens to the orienting role of the Orient when the Orient ceases to be the Orient because its attributes have been dispersed in the real and symbolic determinations of the West?

In the complex turn from the rhetorics of credit, innocence, and freedom to those of debt, guilt, and failure, we pointed to the return in Europe of most of those features that had sustained its self-representation in post-war times, allowing the crisis of Europe to be first and foremost an identity crisis, a detour of its own imaginary, a moment of suspension and interregnum.[46] Hence, new discourses appear aimed to separate and decide about what constitutes the field of *Europeanness* and consequently redesign the field of *Orientness*. We testify here to a certain reactivation and intensification of orientalist projections at an *intra*-European level. We saw, in this respect, the way in which in the wake of the Greek debt crisis, accusations of 'egoism' and 'lack of solidarity' towards Northern European partners have largely been juxtaposed by narratives portraying the ultimate corrupted, irresponsible, and somehow 'oriental' traits of South Europe and the so-called PIGS (Portugal, Italy, Greece, and Spain) in what has been called a 'spaghetti Orientalism'.[47]

More than simply calling into question old rivalries between European countries, such discourses seem to stand as the natural effects of the generalized reorganization of European subjectivities that austerity has enacted under the rule of an economy of anxiety and the indebted man. What if these discourses reveal, then, the very *dis-orienting* function of austerity in times of European detours? What if they reveal the ultimate enfeeblement of the orienting function of the Orient at the time of a new *critical* moment of redefinition of Europe's own imaginary and identity; in a word, a new traumatic encounter with the uncoded?

The Indebted Citizen

To answer this set of questions, emphasis should be put on the type of libidinal economy that we examined in the first part of the article, when we addressed the range of conflicting affects that sustain austerity discourses in Europe. We pointed to the affirmation of a new subject, who is constitutively indebted and anxious, and whose 'entrepreneurship', as required by the dispositif of debt, is now directed at the management of an unsolvable 'knot' intertwining conflicting passions such as sacrifice and gratification, pain and pleasure, restraint and indulgence. What makes this knot unsolvable is the immensurability and immeasurability that the logic of debt enacts in this framework, a debt that escapes any possibility of quantification, standing as a function, not a concrete quantifiable exchange. This allows for an ongoing circulation of consumption and consummation which nullifies any possibility whatsoever of a final fulfilment of debt. More than simply mobilizing a classic negative dialectic at an infra-European level (Southern Europe fulfilling the role of an orienting constitutive outside towards Northern Europe and vice versa), discourses on PIGS and the like point to the construction of a new 'soul' of Europe morally 'responsible' for a condition of generalized *indebtedness*. The parsimonious distribution of 'benefits' that neoliberal economy has granted in substitution of old twentieth-century 'rights' – replacing the 'general' and 'abstract' character of rights with the 'particularistic' and 'conditional' character of the benefit – goes in this direction, contributing to the ultimate transition from the post-war figure of the *entitled citizen* to the neoliberal figure of, we would call here, the *indebted citizen*, the new soul of Europe.

We argued that the anxiety of Europe is, among other things, partly elucidated above, the anxiety of a return in Europe of that which was either projected in the figure of the phantasmatic and excessive other or repressed in the distorted shadows of its own history and politics. More than simply entailing the abandon of old narratives of prosperity, liberality, and credit, we suggest that this return coincides in Europe with the emergence of the indebted citizen, who stands as the new paradigmatic figure of the disoriented development described above. While denoting the construction of a new 'European' upon whom rests now the 'responsibility' to administrate the inextricable knot of its own indebtedness, with its conflation of guilt and satisfaction and the impossibility to gain final redemption, an economy of anxiety is once again what the biopolitical dispositif of debt mobilizes. This is well evidenced by the conditional logic organizing the discourse on benefits. While their allocation assumes more and more the form of conditional gift – dependent on acceptance of the new harsh rules of the labour market, neoliberal structural reforms, and so on – their enjoyment remains irremediably subjected to endless revisions and evaluations, which can lead to their withdrawal at any moment. We see here how the critical encounter between an offer of enjoyment and the possibility of its withholding that we posited at the centre of this economy of anxiety is activated in this context, producing once again an inevitable interplay of guilt and satisfaction. The very acceptance of these same benefits by the indebted citizen entails in fact discriminating between the recipients of the benefits and those who remain suspended in an interval of precarity, so reproducing a vicious circuit of privilege, consumption, and guilt.

The logic of confession, when thought of in association with the apparatus of indebtedness, offers a good perspective from which to consider the dynamics mobilized here. In his recent work, Andrea Teti has drawn on Foucault's analyses of *confession* to explore the operation of democratization as a discourse with regards to the Middle East. In this space, orientalist characterizations are said to rely on positionalities that parallel those of Confessor and Sinner in the first volume of Foucault's *History of Sexuality*,[48] allowing for forms of cultural essentialism on Arabo-Islamic 'deviant' alterity. Within this perspective, 'disciplinary interventions are framed in order to generate a productive failure, which provides the root mechanism through which confessional – and thus Orientalist – discourses are capable of (re)producing their specific subject positions and relations of power'.[49] Whether with discourses on modernization or democratization, a 'polymorphous and deviant causality' constantly fails and reproduces an emancipatory/reformatory agenda instantiated by the Occident and introjected by the Orient, transforming 'any Orientalist discourse into a carceral space, the fundamental function of which is to govern the other by framing its purpose as emancipation on this confessional discourse's own terms, and by disciplining its (inevitable) failures'.[50]

This enacts a circularity between failure, care, and discipline, whose operational workings, seemingly, we saw transposed in the European activation of an 'unpayable debt' mobilizing the anxious circuit between semiotics of guilt and semiotics of innocence just described. Only ten years ago, discourses about the renegotiation of Third-World debt and the disciplinary effects of foreign aid (with its necessary links to neoliberal structural reforms and confessional strategies) denoted the centrality of the 'indebtedness paradigm' in the relation between Europe and its others, contributing to sustain the image of a Europe of prosperity and credit and to reproduce the 'indebted' and 'failing' position of the Third World. The return of the indebtedness paradigm from the 'laboratory' of emerging economies to Europe helps us to identify a further sign of detour in the European crisis.

This return figures, as we put it, as a return in Europe of that which, from outside, allowed Europe to be constituted as a unified symbolic reality: Europe, a space of prosperity, democracy, labour, and social protection, opposed to the authoritarian quality of Asiatic *despotic* states and *despotic* capitalisms; Europe, as a space of credit, abode of creditors, as opposed to a Third World, to whom *aid* had once to be granted – on condition, of course, of *rights* being transformed into *benefits* after neoliberal structural reforms; Europe as the house of the *modernist* paradigm yielding shelter to industrialization, belief in progress, social and institutional differentiation – all features missing in the 'primitive' sociality of the Rest and now leaving a vacuum in the current context of uncertainty, stagnation, deindividualization, and deinstitutionalization of Europe. The anxiety of the critical turn that the crisis has instantiated is the anxiety of the return of all those elements that had once marked the field of the other, and that now populate the social life of most Europeans, making old orientalist narratives somehow enfeebled, if not untenable. How to talk about authoritarian capitalism, in fact, in the face of today's European 'need' for flexibility, a flexibility that serves, more and more, as a masquerade of the precariat?

This is not to say that these elements were absent before European austerity. But the hegemonic position that austerity discourses have granted them produces a fundamental encounter at the level of symbolic inscription, allowing for a general reshaping of European subjectivities. If, as Foucault put it, 'in the universality of Western Reason [*ratio*], there is a split [*partage*] which is the Orient: the Orient thought of as origin, dreamt of as the vertiginous point from which are born nostalgias and promises of a return', an encounter with this split, with this original constitutive truth, can only stand as an encounter with the uncoded, with that 'lack of lack' that we posited as a crucial condition for anxiety.[51] It is here, in this crucial movement of turns and reversions, with Europe somehow compelled to confront the Orient inside itself (that is, the reversion and return of all those paradigms that bestowed on Europe its ontological consistency) that we can detect the crisis of Europe and envisage the interplay of different strategies at work. Hence, once again, the deployment of paranoid solutions aimed at imposing an hypertrophic line of separation between the Orient and the Occident, with the effect of recompacting the idea of Europe along a logic of rejection in a critical context of social and cultural dis-*orientation*. This tendency, however, combines with other disciplinary frameworks mobilizing different libidinal economies. When thinking about al-Qaeda in the aftermath of 9/11, it is easy to detect, for instance, the instantiation of a paranoid strategy sustaining the persecutory phantasm of an illiberal Islam, while, at the same time, testifying to a perverse mobilization of al-Qaeda's spectre as a vehicle of anxiety in a framework organized upon the production, consumption, and consummation of insecurity and fear. Similarly, the recent surfacing of ISIS (Islamic State of Iraq and Syria; English acronym for DAIISH, *Al-Dawla al-Islamiya fi al-Iraq wa al-Sham*) in the international scene, right at the moment of a crucial passage with the 2014 European elections and the utmost eruption of anti-European feelings, seems to produce a twofold effect. On the one side, it helps to recompact the European field in the aftermath of a harsh electoral campaign dominated by populist movements, rekindling the old civilizational position of the West against a barbarian Islamic terror; on the other, it re-enacts a confessional logic revitalizing the same rhetoric that was used following September 11, with European Muslims asked, on a daily basis, to *confess* what they stand for: to unremittingly declare their abhorrence of Islamic terror (e.g., recent demonstrations declaring: 'Not in our names!'); to publicly stand against the ISIS, so reproducing the *impossible* task for the *indebted* Muslim, whether outside or inside Europe: to keep pace with and finally prove compatibility with democracy and tolerance. We see reproduced here a generalized mechanism of production and consumption of failure at work in the debt economy, with the crucial nexus between orientalism and citizenship reconfigured along the paradigm of the new indebted citizen of Europe, which now extends to the whole society. It is here that we locate the *dis-orienting* function of austerity and its ability to mobilize a typical transferral of sadistic perversion by which the symbolic experience of castration is turned over to the other, and an 'inassimilable' core of anguish (*anxiety*) is passed on, as Lacan would say, in the imperturbable and 'soulless' location of God:[52] the irresponsible Muslim, Christian, or lay European citizen now remodelled, through an *unsolvable* knot, in the figure of the indebted citizen, responsible in the end for a new soul to be provoked, blamed, cared for, and disciplined.

Notes

1 A. Gramsci, "'Wave of Materialism' and 'Crisis of Authority'," (1930/1972), 275–6.
2 Z. Bauman, "Times of interregnum," (2012), 49.
3 Ibid.
4 Ibid., 51.
5 http://www.theguardian.com/commentisfree/cifamerica/2010/jun/30/useconomy-georgeosborne
6 http://www.theguardian.com/business/2010/jun/13/europe-embraces-cult-of-austerity
7 http://www.telegraph.co.uk/finance/budget/7846849/Budget-2010-Full-text-of-George-Osbornes statement.html
8 http://www.nytimes.com/2010/05/04/business/global/04iht-euro.html?_r=0
9 Ibid.
10 http://www.theguardian.com/commentisfree/2010/jun/25/g8-g20-europe-deficit-hawks
11 http://www.nytimes.com/2010/05/04/business/global/04iht-euro.html?_r=1&
12 R. Koselleck, *Critique and Crisis* (1952/1988).
13 A. Gramsci, "Q 15 (II) § 5, Passato e presente. La crisi," (1933/2001), 1756; translated by the author.
14 This section draws material from a previously published article, which examines the biopolitical workings of indebtedness from the viewpoint of Lacan's discourse of the capitalist: A. Mura, "Lacan and Debt: The Discourse of the Capitalist in Times of Austerity," *Philosophy Today* 59 (2015): 2. For an in-depth analysis of this relation, please refer to this article.
15 M. Lazzarato, "The Making of the Indebted Man: Essay on the Neoliberal Condition" (2012).
16 Ibid., 29.
17 For instance, A. Badiou, *Metapolitics* (2006); and J. Ranciére, *On the Shores of Politics* (2007).
18 For instance, F. Declercq, "Lacan on the Capitalist Discourse: Its Consequences for Libidinal Enjoyment and Social Bonds," (2006).

19 M. Lazzarato, "The Authoritarian turn of neoliberalism – Preface to the Italian edition," *La Fabbrica dell'Uomo Indebitato* (2012), 5–27, translated by the author.
20 Ibid., 18.
21 C. Melman, *L'homme sans gravité: Jouir à tout prix* (2002).
22 Roughly, expressions like 'paternal law' or 'symbolic castration' refer to the requirement of a certain drive renunciation that Freud posited as conditional for the inclusion of the subject in the programme of civilization. The 'oedipal' institution of the law in the forms of social and moral norms (but also the very function of language in Lacanian psychoanalysis) while 'limiting' the subject, 'humanizes' and 'socializes' it through that very request for sacrifice and renunciation. Although negative, this prohibition is therefore also productive, as it allows the subject to develop 'desire' (for instance, the desire to recover the very object that has been lost or sacrificed). Because of this sacrifice and drive renunciation, 'lack' is established as a fundamental constitutive feature of the subject.
23 J. Lacan, "The Subversion of the Subject and the Dialectic of Desire in the Freudian Unconscious" (1960/2006), 700. *Jouissance* (in English, 'enjoyment') figures in this context as a 'painful pleasure' that is always excessive for the physical survival of the subject: see, for instance, J. Lacan, *The Seminar Book VII, The Ethics of Psychoanalysis* (1959-1960/1992), 184.
24 J. Lacan, "Del discorso psicoanalitico," (1972/1978).
25 S. Freud, "Extracts from the Fliess Papers," (1894/1953-74), 191.
26 S. Freud, "Inhibitions, Symptoms and Anxiety," (1926/1953-74), 140.
27 J. Lacan, *Anxiety: The Seminar of Jacques Lacan, Book X* (1962-63/2014), 42.
28 Ibid.
29 Ibid., 3.
30 J. Lacan, "The Subversion of the Subject," 700.
31 J. Lacan, *Anxiety*, 104
32 R. Salecl, *On Anxiety* (2004).
33 M. Lazzarato, "The Authoritarian turn of neoliberalism – Preface to the Italian edition," (2012), 14.
34 G. Standing, "The Precariat: The New Dangerous Class" (2011).
35 A. Corsani and M. Lazzarato, *Intermittents et précaires* (2008).
36 R. Jackson, *Writing the War on Terrorism: Language, Politics and Counter-Terrorism* (2005), 120.
37 Deleuze, "Cours Vincennes – 16/11/1971: Capitalism, flows, the decoding of flows" (1971).
38 M. Lazzarato, "The Authoritarian turn of neoliberalism," 7.
39 E. Said, *Orientalism* (1978).
40 M. Hardt and A. Negri, *Empire* (2000), 128.
41 A. Grosrichard, *The Sultan's Court: European Fantasies of the East* (1979/1998).
42 J. Lee, "Western vs. Authoritarian Capitalism" (2009). For a critical reading on this point, see also, P. Bowles, *Capitalism* (2012).
43 P. Heller, *The Labor of Development: Workers and the Transformation of Capitalism in Kerala* (1999), 42.
44 G. Hamilton, *Commerce and Capitalism in Chinese Societies* (2006).
45 S. Žižek, "China's Valley of Tears – Is authoritarian capitalism the future?" (2007).
46 For a detailed account of the economic and social causes of the crisis and its impact on the narrative of prosperity and 'necessary' growth at the core of Europe's self-representation in post-war times, see I.T. Berend, *Europe in Crisis: Bolt From the Blue?* (2013). The debate about the crisis has touched upon the role

of the European Union vis-à-vis national members. In a recent analysis on the crisis and its effects on the European social model, Marie-Ange Moreau pointed to a rejuvenated function of the nation-state as 'important generator of policies to fight the effects of economic crisis', observing a higher reliance on national law over EU law by members, M.A., Moreau, ed., *Before and After the Economic Crisis: What Implications for the 'European Social Model'?* (2011), 4. From a critical angle, Wolfgang Streeck advocated a stronger role of those institutions – included revitalized national institutions – able to regulate financial markets, denoting a fundamental recasting of the European state system during the crisis, with the incipient formation of a European multilevel governance regime subsuming debt states, Wolfgang Streeck, *Buying Time: The Delayed Crisis of Democratic Capitalism* (2014). While cautioning against the risks of 'nostalgic' views across leftist readings of the crisis and their critique of Europe, Habermas proposed re-enacting constructive engagements with the European project able to promote a truly democratic 'transnational' view, J. Habermas, *The Crisis of the European Union: A Response* (2013).

47 A. Teti, "Spaghetti Orientalism: From Tunis to Schengen" (2011)
48 M. Foucault, *The History of Sexuality: An Introduction* (1976/1990).
49 A. Teti, "Orientalism as a Form of Confession" (2014), 194.
50 Ibid., 207.
51 Foucault, *Dits et Ecrits, Tome I*, (1961/2001), 189; translated by Andrea Teti and quoted in Teti, "Orientalism as a Form of Confession," 208.
52 J. Lacan, *Anxiety*, 164.

References Cited

Badiou, A. *Metapolitics* (London: Verso, 2006).

Bauman, Z. "Times of interregnum," *Ethics & Global Politics* 5, 1 (2012): 49–56.

Berend, I.T., *Europe in Crisis: Bolt From the Blue?* (Abingdon, UK: Routledge, 2013).

Bowles, P. *Capitalism* (London: Pearson, 2012).

Corsani, A., and M. Lazzarato. *Intermittents et précaires* (Paris: Editions Amsterdam, 2008).

Declercq, F. "Lacan on the Capitalist Discourse: Its Consequences for Libidinal Enjoyment and Social Bonds," *Psychoanalysis, Culture & Society* 11 (2006).

Deleuze, G. Cours Vincennes. "Capitalism, flows, the decoding of flows," www.webdeleuze.com (16 November 1971) http://www.webdeleuze.com/php/texte.php?cle=116&groupe=Anti%20Oedipe%20et%20Mille%20Plateaux&langue=2

Foucault, M. *Dits et Ecrits, Tome I*, texte n. 4 (Paris: Gallimard, 2001); originally appeared in Foucault, M. 'Préface,' in *Folie et Déraison. Histoire de la folie à l'âge classique* (Paris: Plon, 1961/ 2001), I-XI.

Foucault, M. *The History of Sexuality: An Introduction* (New York: Vintage, 1976/1990).

Freud, S. "Extracts from the Fliess Papers," Volume 1 of *The Standard Edition of the Complete Psychological Works of Sigmund Freud* (London: Hogarth, 1894/1953–74).

Freud, S. "Inhibitions, Symptoms and Anxiety," Volume 20 of *The Standard Edition of the Complete Psychological Works of Sigmund Freud* (London: Hogarth, 1926/1953–74).

Gramsci, A. "Wave of Materialism" and "Crisis of Authority," *The Prison Notebooks* (New York: International Publishers, 1930/1972).

Gramsci, A. Q 15 (II) § 5, Passato e presente. La crisi. *I Quaderni dal Carcere, Volume Terzo* (Torino: Einaudi, 1933/2001). (*Prison Notebooks*).

Grosrichard, A. *The Sultan's Court: European Fantasies of the East* (London: Verso 1979/1998).

Habermas, J. *The Crisis of the European Union: A Response* (Cambridge, UK: Polity Press, 2013).

Hamilton, G. *Commerce and Capitalism in Chinese Societies* (Abington, UK: Routledge, 2006).

Hardt, M., and A. Negri. *Empire* (London, UK: Harvard University Press, 2000).

Heller, P. *The Labor of Development: Workers and the Transformation of Capitalism in Kerala, India* (Ithaca, NY: Cornell University Press, 1999).

Jackson, R. *Writing the War on Terrorism: Language, Politics and Counter-Terrorism* (Manchester, UK: Manchester University Press, 2005).

Koselleck, R. *Critique and Crisis: Enlightenment and the Pathogenesis of Modern Society* (Cambridge, MA: MIT Press, 1952/1988).

Lacan, J. *Anxiety: The Seminar of Jacques Lacan, Book X* (Cambridge: Polity Press, 1962–1963/2014).

Lacan, J. *The Seminar Book VII, The Ethics of Psychoanalysis, 1959–1960/1992* (London: Routledge, 1959–1960/1992).

Lacan, J. "The Subversion of the Subject and the Dialectic of Desire in the Freudian Unconscious," *Écrits: The First Complete Edition in English* (New York: W.W. Norton & Company, 1960/2006), 671–702.

Lacan, J. "Del discorso psicoanalitico," *Lacan in Italia, 1953–1978. En Italie Lacan* (Milan: La Salmandra, 1972/1978), 27–39.

Lazzarato, M. *The Making of the Indebted Man: Essay on the Neoliberal Condition* (Los Angeles, CA: Semiotext(e), 2012).

Lazzarato, M. "The Authoritarian turn of neoliberalism – Preface to the Italian edition," *La Fabbrica dell'Uomo Indebitato* (Roma: DetriveApprodi, 2012), 5–27.

Lee, J. "Western vs. Authoritarian Capitalism," *The Diplomat* (18 June 2009) http://thediplomat.com/2009/06/western-vs-authoritarian-capitalism

Melman, C. *L'homme sans gravité: Jouir à tout prix* (Paris: Denoël, 2002).

Moreau M.A. *Before and After the Economic Crisis: What Implications for the 'European Social Model'?* (Cheltenham: Edward Elgar Publishing, 2011).

Ranciére, J. *On the Shores of Politics* (London: Verso, 2007).

Said, E. *Orientalism* (Harmondsworth: Penguin, 1978).

Salecl, R. *On Anxiety* (Abingdon, Oxon: Routledge, 2004).

Standing, G. *The Precariat: The New Dangerous Class* (London: Bloomsbury Academics, 2011).

Streeck, W. *Buying Time: The Delayed Crisis of Democratic Capitalism* (London: Verso, 2014).

Teti, A. "Orientalism as a Form of Confession," *Foucault Studies*, 17 (April 2014): 193–212.

Teti, A. "Spaghetti Orientalism: From Tunis to Schengen," *The Weave – Mediocracy Unspun* (23 May 2011) http://weavenews.org/blogs/andreateti/1624/spaghetti-orientalism-tunis-schengen

Žižek, S. "China's Valley of Tears – Is authoritarian capitalism the future?" *In These Times* (3 December 2007) http://historynewsnetwork.org/article/45381

4
The Imperial Citizen: British India and French Algeria

Jack Harrington

Abstract

This chapter explores empire as a historical context for understanding what activities are deemed to constitute citizenship and by what characteristics or identities it is supposed to be conferred. It broadly examines the ways in which such ideas were applied through the government of societies under imperial rule with reference to British India and French Algeria between the 1830s and mid-twentieth-century independence. These are not simply significant examples. They represent the most widely discussed and theorized sites of British and French imperial control. The historical contingency of these two sites has shaped differences and similarities between Anglophone and Francophone critiques of the effects of colonialism and orientalism on the postcolonial subject. The problem of inclusion and exclusion inherent to political theory of citizenship must therefore be analysed in terms of the complex and conflicting interplay between national and imperial histories rather than treating them as separate or even opposite trajectories. The apparent novelty of the concept of imperial rather than national citizenship is simply one example of the way mainstream Western political theory has both been shaped in the context of extra-European expansion and, at the same time, failed to acknowledge the extent or full consequences of this connection. This chapter is intended as a historical contribution to the question of what the political theory of citizenship after orientalism might look like.

What Is Imperial Citizenship?

The question of who could be called a citizen under empire relates closely to Western political theories of what activities constitute citizenship and what characteristics or identities should confer it.[1] How political theories of citizenship developed in national and colonial contexts were not temporally or geographically distinct. To take the example of Britain and France, the crucial period between the 1830s and 1950s witnessed not only the consolidation and collapse of their imperial projects but also the constitution of a recognizably modern citizenship regime. Many of the debates about who could be a citizen, particularly conceptions of capacity, gender, race, and minority identity emerged from efforts to define and enact not national but imperial citizenship.[2] Without a proper acknowledgement of their imperial lineages, national histories of citizenship cannot offer a sound basis for understanding the complex bundles of overlapping and unstable citizenships that characterize the experience of most people today.[3] This chapter critically assesses the supposedly radical differences between ideas of the citizen, state, and society in Britain and France and their colonies up to the eve of decolonization. The chapter draws together incisive examples of how such ideas were applied through the government of societies under imperial rule with reference to British India and French Algeria. A formal comparison would only reassert the analytical framework of nationally distinct experiences of imperial citizenship. Rather, my purpose here is to use the richness, complexity, and contemporary resonances presented by these two cases to point to some of the most striking features of imperial citizenship as a forerunner of the modern institution of citizenship.

More than significant examples, French Algeria and British India represent the most widely theorized sites of British and French imperial government and anti-colonial struggle. This chapter suggests ways in which the historical contingency of these two sites has shaped differences and similarities between Anglophone and Francophone critiques of the effects of colonialism and orientalism on the transitions from the imperial citizen to the postcolonial subject.[4] A combined approach invites us to re-examine supposed commonalities such as nationalist struggle, supposed contrasts such as between republican and liberal theories of the political subject, or even supposed ruptures such as between the colonial and postcolonial. More importantly, by studying not simply comparisons and contrasts but also connections and confluences between supposedly distinct national enterprises, we have the opportunity to analyse the formation of 'European-ness'.[5] This we can understand as an unstable and fluid discourse that attempted to constitute the sameness of British and French metropolitan cultures and the 'otherness' of those societies and those peoples who were encountered and governed through imperial enterprises. In many respects, it was the concept of the 'European' as a privileged subject of rights and obligations that fundamentally foreclosed efforts to realize an ideal of imperial citizenship.

What is imperial citizenship? If citizenship has been historically constituted as membership of a polity, then clearly, exclusion and inclusion from the imperial polity must be understood as distinct from, albeit related to, membership of the metropolitan or postcolonial nation-state.[6] In contemporary political theory, the history of citizenship is still only partially understood as an aspect of the history of colonialism. Overwhelmingly, the history of citizenship in this context is still understood in terms of the reordering or constitution of postcolonial or metropolitan national citizenship.[7] As has been argued in both the British and French cases, this process of 'reinventing' national citizenship in the wake of decolonization has entrenched many elements of exclusion inherent to citizenship's imperial legacy, without adequately acknowledging their presence or historic origins in empire.[8] Nor does the national perspective provide a sufficient vocabulary for understanding how people acted as members of an imperial polity, however degraded, restricted, and localized the rights they may have claimed were.[9] Imperial citizenship engendered racialized and cultural criteria for citizenly capacity which belie the liberal tradition associated with Britain and the republican tradition associated with France. At the same time, the examples of British India and French Algeria reveal the complex, contingent, and contested ways in which citizenship and political being are actually formed. Crucially, such formations were unsystematic, inconsistent, and in flux. The legacies of contemporary national citizenship in Britain, France, Algeria, and South Asia are well documented, but do we fully understand the historic polities that begat them?

Theories of citizenship primarily understood as nationality or status inevitably obscure the extent to which those we call 'colonized' and 'colonizing' subjects attempted to enact rights and obligations as members of an imperial polity.[10] Examples of such attempts include the Aligarh movement in late-nineteenth-century India or the interwar Young Algerian movement. Such movements have been viewed alternatively as proto-nationalist or as superseded by anti-colonial nationalism.[11] I argue that by attempting to invest imperial forms of citizenship with the universality they reluctantly or perhaps unintentionally promised, such movements exemplify how imperial citizenship regimes functioned dynamically as well as how they bifurcated into contemporary national citizenships. Even as they embed and memorialize moments of rupture, such as partition in South Asia, the coherence of national histories papers over the negotiation of political subjectivities under empire whose legacy is contemporary citizenship.[12]

In the following section I examine British India and French Algeria as types of imperial polity. I contrast how the ideal types of membership to these polities were conceived. The key concepts of assimilation and association as approaches to managing and 'improving' colonial populations are also discussed. The two major categories that divided members of the polity in both cases were 'European' and 'native'. Crucially, the subsequent two sections show that these identities were not homologous to racial binaries or to full and partial enjoyment of the rights and obligations of the British Subject or the French Citizen. Analysis of the interplay between imperial and anti-colonial political subjectivities provides an overview of the nationalist periods in each case. Crucially, the tensions between anti-colonial and imperial citizenship involve not simply the rejection of colonial rule but also of colonial stratifications of peoples in terms of access to political and civil rights. The nationalist demand to reconfigure racialized and ethnic structures involved efforts to supress or elide strategies of cultural integration or difference management under empire. This can be seen, for example, in the 'repatriation' to France of almost one million *pieds-noirs* (settlers) after Algerian independence which reflected the impossibility of their continued identity as 'Algerian French'.[13] Initial efforts to put aside differentiated citizenship rights when forming the Indian constitution of 1950 are another example. Lastly, I suggest ways in which 'imperial citizenship' is a useful category for understanding how the contemporary concept of the citizen has been historically constituted.

Between Association and Assimilation

If we understand contemporary citizenship as constituted through historic social struggles over the content (rights and obligations) and extent (criteria of inclusion) of being political, how are we to frame the ways membership of the imperial polity was managed in British India and French Algeria?[14] It is a commonplace that most of British India was characterized by indirect rule and the careful maintenance and management of indigenous structures and of political and cultural difference, not only between 'Europeans' and 'natives' but between supposedly homogenous and agonistic populations such as 'Hindus' and 'Muslims'. According to the same generalization, French Algeria was a failed experiment in assimilating its native population into French citizens, characterized ethno-linguistically by their use of French, and in political and civic terms by their obligations and rights under the republic and the marginalization of religious and customary laws. These two opposing ideals have been labelled 'association' and 'assimilation'.[15] As we shall see, both the British and the French experimented with both assimilation and association at different times. Moreover, both theories fail to convey commonalities and differences in practical experiences of empire or the aspirations that animated these two imperial polities for most of this period.[16] More importantly, these theories tell us little conceptually about how we are to interpret the ways in which imperial citizenship itself was constituted by those colonial subjects who enacted it, for example through volunteering in World War I or standing for elected office in the metropole.[17] Clearly the model of citizenship as a status or identity or set of rights and privileges conferred or withheld by the state fails to capture this dynamic.

Assimilation in the imperial context exposes a tension between a universalizing progressive model of what the citizen can be, using the metropole as its frame of reference, and the ways in which empire and the migrations it engendered expose the de facto gradation and disaggregation of rights that has been the experience of most people under nineteenth-century European state-building (whether imperial or national).[18] Assimilation should not be understood merely as acculturation to a dominant discourse – not simply, for example, 'making French citizens'. In fact, the discourse of assimilation frequently endeavoured to attain a perfectibility among colonial peoples that was deemed less easily achievable in the metropole.[19] This is evident in the aspirations of the British radicals to furnish India with a utilitarian penal code, free of the obscurities and anachronisms that made English law an unequal, unpredictable, and frequently iniquitous instrument of justice.[20] In this sense, assimilation has historically aimed at eroding not simply difference but also gradation in political and civil rights. This is significant when we think of assimilation in terms of the strengthening of the presence of the imperial state. As has recently been argued in the case of the Mediterranean, French centralization has hidden or attempted to obliterate the liminal subjectivities that proliferated in this region, replacing them instead with more rigid definitions of European and non-European spaces and peoples.[21]

Association, in contrast, recognized differences in populations that translate into differences in being governed. The argument that certain peoples were 'not ready' for the full set of rights and obligations enjoyed by citizens and subjects of the metropole is a well-known aspect of the racializing discourses of both British and French imperial governance of the late nineteenth century. Yet, association had developed out of a romantic conservatism exemplified in India by administrators such Sir John Malcolm and Sir Thomas Munro and later adapted by Sir Henry Maine.[22] In the mid-nineteenth century, the French ruler Napoleon III, admiringly looking to British India for guidance, attempted to build Algeria as an Arab kingdom under French rule. This vision, inimical to most French settlers, was rapidly dismantled with the establishment of the Third Republic (1870–1940).[23] In the same period, biological racism and religious revivalism encouraged a differentiated approach to the granting of rights to colonial peoples in the British as much as the French empire.[24] As will be seen, the associationist aim to protect difference – specifically religious codes for conducting civic life – became an important aspect of the late-nineteenth-century struggle for imperial citizenship rights across both empires.[25]

The differences between French Algeria and British India as polities are striking enough. In 1830, when the French invaded the city of Algiers and its environs, the British presence on the coasts of India and in large swathes of the north had been established for almost 70 years. French expansion was checked by Berber and Arab forces on all sides until the 1840s. Over the next 20 years, significant efforts were made to populate areas under French control with agricultural colonists. This trend would be repeated in the years after 1870.[26] In contrast, the colonization of India, though it never materialized, had been a popular scheme amongst radical reformers in the 1820s and 1830s. It was generally resisted by the East India Company up to its abolition after 1858. Flanked by the protectorates of Morocco and Tunisia, after 1847, all of Algeria was nominally governed directly by the French imperial administration. Even at independence, 40 per cent of India was administered by an elaborate network of princes and chiefs with varying degrees of autonomy.[27] In the 1860s, it was possible to travel from Paris to Algiers in four days.[28] Journey times from London to Calcutta would still be counted in months for most of this period. Even by the 1870s, with the construction of the Suez canal, the lead character in Jules Verne's *Around the World in 80 Days* seemed rash to propose covering the distance in 23 days.[29] In 1870, the last time there was a major insurrection in Algeria before 1945, the ratio of 'natives' to 'Europeans' was nine to one. In India, it was more like 10,000 to one.[30] In both places, the high concentrations of Europeans in cities and military encampments made them a rare sight in most of the country.[31]

When considering Britain and France as loci of imperial polities, a complex distinction is that between the subject under the crown and the citizen. In the former case, those born in British territories were subjects of the crown and thus entitled to its protection.[32] From 1836, the native population of Algeria were deemed to be French, but the Muslim population could only become citizens by renouncing their Muslim religious code.[33] This is not simply a case of republican secularization. The Cremieux declaration of 1870 made most Algerian Jews French citizens *en masse,* without the expectation that they should renounce their *statut personnel.* Nor should it be seen as an unambiguous statement on the inimical place of Islam under the French Republic. In other parts of the French empire, it was possible to be a French citizen and retain Muslim *statut personnel.* Legislation in 1833 and 1848 made inhabitants of the *Quatre Communes* of Senegal and the French Indian ports full French citizens without renouncing their status as Muslims.[34] While such distinctions were not uniform either in the French or the British empire, throughout the period an increasing body of legislation distinguished between 'Europeans' and 'non-Europeans'. In India, native legal systems appertained only between natives and not in cases involving 'Europeans'. While the same pattern is broadly discernible in French Algeria, the possibility of full rights was held out to indigenous peoples willing to renounce their religious *statut personnel.*[35] The key point is that Algeria was conceived as part of France.[36] If the subject peoples of India ever felt like or could imagine being British subjects, it was always as members of an imperial dependency.[37]

Europeans and the Making of Imperial Space

Imperial space was created by the presence not only of the subjects of imperial rule but also that of other transitory and permanent populations.[38] This heterogeneity of practices and regulations was a major feature of the experience of imperial citizenship, just as it is necessarily absent in discourse derived from the orientalist logic of an impermeable and immutable division between Europe and its other. The dyad 'colonizer' and 'colonized' fails to capture the complex range of peoples and the different ways in which they were governed by imperial regimes. An obvious example is the category 'Europeans', which developed in the context of imperial citizenship. For much of the nineteenth century, nationals of other European powers present in British India or French Algeria (or indeed many other similar imperial jurisdictions) lived under much the same legal regime as they would had they been in metropolitan Britain or France respectively.[39] As British and French legal spaces, each was a site for the operation of European norms on individuals defined as 'Europeans'. In both cases, the imposition of European rule ended extraterritorial privilege, meaning the exemption of European nationals from local jurisdictions.[40] Although in both cases this was because Europeans would be subject to French and English law respectively.

This then raises the question, who was a European? If we take the example of British subjects in French Algeria, according to an official return of 1838, the vast majority of these were Jews born in Gibraltar or Malta.[41] They fully enjoyed the same rights as any other British subject abroad, even if in the British metropole they would have faced legal and social prejudice. This is a particularly rich example of how the European-ness of these marginal identities ('Maltese' and 'Gibraltarian Jewish') was constituted by their presence in the imperial space of another European power. As Julia Clancy Smith has shown for neighbouring Tunisia, such protégés frequently included people from areas not formally under British rule (such as mainland Greeks).[42] Equally, as Smith has illustrated with the case of Algerians in Tunisia under French protection in the mid-nineteenth century, it was the protection of a European power rather than any supposed racial or linguistic traits that defined them as European.[43] Adam McKeown's analysis of how national citizenship regimes appeared to counter the free migration flows made possible by imperial subjecthood reminds us of how the growth of national borders in the late nineteenth century was, in part, an explicit response to the need to control the movement of non-European imperial subjects.[44]

Europeans, whether nationals of the home country or not, frequently subverted the aim of their imperial polity. The case against colonization in India was largely on the grounds of the unruliness of likely settlers.[45] One expert imperial administrator, Sir John Malcolm, feared that native elites would see settlers as 'invaders of their rights, and no benefit they could derive from the introduction of capital, or the example of industry and enterprise, would reconcile any to the change, except the very lowest of the labouring classes'.[46] Frequently, the military in Algeria saw themselves as protecting native rights from the encroachment of settlers.[47] Europeans in French Algeria and British India frequently complained that the military occupation curtailed the rights they supposedly enjoyed under metropolitan law. In other words, they were unwilling to acknowledge a different, restricted set of rights as imperial citizens. We can see this in the debate about the freedom of the Anglophone press in India in the 1820s and the Francophone press in Algeria in the 1860s.[48] As Thomas Macaulay wrote when calling for the end of press censorship in India in 1835, 'Possessing as we do the unquestionable power to interfere, whenever the safety of the State may require it, with overwhelming rapidity and entry, we surely are not, in quiet times, to be constantly keeping the office and ceremonial form of despotism before the eyes of those whom, nevertheless we permit to enjoy the substance of freedom.'[49] In both cases, such freedoms were seen as part of and indeed a guarantor of the liberty of a natural born English subject in the one case and a French citizen in the other. Both groups of Europeans were unwilling to acknowledge the limits placed on their rights by the operation of an authoritarian imperial regime and, in this sense, both illustrate the distinction between imperial and national belonging, even when talking about 'colonizing' populations.

The near total removal of the *pied-noir* or European settler population from Algeria distorts the historical significance of their presence and of the rupture in the logic of imperial citizenship created by Algerian independence. The 'settler' problem in Algeria compounded the issue of identifying who was European with one of identifying who was French. Legally part of France and the home of a permanent 'French population', Algeria failed to attract sufficient numbers of ethno-linguistically French settlers. Panic about the demographic marginalization of French settlers led in 1889 to the widespread naturalization of non-French Europeans.[50] The apparent neat racial binary implicit in this move belies the complex network of non-French and often non-Catholic peoples that became citizens of the Third Republic. The subversive challenge embodied by such 'foreign' French citizens to the assimilationist policies of Third Republic France can be seen in government efforts to regulate and restrict the 'cruel' aspects of bull-fighting amongst Spanish colonists in French Algeria.[51] Tensions were created by the efforts to incorporate marginal or liminal groups into a nationally defined body of Europeans. As Julia Clancy Smith has argued, there remains an unwillingness to treat Southern European settlers in North Africa as comparable to European populations in the Americas or Australasia in this period.[52] Writing in 1958, Albert Camus, himself a *pied-noir,* and by this time one of the only leading figures on the French left to resist Algerian independence wrote: 'There has never been an Algerian nation. The Jews, Turks, Greeks, Italians, and Berbers all have a claim to lead this virtual nation... In particular, the French population is large enough and it has been settled here long enough, to create a problem that has no historical precedent.'[53] The problem according to Camus was that no one group of people, whether labelled 'Arabs' or 'Muslims', could justly claim an independent Algeria for their own to the exclusion of another. Camus's observation (coupled with his marginalization stemming from his unpopular political stance) hints at both the conceptual problems involved in tracing the histories of imperial citizenship and the consequent importance of doing so.

Reluctance to compare the historical trajectories of states that suppressed or ejected their settler populations and those that remain dominated by them is unsurprising given the anti-integrationist tone of the dominant Algerian independence party, the *Front de Libération Nationale* (FLN), and most pro-independence opinion by the late 1950s. Equally, the need to absorb a relatively diverse and, in many cases, impoverished 'French' population into post-independence France encouraged a similar silence on the French side.[54] Strictly in terms of the link between citizenship and national identity, the intermittent efforts of the FLN, both before and after Algerian independence, to Arabize the Berber population and to replace French as the language of higher education can be seen as at least analogous to the efforts to remove or minimize minority populations from post-World War II Europe.[55] Such a comparison emphasizes the common effects of post-1945 state-building on the figure of the citizen, challenging the supposed fundamental differences between 'East' and 'West'. In doing so, it also invites us to downplay or rather give a new context to supposed difference between the 'postcolonial' and the 'European' experience.

The Imperial Polity in French Algeria and British India

In what ways could 'natives' be part of the imperial polity? Imperial space was delimited by the exclusion of subject peoples from certain rights, chiefly political, but also by the limited granting of rights. In the context of French Algeria or British India, such rights were differentiated from, and one must add inferior to, not only those granted to Europeans in the colony but in some respects to colonial subjects in the metropole. This last point is a significant feature of imperial citizenship. As Sukanya Banerjee has ably demonstrated in the case of late Victorian Indians, London could be a better site of imperial citizenship than Calcutta.[56] The situation is more complex with Algeria, where from 1836 onwards Algerians had French nationality without citizenship – an inequality that pertained in mainland France as much as in French Algeria.[57] One can find examples of where restrictions on Europeans did not apply to subject peoples. The prohibition of nominal ownership of property by European foreigners is an obvious example. In India during the 1820s, the East India Company's regulations on press censorship could only apply punishment to Europeans (that is those who resided in India under license from the Company).[58] Native or mixed-race editors or proprietors could therefore enact freedom of the press with greater freedom than Europeans. All of this is to say that rhetoric of political exclusion often belied ways of being political and of enacting civil rights under empire.[59] To ignore these supposed anomalies is to invest too much monolithic and stable power in that rhetoric and those strategic discourses that supported it, such as orientalism.

Another, more significant, case is those who claimed rights as imperial citizens with reference not to the norms of the metropole but of the colony. Macaulay's famous vision of 'Englishman, brown in skin and blood but English in taste' seems to be an obvious corollary to the French ideal of assimilation.[60] Yet it is interesting to note that a striking feature of 'imperial citizenship' in the late nineteenth century and in the twentieth century was the desire to claim universal rights with cultural protection. Obvious examples of such rights-claims in India would include the Aligarh movement of Sir Syedd Ahmaden Khan.[61] On Algeria, Albert Camus, who ultimately defied the pro-FLN consensus on the French Left, wrote: 'If there is any excuse for the colonial conquest it has to lie in helping the conquered peoples retain their distinct personality.'[62] For the Young Algerians movement of *Évolué* Algerian professionals and intellectuals that emerged in the interwar years, the revolutionary heritage of the French was there to be subversively appropriated as a legitimate framework for claiming the rights of the citizen.[63] Crucially for Abbas, the possibility of incorporating Islam into the Algerian polity would remain a point of tension with the logic of assimilation and a locus for his political activism. As he wrote in 1930, 'To the theory of racial superiority, invented by Western imperialism, must be added the misunderstanding of Muslim civilization. In reality, the social work of Islam is immense. It has realised the miracle that to educate intelligence is to educate sentiment. Between diverse peoples it has created an indissoluble link.'[64] If the Young Algerian movement of the 1920s began by desiring full assimilation, by saying that there can no longer be an Algerian nation under French rule, it ended with Ferhat Abbas asking for a semi-independent Algeria under a French union.[65]

One can compare this to the movement for dominion status for India. This was an argument for granting India comparable status and autonomy within the British empire to that of Australia, Canada, New Zealand, or South Africa. In both cases, imperial citizenship was seen to include an equality of rights, as subjects under the crown in the British imperial case and as French nationals with the right to be citizens in the French imperial case. But in each instance, there was a demand for cultural protection. Moreover, both sought accommodation as an alternative to the severe prejudices and handicaps the populations they represented faced under imperial regimes. It is this desire for integration, however partial and nuanced, that distinguishes imperial citizenship from nascent nationalist or anti-colonial forms, while not precluding or diminishing their historical significance.

Imperial Citizenship and Anti-colonial Nationalism

The trajectories of imperial citizenship and anti-colonialism continue to create controversy and tension precisely because of the centrality of the anti-colonial in narratives of national liberation. No neat dividing line exists on the spectrum between critical radical reformism and anti-colonial thought – a fact exemplified by the shifts within the careers of many individuals. The reinterpretation and resignification of key historical figures from Abd al-Qādir and Messali Hadj in Algeria to Ram Mohun Roy and Mahatma Ghandi in India become the loci for such controversies.[66] That said, broad shifts in the political organization of opposition to restricted rights under empire are clearly observable in the post-World War I era, even as the lineages of the dominant discourses of the decolonization era are discernible in the earliest resistance movements in colonial Algeria and India. The Indian Congress' willingness to reform within empire before 1915 is one example of this. The marginalization of competing anti-colonial movements by the FLN after 1954 is another.[67] Many movements that are relevant to anti-colonial, nationalist discourse formations had their origins in claims for rights within the imperial polity.

The interwar period sharply exposed the limits of imperial citizenship. In part, the expectation that war service would and should be repaid with expanded civil and political rights was insufficiently realized.[68] The piecemeal attempts to expand the political and civil rights of war veterans, land owners, and professionals in Algeria were ultimately outweighed by the fact most Algerians still suffered the severe and arbitrary restrictions of the Code de l'indigénat.[69] In India as in Algeria the placation of a native elite was ineffectual. The post-war moment also witnessed the apogee of a debate about the access of colonized peoples to rights enjoyed by free citizens of independent states – inasmuch as the shortcomings of any such accommodation soon became apparent.

The nationalist movements that evolved in this period expressed, in varying and often conflicting ways, a tension between universal concepts of freedom (not entirely dissimilar to the unfulfilled promise of full and equal imperial citizenship) and the specific challenges faced by the incipient nation. This can be seen, for example, in the FLN's rejection of integration and collaboration and the increasing anachronism of figures like Abbas, who imagined a future for Algeria that acknowledged its cultural, social, and political indebtedness to French civilization or like Camus who, as late as 1958, saw the 'French' (meaning the European settlers) of Algeria as 'an indigenous population in the full sense of the words'.[70] As in India, the tension between the promise of a new nation for all and the intensified communal structures of the late colonial state can be understood in terms of a debate about the need to supplant an imperial with a national sense of political belonging.

The conscientious development of revolutionary subjectivities antithetical to membership of an imperial polity was a central pillar of nationalist activity in India and Algeria as in so many other anti-colonial struggles. Ghandi's development of Satyagraha (the philosophical underpinning of his arguments for non-resistance and civil disobedience) is one example of this, which had an influence on later colonial struggles, including to some extent in Algeria before the mid-1950s.[71] It is in this context that we should understand the intensification of the binary colonizer and colonized and its deployment by anti-colonial writers such as Nehru, Memmi, and Fanon, to name only some of the most relevant for our current focus.[72] The heterogeneous world of multiple identities under the imperial polity described and defended as historically indissoluble by writers such as Camus was an inappropriate tool for describing the lived experience of colonial violence. Another tension is also apparent here. As Rahul Rao has identified in the writings of Frantz Fanon, Rabindranath Tagore, and, one should add, Edward Said, nationalism was recognized as a transitory phase through which colonized peoples might pass to recuperate a sense of self.[73] This explains, in part, the need to study imperial citizenship formation through its complex relationship to that of the nation and the range of subjectivities produced through rights claiming on a range of overlapping scales.

After and Before: Imperial Citizenship

If inclusion in imperial citizenship was an unfulfilled aspiration, it was one that had been enacted to some degree by various peoples at certain moments. In the French case, the assumed assimilability of Jews justified the Cremieux declaration which made Algerian Jews citizens *en masse*, without the expectation that they should give up their *statut personnel*.[74] The point is that the attempt to legislate according to legally definable cultural identities necessarily involved gradation – degrees of the ability to become a full citizen.[75] If this was the case with racialized or orientalized subjects such as 'French Muslims in Algeria', it was also the case for those whose belonging to the white ethno-linguistic national group was marginal, such as Catholics, mixed-race people relocating to the metropole, and ethno-linguistic foreigners. Even if the French model of citizenship was more clearly and more systematically theorized, in both cases the boundaries between European and non-European and between citizen and subject were negotiated and contingent.

As we are increasingly realizing, in contemporary citizenship, exclusion from political participation and exclusion from the category of full citizen do not prevent people from claiming at least some of those substantive rights that make one a *de facto* member of a polity. In fact, such exclusion often mobilizes such claims. Thus, it is not enough to begin with the nominal absence of full citizenship among colonial subjects.[76] That such rights-claims were necessarily limited or degraded, that they were often permitted by governments in order to entrench inequalities, and that they were often completely denied *de jure* by the imperial regimes concerned are all pressing reasons why this aspect of the history of citizenship must be part of a broader perspective on political theory of citizenship. The study of citizenship after orientalism must overlay the histories of national citizenship with their imperial, multiple, and transnational histories.

Notes

1 Many of the chapters in this volume address this question of what activities constitute citizenship; see for example Atluri, Barbero, Dajani, Ikegame, Marino, and Pilgram.

2 For the complex contemporary implications of the contingent nature of how citizenly capacity is defined, see the chapter on autonomy in this volume by Sabsay.

3 Paul Gilroy, *Postcolonial Melancholia*, 15.

4 Paige Arthur, *Unfinished Projects*, 228.

5 Edward Said, *Culture and Imperialism*, 182.

6 Reiko Karatani, *Defining British Citizenship*, 49.

7 See for example Ranabir Samaddar, *The Emergence of the Political Subject*; Reiko Karatani, *Defining British Citizenship*, 43–9.

8 Benjamin Stora, "La gangrène et l'oubli. La mémoire de la guerre d'Algérie," 11; Olivier Le Coeur Grandmaison, "Exterminer. Coloniser Sur la guerre et l'Etat colonial," 4–10; Todd Shepard, *The Invention of Decolonization: The Algerian War and the Remaking of France*, 8.

9 Sukyana Banerjee, *Becoming Imperial Citizens*, 191.

10 Lauren Benton, *A Search for Sovereignty*, 279–84; Zoë Laidlaw "Breaking Britannia's Bounds? Law, Settlers, and Space in Britain's Imperial Historiography," *The Historical Journal* 55, 3 (2012): 817.

11 For important recent reappraisals see Bayly, *Recovering Liberties;* Belmessous, *Assimilation and Empire*, 179–201; Faisal Devji, "Apologetic Modernity," *Modern Intellectual History* 4, 1 (2007): 61–76.

12 Lauren Benton, "A Search for Sovereignty," op. cit.

13 Alice Kaplan, "Introduction" in Albert Camus, *Algerian Chronicles*, 5.; Jacques Derrida, *Monolingualism of the Other*, 16, 38; Todd Shepard, *The Invention of Decolonization*, 205.

14 Engin Isin, *Being Political*, 15.

15 Recent scholarship that challenges such simplifications includes Niraja Gopal Jayal, *Citizenship and Its Discontents: An Indian History* (Cambridge, Mass.: Harvard University Press, 2013); William Gallois, "Genocide in nineteenth-century Algeria," *Journal of Genocide Research* 15, 1 (2013): 70.

16 See Isin in this volume on Arendt and the superficiality of differences between the British and French empires.

17 Sukyana Banerjee, *Becoming Imperial Citizens*, 36–40; Stora, *Les immigrés algériens en France*, 15.

18 For national contexts, see for example Boyd Hilton, *A Mad, Bad, and Dangerous People?: England 1783–1846*, 13; Pierre Rosanvallon, *Le sacre du citoyen*, 288; Weil, *How to Be French*, 20.

19 Sahila Belmessous, *Assimilation & Empire*, 206.

20 Jack Harrington, "Orientalism, political subjectivity and the birth of citizenship between 1780 and 1830," 580.

21 Julia Clancy Smith, *Mediterraneans*, 245; Gillian Weiss, *Captives and Corsairs*, 4.

22 Karuna Mantena, *Alibis of Empire: Henry Maine and the Ends of Liberal Imperialism*, 141.

23 I am grateful to Gavin Murray-Miller for sharing his insights into settler politics and the founding of the Third Republic.

24 Alice Conklin, *A Mission to Civilize* (1998), 11–13.

25 Christoper Bayly, *Recovering Liberties*, 214 ; Erez Manela, *The Wilsonian Moment: Self-Determination and the International Origins of Anticolonial Nationalism*,

93–4; James D. Le Sueur, *Uncivil War: Intellectuals and Identity Politics During the Decolonization*, 30.

26   John Reudy, *Algeria*, 79.

27   Douglas M. Peers, *India Under Colonial Rule*, 42.

28   Mabel Crawford, *Through Algeria*, 354.

29   Jules Verne, La Tour du Monde en quatre-vingt jours.

30   Theodore Zeldin, *France: Taste & Corruption*, 141.

31   John Reudy, *Modern Algeria*, 94.

32   Jose Harris, "Nationality, Rights and Virtue: Some Approaches to Citizenship in Great Britain," 76; Reiko Karatani, *Defining British Citizenship*, 49; Ann Dummett and Andrew G. L. Nicol, *Subjects, Citizens, Aliens and Others: Nationality and Immigration Law*, 72.

33   Sahila Belmessous, *Assimilation & Empire*, 138.

34   Ibid., 140

35   Todd Shephard, *The Invention of Decolonisation*, 27.

36   It is well established that the metropolitan attitude to the assimilation of Algeria was comparable to that of regions such as Brittany during the Third Republic. See for example Jan C. Jansen, "Celebrating the 'Nation' in a Colonial Context: 'Bastille Day' and the Contested Public Space in Algeria, 1880–1939," 45.

37   Duncan Bell, *The Idea of Greater Britain*, 171–8.

38   Lauren Benton, *Law and Colonial Cultures*, 251–5; see also Isin in this volume on extraterritoriality.

39   Reiko Karatani, *Defining British Citizenship*, 49.

40   G. Murray to R. W. St. John, 10 Jan 1831, National Archives, PRO FO112/05, p. 91; Harrington, "Making imperial subjects across borders: Britain and French Algeria, 1830 to 1870" (forthcoming).

41   Sir Grenville Temple, "Konstantinah in 1837" in *The United Service Magazine* 30 (1839): 67.

42   Julia Clancy Smith, *Mediterraneans*, 104.

43   Andrea L. Smith, "Citizenship in the Colony: Naturalization Law and Legal Assimilation in 19th Century Algeria," 37.

44   McKeown, *Melancholy Order*, 210.

45   Elizabeth Kolsky, *Colonial Justice in British India: White Violence and the Rule of Law*, 70.

46   Sir John Malcolm quoted in Jack Harrington, *Sir John Malcolm and the Creation of British India*, 149.

47   For an important reappraisal of the political language of the settlers see Gavin Murray-Miller, "Imagining the Trans-Mediterranean Republic: Algeria, Republicanism and the Ideological Origins of the French Imperial Nation-State, 1848–1870," in *French Historical Studies* 37, 2 (Spring 2014).

48   C.A. Bayly, *Recovering Liberties;* Gavin Murray-Miller, "Imagining the Trans-Mediterranean Republic."

49   G.O. Trevelyan, *Life of Lord Macaulay*, 1, 189.

50   Andrea L. Smith, "Citizenship in the Colony: Naturalization Law and Legal Assimilation in 19th Century Algeria," op. cit.

51   Jan C. Jansen, "Celebrating the 'Nation' in a Colonial Context," 54.

52   Julia Clancy Smith, *Mediterraneans*, 245

53   Albert Camus, *Algerian Chronicles*, 177.

54   Shepard, *Inventing Decolonization*, 201–10.

55   On this aspect of shift in European minority policy between the aftermaths of World War I and World War II see Hannah Arendt, *The Origins of Totalitarianism*,

276–8; Mark Mazower, *Dark Continent*, 312–45; on post-Independence Algeria see James D. Le Sueur, *Uncivil War: Intellectuals and Identity Politics During the Decolonization*, 201–25; Delphine Perrin, "Citizenship Struggles in the Maghreb," in *The Routledge Handbook of Global Citizenship Studies*, 233.

56   Banerjee, *Becoming Imperial Citizens: Indians in the Late-Victorian Empire*, 26–40, 116–20.
57   Andrea L. Smith, op. cit.
58   Colonel Stanhope, *Sketch of the History and Influence of the Press in British India* (London: C. Chapple, 1823), 57.
59   Thomas Love Peacock, "Evidence to the Select Committee," delivered on 2 March 1834 in H/536, f. 407, Asian and African Collections, British Library.
60   For an example of this analysis of the famous quotation from Macaulay's 1833 speech on the government of India see Uday Singh Mehta, *Liberalism and Empire: A Study in Nineteenth-Century British Liberal Thought*, 15.
61   Christopher Bayly, *Recovering Liberties*, 253.
62   Albert Camus, *Algerian Chronicles*, 83.
63   Jan C. Jansen, "Celebrating the 'Nation' in a Colonial Context," 53–4.
64   Ferhat Abbas, *Le jeune Algérien*, 89. My translation.
65   Sahila Belmessous, *Assimilation & Empire*, 207.
66   Faisal Devji, "Apologetic Modernity," *Modern Intellectual History* 4 (2007): 61–2; C.A. Bayly, "Response," *Britain and the World* 5, 2 (2012): 310; John Ruedy, "Chérif Benhabylès and Ferhat Abbas: Case Studies in the Contradictions of the 'Mission civilisatrice,'" *Historical Reflections / Réflexions Historiques*, 200–1.
67   Allison Drew, *We are no longer in France: Communists in colonial Algeria*, 5.
68   John Ruedy, *Modern Algeria*, 112; Sugata Bose, Ayesha Jala, *Modern South Asia: History, Culture, Political Economy*, 106.
69   Matthew Connelly, *A Diplomatic Revolution: Algeria's Fight for Independence and the Origins of the Post-Cold War Era*, 24; John Ruedy, *Modern Algeria*, 89.
70   Albert Camus, *Algerian Chronicles*, 177.
71   Kate Marsh, "Gandhi and le gandhisme: Writing Indian Decolonisation and the Appropriation of Gandhi 1919–48," 48.
72   Vijay Prashad, *The Darker Nations- A Biography of the Short-Lived Third World*, 24–7.
73   Rahul Rao, *Third World Protest*, Ch. 4.
74   More generally on Jews and assimilation see Wendy Brown, *Regulating Aversion*, 48–77.
75   Jacques Derrida, *The Monolingualism of the Other*, 17.
76   Patrick Weil, *How to Be French*, 240.

References Cited

Abbas, Ferhat. *De la Colonie vers la province* (Paris: Garnier, 1980).
Arthur, Paige. *Unfinished projects: Decolonization and the philosophy of Jean-Paul Sartre* (London: Verso, 2010).
Banerjee, Sukanya. *Becoming Imperial Citizens: Indians in the Late-Victorian Empire* (Durham, NC: Duke University Press, 2010).
Bayly, Christopher. *Recovering Liberties* (Cambridge, UK: Cambridge University, 2012).
Bayly, Christopher. "Response," *Britain and the World* 5, 2 (2012): 308–13.
Bell, Duncan. *The Idea of Greater Britain* (Princeton: Princeton University Press, 2010).
Belmessous, Sahila. *Assimilation and Empire* (Oxford: Oxford University Press, 2013).
Benton, Lauren A. *Law and Colonial Cultures: Legal Regimes in World History, 1400–1900* (Cambridge, UK: Cambridge University Press, 2002).

Benton, Lauren A. *A Search for Sovereignty: Law and Geography in European Empires, 1400–1900* (Cambridge, UK: Cambridge University Press, 2010).

Blévis, Laure. "La citoyenneté française au miroir de la colonisation: étude des demandes de naturalisation des 'sujets français' en Algérie coloniale," Genèses, dossier "Sujets d'Empire" (2003), 53.

Brown, Wendy. *Regulating Aversion: Tolerance in the Age of Empire* (Princeton, NJ: Princeton University Press, 2008).

Clancy Smith, Julia. *Mediterraneans: North Africa and Europe in an Age of Migration, c. 1800–1900* (Berkeley, CA: University of California Press, 2012), revised paperback.

Conklin, Alice. *A Mission to Civilize: The Republican Idea of Empire in France and West Africa 1895–1930* (Stanford, CT: Stanford University Press, 1998).

Derrida, Jacques. *The Monolingualism of the Other*, trans. Patrick Mensah (Stanford, CT: Stanford University Press, 1996).

Drew, Allison. *We are no longer in France: Communists in colonial Algeria* (Manchester, UK: Manchester University Press, 2014).

Dummett, Ann, and Andrew Nicol. *Subjects, Citizens, Aliens and Others: Nationality and Immigration Law* (London: Weidenfeld and Nicolson, 1990).

Gilroy, Paul. *Postcolonial Melancholia* (New York: Columbia University Press, 2004).

Hall, Catherine. *Macaulay and Son: Architects of Imperial Britain* (London: Yale University Press, 2012).

Harrington, Jack. "Orientalism, political subjectivity and the birth of citizenship between 1780 and 1830," *Citizenship Studies* 16, 5-6 (2012).

Harrington, Jack. *Sir John Malcolm and the Creation of British India* (London: Palgrave Macmillan, 2010).

Harris, Jose. "Nationality, Rights and Virtue: Some Approaches to Citizenship in Great Britain," in *Lineages of European Citizenship: Rights, Belonging and Participation in Eleven Nation-States*, eds. Richard Bellamy and Dario Castiglione (London: Palgrave Macmillan, 2004).

Hilton, Boyd. *A Mad, Bad, and Dangerous People?: England 1783–1846* (Oxford, UK: Oxford University Press, 2006).

Isin, Engin. *Being Political* (Minneapolis, MN: University of Minnesota Press, 2002).

Jansen, Jan. C. "'Nation' in a Colonial Context: 'Bastille Day' and the Contested Public Space in Algeria, 1880–1939," *The Journal of Modern History* 85, 1 (2013): 36–68.

Karatani, Reiko. *Defining British Citizenship* (London: Frank Cass, 2002).

Le Coeur Grandmaison, Olivier. *Exterminer. Coloniser Sur la guerre et l'Etat colonial* (Paris: Fayard, 2006).

Marsh, Kate. "Gandhi and le gandhisme: Writing Indian Decolonisation and the Appropriation of Gandhi 1919–48," *Modern and Contemporary France* 14 (2006): 33–49.

Rosanvallon, Pierre. *Le sacre du citoyen – Histoire du suffrage universel en France* (Paris: Folio Histoire, 2001).

Ruedy, John. "Chérif Benhabylès and Ferhat Abbas: Case Studies in the Contradictions of the 'Mission civilisatrice'," *Historical Reflections / Réflexions Historiques* 28 (2002): 185–201.

Ruedy, John. *Modern Algeria: The Origins and Development of a Nation State* (Bloomington, IN: Indiana University Press, 2005).

Said, Edward. *Culture and Imperialism* (London: Random House, 1994).

Samaddar, Ranabir. *The Emergence of the political subject* (London: Sage, 2010).

Smith, Andrea L. "Citizenship in the Colony: Naturalization Law and Legal Assimilation in Nineteenth-Century Algeria," *Political and Legal Anthropology Review* 19, 1 (1996): 33–49.

Stora, Benjamin. *La gangrène et l'oubli. La mémoire de la guerre d'Algérie* (Paris: La Découverte, 1991).

Stora, Benjamin. *Les guerres sans fins* (Paris: Pluriel, 2005).

Stora, Benjamin. *Les immigrés algériens en France: une histoire politique (1912–1962)* (Paris: Hachette Littératures, 2009).

Weil, Patirck. *How to Be French*, trans. Catherine Porter (Durham, NC: Duke University Press, 2008).

5
Haredi Settlers: The Non-Zionist Jewish Settlers of the West Bank

Dana Rubin

Abstract

The project to create a modern Jewish nation on Palestinian land provoked fierce opposition not only from Palestinians but also from Jewish groups that rejected or did not 'fit' into it – in particular the Haredi (ultra-Orthodox) Jews. The latter's opposition is less debated in contemporary literature; yet, this history underlines the impossibility of forming a homogenous state as envisaged by the Zionist movement. One paradoxical aspect of the transforming Israeli colonizing project is that since the end of the 1980s, Haredi groups have been establishing their own settler-cities in the Israeli-occupied West Bank and are the fastest-growing settler group today, despite being theologically and culturally opposed to the Zionist project. The very groups that destabilize the project of a modern Jewish state from within are now at the heart of the most disputed political issue today – the West Bank settlements. Definitions of a single people, sovereignty, and territory remain unstable in Israel.

Introduction

When approaching the issue of Israeli settlements in the West Bank or more broadly the so-called Israeli-Palestinian conflict, there is a commonly held image in the UK, and elsewhere, of two homogenous, ethno-national people, the Arabs and Jews, fighting each other. This image fails to take into account the existence of Jewish groups living within Israel whose attitude to the Zionist political project exposes its inherent contradictions. The definition of Israel as a 'Jewish' state belies the contradiction in the notion of a modern citizenship that tries to establish a link between an ethnic group, territory, and sovereignty, and still claim universalism. As is well known, this attempt to create a modern Jewish nation-state on Palestinian land provoked fierce opposition from Palestinians. What is less known or debated is that there are different Jewish groups that also reject or simply fail to 'fit' into this project – in particular ultra-Orthodox Jews. The impossibility of forming a homogenous modern Jewish nation-state, therefore, further complicates the accepted narrative on Israel/Palestine.

Let us begin with a quote from a text posted on the official website of Beitar Ilit, a West Bank Haredi-exclusive settler city:

> Beitar Ilit was planned according to local outline plan 426, which was approved in 1988. The plan includes state lands on three parallel hills: A, B, C. According to these plans, 17,500 housing units are expected to be built on a 4,300 dunam area, most of them in saturated construction. [...] In recent years, several private building lots have been allocated to people who wish to build their own homes. Throughout the years, additional lots were approved for construction and added to the local outline plan, with all of them officially being recognized as state lands. [...] Each hill features commercial areas, public facilities and multipurpose areas. *Beitar Ilit is the first city to be established specifically for the Haredi population*, and was acknowledged as one of the most optimal solutions for the severe housing problem of the Haredi community, within the framework of *modern, secular surroundings*. The city founders believe that *territorial separation is the most appropriate approach to maintaining an independent lifestyle*.[1]

This opens up some intriguing questions regarding different Jewish positions within Israel and the Zionist settlement project. The history of the establishment of this West Bank settlement (surrounded by Palestinian villages that are not mentioned in the text) describes the mechanism of colonizing lands that are 'officially being recognized as state lands'. Another element is added, however, to this well-known narrative of settlement planning and land colonization: a housing solution for Haredim in the form of a *territorial separation* from the rest of Israeli society – a separation in order to maintain a Haredi lifestyle that is independent from that of a secular, modern Israel. It is not only the paradoxical position of the Haredim within the Zionist political and colonial project that makes their settlements an important political issue today; it is also the fact that the population of Haredi settlers in the West Bank has increased more than 18-fold over the last two decades, making them the fastest-growing group within the West Bank settler population. They now represent one-third of the Jewish settler population in the West Bank.[2] The Haredi settlers live in the largest settler cities in the West Bank today, both of which are exclusively Haredi: Modi'in Ilit and Beitar Ilit.[3] Other Haredi West Bank settlements include Tel Zion, Emanuel, Matityahu, Ma'ale Amos, and Asfar, and there are also Haredi settlements that are considered as 'neighbourhoods' of Jerusalem. This significant change in the demographics of the West Bank settlements, and accordingly in the politics of this area, call for an examination of the Haredi settlement in particular and a more comprehensive examination of the place of Haredim within Israel and Zionism in general.[4]

The trend of construction of Haredi cities also becomes a part of the process of colonization that extends beyond the West Bank. For example, the Haredi city of Elad was built in 1990 close to the Green Line.[5] Although not located inside the West Bank, the city is part of the Stars Plan introduced by former Israeli Prime Minister Ariel Sharon, which aimed to create 'Jewish continuity' across the Green Line. Additionally, over the last decade, the Ministry of Housing promoted the extensive construction of cities for Haredim, such as Harishin Waddi Ara. There are also plans to build the Haredi-only city of Kasif in Naqab on Bedouin lands.[6] These projects that produce a double segregation of Haredim from the rest of Israeli society and from Palestinians are created by a combination of state-subsidized and planned housing programs for Haredim and of investment by private developers. To this day, few academic works focusing on the topic of Haredi settlements have been published, and the topic is rarely mentioned in the extensive debate on the settlements. This chapter takes up the task of examining this phenomenon and its implications.[7]

To give a brief definition of 'Haredi', it translates from Hebrew as 'he who trembles' (meaning trembles at the word of God).[8] The Haredi lifestyle is centred on the Torah, the strict interpretation and practice of Halacha, Jewish law, and a life devoted to religious studies. The term 'Haredim' refers to traditional Jewish religious groups that object to the modernization of Jewish life.[9] The literature on Haredim refers to a distinct lifestyle and subjectivity that was formed in the period of Jewish assimilation in European societies that ended with World War II (WWII), which marked the decline of Eastern European Jewish towns. However, although the literature on Haredim largely points to this period as formative, the Haredi lifestyle continued to transform in response to the different economic, technological, political, and social upheavals in the non-Jewish and Jewish societies surrounding the Haredim. Viewing Haredim simply as a static form of Jewish tradition overlooks the Haredi process of rearticulating Jewish lifestyle and identity in response to secularization and modernization, as well as in response to Zionism. The structure of Haredi society as a learning society based on *yeshivas* was one of the main tools in preserving a traditional Jewish religious community as it created a totalizing institution that could mark a closed community separate from non-Jewish and secular Jewish societies.[10] My focus here is mainly the history of the Ashkenazi Haredim (Lithuanians and Hasidim), but in addition to this group, there are the Sephardi Haredim, of which the Mizrachi Haredim form a part. The histories of these groups are distinct and are positioned differently within Israeli society, particularly in relation to the nexus of class, ethnicity, and religion. However, as a Jewish group that rejects modernization and a secular culture, all Haredim share a distinctive position within the modern project of Zionism and the state of Israel.

Zionism as a settler-colonial project has given rise to many configurations of settlement. Different forms of settlement correspond to changing local and global circumstances and discourses, from socialism to Jewish religious Messianism, to name two examples. Today, the West Bank settlements are one of the most disputed issues in the politics of Palestine-Israel, and they are often presented as the core obstacle on the road to a resolution of the so-called 'Israeli-Palestinian conflict'. To better understand Haredi settlements, we must move beyond the narrow context of the 1967 settlement enterprise. The settlements, and the segregation between Jewish-Israelis and Palestinians that they endorse, also provide a means for Haredim to separate from the rest of Israeli-Jewish society; for the latter, it is a means of isolating the Haredim that are considered to pose a threat to the modern Jewish state. This segregation could also be seen as a mode of incorporation. That is, the Israeli state promotes and encourages Haredi settlers as they are willing to invest in the colonial project by actively establishing new settlements on Palestinian lands on the West Bank. Yet, this incorporation into the colonization project also runs the risks of estrangement and alienation by paradoxically encouraging autonomous settlements. In other words, although the settlements serve the purposes of both sides, they do not resolve the conflicts between them but rather provide new modes of segregation.

In order to examine the position of Haredim within Zionism and Israel, and the recent emergence of the Haredi city, I will explore two evidently problematic vocabularies that are used extensively in Israel today: 'non-Zionist' and 'non-ideological'. 'Non-Zionist' is used to describe the political position of most Haredim in Israeli society. 'Non-ideological' describes the transformation in settlement activity in the West Bank with the construction of vast settlements close to the Green Line to which settler-groups have relocated since the 1980s. 'Non-ideological' also refers to the ideology of Gush Emunim (which translates as 'Block of the Faithful') by the negation of their ideology, in other words, 'non-ideological' refers to settlers who are not part of the religious-nationalist settler movement and who do not share its views. On the other hand, as mentioned, it also refers to a process of economization and liberalization of settlements and to settlers who were attracted by the *quality of life* (another prevalent description of this group of settlers in Israel) and the cheap housing offered within these territories. Arguably, these processes brought about the establishment of homogenous and segregated Haredi communities pursuing 'an independent lifestyle' separate from Israeli society.[11] However, there are many more factors involved in these processes than this chapter can possibly cover. The chapter selectively touches on some aspects of these processes in order to offer a perspective on contemporary Israeli-Jewish society and the dynamics of ongoing colonization.

Zionist Settler-Colonialism

Zionism as a settler-colonial project has been the focus of a growing body of scholarship in recent decades. These works examine the early Zionist settlement, the *yishuv*, and the state of Israel as a settler-colonial project.[12] Maxime Rodinson's *Israel: A Colonial Settler-State*, published in 1967 (in English 1973), established a framework in the West for discussing the colonial project of Israel that continues to have ramifications for the political legitimacy of the state of Israel today. Israeli revisionist scholars, who have been called 'new historians' and 'post-Zionist', have challenged Zionist narratives such as those of *hityashvut*, the Zionist settlement activity. These scholars did not focus on the 1967 occupations but rather questioned Zionist settlement altogether.

Settler colonialism is a distinct form of colonialism. As argued by Patrick Wolfe, it 'is at base a winner-take-all project whose dominant feature is not exploitation but replacement'.[13] Accordingly, settler colonialism can be distinguished from other forms of colonialism or other forms of migration and has unique characteristics.[14] According to Mamdani, the difference between colonialism and migration is evident when a state is structured around the *native-settler distinction*, and it privileges the settler and isolates the native.[15] Furthermore, Wolfe argues that settler-colonialism is not an *event* constrained within the temporality of colonization but is a dynamic structure that reproduces the *native-settler distinction* on which it was founded.[16]

It is important to examine Haredi settlements within the framework of settler-colonialism, as it is this native-settler distinction that is imbedded in the process of *hityashvut* in Palestine. *Hityashvut* within Haredi and other settlements was always molded by the political and economic forces of the time, beginning with *Hovevy Zion* settlers in the last two decades of the nineteenth century and continuing until today. Baruch Kimmerling, in his works on Zionism and territory, developed the notion of the Zionist frontier and the mechanisms in which *hityashvut* acquired territories and was legitimized.[17] Gershon Shafir argues that the socialist ideology of Labour Zionism, which established the *kibbutzim*, was integrated within and endorsed by the settler-colonial project of a homogeneous Jewish settler-colony.[18] If in the *yishuv* period the *hityashvut* was part of the pragmatic Zionist ideology of 'putting facts on the ground', after the establishment of the state of Israel, *hityashvut* was focused on the process of 'Judaizing' the territory.[19] Examples of this process include the 'Judaizing Galilee' program that was initiated at the end of the 1970s, as well as earlier programs of the 1950s that involved settling newcomers from the Middle East and North Africa in 'development towns' within Palestinian communities such as the Naqab and the Galilee. 'Judaizing' through *hityashvut* continues today both in the West Bank and throughout Israel through, inter alia, the construction of Haredi cities. *Hityshvut* also encompasses significant processes in addition to acquiring land for settlement. It involves creating affinity between diasporic Jews and the territory (i.e., Palestine). The creation of different modes of affinity to the territory has contributed to the transformation of the settler as a type. Thus, the agricultural settlements of *kibbutzim* and *moshavim* created a 'settler-labourer'. *Homa u'migdal* (tower and stockade) settlements of the second half of the 1930s created a 'settler-warrior'. Both aimed to construct a new Hebrew man, different to the diasporic Jew. While *hityashvut* refers to the Zionist settlement activity, the twofold aim of this activity involved the construction not only of settlements but also of a new identity, as suggested by the Hebrew phrase *livnot u'lehibanot*, meaning 'to build and to be built'.

Gershon Shafir and Yoav Peled, in their study on Israeli citizenship, suggest that there are three discourses of citizenship in Israel: republican, ethno-national, and liberal.[20] This creates a setting in which, alongside the distinction between native and settler, there are different forms of incorporation of various groups into the settler society in relation to their position within each citizenship discourse. Haredim's position in society, Shafir and Peled maintain, corresponds to and provides one justification for the ethno-national discourse. The degree of incorporation, as Oren Yiftachel's work on Israeli geography lucidly demonstrates, corresponds with the groups' geographical and political position within the territory.[21] Yiftachel shows how Mizrahim were settled in peripheral towns in order to 'Judaize' the land as a 'division' between Palestinians and the hegemonic group of Israeli secular Ashkenazim, which produced *Jewish ethno-classes* that comprise what he calls Israel's 'ethnocracy'. Thus, while retaining the settler-native distinction, changing discourses of *hityashvut* and citizenship reshape the space and the social and political organization of Israeli society, while extending the dispossession of the Palestinians. Accordingly, the place of Haredim in the West Bank was produced through transformations in *hityashvut* and citizenship discourses which reflect the changing place of Haredim in Israeli society.

The 1967 settlements reshaped once again the Zionist settler-colonial project. The 1967 war was followed by Israel's occupation of vast territories.[22] Soon after the occupations, Israel began extensive settlement activities in these territories. Studies of Israeli settlements mostly focus on the West Bank and stress their military function within the Israeli occupation.[23] Alongside the military function of the occupation, *hityashvut* after 1967 corresponds to tensions and instabilities within Israeli society. As I later demonstrate, it was the process of the liberalization of *hityashvut* that enabled new settlement spaces to emerge and certain groups to change their position within Israeli society by settling in these territories.

The 1967 settlements are often divided into three main phases that are to some extent overlapping. The first phase is the Alon program of so-called 'security' settlements built in the Jordan Valley, such as *moshavim* and *kibbutzim*. The second phase is the movement of religious-nationalist settlers, Gush Emunim, which had a large impact on the settlements and continues its activities today under Amana and Moetzet Yesha, among other bodies. The third phase, which began in the 1980s, is recognized as the creation of 'non-ideological' settlements, also known as 'quality of life', 'housing solution', or 'economic' settlements. In other words, settlers are driven by the reality of the cost of housing rather than by a nationalist-religious ideology of rightful land ownership. Unlike many nationalist-religious settlers, the 'non-ideological' settlers live proximate to the Green Line. The Haredi group today comprises a large part of these settlers. Neve Gordon expresses a view held by many scholars working on the West Bank settlements in regard to the 'non-ideological' settlements: 'Whether a settler moved to the OT [occupied territories] for ideological reasons and was interested in dispossessing the Palestinians or whether he or she was encouraged to leave Israel and to relocate to the West Bank and Gaza Strip in order to buy an affordable single-family home is beside the point; in both cases the settlers have been mobilized to serve the purpose of military domination.'[24] However, a growing body of recent work on the 1967 settlements, within which my argument is positioned, challenges this line of argument.

There are two main arguments for challenging the position that highlights merely the military function of the settlements. First, the 1967 occupations and settlements open up the older question of the legitimacy of the settler-colonial project of Israel as a whole. The 1948 Palestinian dispossession of the *Nakba* was challenged: 'If land seized in 1967 must be given back, then why not land seized the same way in 1948? If the exclusive Jewish claim to any part of Palestine can be challenged, then is the claim to any other part secure?'[25] Second, in recent decades questions have also been raised regarding Israel's 'ethno-classes' in relation to settlement activities.[26] These two elements blur the former conventions regarding right and left in Israel. Michael Feige has observed that the 'appropriation' or 'estrangement' of the 1967 occupied territories developed in the Israeli-Jewish geopolitical 'mental-map' as a division between the camps of the secular-liberal versus the religious-nationalist.[27] In the same vein, Joyce Dalsheim observes that the settlers in the 1967 occupied territories confronted the secular-liberal camp with

> a deep anxiety that the entire Zionist project may be called into question. The fear that Jewish presence and sovereignty on this territory stands to lose its moral and rational legitimacy in the eyes of the international community may be the driving force behind the hatred aimed at the post-1967 religiously motivated and right-wing settlers.[28]

However, a critique of this construction of the settlements as a moral division between religious-nationalists and secular-liberal Israelis has been growing since the 1980s and 1990s, when new groups of settlers that did not belong to either the religious-nationalist Israelis and/or secular-liberal Israelis relocated to the settlements. Yehuda Shenhav, in response to Gordon et al., views the circumstances in which the settlers relocated, and the ways in which they shaped Israeli and Palestinian societies, as anything but 'beside the point'.[29] Shenhav argues that the new settlers have a potential to cut themselves off from the old political paradigms that have immobilized the political situation in Israel/Palestine for decades. The Green Line, according to Shenhav, indicates a cultural-economic and political paradigm supported by Israeli hegemony.[30] It is a cultural myth that is tied to the economic and political interests of liberal Israel that prefers to articulate the problem as 1967 (the 1967 war and occupations) and not 1948 (the formation of the state). Shenhav continues by arguing that since 1993, with the Oslo Accords, the idea of separation has widened and pushed away questions regarding Palestinian refugees, the status of Palestinians within the Jewish state, and the place of Israel's non-hegemonic groups (third Israel), which include Haredim, Mizrachim, and newcomers who relocated to the settlements. Since the 1980s, he argues, third Israel was shaped *by* the settlements. Thus, the Green Line has had little hold on the ground as a result of the settlement enterprise, but it remained in the Israeli imaginary, separating both the Palestinians from the Israelis and 'moral' Israel from the 'immoral' settlers.[31] In the attempt 'to make sense' of the Haredi settlements and the wider group of the so-called 'non-ideological' settlements, while attending to the social, political, and also ethical questions embedded within them, this chapter follows Shenhav by trying to move away from the hegemonic discourse on settlements. I now trace the paradoxical positions of Haredim within Israel and Zionism in order to provide a wider framework for the emergence of the Haredi settlements and the depiction of Haredim as 'non-Zionist'.

Non-Zionist?

The histories of Haredim and Zionism or Haredim and Israel are long and complex, but I want to highlight here the longstanding tensions and contradictions. Different imaginaries, at times contradictory, were poured into the proposals for a Jewish colony. The ethos of settlement on the frontier as a means of breaking away from the existing social and political order has characterized many settler societies.[32] In the Zionist case, breaking away from Europe meant leaving behind not only the place allocated for Jews within European societies but also Jewish traditional-religious society. Jewish intellectuals who were driven by a keen awareness of what they understood to be the cul-de-sac of assimilation wished to establish a semi-European modern state for Jews outside of Europe as revealed in the words of the founder of 'cultural Zionism', Ahad Ha'Am: 'What Hertzel understood is that only by leaving Germany and settling in the Jewish state could the Jew finally become a real German'.[33] For some, it was also a search for a new life for Jews by leaving Jewish tradition behind: 'Zionism was an invention of intellectuals and assimilated Jews [...] who turned their back on the rabbis and aspired to modernity, seeking desperately for a remedy for their existential anxiety'.[34] At the heart of this colonial imagination stood the question regarding the possible place of European Jewry in modernity.[35] Zygmunt Bauman describes how the Jew, departing from the ghetto in time of modern nationalism, was 'cut from his origin but not yet admitted to any other home'.[36] Zionist scholar Shlomo Avineri reinforces the myth of Zionism's success in reviving the Jewish public sphere by replacing the religious community and its institutions and finally 'placing the Jews in modernity' where they are no longer subjected to historical passivity.[37] Nevertheless, Zionism evolved under the rapidly changing circumstances of Jewish life and was developed into a wide diversity of ideologies, which were then rejected or adopted by different segments of Jewish religious groups. While some religious groups saw Zionism at times as a political solution for Jews and others also incorporated Zionism into religious ideas such as salvation or *halacha* sovereignty, the majority of orthodox-religious Jews viewed Zionism as an *anti-Jewish* movement.

The religious-orthodox (now named Haredi) response to Zionism comprised two essential elements. Firstly, Zionism poses the threat of the modernization and secularization of Jews. Secondly, it has brought the threat of a false messiah. Zionism sought to *modernize* Jews as a *collective* during a time in which European assimilation sought to modernize Jews as *individuals*. The logic of European liberal assimilation, as pointed out by Hannah Arendt, was directed at *individuals*, which meant the intolerance of Jews as a *collectivity*.[38] This is where Zionism offered a *collective* secular Jewish identity as an alternative to religious Jewish identity *and* an alternative to individual assimilation.[39] The second orthodox- religious response to Zionism was based on the 'messianic question'. The dialectics between the Jewish duty of *Galut* (diaspora) and the desire to change it shaped Jewish communities and discourses before and during modernity.[40] Zionism was to be rejected utterly because it stood in the way of the Jewish messianic belief that human interference in the process of redemption will prevent the long-awaited divine redemption. According to this logic, diaspora and its burdens must be accepted before the redemption will take place. The Zionist political project of establishing a Jewish state in the Holy Land sought to break the dichotomous logic in Jewish religious thought between absolute diaspora on the one hand and absolute redemption on the other. The notion of redemption and the return to the Holy Land played a central role in the Zionist movement by making a claim for a right over a land and constructing a national narrative and indeed a nation.[41] Zionism's Jewish religious opponents considered its attempt to 'change Jewish history' through the Zionist political project as a 'false redemption'.[42] Henceforth, Zionism could only lead to religious 'conversion'. These views are held by most Haredim and as such represent the Haredi position to this day.

Nevertheless, since the beginning of the twentieth century, Haredi leaders and organizations have had a dynamic relationship with Zionist organizations and later the Israeli state institutions that have evolved around sites of strain as they try to secure the conditions and a degree of autonomy for Haredi groups. This is manifested, for example, in the varying positions of some of the *yishuv* institutions during the pre-state period over issues of migration permits on the one hand and education and the separation of institutions on the other. The poles of this dynamic relationship oscillate between Haredi negotiations with Arab leaders (for example, Jacob Israël de Haan in the 1920s or more recently the Jerusalemite Haredi collaborating with Iran), to attempts by a segment of the Haredi *Agudat Yisrael* (*Poalei Agudat Yisrael*) to build Haredi *kibbutzim*.[43] Hence, Haredi attitudes towards the Zionist pre-state movement and institutions have subsequently evolved into complex, varying attitudes towards the Israeli State today. Either willingly or unwillingly, they comprise part of the Jewish population of Israel. Some Haredi groups such as *Edah Haredit* and *Neturei Karta* vehemently refuse to cooperate with the state. Most of the other Haredi groups identify as non-Zionist or anti-Zionist and approach Israel not as a Jewish state but as the state in which they live, in other words, a 'hosting society'. This is manifest in an independent education system; parliamentary participation and legislation that relates directly to Haredim (which has increased since 1977); extra-parliamentary protest regarding issues such as military service; and religious institutions (such as the *Rabbanut*).[44] However, this has led to a permanent tension over the possibility of a stable settlement between the Israeli state and the Haredim and regarding the place of this group within Israeli society, given that they do not identify with Zionist ideology, or with Israeli state institutions, or with the idea of a modern nation-state altogether.

Aziza Khazzoom argues that a modern Jewish state in Palestine has been threatened by two elements that were to be 'managed' in order to assure its success.[45] The first was the non-modern Middle East and its Palestinian population, and later the Mizrahim (Jews from Muslim countries) as well. The second was the Jewish religion that was in itself a threat to the project of Westernization and modernization while also representing the diaspora.[46] However, this was a contradictory process since the definition of the state as a Jewish one seemingly keeps Israel from the 'accomplishment' of the project of modernization. Yet, it constantly requires the (re)definition of 'Jewishness' as a category in order to justify its existence as a *Jewish* state. This goes back to the settler-colonial distinction of the native and settler as well as to the project of the non-assimilative, modern *Jewish* nation-state. Israel, as a Jewish state but also as a settler-colonial project, defines the place of religion and also accordingly its Jewish subject in opposition to the non-Jewish Palestinian. Religion is thus where the distinction between the Jewish and Palestinian subject is maintained. Therefore, the debate over the role of religion in Israel and the definition of a *Jewish* state echoes this genealogy of European orientalism and the logic of assimilation, as well as the settler-colonial structure, which is formed around the settler-native distinction. Consequently, the Jewish religion and hence religious Jewish groups become at the same time both the problem and the justification for the Jewish state.

As argued, Haredim are constructed as a threat to modern Western society in the Israeli political debate. The next section follows recent examples of this discourse. It is revealing that in 2011, the former director of Mossad, the Israeli intelligence agency, Efraim Halevy, declared that internal 'growing haredi radicalization poses a bigger risk' to the state of Israel than Iran and its then president Ahmadinejad. He complained that 'ultra-Orthodox extremism has darkened our lives'.[47] Yaron London, a prominent Israeli journalist, has written of the high birthrate within Haredi communities as the 'Haredi bomb', elaborating that

> [o]nly a fool would avoid the reasonable assumption that in the next generation the Zionist share of the population would be a minority. If the Haredi community's spirit and lifestyle don't change, it would be doubtful whether Israel would be a political entity that is different than surrounding states: a theocratic county, poor in economic and spiritual terms, and incredibly crowded.[48]

The Haredim are the subject of many demographic studies in Israel as they are seen as threatening Zionist Israeli Jewish society. The Chaikin Chair in Geostrategy at the University of Haifa published a report in 2012 entitled 'Israel: Demography 2012-2030 On the Way to a Religious State'. Highlighting the growth in Palestinian and Haredi populations, the report warns that

> [t]he state of Israel as a Jewish and democratic state can continue to exist only if it has a clear Jewish majority, which supports modernity, lives in territory whose dimensions and borders permit actualization of the state's sovereignty and defense, and if it enjoys a quality of life that befits a Western society. Attainment of these essential conditions of supporting democratic and liberal values is not self-evident; demographic processes [...] threaten the capacity to realize them.[49]

Moreover, such discourse on Haredim and Israel has often questioned the latter's authenticity as Judaism. For example, in July 2012 an article in the *Ha'aretz* newspaper argued that 'Haredi Judaism isn't our forefathers' religion, but a radical and dangerous new cult'.[50] The article continues, 'This is among the most strongly held and unfounded myths in Israel society' and warns that 'a large portion of the Haredi public continues to go to further extremes until it resembles nothing as much as a Taliban-like cult'.[51]

The two 'projects', of 'guarding' the tradition of Haredim and 'securing' a Jewish identity through the modern national and colonial political project of Zionism, contradict one another. These tensions are reflected at every stage of the relationship between Haredim, Zionism, and the state of Israel. The constructions of Haredim as premodern, as similar to 'primitive' neighbouring societies and of course the Palestinians, as a growing threat to Zionism and the 'Jewish and democratic' state, and as a dangerous cult illustrate their extremely ambivalent position in Israel. But, if Israel were to occlude its

Jewish definition, it would sacrifice the defining signifier that distinguishes between settler and native, and it also runs the risk of increasing the autonomy of Haredi groups. The Haredi settlement represents yet another configuration of a colonization, whose historical traces I have presented here. While keeping and deepening the settler-native distinction, the tensions between the Haredi settlement and the Israeli state were reworked through the liberalization of the 1967 frontier, as I articulate in the next section.

Non-ideological?

As argued earlier, *hityashvut* was underlined by the strategic expansion of colonization, maintaining the settler-native distinction and the shaping of divisions among Jewish 'ethno-classes' through different positioning of groups on the frontier. Nevertheless, over time, economic and political objectives formed different discourses of *hityashvut*. This section looks at the transformation of *hityashvut* in the West Bank in order to elucidate the emergence of the Haredi settlements as part of a wider phenomenon labelled 'non-ideological' settlements within Israeli political debate. From the 1970s, the *hityashvut* has moved away from former rural and agricultural forms of settling to the formation of suburban communities. This has been accompanied by the liberalization of settlement activities, which were now opened to private investors and developers. This section discusses neoliberalism – while not being able to engage expansively with its many aspects – in order to articulate the recent changes in *hityashvut* and the emergence of the term 'non-ideological' settlements.

Without doing an injustice to the extensive scholarship on neoliberalism, its many definitions could be mapped in two main directions. The first is the economic logic of late capitalism that advances corporatization and state reform towards privatization and economization. The second, which largely follows the work of Michel Foucault, views neoliberalism as a social formation. This refers to the ways in which people govern themselves and others that are implicated in what we can call 'market values'. The latter approach also emphasizes the local and hybrid configurations of neoliberalism rather than viewing it as a 'wave' spreading on a global scale replicating the same model. I argue that the transformation of *hityashvut* in the West Bank since the 1970s cannot merely be viewed as a project of privatization and economization, as suggested by the first school of thought. The West Bank *hityashvut* has involved the extensive role of state settlement plans and 'housing programs' for Israeli-Jews in the West Bank as well as legislative and military actions. At the same time, it involved changes that can certainly be thought of as the economization of settlement activity, which feeds into a discourse of individual and 'privately undertaken colonization'.[52] The two main processes that shall be observed here are, first, the creation of settlement forms that enable extensive segregated homogenous communities, and second, a discourse of settlement that casts settlement activity seemingly away from the state and away from the realm of the 'political/ideological'.

Principally, until the 1970s, *hityashvut* was based on a division between urban and rural settlements. Rural settlements were regarded as the flagship of the Zionist settlement venture, important for their ability to occupy land on a large scale, and as argued earlier, for their transformative role in the construction of the settler as a new 'Hebrew Man'.[53] Both early Zionist settlement activity in Palestine and that conducted after the establishment of the state were largely centralized. Hence, only limited forms of settlements were approved, granted institutional support, and allocated land. These settlements were then established by the settlement division of the Jewish agency, the settling bodies (*gufim meyashvim*), and after the establishment of the state also the Ministry of Agriculture and the Ministry of Housing. Thus, settlement that fitted the criteria introduced by the World Zionist Organization was approved and received land and support.[54]

In the late 1970s, suggestions were made to the World Zionist Organization regarding new forms of settlements such as the *private* and the *community settlement* (*yishuv kehilati*) that did not fit into the previous urban and rural categories. These forms were recognized by the organization in 1977 and became eligible for funding.[55] The new settlements' characteristics were described by Aharon Kellerman as: 'homogeneously structured, along one or more political, religious or professional lines [...] characterised by individual rather than collective decision making [...] and economic freedom. [...]'.[56] The title *community settlement* is misleading, as the idea was, unlike the former *kibbutz* and *moshav*, to loosen the economic ties between settlement residents. The 'communal' aspect lay in the creation of a homogenous community maintained by exclusive selection committees, which controlled who could join. Uzi Gdor, a leading planner of the new settlement forms, recalled in an interview that he realized the only way to sustain the Zionist project of settlement was to create a new form of *community* and accordingly a new form of *settlement* that would offer people life among 'people like them' without the 'burden' of a shared economic system, whilst advancing the *hityashvut* goals.[57] The new form of *community settlement* was first adopted in the establishment of Gush Emunim settlements.[58] It later became a model for the establishment of many settlements close to the Green Line to which other groups of Israeli-Jews now relocated.[59] In only five years, about 60 of the *community settlements* were established around the West Bank, and by 1992, 118 *community settlements* were already established, ten of which were funded entirely through private initiative and investments.[60]

The new forms of settlement were part of a wider transformation in the process of settlement planning and construction. One of the main changes came in 1980, when land purchased by individual Israelis was made available in the West Bank.[61] One year later, the 1981 plan of Mattityahu Drobless, then head of a new settlement division in the Jewish Agency, was initiated. Shafir and Peled describe it in these words: 'To encourage this process, Drobless, with the active support of Ariel Sharon as chair of the ministerial settlement committee, turned settlement, for the first time in Zionist history, into a capitalist venture, encouraging the employment of private funds and private initiative in the construction of settlements.'[62] The new settlement forms were also expanded into larger settler-urban suburbs close to the Green Line and attracted private developers who were offered land at almost no cost and assumed many of the roles of the former settling bodies. Additionally, settlers were offered tempting benefits and loans in the new settlements.

Nonetheless, settlement activity was not simply 'handed' to private developers but was bound to housing policies, settlement plans, programs to increase the population, and regulations and policies that accompanied the private initiatives.[63] The 'capitalist venture' was an intersection of governing activities – or settling activities that were recast as market ventures – that alter and blur the roles of the state versus private developers. Market rationality contributed to casting the new settlements as 'non-political' and 'non-ideological'. However, they can be thought of not as the absence of the state or 'politics' but as a reconfiguration of the role of the state, of private developers, and of settlers.

Shafir and Peled have called the new forms of *hityashvut* 'privately undertaken colonization'.[64] They maintain that 'whereas pioneering was hailed as dedication to the common good that overrode individual interests, the new settlement drive was undertaken by *individuals for their own benefit*'.[65] Again, this is an example of understanding the new settlements through the market logic of individuality that 'pushes away' the role of the state, returning to the role of *hityashvut* in the geographical 'distribution' of different 'Jewish ethno-classes' and to the reproduction of the division between settler and native (by the dispossession of the latter). Gutwein sees the new settlers as part of a wider structure that is strongly related to the privatization process in Israel and to economic inequalities in Israeli-Jewish society. He calls the settlements 'compensation' for the inequalities that were widened even further by the process of the privatization of the Israeli welfare state. Gutwein's understanding of the wider political and economic framework of the new West Bank settlements echoes Shenhav's analysis of the 1967 settlements as another phase of reshaping Israeli society and hegemony. Hence, in this process, non-hegemonic groups such as Mizrahim and newcomers from the former Soviet Union (and later the Haredim) relocated to settlement-suburbs such as Ma'ale Adumim and Ariel, two of the largest four West Bank settlements (after the Haredi settlements) and to many smaller community settlements close to the Green Line.

It is worthwhile to consider Foucault's theorization of neoliberalism in relation to the inseparability of the economic and the political that are constructed as a 'regime of truth'. This 'regime of truth' makes itself invisible through ideas of 'freedom'. Foucault argued that '[...] governing people is not a way to force people to do what the governor wants; it is always a versatile equilibrium, with complementarity and conflicts between techniques which assure coercion and processes through which the self is constructed or modified by himself'.[66] In the new phase of settlement, settlers are not seen as part of a program but as individuals who follow their own private (economic and social) interests and exercise their freedom of choice. This is why Shafir and Peled can view the new settlements as a private and individual venture. This idea of freedom is also neatly conveyed in a statement that appeared on the website of the Israeli Foreign Ministry regarding the settlers' relocation to the West Bank: 'It should be emphasized that the movement of individuals to the territory is entirely voluntary.' Thus, the movement of settlers to the West Bank is not achieved by 'forcing' them 'to do what the governor wants', but rather, it is through complex and contradictory dynamics that West Bank settlements are now presented as market ventures and as the free choice of the individual. This process thus 'mak[es] invisible' the traces of the settler-colonial structure and of the economic and political formations of Israeli-Jewish hegemony.

This section has demonstrated how the transformation of *hityashvut* in the West Bank (in other words, the new forms of settlement), the suburbanization process, and the policies and settlement plans brought both private developers and funds as well as a new discourse to the West Bank and located these settling activities within market rationality. The settlements were thus recast as 'non-political' and the settler as 'non-ideological' (unlike the former Zionist 'pioneers' or the religious-nationalist settlers).

Moreover, this process made invisible the settler-colonial structure as hegemonic formations were articulated in the rhetoric of choice, individuality, and freedom. Earlier I described the complex position of Haredim in the ambivalent dialectics of the Jewish definition of the state, which involved maintaining the settler-native distinction on the one hand and Israel's aspiration to be a modern Western state on the other. Chava Pinchas-Cohen, a West Bank settler, describes her relocation to the West Bank in terms that echo the ideas of individuality and the 'non-political' in what she sees as the possibility to live a 'non-political' Jewish way of life in the West Bank: 'For me it was the only possible way to live my life as an individual in a community and to observe a Jewish way of life without being pushed into a political category [...].'[67] The statement of pursuing a 'Jewish lifestyle without being pushed into a political category' resonates with the statement this chapter began with, taken from the website of a Haredi settlement: 'The city founders believe that territorial separation is the most appropriate approach to maintaining an independent lifestyle.'[68]

The next section brings together the 'non-political' Jewish way of life, the 'non-ideological' settlement (implicated in market rationality), and 'non-Zionist' Haredim (in their contradictory position in the modern, Western state).

Haredi Settlement

I now want to examine the Haredi settlements as an intersection of four major themes discussed above: firstly, the position of Haredim within Israeli society; secondly, the transformation in *hityashvut* in the West Bank; thirdly, the role of the settlements in keeping the native-settler distinction; and fourthly, the reshaping of Jewish ethno-classes. Furthermore, I have argued that the construction of Haredim as 'non-Zionist' and of settlements as 'non-ideological,' since the 1980s, is implicated in market rationality. The 'non-Zionist' and the 'non-ideological' conjoin in the creation of the new Haredi settlement spaces that enable a seemingly 'non-political' (Haredi) Jewish lifestyle within the framework of Zionist settler-colonialism.

While each Haredi settlement in the West Bank has a different story behind its establishment, together they constitute a process. This process grew out of a 'failed' endeavour to construct private Haredi-settler towns, through a large-scale, planned project by the Ministry of Housing, as a result of which failure the largest settler-city in the West Bank was built using private capital. Each of the settlements operates within a similar dynamic: new settlers relocate to them and establish the kind of homogenous community and lifestyle that they were set up to create and maintain. The location of the two largest Haredi settlements – in terms of their proximity to the Green Line (and therefore to centres such as Jerusalem and Bnei Brak) – plays a major role in their growth. This is also true of the other, later-phase West Bank settlements discussed in the previous section. Haredi settlements, like many other settlements in the West Bank, are built mainly by Palestinian labour sourced from the surrounding cities and villages. Like these other settlements, they form part of the continuous process of land colonization that is executed through a variety of judicial mechanisms.[69]

The Haredi settlements, in ways similar to the private and community forms of settlement that were developed at the end of the 1970s and continued throughout the 1980s, guarantee their homogenous Haredi-only population through selection committees (also known as populating committees). Unlike the smaller-scale community and private settlements, the Haredi settlement of Beitar Ilit and Modi'in Ilit have populations of 42,500 and 55,500 respectively. New settlers who wish to move to these cities do so principally by one of the two following ways. Firstly, they can engage the services of property agencies that refer them to selection committees for approval before they can move to the city or buy property. Those who wish to receive this approval have to provide information regarding their affiliation to a certain Haredi community, place of prayer, information about their families, and, in some cases, their consent to the separation of women and men on public transport. The second way that new settlers are recruited and Haredi homogeneity is maintained is through voluntary associations (*amuta*) that organize groups of potential buyer-settlers and negotiate with the private developers on their behalf. As part of the agreement, the association maintains a right of veto over the people who will live in the development (for example, a block of flats or a neighbourhood). The role of these Haredi associations is significant. One study revealed that over half of Haredi housing purchases are organized through these associations or some form of organization.[70] In addition, developers who wish to attract Haredi buyers will avoid selling property to non-Haredim. Another aspect is the influence of religious leaders on the choice of residency by individuals and families, as expressed by one of my interviewees: 'How does the Haredi population move to another place? Whenever a Rabbi is asked advice on where to live he recommends Beitar Ilit or Modi'in Ilit. Instantly hundreds would move, whoever gets married comes to live there.' Furthermore, some Haredim relocate as a group – as is the case with the Boyan Hasidic dynasty in Beitar Ilit – and establish their own *yeshivas* and synagogues.

The three largest Haredi settlements are Emanuel, a town built by private developers; Beitar Ilit, which was the first state planned Haredi-only city project of the Ministry of Housing; and Modi'in Ilit, which was built by private developers following the success of Beitar Ilit. Nevertheless, the West Bank Haredi cities are situated in the lowest cluster (poorest) of Israel's socioeconomic ranking.

Income is a major factor in the relocation of many Haredi settlers. In Emanuel, the first Haredi town, the average income constitutes half of Israel's national average income.[71] An average price for a new three-bedroom apartment in 2013 in Bnei Brak (which is not in the West Bank but is a city close to Tel Aviv with a large Haredi population) was 1,105,000 NIS. In comparison, the same property in Beitar Ilit cost 639,000 NIS, and in Emanuel a three-bedroom apartment could be bought for only 234,000 NIS. Lower property prices and the relative lower socioeconomic position of many Haredim influence their decision to relocate, as suggested by one of my interviewees: 'If a Haredi city were established within the Green Line and it was ten shekels [less than £2] cheaper – they would go.'

The first Haredi town, Emanuel, was established in the West Bank in 1983 by three private developers from Samaria Star Limited who designed a town to accommodate the Haredi lifestyle. As a result, Emanuel was designed with a higher number of Haredi educational and religious institutions than other Israeli towns. The process of establishing the Haredi settler-town Emanuel is described in an interview with the architect and town-planner, Thomas Leitersdorf:

A group of ultra-Orthodox developers came to me with a map, with six points marked on it [...] and they told me that they wanted to build a town. [...] I took their map and said, 'What you have shown me is not a town'. Then they asked, 'What do you need for a town?' So with a 6B pencil I drew on the map what the size of the town should be, and they told me, 'It's yours, start planning.'[72]

Emanuel was considered a 'failure' due to the choice of location, which is far from the Green Line, and the financial mismanagement of the company responsible for establishing the settlement. This resulted in the settlement attracting only a small and relatively poor population and the eventual bankruptcy of Samaria Star Limited. However, a new public housing policy in the 1980s designated the Haredim as a separate, non-integrative group for the first time.[73] This meant that Haredi housing was now addressed for the first time as a *public problem*, which was solved, in part, through the construction of housing in Haredim-only cities and neighbourhoods.

In 1988, the second Haredi city, Beitar Ilit, was established as the first large-scale project built to address the 'Haredi housing problem'. Beitar Ilit began as an initiative of Yosef Rosenberg, a private investor who sought religious-nationalist settlers, and was later adopted as a project of the Ministry of Housing for Haredim and executed by Ashdar Limited.[74] In order to ensure its success, Beitar Ilit was located in close proximity to the Green Line as a settler-suburb of Jerusalem and granted extensive subsidies by the government. In addition to the land allocation and subsidies provided by the Ministry of Housing, the government's priority 'developing areas' have received a new designation as 'National Priority Areas' since 1993.[75] Under this government policy of population distribution, areas such as Beitar Ilit receive benefits such as loans and tax exemptions that are distributed according to what are considered to be the national priorities of the time.[76]

Haredi Modi'in Ilit, now the largest settlement in the West Bank, was established in 1990 (and recognized as a city by Israel in 2008). The city was built with no official planning but rather as an initiative of private entrepreneurs under the umbrella of Kiryat Sefer Limited as a way of 'putting facts on the ground'. It only submitted guidance plans to the governmental committees at a later stage in its development. Gadi Algazi (2010) describes the influential private developers who stood behind the construction of the city and the industrial area built in it including the businessman Lev Leviev, who is the owner of one of the biggest construction companies in Israel, Africa Israel Investments Ltd. Algazi shows how the dynamics of land colonization were influenced and pushed by the private investors. Furthermore, even the route of the separation wall's construction around Modi'in Ilit was decided in accordance with the private investors' wishes.

Following on from the previous section that described how the 'non-ideological' settlements and settlers are positioned as merely a 'capitalist venture' – wherein the roles of the state, the private developers, and the settlers are reconfigured and contribute to a process that makes the settler-colonial structure invisible – Haredi cites, including Modi'in Ilit and Beitar Ilit, became a major part of this new discourse. Thus, in the *Yedioth Ahronoth* newspaper in September 2009, an article cites a series of public personalities arguing that the West Bank Modi'in Ilit is not a settlement. Ehud Barak, the former Minister of Defence argues that 'Modi'in Ilit is not a settlement, it is a city'. Modi'in Ilit's mayor, Ya'akov Guterman, states that 'we are part of the consensus, therefore we are not a settlement'. In addition, even the secretary-general of the Peace Now movement, Yariv Openheimer, is cited as saying that unlike the other settlements, 'the grounds for the establishment of Modi'in Ilit is not ideology but real estate'. Here, the discourse of a capitalist venture makes real estate free of (colonial) ideology and reflects the way that Haredi settlements are represented in Israel and how these settlements represent themselves. In a later interview, Ya'akov Guterman says, 'If I thought this was a settlement, I would never have come here [...]. We are not here for political reasons. [...] Ninety percent of the people are here for the affordability, not for ideology.'[77] One of my interviewees, a resident of Modi'in Ilit, explains what the line is between 'ideological' and 'non-ideological' settlers in his opinion:

> Nobody lives here and sees it as a redemption of the Land of Israel or a defense of the borders. [...] Most of the inhabitants of Modi'in Ilit don't know where the Green Line runs. I take a bit more interest, but they don't know and aren't interested. It isn't a question that comes up before they move here.

The idea that Haredi West Bank settlements are 'non-ideological' is articulated not only through the motivation for moving to the settlements (i.e., affordability or the desire to live in a Haredi-only environment) but also in relation to the Haredim's position in Israel. This reasoning is conveyed by the words of Yitzhak Zeev Pindrus, Beitar Ilit's former mayor, in an interview to *Ynet* in 2005:

> No one moves here because they want to 'cross' the green line. People are looking for quality of life and that's what they get here. The Haredim never truly felt part of the state. They were never part of its leading elite, even when we were represented in the coalition government. We're not involved in the state's management, we are not part of it, and therefore we don't deal with these questions [policy questions relating to the settlements].[78]

The mayor's statement that the Haredim are not part of the Israeli state is put in even stronger terms by MK Yisrael Eichler, from the United Torah Judaism Party, who – responding to the removal of Beitar Ilit from the list of National Priority Areas (meaning that the city would lose benefits offered under this policy) in August 2013, as well as to other changes in government policies touching on Haredi communities – presented the Haredim as 'subjects' colonized by the 'secular government':

The secular government treats the Haredim with brutality; they are like helpless subjects colonised by it. [...] The evil government has police forces and weapons, and prisons to impose its rule on its subjects. But we [the Haredim] have the answer that David gave to Goliath: Thou comest to me with a sword, and with a spear, and with a javelin: but I come to thee in the name of the Lord of hosts, the God of the armies of Israel, whom thou hast defied... that all the earth may know that there is a God in Israel.[79]

This discursive division of 'non-ideological' settlers or even 'non-settlers' is also evident in the way the Haredi settlements position themselves in relation to the religious-nationalist settler movement (or the 'ideological' settlers). Yitzhak Ravitz, a Haredi settler-resident of Beitar Ilit, articulates this position in an interview in *Ha'aretz*: 'We don't identify with the settlers. You won't see us demonstrating alongside them. We've nothing in common with the "hilltop youth" [...] They may have drawn closer to us, but not vice versa.'[80] However, the leaders of the nationalist-religious settlers reject any distinction. In the same article, Pinhas Wallerstein, former head of the West Bank settler body Binyamin Regional Council, is quoted as saying in September 2003: 'It is my ideal [...] to see every Jew living in the territories. I expect nothing from the Haredi settlers. But even if they didn't come here for ideological reasons, they won't give up their homes so easily.'[81] Conversely, when a group of religious-nationalists wanted to settle in Beitar Ilit, the selection committees prevented them from doing so.

Since the 1980s, the liberalization of the West Bank settlements has shaped the positions of non-hegemonic groups in relation to the liberalization of Israel's economy, leading to the segregation of Jews and Palestinians and between Jewish ethno-classes, and creating a space of non-hegemonic 'third Israel' that is positioned 'outside' of 'moral Israel'.[82] On the Haredi website *Kicker Ha Shabat*, Yossi Elituv, a Haredi journalist, published a column in 2009 that argues it is not by chance that Haredi settlements are at the centre of an international dispute over the freeze of West Bank settlement construction as the Haredi settler-cities are almost the only available housing solution for the Haredi population. He blames the Israeli government for pushing the Haredi housing solution 'outside' the Green Line by 'navigating' and exploiting the high birth rate of Haredim as cannon fodder in the settlement enterprise. Elituv continues,

Now this business has to stop. The Haredi representatives must insist upon it. Not Harish, not Katzir and not Kasif. Don't send us to the territories, not to the Arad region and not to Wadi Ara. [...] we are not chunk[s] of meat [...] like putty in the hand of the Israeli government to settle any area that occurs to them.[83]

An article that was published in the Haredi daily newspaper *Yated Ne'eman* on July 1991 (soon after the establishment of the two major West Bank Haredi settler-cities) had gone further in arguing that the construction of Haredi settlements was not only part of the government's settlement policy but also a plan of 'thinning out' Haredim in Jerusalem.[84] 'Thinning out' Haredim from Jerusalem feeds into the discourse that constructs Haredim as a threat to the Israeli state and society.

However, segregation (from the rest of Israeli society and from the Palestinians) is also a motivating force for some Haredim to move to the settlements. As I have demonstrated, financial considerations play an important role in the decision of settlers to move to a Haredi settlement. But, an additional consideration for settlers is the desire to maintain a homogenous cultural space. An interviewee expressed his and his wife's considerations before moving to the Haredi settlement: 'First of all we looked for a Haredi city so our children's education would be *clean and pure* and the second problem was financial. Jerusalem wasn't an option, very high prices. Modi'in [Ilit] was a good option.' As this quote suggests, Haredi-only cities offer Haredim segregation from the secular environment. The interviewee continues, 'Modi'in Ilit is entirely Haredi, it is actually the most Haredi city in the world. There are no "knitted kipot" [commonly meaning Zionist orthodox] and certainly no secular people.'

The liberalization of West Bank settlements, Israel's settlement policy, and its policy regarding the Haredim together made possible the large-scale homogenous spaces of Haredim on Palestinian lands, segregated from the rest of Israeli society. These settlements are an assemblage of extensive planning on behalf of governments (such as Beitar Ilit), or of providing a space for private developers to 'put facts on the ground'. An important element in the creation of these settlements is the designation of Haredi housing as a *public problem*. The creation of controlled homogenous communities maintains segregation from Palestinians, and from most Israelis, and therefore makes these cities attractive for those who seek a 'pure' environment. The desire to live a 'non-political' Jewish (Haredi) lifestyle is another articulation of a discourse of 'non-ideology', which intersects with the fact the Haredim do not identify with Zionist ideology or with Israel. It is made possible by ideas of freedom or 'privately undertaken colonialism', enabling many Haredi settlers to purchase relatively cheap housing and to segregate themselves from the 'secular society' or 'secular state'.

Conclusion

Several factors enable the extensive presence of the Haredim in the West Bank. First, while Israel has classified the Haredi housing problem as a distinct one requiring a solution, private developers and entrepreneurs have seen the demand for cheap Haredi housing as a good investment opportunity. This has made the idea of Haredi settlements in the West Bank attractive to both private investors and state authorities. Second, the Haredi aspiration of autonomous living in spaces ostensibly separated from secular and modern Israeli society has been compatible with a popular view in Israeli society that the Haredi lifestyle poses a threat to its image as secular and modern. These two main factors cannot exist outside of the broader historical context of ongoing tensions between Zionism and Haredim. Similarly, they cannot be understood outside the context of economic and political changes in the *hityashvut,* the settlement activity, as a whole, or in other words, the move towards homogenous settler communities that are part of a discourse of individualism and economic freedom.

Haredim are the fastest-growing settler population, and will soon become the largest settler group in the West Bank, and should therefore no longer be neglected in analyses of West Bank settlements. As I have shown, this neglect can be explained by the fact that they are cast in Israeli internal discourse as 'non-ideological' (which follows a market rationality of individualism and is opposed to the religious-nationalist ideology) and 'non-Zionist'. In addition, international political discourse and academic scholarship tend to see the settlement enterprise as a unified entity, which again omits Haredim from discussion of the settlements despite their growing demographic and political significance. Bringing political factors to bear upon the economic and social circumstances enables us to analyse the emergence of these settlement spaces and to develop a deeper understanding of the contemporary West Bank colonization and settlement project as a whole.

When looking at how Zionism was formed as a way of breaking away from both Jewish traditional-religious communities and European assimilation through the creation of a modern Jewish nation-state in the colony, we may be tempted to view the 1967 frontier as a way for different Jewish groups to further 'break away' from modernized Jewish society. This is also where we encounter the desire to live a 'non-political' Jewish lifestyle in the colony. The idea of a 'non-political' Haredi Jewish lifestyle was constructed, as I have argued, through the articulation of the notion of 'non-Zionist' and 'non-ideological' settlements. This chapter began with a view that presented the Haredi settler-city as 'one of the most optimal solutions for the severe housing problem of the Haredi community, *within the framework of modern, secular surroundings.* The city founders believe that *territorial separation* is the most appropriate approach to *maintaining an independent lifestyle'.*[85] Haredi settlements may therefore be understood, firstly, as an expansion of colonial space and, secondly, as an *agreement* regarding the semi-independent place of Haredi-settlements within Israel, which, I argue, challenges the people, sovereignty, and territory principle of the modern Israeli state.

Notes

1 "About Us," *Official Website of Beitar Ilit*, http://betar-illit.muni.il/eng/?CategoryID=167 (accessed 30 October 2013) – my emphasis.

2 N. Gordon and Y. Cohen, "Western Interests, Israeli Unilateralism, and the Two State Solution," *Journal of Palestine Studies* 41, 3 (2012): 6–18.

3 According to the 'Statistical Abstract of Israel 2013' published by the Israeli Central Bureau of Statistics, in 2012 Beitar Ilit had a population of approximately 42,500 residents.

4 *Haredim* is plural of *Haredi*.

5 The 1949 Armistice Green Line, which following the 1967 war and occupations became known as the 1967 borders, meaning the pre-1967 war borders.

6 A Shauli, "The New Haredi Bonanza? 20 Thousand Apartments in the Negev," *Yedioth Ahronoth*, http://www.ynet.co.il/articles/0,7340,L-4437563,00.html (accessed 30 October 2103).

7 See Gorden and Cohen, "Western Interests"; Gadi Algazi, "Matrix in Bil'in," *Who Profits*, http://www.whoprofits.org/content/matrix-bil%E2%80%98-gadi-algazi (accessed 30 October 2013); and Y. Shilhav, *Ultra-Orthodoxy in Urban Governance in Israel* (Jerusalem: Floersheimer Institute For Policy Studies).

8 The source of the term 'Haredi' is commonly thought to be the verse 'Hear the word of God, (you) who tremble at His word' (Isaiah 66:5).

9 Haredim see themselves as distinct from Modern-Orthodox Jews.

10 See M. Friedman, "Life Tradition and Book Tradition in the Development of Ultraorthodox Judaism," in *Israeli Judaism: The Sociology of Religion in Israel*, eds. Š.A. Dešen, C.S. Liebman, and M. Shokeid (New Brunswick, NJ: Transaction, 1995), 127–47; and M. Friedman, *The Haredi (Ultra-Orthodox) Society: Sources, Trends and Processes* (Jerusalem: Jerusalem Institute for Israel Studies, 1991).

11 Beitar Ilit website.

12 See for example G. Shafir, *Land, Labor and the Origins of the Israeli-Palestinian Conflict 1882–1914* (Cambridge: Cambridge University Press, 1989); L. Veracini, *Israel and Settler Society* (London: Pluto Press, 2006); N. Masalha, *Imperial Israel and the Palestinians: The Politics of Expansion* (London: Pluto Press, 2000); J.A. Massad, *The Persistence of the Palestinian Question: Essays on Zionism and the Palestinian* (New York: Routledge, 2006).

13 Quoted in Veracini, *Israel and Settler* Society, 8. See also P. Wolfe, "Settler Colonialism and the Elimination of the Native," *Journal of Genocide Research* 8, 4 (2006): 387–409 who quotes Theodor Herzl on the logic of 'replacement': 'If I wish to substitute a new building for an old one, I must demolish before I construct.'

14 Veracini, *Israel and Settler Society*.

15 M. Mamdani, *When Does a Settler Become a Native?: Reflections of the Colonial Roots of Citizenship in Equatorial and South Africa* (Cape Town: University of Cape Town, 1998), 4.

16 Wolfe, "Settler Colonialism."

17 Kimmerling (1983 and 1989) B. Kimmerling, *Zionism and Territory: The Socio-Territorial Dimensions of Zionist Politics* (Berkeley: California University Press, 1983). And B. Kimmerling, "Boundaries and Frontiers of Israeli Control System," in *The Israeli State and Society: Boundaries and Frontiers*, ed. B. Kimmerling (Albany, NY: Suny Press, 1989), 265–84.

18 Shafir, *Land, Labor and the Origins*.

19 A distinction is often made in the literature between what was later termed the 'old *yishuv*' (i.e., pre-Zionist but also anti- and non-Zionist Jewish settlements in Palestine) and the 'new *yishuv*' or *ha'yishuv* (the *yishuv*) meaning Zionist settlement and institutions in Palestine before the establishment of the state of Israel.

20 Y. Peled and G. Shafir, *Being Israeli: The Dynamics of Multiple Citizenship* (Cambridge: Cambridge University Press, 2002).

21 O. Yiftachel, *Ethnocracy: Land and Identity Politics in Israel/Palestine* (Philadelphia, PA: University of Pennsylvania Press, 2006).

22 These territories include the Sinai Peninsula and Gaza Strip from Egypt, Golan Heights from Syria and East Jerusalem, and the West Bank from Jordan.

23 See for example N. Gordon, *Israel's Occupation* (Berkeley, CA: University of California Press, 2008) and E. Weizman, *Hollow Land: Israel's Architecture of Occupation* (London: Verso, 2007); or for focus on the religious-nationalist strand of the settlement movement Gush Emunim, see M. Feige, *Settling in the Hearts: Jewish Fundamentalism in the Occupied Territories* (Detroit: Wayne State University Press, 2009); I. Zertal and A. Eldar, *Lords of the Land: The War Over Israel's Settlements in the Occupied Territories, 1967–2007*, trans. V. Eden (New York: Nation Books, 2007), and Inbari, "The End of the Secular Majority," *Haaretz*, http://www.haaretz.com/weekend/magazine/the-end-of-the-secular-majority-1.410880 (accessed 22 January 2015).

24 Gordon, *Israel's Occupation*.

25 P. Buch, "Introduction," in *Israel: A Colonial-Settler State?* ed. M. Rodinson (New York: Monad Press, 1973), 18.

26 Yiftachel, *Ethnocracy*.

27 Feige, *Settling in the Hearts*.

28 J. Dalsheim, *Unsettling Gaza: Secular Liberalism, Radical Religion, and the Israeli Settlement Project* (Oxford: Oxford University Press, 2011), 48.

29 Y. Shenhav, *The Time of the Green Line: A Jewish Political Essay* (Tel Aviv: Am Oved, 2010).

30 Shenhav, *The Time of the Green Line*, 12.

31 Ibid.,17.

32 See for example Frederick Jackson Turner's notable Frontier Thesis in *The History of The American Frontier* (1920).

33 Quoted A. Khazzoom, "The Great Chain of Orientalism: Jewish Identity, Stigma Management, and Ethnic Exclusion in Israel," *American Sociological Review* 68, 4 (2003): 500.

34 Barnavi quoted in Y.M. Rabkin, *A Threat from Within: A Century of Jewish Opposition to Zionism* (London and New York: Zed Books, 2006), 7.

35 Furthermore, it was the same logic of order, exclusion, and segregation that formed the modern European nation-states and now was part of the aspiration and practice of the Jewish nation-state first in the Zionist *yishuv* and later in the state of Israel.

36 Z. Bauman, *Modernity and Ambivalence* (Ithaca, NY: Cornell University Press, 1991), 169.

37 Avineri, *The Making of Modern Zionism: Intellectual Origins of the Jewish State* (New York: Basic Books, 1981).

38 H. Arendt, *The Jewish Writings*, eds. J. Kohn and R.H. Feldman (New York: Schocken Books, 2007).

39 Friedman, *The Haredi*, 19.

40 A. Ravitzky, *ha-Kets ha-meguleh u-medinat ha-Yehudim: Meshihiyut, Tsiyonut ve-radikalizm dati be-Yisrael* (Tel Aviv: Am Oved, 1993).

41 A possible argument is of course that these religious doctrines of redemption and return were not merely instrumental.

42 Ravitzky, *ha-Kets ha-meguleh*.

43 See G. Cohen, C. Levinson, Y. Ettinger, and N. Hassom, "Anti-Zionist Haredi sect member charged with offering to spy for Iran," *Ha'aretz*, http://www.haaretz.com/news/national/.premium-1.539196 (accessed 30 October 2013).

44 It is worth noting that the division in family and civil law of different communities was based on the former Ottoman millet system and a later variation that was

altered and recognized during the period of the British Mandate. The Haredim kept this relative autonomy through the status-quo agreement in June 1947. The status-quo agreement is considered in Israel to be a milestone in Haredi and Israeli settlement.

45   Khazzoom, "The Great Chain of Orientalism."

46   An example for the treatment of Mizrachim, who did not 'fit' into the aspiration of a modern and Western society, is the cutting by state officials of the sidelocks of the Yemeni newcomers in camps (*ma'abarot*) in the 1950s.

47   Y. Zitun, "Iran far from posing existential threat," *Ynet*, 11 April 2011, http://www .ynetnews.com/articles/0,7340,L-4143909,00.html (accessed 30 October 2013).

48   Y. London, "The Ultra-Orthodox Bomb," *Ynet*, 11 August 2012, http://www .ynetnews.com/articles/0,7340,L-4145351,00.html (accessed 30 October 2013).

49   E. Bystrov and A. Soffer, *Israel: Demography 2012-2030 On the Way to a Religious State* (Haifa: Chaikin Chair in Geostrategy, University of Haifa, 2012), 15.

50   S. Ilan, "The myth of Haredi moral authority," *Ha'aretz*, 12 July 2012, http://www .haaretz.com/the-myth-of-haredi-moral-authority-1.450670 (accessed 30 October 2013).

51   Ilan, "The myth of Haredi moral authority."

52   Peled and Shafir, *Being Israeli.*

53   And after 1949, rural settlements were also used to settle newcomers in abandoned and evacuated Palestinian villages throughout the country.

54   D. Newman, "The Changing Rural Landscape, 1967–1992," in *Settlement Geography of Israel: Spatial Experiments*, ed. S. Reichman Ramat (Tel Aviv: Open University of Israel, 1997), 122.

55   Benvenisti quoted in Peled and Shafir, *Being Israeli,* 170.

56   A. Kellerman, *Society and Settlement: The Jewish Land of Israel in the Twentieth Century* (Albany: State University of New York Press, 1993), 95.

57   From a series of interviews I conducted with Uzi Gdor in August 2012, Israel.

58   Amana, the settling body of Gush Emunim movement, explicates in one of its publications that by promoting *individualism* and *homogeneity,* the *community settlement* aimed to open the 'gateway of *hityashvut*' for a public who did not fit into the former framework of socialist *kibbutz* and *moshav.*

59   This form later also became popular west of the Green Line.

60   Newman, "The Changing Rural Landscape," 89.

61   Kellerman, *Society and Settlement*, 93.

62   Peled and Shafir, *Being Israeli,* 173. Peled and Shafir further cite from the Drobless plan: 'The dominant incentives for migration [...] purchasing high standard housing with land attached, at lower costs'.

63   For example, the Stars Plan of Sharon that aimed to blur the Green Line and later the construction of the separation wall. See also the National Priority Area and Haredi housing policies.

64   Peled and Shafir, *Being Israeli,* 178.

65   Ibid. – my emphasis.

66   Foucault quoted in T. Lemke, "The Birth of Bio-Politics: Michel Foucault's Lecture at the Collège de France on Neo-Liberal Governmentality," *Economy and Society* 30, 2 (2001): 204.

67   C. Pinchas-Cohen, "A Dangerous Relationship: Israeli Society and the Settlers," *Eretz Acheret* 10 (2002).

68   Beitar Ilit website.

69   See for example "Land Grab: Israel's Settlement Policy in the West Bank," *B'Tselem,* http://www.btselem.org/download/200205_land_grab_eng.pdf. (accessed 30 October 2013).

70 A. Dgani and R. Dgani, *Hbikush Limgurim Bamigzar Ha'Haredi* (Tel Aviv: Geocartography: Institute for Spatial Analysis, 2000), 17.
71 "Report 1531," *Central Bureau of Statistics*, 2011 http://www.cbs.gov.il/publications 13/local_authorities11_1531/pdf/637_3660. pdf. (accessed 30 October 2013).
72 Quoted in R. Segal and E. Weizman, *A Civilian Occupation: The Politics of Israeli Architecture* (Tel Aviv: Babel; London and New York: Verso, 2003), 157–8.
73 Shilhav, *Ultra-Orthodoxy in Urban Governance.*
74 Ibid.
75 24 January 1993, government decision 721.
76 Beitar Ilit was considered a National Priority Area until August 2013.
77 E. Bronner, "In West Bank Settlements, Sign of Hope for a Deal," *New York Times*, 26 July 2009, http://www.nytimes.com/2009/07/27/world/middleeast/27settlers .html?pagew anted=all (accessed 30 October 2013).
78 D. Shefer, "There Was No Place for Us in Bnei Brak, So We Came to Beitar Ilit," *Ynet*, 26 August 2005, http://www.ynet.co.il/articles/0,7340,L-3133299,00.html (accessed 30 October 2013).
79 H. Lev, "We Were Here Before This Government and We'll Be Here After It Is Gone," *Arutz Sheva*, 4 August 2013, http://www.inn.co.il/News/News.aspx/260290 (accessed 30 October 2013).
80 T. Rotem, "The Price Is Right," *Ha'artez*, 25 September 2013, http://www.haaretz .com/print-edition/business/the-price-is-right-1.101174 (accessed 30 October 2013).
81 Ibid.
82 On how the liberalization of the West Bank settlements has shaped the positions of non-hegemonic groups see D. Gutwein, "Comments on the Class Foundations of the Occupation," *Theory and Criticism* [Teoria Ubikoret] 24 (2004): 203–11; on the segregation of Jews and Palestinians and between Jewish ethno-classes see Yiftachel, *Ethnocracy;* and on creating a space of non-hegemonic 'third Israel' 'outside' of 'moral Israel' see Shenhav, *The Time of the Green Line.*
83 Y. Elituv "No More Settlements," *Kikar HaShabat*, 4 June 2009, http://www .kikarhashabat.co.il/1042.html (accessed 30 October 2013). Note: Harish, Katzir, and Kasif are the names of the new Haredi cities that have recently been constructed or will be constructed in the coming years.
84 Quoted in Shilhav, *Ultra-Orthodoxy in Urban Governance*, 26.
85 Beitar Ilit website – my emphasis.

References Cited

Arendt, H. *The Jewish Writings*, eds. J. Kohn and R.H. Feldman (New York: Schocken Books, 2007).
Avineri, S. *The Making of Modern Zionism: Intellectual Origins of the Jewish State* (New York: Basic Books, 1989).
Azoulay, A., and A. Ophir. *This Regime Which Is Not One: Occupation and Democracy Between the Sea and the River (1967–)* (Tel-Aviv: Resling Publishing, 2008).
Bauman, Z. *Modernity and Ambivalence* (Ithaca, NY: Cornell University Press, 1991).
Buch, P. "Introduction," in *Israel: A Colonial-Settler State?*, ed. M. Rodinson (New York: Monad Press, 1973), 9–26.
Bystrov, E., and A. Soffer. *Israel: Demography 2012–2030 On the Way to a Religious State* (University of Haifa: Chaikin Chair in Geostrategy, 2012).
Dalsheim, J. *Unsettling Gaza: Secular Liberalism, Radical Religion, and the Israeli Settlement Project* (Oxford, UK: Oxford University Press, 2011).

Dgani, A., and R. Dgani. *Hbikush Limgurim Bamigzar Ha'Haredi* (Tel Aviv: Geocartography, Institute for Spatial Analysis, 2000).

Feige, M. *Settling in the Hearts: Jewish Fundamentalism in the Occupied Territories* (Detroit: Wayne State University Press, 2009).

Feige, M., and S. Mapot. *One Space, Two Places: Gush Emunim, Peace Now and the Construction of Israeli Space* (Jerusalem: Magnes Press, The Hebrew University, 2002).

Friedman, M. *The Haredi (Ultra-Orthodox) Society: Sources, Trends and Processes* (Jerusalem: Jerusalem Institute for Israel Studies, 1991).

Friedman, M. "Life Tradition and Book Tradition in the Development of Ultraorthodox Judaism," in *Israeli Judaism: The Sociology of Religion in Israel*, eds. Š.A. Dešen, C.S. Liebman, and M. Shokeid (New Brunswick, NJ: Transaction, 1995), 127–47.

Gordon, N. *Israel's Occupation* (Berkeley, CA: University of California Press, 2008).

Gordon, N., and Y. Cohen. "Western Interests, Israeli Unilateralism, and the Two State Solution," *Journal of Palestine Studies* 41, 3 (2012): 6–18.

Gutwein, D. "Comments on the Class Foundations of the Occupation," *Theory and Criticism [Teoria Ubikoret]* 24 (2004): 203–11.

Kellerman, A. *Society and Settlement: The Jewish Land of Israel in the Twentieth Century* (Albany, NY: State University of New York Press, 1993).

Khazzoom, A. "The Great Chain of Orientalism: Jewish Identity, Stigma Management, and Ethnic Exclusion in Israel," *American Sociological Review* 68, 4 (2003): 481–510.

Kimmerling, B. *Zionism and Territory: The Socio-Territorial Dimensions of Zionist Politics* (Berkeley, CA: University of California Press, 1983).

Kimmerling, B. "Boundaries and Frontiers of Israeli Control System," in *The Israeli State and Society: Boundaries and Frontiers*, ed. B. Kimmerling (Albany, NY: Suny Press, 1989), 265–84.

Lemke, T. "The Birth of Bio-Politics: Michel Foucault's Lecture at the Collège de France on Neo-Liberal Governmentality," *Economy and Society* 30, 2 (2001): 190–207.

Mamdani, M. *When Does a Settler Become a Native?: Reflections of the Colonial Roots of Citizenship in Equatorial and South Africa* (Cape Town: University of Cape Town, Department of Communication, 1998).

Masalha, N. *Imperial Israel and the Palestinians: The Politics of Expansion* (London: Pluto Press, 2000).

Massad, J. A. *The Persistence of the Palestinian Question: Essays on Zionism and the Palestinian* (New York: Routledge, 2006).

Newman, D. "The Changing Rural Landscape, 1967–1992," in *Settlement Geography of Israel: Spatial Experiments*, ed. S. Reichman Ramat (Tel Aviv: Open University of Israel, 1997).

Peled, Y., and G. Shafir. *Being Israeli: The Dynamics of Multiple Citizenship* (Cambridge, UK: Cambridge University Press, 2002).

Pinchas-Cohen, C. "A Dangerous Relationship: Israeli Society and the Settlers," *Eretz Acheret* 10 (2004).

Rabkin, Y. M. *A Threat from Within: A Century of Jewish Opposition to Zionism* (London and New York: Zed Books, 2006).

Ravitzky, A. *ha-Kets ha-meguleh u-medinat ha-Yehudim: Meshihiyut, Tsiyonut ve-radikalizm dati be-Yisrael* (Tel Aviv: Am oved, 1993).

Rodinson, M. *Israel: A Colonial-Settler State?* (New York: Monad Press, 1973).

Segal, R., and E. Weizman, eds. *A Civilian Occupation: The Politics of Israeli Architecture* (Tel Aviv: Babel; London and New York: Verso, 2003).

Shafir, G. *Land, Labor and the Origins of the Israeli-Palestinian Conflict 1882–1914* (Cambridge, UK: Cambridge University Press, 1989).

Shenhav, Y. *The Time of the Green Line: A Jewish Political Essay* (Tel Aviv: Am Oved, 2010).

Shilhav, Y. *Ultra-Orthodoxy in Urban Governance in Israel* (Jerusalem: Floersheimer Institute For Policy Studies, 1998).

Shlomo, A. *The Making of Modern Zionism: The Intellectual Origins of the Jewish State* (New York: Basic Books, 1981).

Veracini, L. *Israel and Settler Society* (London: Pluto Press, 2006).

Veracini, L. *Settler Colonialism: A Theoretical Overview* (Basingstoke, UK: Palgrave MacMillan, 2010).

Weizman, E. *Hollow Land: Israel's Architecture of Occupation* (London: Verso, 2007).

Wolfe, P. "Settler Colonialism and the Elimination of the Native," *Journal of Genocide Research* 8, 4 (2006): 387–409.

Yiftachel, O. *Ethnocracy: Land and Identity Politics in Israel/Palestine* (Philadelphia: University of Pennsylvania Press, 2006).

Zertal, I., and A. Eldar. *Lords of the Land: The War Over Israel's Settlements in the Occupied Territories, 1967–2007*, trans. V. Eden (New York: Nation Books, 2007).

Part II
Uncovering Citizenship

6
Overlapping Sovereignties: Gurus and Citizenship

Aya Ikegame

Abstract

Political anthropologists have been arguing that the actual working of the state or sovereign-like figures such as big-men and gangsters are quite different from a normative understanding of a compact, centralized, and unifying sovereignty. The distinction should not, though, be drawn between a Western norm and an Eastern anomaly, as political orientalism has tended to do. The difference should instead be found between molar and molecular forms of sovereignty. While molar sovereignty insists on its own exclusive and indivisible nature, molecular sovereignties connect each other and constantly change their original forms. By examining an ethnographical example of an informal arbitration court run by a religious ruler, or guru, in southern India, this chapter argues that the ways in which a guru as a sovereign performer interacts with other performers – in this case, the state, politicians, mining companies – opens up a space where a more inclusive and possibly democratic ethos could emerge.

Introduction

Citizens living in many parts of the world, especially places referred to as the 'global South', seem to have different relationships with the state to those that are most commonly discussed in Western political theory. In fact, many if not most of these citizens continue to experience the legacies of colonialism, imperialism, then anti-colonial-inspired nationalism, and many endure internal conflicts based on religious, ethnic, linguistic, and regional 'differences' while maintaining precolonial equally diverse political cultures. To make matters more complicated, those 'differences' themselves did not predate colonial encounters nor can they simply be described as 'natural'. Rather, these differences between people were often drawn by their colonial masters.[1] Clifford Geertz has stated that in these 'complicated places' something possibly called 'the state' is quite different from the normative definition of sovereign state that is characterized as a vested authority enjoying the monopoly of legitimate violence in a territory with clear boundaries.[2]

Weak state, failed state, quasi-state, rogue state, tribal state, or civilizational-state are the names some political theorists have given to 'the state' in these complicated places. At the same time, anthropologists have embarked upon the serious study of something like a state or something behaving like a state in those same places especially since the 2000s. From vigilantism in post-apartheid South Africa, big-men or political brokers in western India, to street gangs in Africa and a 'public' transport system provided by local mafia in Siberia, anthropologists have begun to reveal the working of sovereign-like figures that provide vital social services, maintain some degree of social stability, and bring justice through the use of legal and illegal means in places where legal state provisions are not accessible or nonexistent.[3] Political anthropologists, who came out of a long tradition of analysing the political institutions of 'tribal' societies, have brought a sensitivity to seeing political institutions of postcolonial societies not simply as an early developmental stage of European society nor its simple mirror image. The ethnographical investigations they have carried out enabled them to see how such sovereign-like figures actually function in complex social and cultural contexts. In the same period, political anthropologists also began to dissect the workings of the so-called modern state and to reveal the increasingly complex and contradictory faces of the state, which show it to be far from singular or cohesive.[4] Geertz thus notes, this was 'a shift away from looking at the state first and foremost as a leviathan machine, a set-apart sphere of command and decision, to looking at it against the background of the sort of society in which it is embedded'.[5] He further states that we need to see here 'less Hobbes, more Machiavelli; less the imposition of sovereign monopoly, more the cultivation of the higher expediency; less the exercise of abstract will, more the pursuit of visible advantage'.[6] Here Geertz does not suggest that we abandon the concept of sovereignty altogether but alerts anthropologists to 'the variousness of the forms that really existent statehood can and does nowadays take'.[7]

Performing Sovereignties

Anthropologists, such as Geertz, who examine the 'irregularity and divisions' of a supposedly unified and unifying sovereign nation-state, treat the state not as static but instead as 'performance': their focus has been, for example, the imagining of the state, discursive lives of the state, and their practical effects.[8] Sovereign performers (Hansen 2006) or localized sovereigns (Humphrey 2004) all interact and negotiate with these performative effects of the state, which are often confusing and contradictory. I want to argue that ethnographic accounts produced by anthropologists with their 'ingrained obsession with detail and difference'[9] should be more seriously accounted for in our rethinking of the political theories of sovereignty.[10] It seems, however, that there are some shortcomings or traps to be foreseen in a possible conversation between the anthropology of sovereignty and political theory.

While anthropologists tend to bundle up theories of sovereignty into a coherent and Eurocentric whole, the ideas of sovereignty developed in Europe actually have a variety of mutually contradictory historical trajectories. As Raia Prokhovnik has rightly noted, there is also 'a politics of the tradition of thinking about sovereignty going on in the canon, in that what we choose to remember of that tradition is a useful cultural indicator'.[11] Recent interest in sovereignty clearly demonstrates a growing awareness of this contingency and the politics with which different theories of sovereignty are aligned. Even the description of what sovereignty actually is or does differs radically from one position to another. For some, sovereignty is equated with rule and jurisdiction of law; for others, sovereignty is a capacity to violate the very law it creates.[12] For some, sovereignty is a unifying force for autonomy and self-rule, while for others it is suppressive power against citizens who demand political freedom. Some insist on its absolute and indivisible nature as its core, and some suggest it can be sharable, partial, and divisible.[13]

Wendy Brown has claimed that the origin of the wildly opposing contemporary views on sovereignty come from the fact that sovereignty always holds two very different faces – supremacy and autonomy.[14] Within the space which sovereign itself demarks, sovereignty represents supremacy of power or authority, while outside of this space, sovereignty projects autonomy or self-rule and the capacity for independent actions.[15] A number of the ambiguities and paradoxes of sovereignty mentioned above are, according to Brown, subsets of its contradictory two characters.[16]

Opposing views on sovereignty thus not only stem from disciplinary or political differences but also the paradox at the very core of sovereign configuration. Some theorists, such as William Connolly, see potentiality in the very gaps and fissures that occasionally emerge between the two contradictory faces of sovereignty. Connolly asks if we could perhaps envisage a more inclusive and democratic ethos in this very paradox itself.[17] This places Connolly at a distance from the sovereign paradigm described by Giorgio Agamben, in which sovereignty is closely tied up with biopolitics, with which it forms an inescapable conjunction. We could instead examine a different aspect of the sovereign-performers that operate in the very contradictory terrain of sovereignty.

Sovereignties: The One and the Multiple

I consider the contributions of political anthropology in a slightly different light from the main players within this trend. One of the issues to acknowledge is whether anthropological critiques of the conventional definition of sovereignty really challenge the Eurocentric foundation of such theories. Geertz, for example, with his usual clarity and wit, has claimed that sovereign nation-states in 'complicated places' are not 'compact, centred and inclusive', even within the domain of the jurisdiction that they themselves demarcate.[18] It seems that 'complicated places' are somewhere outside of where the state can be compact, centred, and inclusive, but this contrast, between complicated and less complicated spaces, does not disrupt or necessarily contradict the usual dividing line between the East and West. Nor does this necessarily destabilize the supposed universality of sovereign theory that this anthropological claim wishes to criticize. Rather it might just do the reverse. Explicitly and implicitly, many anthropologists suggest that multiple, divisible, and overlapping sovereignties have existed and still exist despite the colonial expansion and modern nation-state building. Admittedly this often comes from empirically based investigations with sympathy and sensitivity, but this does not change the very common binary of 'the One and the Multiple'.[19] If anthropologists and others continue to rely on the contrast between less complicated places and more complicated places, then the very existence of multiple others only serves to affirm that the single coherent One is the norm and others are mere deviant or they have not quite reached this point yet. This is a very deep-rooted political orientalism within the European political genealogy that this volume wishes to deconstruct, destabilize, and transform.

Secondly, many influential anthropological studies of sovereignty tend to take violence as the sole source of authority and power.[20] For example, aligning with the theorizing of Schmitt and Agamben, Hansen and Stepputat, who pioneered the anthropology of sovereignty, propose 'to abandon sovereignty as an ontological ground of power and order, expressed in law or in enduring ideas of legitimate rule, in favour of a view of sovereignty as a tentative and always emergent form of authority grounded in violence that is performed and designed to generate loyalty, fear, and legitimacy from the neighbourhood to the summit of the state'.[21] Violence is certainly a very important aspect of sovereignty in many parts of the world where other forms of security are largely undermined or missing. This is also true within Western democracy as well, when citizens are placed at the margins of the state where they cannot claim rights that they have; Guantanamo Bay is the ultimate example of this.

It is understandable that anthropologists are concerned with violence, but this may restrict our further inquiry into figures performing sovereignty. Important aspects of these 'sovereign-like' figures that we need to pay attention to include not only their ability to kill but other characteristics; for example, their incredible flexibility to change their identity and their abilities to connect with other performers and create new networks and to turn negative aspects of life into something positive. Indeed, strongmen in the street often transform themselves into democratically elected representatives and create a new form of belonging, loyalty, and security in a situation where poverty and the lack of opportunity only increase the sense of desperation and alienation.

Two different forms of multiplicity discussed by Deleuze and Guattari might be useful here to tackle the problematic but persistent story of 'The One and the Multiple' and also to think about alternative forms of sovereignty. Firstly, they rightly argued that the multiple is effective only when it is 'treated as a substantive "multiplicity," that it ceases to have any relation to the One as subject or object'.[22] In order to escape the abstract opposition between the One and the Multiple, they argued, we need to distinguish different types of multiplicity.[23] Molar and arborescent multiplicities are 'extensive, unifiable, totalizable, and conscious or preconscious', while molecular and rhizomatic multiplicities are 'libidinal and unconscious'.[24] What political anthropologists have tried to make a distinction between is the idea of singular and centralized sovereign and the actual practices and performance of state-like institutions and performers. Moreover, what ethnographical examples of anthropologists provide us with is not simply a variety of different anomalies, which can be opposed to the One that the only Western sovereignty represents, but different ways in which such sovereign-like figures interact and compete. If 'compact, centred and inclusive' (Geertz) sovereignty is molar, what attracts anthropologists is certainly the molecular. If we follow Deleuze and Guattari, anthropological understanding of sovereignty can provide truly substantial multiplicity which destabilizes the story of the One and the Multiple, when we see multiple forms of sovereignty everywhere unrestricted to 'complicated places'. Moreover, if possibly more democratic and liberating forms of sovereignty could be found in the very contradictory facets of sovereignty, then ethnographical evidence from complicated places is not a counter-example to the Eurocentric form of sovereignty but an indication of its self-professed possibility.

Secondly, the Deleuzean idea of molecular multiplicities also enables us to think about non-state sovereign performers beyond violence. Molecular multiplicities ought to change 'in nature as it expands its connection'.[25] They 'do not divide without changing in nature, and distances that do not vary without entering another multiplicity and that constantly construct and dismantle themselves in the course of their communications, as they cross over into each other at, beyond, or before a certain threshold'.[26] This description of molecular multiplicities actually fits better with what anthropologists have identified as localized sovereigns. The distinction between centralized sovereignty with clear territorial boundaries and sharable, divisible sovereignties made by anthropologists is better fitted to a molar and molecular distinction than the orientalist distinction of the West and the East.

Western political theories have maintained a polarized idea that only the West has produced a coherent political genealogy of sovereignty, while a variety of different experiences that the East provides only emphasize the universality of canonized Western norms. The molar and molecular distinction made by Deleuze and Guattari helps us to see another possibility of performative aspects of sovereign-like figures that the orientalist distinction simply conceals. While analysing an ethnographical account of an informal arbitration court run by a local religious leader, a guru, in rural south India, this chapter argues that these very partial, connected, and sharable forms of sovereignty make this informal legal space more inclusive and possibly democratic. The contrast drawn here is not between the coherent West and deviant Others but between exclusive claims of sovereigns – molar multiplicities – emerging both in the West and non-West, and more molecular, rhizomatic practices of sovereign power.

Informal Legal Spaces in South Asia

In recent years, the brutality of self-proclaimed informal legal bodies in South Asia has been widely reported in the media. The Khap panchayats of northern India, and Sharia courts run by Taliban associates in Afghanistan, are probably the most notorious. A marital or sexual liaison between a man and a woman belonging to the same *gotra* (a clan-like subset of a caste group) is now strictly prohibited by certain self-claimed community legal bodies such as Khap panchayats. Some groups severely punish and occasionally kill those who violate this taboo. Many Khap panchayats impose ridiculously restrictive dress codes and curfews upon young women in order to 'protect' them from any sexual deviation.[27] Various Taliban groups also employ draconian punishment against those who do not follow their narrowly interpreted Sharia codes (Kadri 2012). Their influence seems to be growing in certain areas of South Asia.[28] The fact that they do claim their exclusive legal sovereign space through religious and community rights challenges the limits of liberal democracy.

It has become obvious that the broad secularization thesis, in which these phenomena would have been treated as a sign of backwardness, and secular democracy, which is believed to eventually bring about the more liberal and effective rule of law, is not as compelling as it used to be (Hadden 1987; Swatos and Christiano 1999). The situation is even more complicated in India, where secularism is primarily understood as a principle by which the state ensures the freedom and rights of each religious community. In order to do so, the 'secular' Indian state actively interferes in religious matters from temple administration to managing religious trusts. Indian citizens belonging to different religious communities are governed by different sets of personal laws in matters relating to marriage, divorce, inheritance, maintenance, and adoption. For many years Indian feminists have regarded personal laws as discriminatory against women and have fought for a uniform civil code, and at the same time any proposal for removal or reform of personal laws is perceived as a threat to community rights and identity.[29]

The debate concerning secularism in India is highly divisive; however, it is too hasty to argue that community legal practices grounded on the bases of religion or ethnicity or caste frustrate the promise of democracy. Many recent examples show otherwise. Innovative non-state legal practices have sprung up in many parts of India. Muslim conflict resolution services under the All India Muslim Personal Law Board, or the alternative legal service, or 'special women's courts' run by Muslim women activists in the states of Uttar Pradesh and Tamil Nadu in India are proving a vital support for citizens who do not have the means to employ the state legal system.[30] This new approach to legal interpretation within religious communities in India has a clear resonance with what is currently emerging in the UK and elsewhere (see the chapter by Pilgram in this volume). These non-state legal activities are often challenged as anti-constitutional and undermining the rule of law and secularism.

In 2005, an alleged case of rape of a young Muslim woman by her father-in-law led to a fatwa issued by a local Islamic legal body declaring she should not be considered the wife of her husband. This incident fuelled the national imaginary of, and anxiety about, Muslim legal bodies in India and subsequently led to a petition campaign demanding that the Supreme Court eradicate all non-state Muslim legal services in India. Jeff Redding (2013) has shown how the discourse of protecting women's welfare and rights becomes justification for the Hindu majoritarian rule. What he calls 'liberal Islamophobia' creeps into a seemingly liberal constitutionalism that tries to uphold secularism and the rule of law. Considering the fact that no such nationwide campaign has been initiated to control Hindu Khap panchayats, liberal Islamophobia needs to be taken into account when such claims are evaluated. What is interesting here is that campaigners for eradication of the non-state Muslim legal bodies do support the Muslim Personal Law, which ensures Muslims maintain traditional customs, but they insist that the adjudication of such laws has to be done by the state. For the opponents of Muslim legal bodies, the existence of non-state legal bodies threatens the very sovereignty of the state. Singularity and indivisibility of sovereignty, they think, is the core of their constitutionalism (Redding 2013).

Many alternative legal practices by Muslim women's rights activists in South Asia have also posed a threat not only to conservative Muslim authorities but also to progressive feminists. The recent demand of Muslim 'feminists' for gender equality within Muslim Personal Law through alternative readings of the Qur'an cannot be easily accommodated within the discourse of secular feminism in India that has long campaigned for a religion-neutral uniform civil code. Sylvia Vatuk (2008) has pointed out that the alternative legal practices led by educated middle-class women is evidence of 'the process of fragmentation of religious authority in the contemporary globalising Muslim world' where digital circulation of religious texts and translation has enabled greater access to them, consequently eroding the knowledge monopoly of religious scholars.[31] Vatuk contrasts these new Muslim women's rights activists with the Islamist reformists who are more concerned about the advancement of Islamization than the promotion of women's rights.[32] They are, according to Vatuk, indeed very critical of reformist efforts to control women's behaviour. What interests us here is that the fragmentation of religious authority has opened a space for a new politics that does not abandon religious and ethical life altogether.

Discussion of non-state legal authorities, most of which are also religious, tends to concentrate on the question of whether these authorities promote democratic rights, especially the rights of women, or consolidate traditional norms and values which are often regarded as non-democratic or anti-women. The question is still relevant to many parts of the world, particularly in South Asia where violence against women still persists in everyday life (see chapter by Atluri in this volume), but we also need to be cautious about the fact that pro-women liberal ideologies could work as another oppressive force against minorities, as we have seen in the case of the campaign against Muslim legal services in India. While this should be seen as a political tension, it is not necessarily between democratic and non-democratic, or between the secular and the religious, but instead between two opposing ideologies: one that insists on the singular and absolute nature of sovereignty – whether it is the nation-state or the centralized religious authority – and the other that challenges the singularity of sovereignty by creating multiple sovereign spaces. Here again Deleuze and Guattari's distinction between molar and molecular multiplicities could be used as a vital analytical tool to see the liberating possibilities of fragmented sovereignties.

Against this background, let us now examine how a non-state legal authority in rural south India resolves local disputes by carefully crafting networks of other sovereign performers. In our example, the guru (Hindu religious leader) acts as a sole judge in an informal court. The ways in which the guru employs his power and authority to settle local disputes may not appeal to the defenders of secular and liberal principles of democracy. Such suspicion is not unfounded, since, as many scholars have demonstrated, many Hindu religious leaders have enthusiastically participated in often violent Hindu fundamentalist movements (Hansen 1999; van der Veer 1994), and some even claim the superiority of 'Hindu science' or 'Hindu modernity' over 'Western' science and universal modernity (Nanda 2003). However, rejecting such religious leaders simply because they represent a certain tradition of beliefs or teaching might be premature. This example illustrates how people of southern India utilize overlapping sovereignties in order to achieve social justice. The gurus could be compared to Rousseau's idea of the 'legislator' (Rousseau 1978). The legislator is a quasi-divine figure who brings a democratic ethos amongst people and enables them to be capable of making their own law, although Rousseau himself was not certain that such a person could be found.[33] With the performance of being such a 'legislator', we still do not know if a guru is a political genius or a charlatan. This indeterminacy and instability of the legislator, however, as some scholars have argued, should not be treated as a failure of democracy but as a positive potentiality that keeps political space open for change (Inston 2010; Honig 2007).

The Guru's Court

Local dispute resolution by religious leaders has a long tradition in rural south India. Gurus backed by their religious organizations, called *mathas,* can be regarded as 'institutional big-men', a very typical local power-holder in south India, who 'attract followers and enact their roles as generous leaders through charitable institutions that they control'.[34] Most gurus are also celibate renouncers who deny themselves worldly pleasures. Since the early twentieth century, mathas, especially Lingayat mathas in Karnataka, have worked extensively to promote education and health care in rural areas where government provisions were scarce or non-existent. Loyalty towards their gurus or their institutions often comes from the fact that people have benefited from free or affordable education or other help given by the mathas. Many prominent Lingayat gurus in contemporary Karnataka built their reputation not only through their own charitable work but also from previous gurus' efforts.

One such prominent Lingayat guru runs a popular informal arbitration court with a very modern flair. The court is called the Nyaya Peetha (seat of justice) and is run by Taralabalu Jagadguru Brihanmath, a Hindu matha in the village called Sirigere in the Chitradurga district of central Karnataka.[35] Dispute settlement has been carried out for many years in the matha in an *ad hoc* fashion, just as in many other mathas in present times. In 2002, Dr Shivamurthy Shivacharya Maha Swamiji (hereafter the Sirigere guru), who is also an internationally renowned Sanskrit scholar, radically modernized this informal settlement. Now each dispute is given a case number, and at the end of each hearing the Sirigere guru dictates the summary of the dispute. His assistant then transcribes it and keeps a record in a computer database. All the petitions, counter-petitions, and related documents are also carefully filed. By late August 2013, the total number of disputes amounted to 3,016 cases.[36] Not all of the cases are resolved. Some of them have gone on for several years; some were simply discontinued because the accused parties did not turn up. The material for this chapter comes from recorded court hearings, interviews with the guru and people involved, and petition and counter-petition letters that they submitted to the Nyaya Peetha. In this informal court, the guru acts as the sole judge. He listens to the claims of both sides and tries to settle their disputes.[37] The nature of the disputes varies: from failed marriages to industrial disputes in which villagers bring lawsuits against mining or other companies. Most cases are family disputes about marriage and inheritance within the Sadaru Lingayats – a relatively low-status sub-caste of the dominant landed Lingayat caste – who are also the devotees of the Sirigere Taralabalu matha.

The fact that this kind of informal arbitration court is becoming increasingly popular indicates that the Nyaya Peetha that we see today is something more than a modern incarnation of the caste panchayat (assembly) for the Sadaru Lingayat. What is particularly interesting is that other castes are also attracted to the Nyaya Peetha and seek the judgement of the Sirigere guru.[38] The reality is that guru courts are becoming an alternative to the formal regular courts which have been a central part of the everyday life of ordinary Indians since the colonial period. So why is this happening? What can these informal courts offer that formal courts and formal legal systems cannot?

One of the attractions of the Nyaya Peetha arises from the fact that the guru creates a moral space beyond the formal legality upheld by the state law. Many cases solved at his court cannot easily be brought to the official state courts. For example, there are surprisingly many cases of so-called 'second marriages' at the guru's court. The 'first wife' who wants to obtain a share of her husband's property or monthly maintenance payment after he has committed himself to an informal arrangement of 'second marriage' cannot possibly go to a formal court to achieve the arrangement she seeks since legally she is still his wife. Neither side wants to bear the shame of a divorce. The guru often persuades the husband's family to deposit a certain sum of money from which she will regularly receive maintenance.

Both during the guru's court hearings and in interviews with the villagers, the contrast between formal law (*kanunu*) and morality (*dharma*) was often emphasized. In the several cases concerning former temple lands, which I have analysed in detail elsewhere (Ikegame forthcoming), villagers who wish to recover their 'common property' could not appeal to a formal court, because it was they who had nominated different individuals as legal cultivators-cum-owners of the land in order to evade the land reform of the 1970s.[39] The guru himself once told me in a private conversation that the reason why his court at his matha works is because he 'has the moral authority'. Morality (*dharma*) is the domain of his sovereignty. He can make the law within this domain. Moreover, the very limitation of the state law creates his domain, where justice is waiting to be recovered. This is not a domain where the state has yet penetrated, but the domain where the state is, as Talal Asad has argued, 'continually both experienced and undone through the *illegibility* of its own practices, documents and words'.[40] The illegibility of the state practices here partly derives from the inflexibility and short-sightedness of the state law. Meanwhile, citizens of south India are far more flexible in circumventing the law and imaginative in creating new arrangements.

The relationship between the state and the guru's informal court is a complex one. The variety of social activities of mathas and their effectiveness invite us to think that some mathas in the state are now acquiring state-like characteristics or have even become a parallel-state (Sood 2006). Indeed gurus and devotees often compare the state government (*sarakaara*) and their mathas; for example, a devotee described the very impressive office building of his matha in Mysore city as 'like Vidhana Soudha [the seat of the state legislature of Karnataka]' and another described their regular donations to the matha as 'more like a tax'.

Apart from the actual and analogical 'stateness' (Hansen and Stepputat 2001) of the matha, the nature of typical cases brought to the guru's court at Sirigere also indicates that his court stands outside of the formal legal system. As we have seen, the causes of the problems brought to the guru are not strictly legal to begin with (e.g., cases of 'second marriage'). The guru's court tries to operate within the state legal system and even seeks to obtain official legal backing for his decisions by using the recently revised Arbitration Act within the state. Voluntary mediators at the guru's court, who are retired state officers or former Panchayat leaders, often make reference to legal processes and regulations regarding the division of the land amongst family members and the legal registration of land rights. The guru sometimes advises people to go to a local civil court and even helps them to find a lawyer who would be sympathetic to their problems. In this sense, the guru's court acts like an extension or an agent of the state.

Overlapping Sovereignty

The sovereign domain of the guru is a space where the distinctions between morality and immorality, legality and illegality, and the personal and impersonal are blurred and one penetrates the other. Only the guru and the state have the authority to draw the line as sovereigns, and yet, these lines are constantly shifting and being redrawn. The nature of the sovereignty of the guru is not exclusive nor absolute but overlapping and sharable.

An example of how the molecular and rhizomatic nature of the guru's sovereignty strengthens his power and authority can be seen in the case of a dispute between local mining companies and four villages located near to the Sirigere matha.[41] The case originally started in 2003, when three local mining companies brought a complaint against four villages, claiming that the villagers had been blocking the road that led to the local railway station for 15 days – preventing lorries carrying iron ore from passing through. During the court hearings, the villagers demanded compensation for crops – mostly for bananas, areca nuts, and maize – which were damaged by pollution from the iron ore, as well as money for repairing the road. They also requested strict regulations concerning the safe driving of lorries and funding for local developmental projects. In his judgement, the guru ordered the villagers to stop any blocking of the road.[42] The villagers immediately obliged. The guru at the same time ordered the mining companies to deposit a sum of money for the purpose of new road construction and rural development. Since 2003, two mining companies have deposited for this purpose the astonishing sum of 220 million rupees, equivalent to 2.2 million GBP or 3.2 million USD.

During an interview, the representatives from one of the mining companies involved in this dispute told me the reason why they went to see the guru to seek his help in the first place.[43] They said that if they had to deal with the leaders of each village, the negotiation would be endless. One of them said, 'There were several villages we had to negotiate with. Each village has not only one but several leaders. And then [we need to think about] different caste groups! But if we go to the guru, all the leaders would listen to him. It made much more sense to go to see the guru.'[44] The Sirigere guru is thus a leader above many other small local leaders. The guru transcends differences of locality, kinship, and caste. The logic of renunciation assures him this transcendent position. As the sociologist Louis Dumont (1980) has argued, the renouncer in Asian traditions attains a transcendent position beyond rigid caste hierarchies. By cutting off kinship ties, a renouncer becomes 'an individual-outside-the-world'.[45] Through renunciation, 'a man can become dead to the social world, [and] escape the network of strict interdependence'.[46] The kinlessness of the renouncer-guru also makes him an incorruptible leader, unlike an elected politician who is, many Indians believe, inevitably corrupt because he needs to support his kin, supporters, and caste community.[47] The actual nature of his sovereignty is not, however, one of complete independence. The renouncer-guru transcends kin networks and caste communities, but he also creates new networks and connections.

Further examination of how the guru actually executes the development projects funded by local mining companies reveals a different aspect of his authority and power. Here the guru cannot act alone but has to rely on the networks of power-holders that he has carefully cultivated over the years. During my visit to the Nyaaya Peetha in late August 2013, people were discussing the construction of a 2 km reinforced concrete road from the local railway station. One of the mining companies was ready to pay for the entire cost of construction, which was 200 million rupees (around 2 million GBP). The tender was given to a local construction company with a good reputation, and they were willing to start the construction as soon as possible. But they still needed a sanction from the state government. The request for the sanction was sent in May, but by late August they had not yet heard a response. The villagers and representatives of the mining company asked the guru to intervene. During the course of the meeting, held in a village school hall, the guru made a phone call to a current state minister and made him promise there and then that he would provide the necessary sanction within a week. The sanction indeed came within three days. The act of calling a politician and fixing things in front of the public was a compelling demonstration of the guru's performative power but also of the effectiveness of his political network and his connections with the state.

The way in which the guru used the political network to get things done was even more impressive when we consider the fact that the then state government was formed only a few months earlier. In May 2013, the Bharatiya Janata Party (BJP) suffered a spectacular electoral defeat, and the rival Congress Party gained a majority within the state assembly. Clearly the guru managed to establish a completely different network of politicians who would follow his orders in a very short amount of time, since it was widely believed, and the guru himself confirmed with me, that he used to support the BJP. The left-leaning Kannada tabloid newspaper *Gauri Lankesh* has reported how effectively the Sirigere guru establishes his alliance with political parties by using a political broker or intermediary.[48] The newspaper claims that a man who was a former government engineer-turned-developer joined the BJP in 2008 in order to forge a tie between the party and the Sirigere matha. The man seemed to be acting as a political broker for the matha for several years. Just before the last election he joined the Congress, probably because many could see the declining popularity of the BJP. The broker was alleged to have given financial support to the Congress candidate in the constituency near Sirigere. After his victory in May 2013, the Congress politician became a state minister. The state minister whom the Sirigere guru called on the day of the meeting with the villagers and mining company representatives was this same politician.

The fact that the guru's sovereignty works precisely because he stands alongside the state does not mean that he can operate without the state. As we have seen in the mining dispute case, the reality is quite the opposite. Many activities of the matha require support or indeed authorization from the state. Although a powerful matha like Sirigere can successfully generate and divert money for local development without going through formal administrative procedures, it nonetheless still needs to penetrate the state apparatus using personal and often informal connections. A journalist based in Bangalore confirmed this point. During an interview in March 2013, he stated that powerful mathas do not require financial support from the state anymore, but they are still compelled to maintain good relations. To obtain government approval for a newly opened school, for example, it was certainly always helpful to have sympathetic officers or politicians within the government.[49]

The state is not at all monolithic or coherent, but a penetrable and to some extent pliable entity. The guru's act of publicly calling an influential politician to get things done is a clear demonstration of the performativity of these informal sovereigns in south India. He can stand outside of society as a renouncer and has the authority to distinguish morality from immorality, but what makes his court effective still largely depends on his ability to manipulate the state apparatus. Of course, the state and informal sovereigns do not always work harmoniously. The state does occasionally declare the moral activities of the guru to be illegal. In 2009, income tax officers from the central government raided Sirigere Talarabalu matha. Allegedly, the large sum of money deposited by the mining companies was suspected to be a form of tax evasion; at least this is the story that villagers believe.[50] Now the money is instead transferred directly to a local development trust that the guru ordered villagers to establish. A tabloid newspaper also called the Sirigere matha a secret banker of the then chief minister B. S. Yeddyurappa, and this was proposed as another reason for the raid by income tax officers.[51] Such accusations may not be baseless, but they miss the point. The very ambiguity of this legal space attracts people whose problems are serious but nonetheless insolvable within the formal legal system or inflexible structure of the state administration. The instability of the guru's sovereignty also makes his domain open and suggests the possibility of multiple means and opportunities for people to change and improve their lives.

Conclusion

The ways in which rural citizens of south India constitute their gurus as their sovereigns are not entirely different from those that citizens of Western societies use. They create a locus of power and authority by submitting themselves to a religious authority. Citizens of other parts of the world might do this less conspicuously towards their state. The aimed for effect is the same. They expect the sovereign to be selfless and to work for society at large. Good gurus and good states do the same. What we need to distinguish is the quality of sovereigns. A molar form of sovereignty, whether it is a nation-state or a self-claimed community vigilante group, insists on its exclusive authority over its territories. The molecular form of sovereign, on the other hand, connects with other sovereigns, shares authority, and creates a new network of power-holders and political actors. Gurus in south India clearly embody the latter form of sovereignty.

The informal legal space created by the guru also presents a similar paradox that is inherent within European political theories of sovereignty. The guru can make his law precisely because he stands alongside the state, while what makes the guru an effective sovereign is his ability to connect with and penetrate into the state apparatus. As a molecular and rhizomatic sovereignty, this is not weakness but strength. He works in an ambiguous area where the distinctions between legality and illegality, morality and immorality, are not clearly defined. He, as a sovereign, decides and draws the line, although never decisively. The legal space he creates is inevitably a murky one, but this does not make this space immoral – quite the opposite. Since he is not restricted by clearly defined legal codes, the grievances that people bring to his court can be interpreted and judged in a number of different ways. Rather than declaring the 'second marriage' illegal and invalid, the guru does not deny the two marriages but supports the 'first wife' who often struggles to make ends meet. Similarly, individual property rights can be compromised by the decision of guru's court in favour of the common property claims of the village temple, even when these are unrecognized by the formal legal system.

In the political landscape of rural south India, there is no single indivisible and absolute sovereignty but several fragmented sovereignties that compete against, negotiate with, and connect to each other. The guru, himself a fragmented sovereign, connects many different political players: village elders, caste leaders, political brokers, politicians, bureaucrats, and powerful industrial corporations. His ability to create networks and to cut them at the right moment is the strength and resilience of the molecular and rhizomatic sovereign. Renunciation gives him a transcendent position above society, but the 'individual-outside-the-world' (Dumont) does not simply remain there. The guru reaches down into the messy layers of local politics and uses his rhizomatic web of political actors for the betterment of society.

The very nature of molecular sovereigns means that the multiple sovereign domains are open to many, including those who are at the margins of society – abandoned wives and labourers in mines – who can access resources and influence that otherwise are not available to them. Citizens can also switch between sovereigns whenever it is necessary. The very same people happily go to the formal civil court if they think they have more advantages to gain there. Similarly, they will go to their caste leader when he is believed to have more influence over other issues. Citizens of rural south India have constituted many sovereigns for their own good. These fragmented and overlapping sovereignties give possibilities and hope for social justice and the potential for the development of a fairer and more equal society.

Notes

1   Dirks, *Castes of Mind*.
2   Geertz, "What Is a State If It Is Not a Sovereign?" 579.
3   For recent political anthropological work on sovereignty, see Buur, "Crime and Punishment," "The Sovereign Outsourced"; Jensen, "Above the Law"; Hansen, "Sovereigns beyond the State," "Performers of Sovereignty"; Humphrey, "Sovereignty."
4   See for example, Das and Poole, *Anthropology in the Margins of the State*; Sharma and Gupta, *The Anthropology of the State*; Spencer, *Anthropology, Politics, and the State*.
5   Geertz, "What Is a State If It Is Not a Sovereign?" 580.
6   Ibid., 580.
7   Ibid., 579.
8   Feuchtwang (2004), 587; see also Das and Poole (2004), Hansen and Stepputat (2001), Spencer (2007), Gupta (2012).
9   Geertz, "What Is a State If It Is Not a Sovereign?" 579.
10 See also Wachspress, "Rethinking sovereignty with reference to history and anthropology."
11 Prokhovnik, *Sovereignty*, 12.

12 Brown, "Sovereignty and the Return of the Repressed," 236.

13 Ibid., 236.

14 Ibid., 236.

15 Ibid., 237.

16 Ibid., 237.

17 Connolly, *Pluralism*, 131–48.

18 Geertz, 579.

19 There are anthropological works on overlapping natures of sovereignty and new forms of governance without the nation-state in the EU (for example, Wilson 2014, Shore 2006). However, there has not been a productive interexchange between the anthropology of sovereign-like figures of non-European societies and the anthropology of European sovereign experiments.

20 Exceptions to the violence centred studies are for example, Mines and Gourishanker (1990), Mines (2014).

21 Hansen and Stepputat, "Sovereignty Revisited," 297.

22 Deleuze and Guattari, *Thousand Plateaus*, 8.

23 Ibid., 32–3.

24 Ibid., 33.

25 Ibid., 8.

26 Ibid., 33.

27 The Khap panchayats claim that they existed for several hundred years as an autonomous and independent legal body in north India amongst the Jat community. They even defend frequent 'honour killings' of couples who have not followed their marriage regulations, and they insist upon the strict surveillance of women within the region as community rights. Contradicting their claim to have an autonomous legal bodies for centuries, a recent study by Bharadwaj shows that village life in pre-modern Haryana and surrounding regions was regulated by multiple layers of legal authorities and that the Khap panchayats are actually a quite recent phenomena, practically unknown until the 1960s (Bharadwaj, "Myth and Reality of the Khap Panchayats").

28 The Pakistan Taliban negotiating team insisted that there was no chance of peace unless Pakistani government officials embraced Islamic Sharia law in February 2014. http://blogs.reuters.com/faithworld/2014/02/28/pakistani-taliban-see-no-peace-unless-islamabad-government-enforces-sharia-law/ (accessed 20 December 2014).

29 For more detailed analysis of the Uniform Civil Code debate in India, see Sundar Rajan, "Women Between Community and State."

30 "Alternative fora," *The Frontline* 30, 17, Special Edition on "Personal Laws," 6 September 2013.

31 Vatuk, "Islamic Feminism in India," 515.

32 Ibid., 517.

33 Connolly, *Pluralism*, 135; see also Matravers, "Introduction," xiii.

34 Mines and Gourishankar, "Leadership and Individuality in South Asia," 762.

35 Professor Janaki Nair of JNU and I researched this case together, and I am thankful to her for sharing her work. I am grateful for her encouragement and comments on my work. I thank Mr Anil Kumar, Mr Ravikumar, and Mr Suresh for their assistance during my fieldwork.

36 I have attended the Nyaya Peetha since 2007 and was given access to the database of the court cases. I have selected several cases and conducted interviews with people involved in these cases. I am deeply indebted to the generosity and support given by Dr Shivamurty Shivachariya Swamiji.

37 Anyone can bring their problems in the form of a petition letter and the court will give them on the same day a date for the first hearing and a case number. The court then informs the other party (or 'defendant') and asks them to come and receive the blessing of the guru on that specific date. Since many cases concern family disputes amongst the Sadaru Lingayat community, who constitute a majority of devotees of the Sirigere matha, most accused parties would not refuse this order from the matha. Even in the case of a non-Lingayat, most of them live in nearby villages so they cannot ignore the guru's order.

38 There are several ongoing cases in which villagers belonging to different caste groups accuse village leaders who are Sadar Lingayat of immoral or illegal practices. There is also a case of a local Bovi (traditionally stonecutters) community complaining of their own caste leader (the Nyaaya Peetha, case no. 2354/2010).

39 The successive land reforms in Karnataka in the 1970s were believed to be relatively successful in terms of enforcement, although it did not bring the more fundamental social transformation that some other states managed to achieve. One of the problems was that they did not exempt common properties, such as land donated for the maintenance of village temples. Many villages, in order to save their temple lands, gave the names of village heads or the names of people directly giving services to the temples as cultivators of the land and they became legal owners of the temple lands. In recent years, these legal owners have begun selling the supposed common temple lands and villagers are facing difficulty in maintaining temple worships and other activities (Ikegame forthcoming).

40 Asad, "Where Are the Margins of the State?" 279, emphasis in original.

41 The Nyaaya Peetha, case no. 398/2003.

42 The Nyaaya Peeta, case no. 398/2003, 30/06/2003, para. 3.

43 From the interview with three representatives of the John Mines, near Sirigere, Karnataka on 3 June 2014.

44 Ibid.

45 Dumont, *Homo Hierarchicus*, 185.

46 Ibid., 184.

47 Ikegame, "The Governing Guru," 56–7.

48 *The Gauri Lankesh* on 28 August 2013 by T.N. Shanukha.

49 From the interview with Bangalore-based journalist and writer Mr Shivasundar on 14 March 2013.

50 Ikegame, "The Governing Guru," 60.

51 Ibid.

References Cited

Asad, Talal. "Where Are the Margins of the State?" in *Anthropology in the Margins of the State*, eds. V. Das and D. Poole (Santa Fe, NM: School of American Research Press, 2004).

Bharadwaj, S.B. "Myth and Reality of the Khap Panchayats: A Historical Analysis of the Panchayat and Khap Panchayat," *Studies in History* 28, 1 (2012): 43–67.

Brown, Wendy. "Sovereignty and the Return of the Repressed," in *The new pluralism*, eds. D. Campbell and M. Schoolman (Durham, NC: Duke University Press, 2008).

Buur, Lars. "Crime and Punishment on the Margins of the Post-Apartheid State," *Anthropology and Humanities* 28, 1 (2003): 23–42.

Buur, Lars. "The Sovereign Outsourced: local justice and violence in Port Elizabeth," in *Sovereign Bodies*, eds. T.B. Hansen and F. Stepputat (Princeton, NJ: Princeton University Press, 2005).

Connolly, William E. *Pluralism* (Durham, NC: Duke University Press, 2005).

Das, Veena, and Deborah Poole, eds. *Anthropology in the Margins of the State* (Santa Fe, NM: School of American Research Press, 2004).

Deleuze, Gilles, and Félix Guattari. *Thousand Plateaus* (London: Continuum, 2004 [1980]).

Dirks, Nicholas. *Castes of Mind: Colonialism and the Making of Modern India* (Princeton, NJ: Princeton University Press, 2001).

Dumont, Louis. *Homo Hierarchicus: The Caste System and Its Implications* (Chicago: University of Chicago Press, 1980).

Feuchtwang, Stephan. "Comments to Geertz," *Current Anthropology* 45, 5: 587.

Geertz, Clifford. "What Is a State If It Is Not a Sovereign? Reflections on politics in complicated places," *Current Anthropology* 45, 5 (2004): 577–93.

Gupta, A. *Red Tape: Bureaucracy, Structural Violence, and Poverty in India* (Durham, NC: Duke University Press, 2012).

Hadden, J.K. "Toward Desacralizing Secularization," *Social Forces* 65, 3 (1987): 587–611.

Hansen, Thomas B. "Performers of Sovereignty: On the Privatization of Security in Urban South Africa," *Critique of Anthropology* 26, 3 (2006): 279–95.

Hansen, Thomas B. *Saffron Wave* (Princeton, NJ: Princeton University Press, 1999).

Hansen, Thomas B. "Sovereigns beyond the State: on legality and authority in Urban India," in *Sovereign Bodies*, eds. T. Hansen and F. Stepputat (Princeton, NJ: Princeton University Press, 2005).

Hansen, Thomas, B., and Finn Stepputat, eds. "Introduction," in *States of Imagination*, eds. T. Hansen and F. Stepputat (Durham, NC: Duke University Press, 2001).

Hansen, Thomas B., and Finn Stepputat, eds. *Sovereign Bodies* (Princeton, NJ: Princeton University Press, 2005).

Hansen, Thomas B., and Finn Stepputat, eds. "Sovereignty Revisited," *Annual Review of Anthropology* 35, 1 (2006): 295–315.

Honing, Bonnie. "Between Decision and Deliberation: Political paradox in democratic theory," *The American Political Science Review* 101, 1 (2007): 1–17.

Humphrey, Caroline. "Sovereignty," in *A Companion to the Anthropology of Politics*, eds. D. Nugent and J. Vincent (Malden, MA: Blackwell, 2004), 418–36.

Ikegame, Aya. "The Governing Guru: Hindu mathas in liberalising India," in *The Guru in South Asia*, eds. J. Copeman and A. Ikegame (London: Routledge, 2012).

Ikegame, Aya. "Trust and trusts: the guru and devotee-citizens in southern India" (forthcoming).

Ikegame, Aya. "Why do backward castes need their own gurus? The social and political significance of new caste-based monasteries in Karnataka," *Contemporary South Asia* 18, 1 (2010): 57–70.

Inston, Kevin. "Representing the unrepresentable: Rousseau's legislator and the impossible object of the people," *Contemporary Political Theory* 9, 4 (2010): 393–413.

Jansen, Steffen. "Above the Law: Practices of sovereignty in Surrey Estate, Cape Town," in *Sovereign Bodies*, eds. T. Hansen and F. Stepputat (Princeton, NJ: Princeton University Press, 2005).

Kadri, Sadakat. *Heaven on Earth: A journey through Shari'a law*. (London: Vintage, 2012).

Matravers, Derek. "Introduction," in *The Social Contract*, J.-J. Rousseau, trans. H.J. Tozer (London: Wordsworth Edition, 1998).

Mines, Mattison. "The political economy of patronage, preeminence, and the state in Cennai," in *Patronage as Politics in South Asia*, ed. A. Pilavsky (Cambridge, UK: Cambridge University Press, 2014).

Mines, Mattison, and Vijayalakshmi Gourishankar. 'Leadership and Individuality in South Asia: The Case of the South Indian Big-man,' *The Journal of Asian Studies* 49, 4 (1990): 761–86.

Nanda, Meera. *Prophets Facing Backward* (Newark, NJ: Rutgers University Press, 2003).

Prokhovnik, Raia. *Sovereignty: History and Theory* (Exeter: Imprint Academic, 2008).

Redding, Jeffrey A. "Secularism, the Rule of Law, and 'Shari'a Courts': An Ethnographic Examination of a Constitutional Controversy," *Saint Louis University Law Journal* 57 (2013): 339–76.

Rousseau, Jean-Jacques. *On the Social Contract*, trans. J. Masters (New York: St Martin's, 1978).

Sharma, Aradhana, and Akhil Gupta, eds. *The Anthropology of the State: A Reader* (London: Blackwell, 2006).

Shore, Cris. "Government Without Statehood? Anthropological Perspectives on Governance and Sovereignty in the European Union," *European Law Journal* 12, 6 (2006): 709–24.

Sood, Aditya Dev. *The Matha State: Kinship, ascetism and institutionality in the public life of Karnataka*, unpublished thesis (Chicago: University of Chicago, 2006).

Spencer, Jonathan. *Anthropology, Politics, and the State: Democracy and Violence in South Asia* (Cambridge, UK: Cambridge University Press, 2007).

Sundar Rajan, Rajeswari. "Women Between Community and State: Some implications of the Uniform Civil Code debate," in *Secularisms*, eds., J.R. Jakobsen and A. Pellegrini (Durham, NC: Duke University Press, 2008).

Swatos, W.H.J., and K.J. Christiano. "Secularization Theory: The Course of a Concept," *Sociology of Religion* 60, 3 (1999): 209–28.

Vatuk, Sylvia "Islamic Feminism in India: Indian Muslim Women Activists and the Reform of Muslim Personal Law," *Modern Asian Studies* 42, 2-3 (2008): 489–518.

van der Veer, Peter. *Religious Nationalism: Hindus and Muslims in India* (Berkeley, CA: University of California Press, 1994).

Wachspress, M. "Rethinking sovereignty with reference to history and anthropology," *International Journal of Law in Context* 5, 3 (2009): 315–30.

Wilson, Thomas M. "Borders," in *A Companion to Urban Anthropology*, ed. D.M. Nonini (London: Wiley-Blackwell, 2014).

7
Contesting Neo-orientalism: Terrorism Detentions, Migrant Activism, and the Claim for Justice

Iker Barbero

Abstract

This chapter outlines the acts of resistance of the relatives of 11 Pakistani and Indian detainees accused of terrorism in Barcelona, Spain, in 2008. These actions were in opposition to the brutal criminalization to which the Muslim community had been subjected. Rather than considering 'orientalization' as an exoticizing strategy or prejudice, this chapter demonstrates that it can be understood as an agonistic strategy of government. Acts of resistance as acts of citizenship play a crucial role in exposing this strategy. Since 2008, not only Muslim migrants but also non-Muslim citizens and non-citizens have mobilized to call for the release of the detainees and the restoration of the presumption of innocence. These acts turned streets, courts, and prisons into sites for contesting the anti-terrorist legislation of exception. These acts also produced new subjects of power: women, youth, and children, who seemingly lacked political subjectivity, had burst onto the scene as political subjects claiming not only freedom and the presumption of innocence of their imprisoned family members but also the dignity of an entire community criminalized by the dominant political and media discourses. This episode in Spain enables us to draw some broader conclusions about Muslims in Europe, neo-orientalization as a strategy of government, and acts of resistance capable of exposing this strategy. Even as they are legally constructed as savage non-citizens incapable of integration, (Muslim) migrants, through their acts of resistance, became activist-citizens against orientalization.

The Scene

On 8 February 2008 in Camaron de la Isla square in the neighbourhood of Sant Roc (five minutes away by metro from the city of Barcelona), various Pakistani women helped by their children gathered around a microphone.[1]

All wore traditional veils and had solemn faces. Behind them, a row of Pakistani men held a banner proclaiming: 'Against terrorism, for the dignity of the immigrant community.'[2] A couple of weeks earlier, on 19 January 2008, at dawn, in the middle of a large police and media presence, 14 men from Pakistan and India had been arrested. As we will see later, they were accused of belonging to a terrorist group that, according to the declaration of a protected witness, had been preparing an imminent attack on the public transport system.

There are different ways of interpreting this act of protest by those women in the square. One would be to see them as veiled women in rage, women who were carried along by emotional impulses, primary, primitive, or even resulting from subordination. Some of the group where not new to claiming rights or to activism.[3] A significant number of those assembled, like most Pakistani women in Spain, had entered the country with a family reunification permit that their husbands or fathers had requested. They spent their daily lives at home, caring for children or occasionally 'helping' in their husbands' business. They had no other chance. The legal situation created by the family reunification permit *de facto* implies a submission of the women to their husbands (Moyano 2000; Cestau 2012), preventing them from any autonomy in doing everyday activities, such as working, through fear of losing the permit. According to Spanish immigration rules, in order to have a separate residence permit from that of their husbands, these women would have to live with their husbands for five years or report domestic violence (this can only be done after two years of marriage) and be able to show independent economic means (something almost impossible for many woman in these circumstances during the economic crisis). These women were also worried because if their husbands fell into irregularity, that is to lose their officially granted rights and status, they and the rest of their family would also become 'illegals'. What would the wives and children of the detainees do if their husbands or brothers were deported? How would they earn their living? Would they also be deported? These were many of the questions they faced.

In effect, a presumably universal-rational-Western norm, here expressed in the Spanish immigration law, creates wives subjected to their husbands. Dominant Western legal and political theory has based its argument on the modern myth of equality, the recognition of rights, the rule of law.[4] By contrast, immigration law not only criminalizes and pursues migrants in general; it also turns migrant women into victims.[5] As the anthropologist Carmen Gregorio says, immigrant women are constructed as 'passive victims' in their patriarchal societies, victims of poverty and of a globalized violence against them, but also as an irrational menace, either as 'constantly pregnant' and therefore over-burdening social and health services or as lewd prostitutes who prey on tourists.[6] Although the security state has been emerging for a while,[7] especially since the security psychosis generated after the 9/11 attacks, 'gendered Islamophobia', as Jasmine Zine calls it, has revitalized orientalist tropes and representations of backward, hyper-religious, politically immature women in need of liberation and rescue through imperialist interventions.[8]

This image of passive, subordinated, outraged, and politically immature women is precisely the result of the emergence of a number of political, institutional, and academic neo-orientalist discourses in Europe and the United States[9] regarding the existence of individuals and groups considered incompatible to Western societies due to their supposed political, moral, or religious differences with regard to values such as democracy, human rights, or the rule of law. In this case, these orientalist discourses operate as an alienating strategy of government through which citizens constitute themselves and others as strangers, foreigners, or aliens[10] in order to legitimize a globalized citizenship and border regime.[11] In *Globalizing Citizenship* (2010), Kim Rygiel, following a line of thought opened by Isin, makes a thorough analysis of how citizenship is increasingly a disciplinary regime for governing the mobility of populations. Faced with the tension between the deterritorialization of the capitalist system and the territorial nation-state system, the regime of citizenship, rather than collapsing, as some authors have pointed out, is being used by some states to implement tighter controls and border mobility, especially after 9/11. In this context, from the moment we consider citizenship as a technology of government for mobility, it has the effect of constructing some citizens that appear to be more reliable and authentic than others. Therefore, this technology enacts its own form of disciplinary power, subjecting certain individuals and groups, particularly those of Muslim and Arab communities, to increased vigilance and instilling fear in these communities.[12]

In the process of becoming a sovereign, modern, European country, Spain has found immigration to have a fundamental role in the revaluation of issues such as identity. In turn, that identity has become eroded in the process of globalization-Europeanization.[13] Spain is one of the few countries in the European Union where Islam has had and still has a historical role in the social and cultural construction of its identity.[14] Certain opinion polls, and political, academic, and media discourses have asserted that particular groups of migrants from North Africa, Latin America, and Eastern Europe, but mainly Muslims, are incompatible with the popular conception of Spanish identity. I argue that the Spanish immigration and citizenship regime is contributing to this construction of otherness, and therefore, to the political and legal (re)definition of what 'being Spanish' means. I will now develop this argument further with a focus on the specific case of the process of orientalization imposed on the detainees in the Raval, their families, and the whole Muslim community in Barcelona.

This chapter also explores the resistances that contest the agonistic side of orientalization strategies. In the second part, I concentrate on those instances when immigrants, women, children, activists, and people generally resist those processes that attempt to extricate them from the legal and political system (detentions, stigmatization, submission, deportation, etc.). In these circumstances, through their actions, they resist this move, and in doing so constitute themselves as subjects of legality and of citizenship. As I conclude in this chapter, another way of interpreting those acts that took place in Camaron Square or later in Rambla del Raval Square in the centre of Barcelona, is to say that perhaps unknowingly or unintentionally these women became political actors. Just as Engin Isin has investigated Ottoman Waqfs as acts of piety (2011), I argue that through these acts, the Pakistani women and their children negated the construction of themselves as passive, reproductive, hidden, subjugated, and apolitical subjects, constituting themselves instead as subjects of citizenship. The static model of Western European formal rights of citizenship and institutional participation is not the site for contesting orientalism because it is precisely the institutional legal and political system that orientalize subjects. The focus of this chapter is instead those who claim rights that are not recognized or not enforced because of this legal and political strategy of alterity.

El Raval: An Orientalized Site

On 19 January 2008, the news of the 14 detainees spread like wildfire through the Raval, the neighbourhood of Barcelona where most of the arrests took place and where the Pakistani community is based.[15] In metropolitan Barcelona only about 13,000 Pakistani nationals reside in addition to those already naturalized as Spanish citizens. About half of these live in the historic district of Ciutat Vella and especially in the Raval. It is the main concentration of Pakistanis in Spain, followed by cities such as Valencia (4,744), La Rioja (2,075), and Tarragona (2,075). Outside Britain, Barcelona is the city with the highest concentration of Pakistani population in Europe.[16]

In 2000, the Pakistani population across Spain was 7,843 people, rising to 14,322 in 2001. The struggles of the *sinpapeles* ('without papers') in churches in Barcelona, and the hunger strike that took place in 2001 that ended in a mass regularization of undocumented migrants, gathered a large group of Pakistanis.[17] From 2004 to 2007, the population doubled again, from 18,072 to 42,630, largely due to the last regularization process of 2005. The association *Papers i Drets per a Tothom* ('Papers and Rights for All' in Catalan language of the region) in 2008 and 2009 organized numerous demonstrations at the doors of the Government Office in Barcelona to denounce the Spanish administration for 'denying residence permits systematically to 4,000 Pakistanis (also Indians, Bangladehises) with no reason'.[18]

Recent immigration patterns combine the arrival of people through clandestine channels with the arrival of younger children in particular and smaller numbers of women through the mechanisms of family reunification. This has led to the consolidation of the social organization of the diasporic community and its contribution to the emergence of so-called 'Islamic business' in the neighbourhood.[19] Pakistanis run around 12 halal butcheries. A Pakistani couple manages the major travel agency that organizes pilgrimage to Mecca for Muslims in and around Barcelona. The most popular Islamic celebrations that take place in the Raval are organized in the local sports centre by one of the two Pakistani Muslim communities. And two main centres of Islamic worship in the Raval were created or are run by Pakistanis: Tariq ben Zyad, related to Tabligh, where the arrests took place, and Minhaj ul-Quran, linked to the international movement of the same name. Because of all this, in recent years the area has disparagingly been called 'Ravalistan' or 'Barcelonistan'[20].

But residents with Pakistani background are not the only inhabitants of the neighbourhood. In this part of the city almost half of the population (25,000) have a foreign origin.[21] As Manuel Delgado says, it provides 'a controlled dose of ethnic diversity – an aesthetic multiculturalism and cosmopolitanism that satisfies the good conscience of those middle and high class sectors interested in the gentrification of old town centres'[22]. Despite the central location of the Raval, close to the main tourist attractions, associations with cabarets, prostitution, and drug trafficking have given it the stigma of a notorious neighbourhood. This has prompted new municipal strategies, including extensive urban planning. These measures of control and government of the local population can be understood as administrative, legal, and criminal technologies of 'criminalization of poverty'. These include the highly contentious and controversial Civic Ordinance of the city of Barcelona, a code that purports to promote peaceful coexistence.

One may think that neighbourhoods like El Raval or Sant Roc (where most of the detainees lived) have become 'abject spaces' (Rygiel and Isin 2009) similar to detention camps, border zones where government strategies have aimed at reducing people into non-existence. However, in opposition to Agamben's concept of 'spaces of abjection', Isin and Rygiel (following Rancière) argue that abject spaces, including stigmatized urban neighborhoods, are also locations for resistance and contestation. In the following discussion we will see how the streets and squares of this stigmatized neighbourhood have become sites for contestation. But before discussing this, we need to reflect on how the 'terrorist issue' is constructed. This, after all, was the original impetus for the detentions.

Political and Media Construction of 'the Terrorist'

It was Saturday at seven o'clock. They brought him out with handcuffs and without covering his face, like a criminal. I was distraught. I'll never forget his eyes. It is not logical to have his face uncovered. It's something they would have never done with a Spanish! Naveed Ayub, son of Muhammad Ayub, detainee[23]

In recent years, a number of arrests ostensibly aimed at jihadist terrorism have taken place in El Raval. Whether in print or on the screen, images of the arrests mingle with those of the local population and especially people with the hijab or headscarf. In fact, the entwinement of the Pakistani community in Catalonia and jihadist terrorism has become a recurring theme. A leaked secret cable from the US ambassador (2 October 2007) described Catalonia as 'the greatest centre of jihadist groups for the Mediterranean'. As stated in the cable itself,

> Heavy immigration – both legal and illegal – from North Africa (Morocco, Tunisia, and Algeria) and Southeast Asia (Pakistan and Bangladesh) has made this region a magnet for terrorist recruiters. The Spanish National Police estimates that there may be upwards of 60,000 Pakistanis living in Barcelona and the surrounding area, the vast majority are male, unmarried or unaccompanied, and without legal documentation. There are even more such immigrants from North Africa. Once here, they share a like fate: they live on the edges of Spanish society, they do not speak the language, they are often unemployed, and they have very few places to practice their religion with dignity. Individually, these circumstances would provide fertile ground for terrorist recruitment, taken together, the threat is clear.[24]

For this, the US government created in 2007 a secret intelligence agency at the consulate in Barcelona to combat Islamist terrorism and organized crime. The decision was made in October 2007. This agency was justified in the following way in the cable:

> The threat in Catalonia is clear. Barcelona [the capital of Catalonia] has become a crossroads of worrisome activities, a natural meeting place and transit point of people and goods moving to and through the region from all countries bordering the western Mediterranean. The U.S. needs an on-site agency to quickly see who and what is passing through the area from places: such as Algiers, Tunis, Rabat, and the south of France. The General Consulate in Barcelona would be the perfect platform for the office because we have the space available, secure communications and a prime location.[25]

On the early morning of 19 January 2008, coinciding with a religious pilgrimage between the two mosques in the El Raval, the anti-terrorist branch of the military police, the Guardia Civil, searched the Tariq ben Zyad mosque run by the religious order Tabligh al Jamaat and the bakery owned by the oldest of the detainees. 'Operation Cantata' had started. The main reason for the detentions was the declaration of a hidden witness and the linkage of these men to the group Tehrik e Taliban Pakistan, who had apparently posted a video with a leader (Maulvi Omar) claiming responsibility for a foiled attack in response to Spain's presence in Afghanistan. The Minister of the Interior Alfredo Perez Rubalcaba assured the public that they had found explosive materials and that the cell was ready to act. And even the Secretary of Defence of the USA, Robert Gates, stated at the NATO Conference for Security Policy (9 February 2008) that Europeans must understand that the Taliban camps in Afghanistan and Pakistan are the seed for future cells such as the one in the Raval that plan to carry out bombings in Europe.[26] On 21 January 2008, Pakistani President Pervez Musharraf, asked by the Spanish MEP Raul Romeva (Greens Parliamentary Group) during his appearance before the Committee on Foreign Parliament, described as 'very sad' the arrest of 12 Pakistanis in Barcelona in an operation against Islamist terrorism.

The media impact was considerable. The arrests in the night and the subsequent transfers of detainees under heavy police guard became the first image that the inhabitants of the city, in Catalonia and in Spain, saw that morning. 'Strike at the heart of El Raval' or 'Aborted imminent Al Qaeda bombing in Barcelona' were the main headlines. The major newspaper *El Periodico de Catalunya* carried on its front page a large '19-E', an analogy to 11-S, 11-M, and 7-J, dates of other attacks attributed to Al Qaeda in New York, Madrid, and London.

On 18 September 2008, Fernando Reinares, professor and analyst on terrorism of the Real Instituto Elcano think-tank, published in the newspaper *El Pais* an article entitled 'Who would attack in Barcelona?'[27] According to Reinares, there were two key reasons that would explain or justify the attack in Barcelona. First, the Pakistani diaspora established in Catalonia create 'environments in which Islamist movements operate as radical guides, well established in Pakistan and introduced in the Pakistani diaspora, often hostile to the integration of immigrants of the same creed and at least ambivalent regarding terrorism called jihad'. The second reason was the imminent state-level elections. On this last point, however, Reinares fails to mention the criticisms against the government of Rodriguez Zapatero, who was accused by sections of the right of being a 'deserter', 'coward', and 'traitor to the West' for withdrawing Spanish troops from Iraq and promoting the political project of the 'United Nations Alliance of Civilizations'.[28] However, the author did not doubt that Tehrik e Taliban Pakistan had claimed responsibility for the attempted suicide bombings in a video (which turned out to be of questionable veracity). In it, one of the spokesmen of the Taliban and Pakistan Tehrik group, Maulvi Omar, claimed that 'the twelve men of Barcelona had sworn loyalty to Baitullah Mehsuh' and that the group Tehrik e Taliban Pakistan 'is responsible for the acts in Barcelona' brought about by the Spanish military presence in Afghanistan.

All these news statements and images left aside the presumption of innocence. Only a handful of newspapers such as *The Guardian,* a UK newspaper, or Catalan alternative newspaper *Directa* talked about the possibility of these being a plot by the dictatorial Pakistani President Mussarraf's secret services to distract public attention after the assassination of the leader of the Pakistan People's Party, Benazir Bhutto, in December 2007. *The Guardian,* under the title 'Terrorist group who turned out to be the president's men',[29] explained how six Pakistani men flew into London Gatwick Airport on 21 January 2008 from Barcelona and were detained by armed police and Scotland Yard detectives 'on suspicion of operating or planning a terrorist activity'. However, soon after their lawyer arrived, the police allowed them to fly back to Pakistan. The Foreign and Commonwealth Office of the United Kingdom initially blamed the debacle on false information from the Spanish authorities but later shifted the blame to French intelligence. However, the injury had already been inflicted. Stigma was already attached to the Pakistani and Muslim community in Barcelona.

The Suspension of Citizenship: Application of Anti-terrorist Law

In the last decade, numerous police operations against terrorist groups have taken place in Catalonia and Spain (Operation Dátil 2001, Operation Dixan 2003, Operation Lago 2003, Operation Nova 2004, Operation Mordisco 2007, Operation Submarino 2008, Operation Pez 2009, Operation Kometa 2012, Operation Kartago 2013). Operation Cantata in 2008 was just another. In all these arrests, anti-terrorist operation protocol was applied. They all share a similar pattern: media impact, political echo, Kafkaesque trial, and either an acquittal or reduction of penalty by a higher judge. Among the more than 180 detentions in the last decade, the Supreme Court has upheld only 21.[30] However, all of the detainees have suffered both media and political accusations for terrorism, police interrogation, and imprisonment awaiting trial.

Exceptionality has marked the trend of fighting terrorism in Spain, and Europe by extension.[31] France, Germany, Italy, and other member states of the European Union (EU) have chosen to sacrifice rights and freedoms of individuals on behalf of a purported collective security.[32] In Spain, although police tactics have evolved, the remnants of Franco's authoritarian regime mark the history of Spanish anti-terrorist actions (special plans for the security forces, exceptional tribunals, suspension of guarantees, and extreme measures of internment). Terrorism offenses are investigated and prosecuted in a specific court within the Spanish judicial structure, the Audiencia Nacional. This court has adopted a very specific strategy to act in cases linked to Basque or international groups. This is called 'preventive justice' and has a double aspect. On the one hand, it allows the criminalization-prosecution of 'sleeping cells', that is groups that have not acted violently yet but could be ready to do so according to police investigations. On the other hand, the accusation is based in the ideological or religious character of the detainees and their personal relations with other people, even in foreign countries.[33]

The sources of this extensive judicial process are numerous and complex, so we will just point out the most relevant documents, laws, and regulations. According to the Guardia Civil police's investigations contained in the Judicial Summary 26/2008,

> A reliable informant of this Service communicated the date of an impending terrorist attack on the territory of Spain. (…) Members of this group had a clear division of roles and specialisms, cohesive ideologically by their adherence to an extremist stance of Islam. There is a parallel between suicide attacks in London in 2005 and the alleged attack in Barcelona. (…) British suicides were aged between 18 and 30 years and the alleged suicide of Barcelona between 24 and 28. Several of the London bombers had recently travelled to Afghanistan and / or Pakistan and those in Barcelona had just come from Pakistan. (…) Between four and five years ago they become more religious and let their beard grow when approaching the Tabligh.[34]

In Spain, most of the anti-terrorist legislation has been elaborated to fight the Basque armed organization ETA (Basque country and freedom) and some others, such as Terra Lliura (Catalan free land) or GRAPO (anti-fascist revolutionary group). The Spanish Constitution approved in 1978 foresees in its article 55.2 the creation of an 'independent body under special law' to deal with the temporary suspension of fundamental rights in order to fight terrorist activities. Since then, a number of organic laws have been passed or reformed in order to narrow the scope of both armed and political dissident activities. This has led to the creation of an exceptional body of norms which not only suspends human rights recognized by international treaties but also attributes capacities to judges and police that result in flagrant rights violations such as lack of due process, torture, and in some cases, death.[35]

One of the main tools that was applied to the detainees is the so-called 'incomunicación' ('without communication') (articles 520 bis and 527 Criminal Prosecution Law). This means that any detainee suspected of terrorism may be kept for 13 days (five plus eight) in police custody without communication with family, lawyers, or even a doctor.[36] The other main tool is the dispersal of prisoners of the same group across different prisons within Spanish territory. This measure is applied to both preventive detainees waiting for trial and to those finally condemned. The main aggravating consequences are first the violation of the right of the prisoner to be kept in the closest centre to his/her home, and second that it impedes the exercise of the right to an effective legal assistance. After spending a few weeks in prisons in Madrid, the detainees were all scattered throughout Spain: Cadiz (900 km from Barcelona), Jaen (650 km), Córdoba (860 km), León (800 km), Palencia

(700 km), Asturias (900 km), Valencia (300 km), and Zaragoza, the closest (255 km).

On 11 September 2009, the III Criminal Chamber of the Audiencia Nacional admitted that the defendants were not preparing any attack and had not acquired the material to do so. But instead, it did confirm that they belonged to the Tehrik e Taliban Pakistan group. For this reason, ten of them were sentenced to eight years and six months imprisonment and one of them to ten years as leader of the cell. The main proof of the trial had been the declaration of a hidden witness (F1) arrived from France who had claimed to have received jihadi training at camps in Afghanistan and Pakistan. Apparently at the last moment he had repented and informed the police of the attack. During the trial investigation, it emerged that F1 was more a police informer than a radical terrorist. Even more, at one moment he declared he was using his hidden identity because he was a 'fugitive' in Pakistan. Since 2009, the so-called Red Book Against Trafficking in Persons of the Federal Investigation Agency (FIA), an office of Pakistani police investigation, included F1 among the 76 immigrant traffickers most wanted in Pakistan. Yet, his testimony was relied upon in the investigation of the detainees.

After filing the appropriate appeal, the detainees were judged again by the Supreme Court (January 2011), which partially granted the appeal of the defence, reducing the sentence to six years in prison for the crime of belonging to a terrorist group, against the wishes of the public prosecutor. In its judgement, the Supreme Court held that, contrary to what was initially announced after the arrest, the detainees were not about to commit an imminent attack. In addition, the high court absolved them from the crime of possession of explosives, considering insignificant the 18 grams of nitrocellulose from a domestic firework found at the scene.

Acts of Citizenship Against Orientalization

Criminalization of immigrants takes many forms, association with terrorism being only one of them. At the same time, there are also many types of migrant contestation of criminalization depending on subjects, the means used, the rights claimed, and the spaces and sites they take place in. Refugees, irregular migrants, and seasonal workers, for example, have been part of campaigns for labour rights, anti-deportation campaigns, demands regularization, occupations, and strikes.[37] The relevance of this chapter is that it adds an almost invisible issue: the struggle for (presumed) innocence and dignity. Both of which have been abused and diminished significantly in the decade and a half since the implementation of the 'War on Terror'.[38] Being universally recognized rights, but at the same time intangible, they cannot easily be restored once the damage has been done. However, claims such as those discussed here are focused on specific rights such as those to legal aid, due process, accurate representation in the media, and the rights of the prisoner.

Nyers and Rygiel rhetorically ask why we hear so little of such migrant mobilization and activism in the media or the academy.[39] Why is it that migrant activism against the global migration regime and the concepts that emerge from this 'citizenship from below' are almost invisible? One possible answer, they argue, is because these acts of resistance exist at the margins of mainstream society. They call into question a dominant and dogmatic model of citizenship. But another possible answer, linked to the previous one, is that it goes unnoticed as a political and legal subjectivity because it is viewed through a conceptual and methodological lens that makes certain subjects or groups invisible. The notion of acts of citizenship instead opens up a whole view to alternative interpretation.[40]

In theorizing acts of citizenship, Isin's interest has been in the relationship between new figures of citizenship and the emergence of new sites, scales, and acts that enable actors to claim rights. In his words, 'what we need to understand is how these sites, scales and acts produce new actors who enact political subjectivities and transform themselves and others into citizens by articulating ever-changing and expanding rights'.[41] We may identify three main characteristics that build the concept of an act of citizenship: 1) the dialogical principle of citizenship; 2) rupture; and 3) the distinction between justice and law. First, the idea of 'being political' derives from a genealogical investigation of political subjectivities through which citizenship is viewed as a dialogical principle that involves certain forms (orientations, strategies, technologies). As mentioned above, otherness is constructed towards strangers, outsiders, and aliens, and acts of citizenship are related to the way in which each of these subjects celebrate, perpetuate, impose, resist, and break the modes of being political with each other. At the same time, this idea differs from the established notion that citizenship is a static concept linked to membership. While this last concept, according to Isin, would be limited to the way of governing conduct within social groups, conceiving citizenship as dialogical implies an investigation of 'conduct across social groups all of which constitute a body politic'.[42]

A second quality that acts of citizenship express is rupture and, subsequently, social transformation. Acts entail a rupture with ongoing situations, such as status (which brings us back again to the idea of membership of an established order), rituals, customs, habits, and routines (in this sense, incorporating Bourdieu's concept of habitus). This notion contrasts with traditional studies of citizenship that have focused on the practices of everyday life and, consequently, have developed the necessity of considering the subject as deserving of the title of citizen. On the contrary, investigating acts of citizenship implies examining the purpose served by an act in breaking with the established order – deviating from the script – in order to change it. The break can be intentional or not, and with or without regard to its possible consequences.

Third, social transformation and rupture are closely related to seeking justice by all means, respectful of the law or not. While most specific acts are not necessarily conceived as emancipatory by their actors (essentially because actors do not typically consider themselves as activists), we, as interpreters, orient the acts towards the claim of justice or against injustice. Acts of citizenship can be enacted by non-citizen subjects who suffer from injustice or by citizens who support non-citizens' struggles as an act of solidarity. However, framing acts of citizenship within the scope of justice does not mean that they need to be founded on law or enacted in the name of the law. Sometimes, the law provides subjects with the tools to claim rights and justice, at other times the law does not recognize claimants as legitimized actors. On occasion, it may even be the case that the law considers actors to be offenders who can be prosecuted according to its remit. This is the reason why, in my view, acts of citizenship can sometimes be enacted through deeds that are considered illegal or go beyond the margins of formal state law.

My aim is not to advocate illegal over legal practices but to analyse how informal practices can be used to claim rights and justice. Construction of otherness, rupture, and struggle for justice are basic characteristics of acts of citizenship, but to be more precise, as Isin notes, acts of citizenship are defined as 'those acts that transform forms (orientations, strategies, technologies) and modes (citizens, strangers, outsiders, aliens) of being political by bringing into being new actors as activist citizens (that is, claimants of rights) through creating or transforming sites and stretching scales'.[43] How did the relatives claim the innocence of their brothers, husbands, or friends? Which scales did the struggles transcend? How did the criminalized immigrants constitute themselves as citizens?

Acts of Mobilization

In the days after the detentions, fear seized the Pakistani community because of possible new arrests and police raids. Going to the mosque, living in a certain neighbourhood, or wearing traditional costumes could make anyone a potential terrorist. This made the community leaders stand back and keep a low profile, at least until the situation calmed down. However, on 8 February 2008, just a couple of weeks after the detentions, some women and children undertook a unique initiative. They met in the square close to the children's school. A meeting after school was deemed the best way to gather most of the Pakistani women in the neighbourhood. They considered that they had to publicize their unfair situation. As one of them said, without their husbands who brought home wages, they were left without sources of income to buy food or pay the rent if they could not work. It was the first time that some of these women had taken to the streets to protest publicly. Along with other relatives and the association *Papers i drets per a tothom*, the Pakistani

Women's Association ACESOP, Pakistan Muslim League in Spain, and the Pakistani Cultural Association of Barcelona all organized a public demonstration under the title 'Against terrorism, for the dignity of the immigrant community'. The call gathered more than 500 people.

Their manifesto had three pillars. First, they wanted to express the Pakistani, Indian, and immigrant community's opposition to terrorism:

> Terrorism, the mass murder of people, has no justification whatsoever. Be it the work of a small group or any state army, these are always abominable crimes. Pakistanis, Indians, immigrants in general are overwhelmingly involved in this condemnation.

Second, the organizers claimed one of the higher values of a democratic legal system: the presumption of innocence.

> The media and even members of the Pakistani government point to us now as potential terrorists. It's a lie. Neither the Pakistani nor the Indian community in Catalonia deserve such treatment. We came to this country precisely because of the terror that hunger, wars and injustices cause. The detainees have overcome death to leave their country and come here to work with dignity and peacefully, and now they are regarded as terrorists. The government stated that prevention is better in these cases. That statement was the justification for the invasion of Iraq, [and] the bombing of civilian populations where terrorist sympathizers may be hiding.
>
> The 14 detainees were arrested without evidence, four have already been released, but the rest are still in prison without strong evidence. The government must always respect the presumption of innocence. No one can be condemned without sufficient evidence. No one can spend years in prison only because of doubts about his innocence. Today the shadow of guilt threatens our future, our children and our families.

The act, expressed in this manifesto and in the public demonstration, aimed to vindicate the dignity of the immigrant community and cease the false accusations made against it. The community were doubly victims: through the media, institutional and social criminalization, and through the arrests themselves.

> The immigrants were and are victims of terrorism, they were on 11 March and in Madrid Terminal 4 at Barajas and they are now when they are indiscriminately criminalized. Terrorism can only be combated through the fight against injustice and discrimination. This is a task for the whole society, immigrants and indigenous. Because all people are equal and deserve the same respect and the same rights.

Many other protests followed this one. A few days later, on 17 February, a much larger demonstration took place in Rambla del Raval Square, the heart of Barcelona. Led by the women and their children, the crowd started walking along the main streets of the neighbourhood (the streets of Hospital de Sant Pau) and finished at the site where the detentions had taken place. As the march went by, some locals decided to close their shops in solidarity with the detainees. As before, it was the families who read the final manifesto. In contrast to the struggles of the *sinpapeles* in Barcelona in 2001, who were mainly men, these demonstrations were much more feminized. The relatives, women and their children, had a strong symbolic role. This was precisely because both the detentions in Raval and the social and legal reality itself placed women in the role of victims, which they were not willing to take, and therefore fought. These acts represented a break: the women and their children moved from a passive role of victim to a rebellious position of action.

Over 1,000 people marched on 23 February 2009 in Barcelona as part of the state-level action days for the rights of immigrants, agreed at the third meeting of the National Network for Immigrant Rights. Events were held simultaneously in other Spanish cities in order to mark the dignity of immigrants. Protesters marched through the Catalan capital under the theme 'We have the right to have rights'. Citizens took to the streets. Amongst other claims, they demanded the right to more flexible conditions for family reunification. The association Papers i Drets per a Tothom and other Paksitani organizations called for the release of prisoners and the restoration of the dignity of the immigrant community.

Acts of Solidarity: Intellectual

On 5 March 2009, about 120 people gathered in the Aula Magna of the Faculty of Geography and History of the University of Barcelona (UB) for the launch of documentary-book entitled *The Dixan Trials. The Construction of Islamophobia and the Enemy after September 11.* The book's title refers to Operation Lago, where 16 people were arrested and later released after an alleged explosive material was later found to be a common commercially available detergent ('Dixan'). This editorial project was an anthology published by Virus Editorial, containing writings by several activists, such as Abdennur Prado (Catalan Islamic Board), Albert Martinez and David Fernandez (*La Directa* newspaper), Iñaki Rivera (Observatory of the Penal System and Human Rights), Benet Salellas (lawyer), and Alberto Lopez Bargados (anthropologist of Islam in the Diaspora Research Group, Universitat de Barcelona). The video was made with images and interviews conducted by Alberto López Bargados, José González Morandi, and Sergi Dies of the detainees' families in other stages of the process. As noted in the introduction by the Vírico Collective, 'the first goal was not to defend the honour of the Muslims as a collective but their complexity as a group: a Muslim should be able be a common criminal, like a Catholic, a Protestant or a Jew (…) to rob a bank or finance a scam without becoming automatically suspected of Islamic terrorism.'[44] The second objective was to 'show how the whole intellectual apparatus deployed by think-tanks, media, "authoritative opinions", [and] police sources acts as magical thinking that does not comply with verifiable facts or reasons, but serves to maintain the proper imagery of a climate of fear and social alarm'[45]. Thirdly, this book represented a 'taking of sides built almost from the underground against the tacit silence to which certain subjects and certain points of view' are condemned.[46]

A diverse body of speakers addressed the launch conference. First, the families of the accused highlighted the contradictions in the charges and the criminalization of immigrants in Barcelona since the arrests of 19 January 2008. Second, relatives affected by other operations against suspected jihadist cells also took part in the launch, as in the case of Khadija Podd, whose husband was arrested in 2006 as part of 'Operation Jackal', which allegedly dismantled a network of recruitment for suicide bombers sent to Iraq. Finally, speeches were given by Professor of Anthropology at the Universitat de Barcelona (UB), Manuel Delgado, the president of the Federation of Neighbourhood Associations of Barcelona, Eva Fernández, Jaume Asens, member of the Defence Committee of the Bar Association of Barcelona, Alberto Lopez Bargados (anthropologist), and Iñaki Rivera (OSPDH).

Acts of Solidarity: Communal

There were a number of acts that fostered solidarity not only with the detainees but also with the relatives. The Pakistani community took up a collection to pay the lawyers and help the family. During March 2009, the relatives and the support group circulated a leaflet in order to collect signatures. All those who signed the manifesto thereby declared, 'We denounce the situation of defencelessness of the detainees and demand the implementation of the necessary measures to correct it'. To do this, the organizations considered necessary the following measures. First, they asked for the immediate release of the detainees, in line with the request made by the defence. The second demand proposed the creation of a commission of jurists, independent lawyers, and human rights organizations to open an investigation on the possible violations of human rights and judicial guarantees of the detainees. Third, the organizations demanded the clarification of the responsibilities in relation to the police proceedings and the imposition of appropriate sanctions if any irregularities or negligence were proved. The group also called for the publication of a correction of all of the information in news coverage of the events that proved to be false. Lastly, the organizations requested a clear statement by the City Council and the Spanish ministries of Interior and Justice of the government in defence of the presumption of innocence of the detainees and release of the detainees until a final judgement was issued.

The families of the detained also showed their support for their brothers and husbands through a range of acts. On the one hand, prison policy had spread the detainees over different prisons throughout Spain, so that family members and defence lawyers were forced to travel hundreds of kilometres to visit them with the expense and danger involved. But on the other, they continued protesting and campaigning in sites such as the streets of Barcelona or at doors of the Court of Exception Audiencia Nacional or the Supreme Court in Madrid (24 November 2009) to claim the innocence and demand the release of their relatives.

Eventually, the main family that had led the campaign in support of the group emigrated to Britain. This was for several reasons. Partly, this was economic. In Spain, the crisis that started in 2008 had been tough, especially for immigrants,[47] while in the UK they had more family ties to Pakistani people. The glut of judicial and police pressure was the other reason. Migrating to UK was a way to close a very difficult chapter in their lives. Migration was again, as Mezzadra would say, an enactment of the right to escape.[48]

Acts of Advocacy

The first lawyer for the detainees was Sebastiá Salellas (1949–2008), a prominent advocate of human rights and alternative social movements. He had previously acted in the case of torture and detention of some young pro-independence Catalans in 1992 before the European Court of Human Rights.[49] The key reason for his involvement was that he had previously been an advocate of Algerian, Moroccan, and Pakistani immigrants accused of belonging to 'Dixan command'.[50] Salellas developed the case with his son, Benet Salellas, also a lawyer, who had been involved in cases such as that of the eviction of an occupied building. In this case, which went to the European Court of Human Rights, he represented the Platform of People Affected by Mortgages in the city of Salt in 2013.[51] After the death of his father, he took over the defence of the detainees (and other jihadist terrorism-related cases) along with the lawyer Jaime Teijelo.

In addition to the procedural act of defending the detainees, as in the cases previously cited, the lawyers also manifested an activist 'case-lawyering' role. As Benet Salellas told us,

> We took a very public role and tried to give voice to people through our interventions in the press and TV. Also I think I tried, especially when I was closer to Barcelona, often go to meetings with the families and Pakistani associations that were supporting the campaign, explaining to them each step of the process and every proof that came from the prosecution. (...) It was to give an ethical and political purpose to our legal action and as a person, I believe that the advocacy is something very beautiful. Compensation also comes within these parameters. We never charge for

> what would correspond to our real work, for all the hours of meetings, for traveling to Madrid, for visits to prisoners (...) But of course I am not working only for an economic compensation, I am working for a cause.

The families were very involved in the judicial process. They engaged with the detailed monitoring of the case and also found means of solidarity with the prisoners and with relatives that were left totally helpless. According to Salellas, there were also prisoners who had no family in Barcelona and had to talk often with family in India and Pakistan; some of them also did much work there pressing the authorities.

Another struggle in which the lawyers and people in the support group took part was to prevent the detainees falling into the administrative irregularity, that is the loss of their papers. Unfortunately, in the end they all lost their residence permits and employment, except the one that had Spanish nationality. The Spanish Government Delegation opened disciplinary proceedings for expulsion according to the Foreigners' Law. At that time, there had been several judgements of the Supreme Court of Catalonia, even by the most progressive magistrates, stating that someone convicted of terrorism did not correspond to the social integration that was expected of a foreigner. Therefore, once the Supreme Court confirmed the sentence, they stopped struggling. One of the main consequences of this process of 'illegalization' was its impact on those relatives, mainly wives and children that depended on the reunification permit of the detainees: those depending on a declined permit would also automatically become irregulars.

After the sentence of the Supreme Court, there was an attempt to present an appeal before the European Court of Human Rights, but the lawyers rejected this option. Considering the time it takes for the European Court to make a ruling, the detainees would have already fulfilled their punishment.

Following the judgement of the Supreme Court, the families chose to hire a Pakistani-English lawyer. The instructions to the new lawyer in regards to the support group was that no contact should be made with the family or with the detainees in order to avoid negative influences to possible procedural benefits that the prison authorities could grant them.

Acts of Liberation

By January 2014, many of those arrested, charged, and imprisoned had served their time, without judicial reduction, as is usual according to prison regulations. Some were transferred to the Aluche detention centre for foreigners in Madrid in order to deport those who were foreign nationals to their countries of origin. Aluche, on the outskirts of Madrid, had previously been a prison and hospital for prisoners. Various reports by human rights organizations[52] have denounced the flagrant violations of rights in the centre (punishment cells, absence of legal assistance or adequate social and health care, poor health, suicide, depression, abuse of women, etc.). Family members and other activists of the support group were assisted by the legal commission of the campaign Cerremos los CIEs ('Let's close the detention centres') in Madrid who helped to find the detainees in the centre of detention and monitored the execution of the expulsion. They wanted to have proof of their state of health before the deportation. One of the worries was that once in India and Pakistan, and having been condemned in Europe for terrorism, the detainees could suffer hard interrogation and once again be sent to prison. Some of the detainees welcomed the visits of the activists and told them that they were physically well, but others rejected the visits. As one of the activists from Madrid said, all of them wanted an end to the nightmare.

Although other inmates normally stay for several days, the detainees where rapidly deported. In some of the cases, deportations took place in less than 48 hours. This meant that the members of the support group and Cerremos los CIEs could not interview all the detainees. One of the defendants, an Indian national, was the first to be handed over to the Indian authorities in Mumbai. There he was interrogated for four hours by the Indian police and was later released. A further five were expelled on a flight with a stopover in Athens between Sunday 19 and Monday 20 January 2014 and were interrogated for several hours. The rest were returned to Pakistan in the following days in a similar pattern. Maruf was to remain in prison for one year more. Mohamed Ayub Elahi Bibi, the oldest of all the detainees, was not to be deported, since he has Spanish citizenship.

Conclusions: Activists Against Orientalization

Beyond what dominant positions in the legal and political fields are intended to construe, empirical reality, both legal practice and the actions carried out by people, brings us to conclude two main things. The first is that the law, despite its modern claims of universality, does not always serve to include all situations under parameters of equality or freedom. There are circumstances, such as with the Immigration Law in Spain and elsewhere in Europe, where the rule operates as an element of differentiation, or differentiated inclusion, one could say. On the other hand, there are subjects, not recognized by the law as legal and political actors, even persecuted, who burst on the scene, raising claims closely related to the treatment that the law gives them. Citizenship as a legal and political basis, from which universal rights are derived, has failed to disengage from those prevailing lines marked by studies in which the citizen was a given subject which was related to others around them. The acts of protest by women and children attempted to remind all concerned that presumption of innocence is a supreme value as well as a right that belongs to people regardless of origin or legal status. And at the same time it showed that immigrant Muslim women, against stereotypes and social and legal constructions of subordination and victimization, can lead demonstrations, present judicial appeals, protest before courts, and give press conferences. If we were to see the scene disclosed in this chapter through the gaze of orientalism, we would never recognize the acts of these women as acts. We would not see political subjectivity in their acts because they were just wives for some and potential terrorists for others. These are contradictory circumstances that only occur in exceptional situations, such as that derived from immigration and security regimes. Although they never thought of it or ever wanted to, the relatives have become activist citizens in spite of their legal status.

Notes

1 Sant Roc is a suburb of the town of Badalona in the Metropolitan Area of Barcelona. The historic settlement of Roma population is one of the characteristic features (see Prieto Flores and Sordé 2010). Together with this fact, in recent years a large immigrant population arrived in the neighbourhood. According to data from the municipal registry, 30 per cent of local residents are foreigners of which around 20 per cent (2,700) are originally Pakistani. They are mainly men (few families) living in precarious conditions. Social exclusion and substandard housing is another feature that adds a 'bad name' to the place (Requena Hidalgo 2003). One of the first decisions of Xavier García Albiol (PP Conservative Party) as mayor was to increase by 77 per cent the officers who patrol the streets of Badalona, with special attention to Sant Roc and Artigas. During the previous elections, the PP in Badalona distributed among city residents a brochure that displayed a photograph of a banner saying: 'We do not want Romanians'. The brochure also had on its cover a picture of two veiled women under the title 'Is your neighbourhood safe? If in 2011 I am the mayor I assure you that we will be able to walk through the neighbourhood with the security of not being harassed. Anyone living in Badalona will have to adapt to our rules and customs.'

2 All translations from Spanish by the author unless otherwise stated.

3 See Iker Barbero, "Orientalising citizenship: the legitimation of immigration regimes in the European Union," *Citizenship Studies* 16, 5-6 (2012): 751–68; or Iker Barbero, *El control selectivo de las fronteras y la transnacionalización de sus resistencias* (Arbor: Ciencia, pensamiento y cultura, 2010), 744, 689–703.

4 Peter Fitzpatrick, *The Mythology of Modern Law* (London and New York: Routledge, 1992); Boaventura de Sousa Santos, *Toward a New Legal Common Sense Law, Globalization, and Emancipation* (Cambridge: Cambridge University Press, 2002).

5 Ruth Mestre i Mestre, "Hilando fino: migraciones autóctonas de mujeres para trabajar en la industria del sexo," in *La condición inmigrante: exploraciones e investigaciones desde la Región de Murcia Manuel,* eds. Hernández Pedreño and Andrés Pedreño Cánovas (Universidad de Murcia, 2005), 313–26; María Helena Bedoya "Mujer extranjera una doble exclusión: Influencia de la Ley de Extranjería sobre las mujeres inmigrantes," *Papers: revista de sociología* 60 (2000): 241–56.

6 Carmen Gregorio, "Mujeres inmigrantes colonizando sus cuerpos mediante fronteras procreativas, étnico-culturales, sexuales y reproductivas," *Viento sur: Por una izquierda alternativa* 104 (2009): 42–54.

7 Didier Bigo, Sécurité, immigration et contrôle social. L'archipel des polices. Le Monde Diplomatique, Octobre 1996, http://www.monde-diplomatique.fr/1996/10/BIGO/5825.

8 Jasmin Zine, "Between orientalism and fundamentalism: The politics of Muslim women's feminist engagement," *Muslim World Journal of Human Rights* 3, 1 (2006).

9 Samuel Huntington, *The Clash of Civilizations and the Remaking of World Order* (New York: Simon & Schuster, 1998); Giovanni Sartori, *Pluralismo, multiculturalismo e estranei: Saggio sulla società multietnica* (Milano: Rizzoli, 2000); Francis Fukuyama, "Identity, Immigration, and Liberal Democracy," *Journal of Democracy* 17, 2 (2006): 5–20.

10 Engin Isin, *Being Political: Genealogies of Citizenship* (Minneapolis: University of Minnesota Press, 2002).

11 Iker Barbero,"Orientalising citizenship: the legitimation of immigration regimes in the European Union."

12 Kim Rygiel, *Globalizing citizenship* (Vancouver-Toronto: UBC Press, 2010), 178.

13 Javier De Lucas, "Discursos de la invisible. Construir la presencia de los inmigrantes," in *Los otros entre nosotros: alteridad e inmigración* (Madrid: Círculo de Bellas Artes, 2003), 213–32; Kitty Calavita, *Immigrants at the Margins: Law, Race, and Exclusion in Southern Europe* (New York: Cambridge University Press, 2005).

14 Eloy Martín Corrales, "El moro, decano de los enemigos exteriores de España: una larga enemistad (siglos VIII-XXI)," in *Los enemigos de España. Imagen del otro, conflictos bélicos y disputas nacionales (siglos XVI-XX)* eds. Xoxe Muñez and Francisco Sevillano (Madrid: Centro de Estudios Políticos y Constitucionales, 2010), 165–82.; Anouar Majid, *We Are All Moors: Ending Centuries of Crusades against Muslims and Other Minorities* (Minneapolis, MN: University of Minnesota Press, 2009); Ricard Zapata-Barrero and De Witte, "Muslims in Spain: Blurring Past and Present Moors," in *Muslims in 21st century Europe: Structural and Cultural Perspectives*, dir. A. Triandafyllidou (London: Routledge, 2010), 181–98.

15 The name El Raval comes from the Arabic word '*rabad*' (suburb).

16 Jordi Bayona and Fernando Gil, "Suburbanisation and international immigration: The case of the Barcelona metropolitan region (1998–2009)," *Tijdschrift voor economische en sociale geografie* 103, 3, (2012): 312–29.

17 Iker Barbero "Expanding acts of citizenship: The struggles of Sinpapeles migrants," *Social & Legal Studies* 21, 4 (2012): 529–47.

18 http://papelesyderechosparatodosytodas.blogspot.com.es/search/label/25% 2F07%2F2009

19 Jordi Moreras, *Musulmanes en Barcelona: espacios y dinámicas comunitarias* (Barcelona: CIDOB, 1999); Jordi Moreras, "¿Ravalistán? Islam y configuración comunitaria entre los paquistaníes en Barcelona," *Revista CIDOB d'afers internacionals* 68 (2005).

20 http://www.interviu.es/reportajes/articulos/barcelonistan-la-casa-de-la-ultima -celula

21 Arkaitz Fullaondo "Inmigración y ciudad. El caso del área metropolitana de Barcelona" in *Pautas de asentamiento de la población inmigrante: implicaciones y retos sociojurídicos*, eds. Cristina Blanco Fernández de Valderrama and Iker Barbero González (Madrid: Dykinson, 2009).

22 Manuel Delgado, *La ciudad mentirosa: fraude y miseria del "modelo Barcelona"* (Madrid: Los Libros de la Catarata: 2007), 166.

23 http://www.abc.es/hemeroteca/historico-22-01-2008/abc/Nacional/no-olvidare -la-vision-de-mi-padre-esposado_1641577642152.html

24 https://wikileaks.org/plusd/cables/07MADRID1914_a.html

25 Idem https://wikileaks.org/plusd/cables/07MADRID1914_a.html

26 "We should also remember that terrorist cells in Europe are not purely homegrown or unconnected to events far away – or simply a matter of domestic law

and order. Some are funded from abroad. Some hate all western democracies, not just the United States. Many who have been arrested have had direct connections to Al Qaeda. Some have met with top leaders or attended training camps abroad. Some are connected to Al Qaeda in Iraq. In the most recent case, the Barcelona cell appears to have ties to a terrorist training network run by Baitullah Mehsud, a Pakistan-based extremist commander affiliated with the Taliban and Al Qaeda – who we believe was responsible for the assassination of Benazir Bhutto." Robert Gates, NATO Munich Conference on Security Policy (9 February 2008, Munich, Germany): http://www.defense.gov/Speeches/Speech.aspx?SpeechID=1214

27 http://elpais.com/diario/2008/09/18/opinion/1221688812_850215.html
28 http://www.hispanidad.com/Editorial/zapatero-traidor-a-occidente-i-2006 1113-14080.html
29 http://www.theguardian.com/uk/2008/feb/09/pakistan.terrorism
30 Miguel Martin, "Pólvora mullada, del comando Dixan als onze del Raval," *La Directa* 374, 4.
31 Guittet Emmanuel-Pierre, "European Political Identity and Democratic Solidarity After 9/11: The Spanish Case," *Alternatives: Global, Local, Political* 29, 4 (2004): 441–64; http://www.hrw.org/reports/2005/spain0105/spain0105.pdf; Cristina Fernández, Manavella A, Jose Maria Ortuño, "The Effects of Exceptional Legislation on Criminalization of Immigrants and People Suspected of Terrorism," Challenge Report 9 (2009).
32 Didier Bigo, Anastassia Tsoukala Terror, *Insecurity and Liberty: Illiberal Practices of Liberal Regimes after 9/11* (London: Taylor & Francis, 2008).
33 Benet Salellas, "El Derecho contra la Justicia," in *Rastros de Dixan Islamofobia y construcción del enemigo en la era post 11-S,* eds. Abdennur Prado, Albert Martínez, Alberto López Bargados, Benet Salellas Vilar, David Fernàndez, Iñaki Rivera Beiras (Barcelona: Virus editorial, 2009), 65-85.
34 Forwarded to the Central Court of Instruction No. 2, 18 January 2008.
35 Cristina Fernández, et al., "The Effects of Exceptional Legislation on Criminalization of Immigrants and People Suspected of Terrorism."
36 On 31 October 2008 the Human Rights Committee of the United Nations in its periodic review of compliance by the Spanish State of the International Treaty on Civil and Political Rights, referred to the incompatibility of the detention formula with the treaty (CCPR/C/ESP/CO/5).
37 Kim Rygiel, "Bordering solidarities: migrant activism and the politics of movement and camps at Calais," *Citizenship Studies* 15, 1 (2011): 1–19; Anne McNevin, *Contesting Citizenship: Irregular Migrants and New Frontiers of the Political* (New York: Columbia University Press, 2011); Vicki Squire, "From Community Cohesion to Mobile Solidarities: The City of *Sanctuary* network and the *Strangers into Citizens* campaign," *Political Studies* 59, 2 (2011): 290–307.
      Peter Nyers, "In Solitary, In Solidarity: Detainees, Hostages, and Contesting the Anti-Policy of Detention," *European Journal of Cultural Studies* 11, 3 (2008): 333–49; Susan Coutin, "From Refugees to Immigrants: The Legalization Strategies of Salvadoran Immigrants and Activists," *International Migration Review* 32, 4 (1998): 901–25.
38 Susan Coutin, "Subverting Discourses of Risk in the War on Terror," in *Risk and the War on Terror,* eds. Louise Amoore and Marieke de Goede (New York: Routledge, 2008), 218–32.
39 Peter Nyers and Kim Rygiel, *Citizenship, Migrant Activism and the Politics of Movement* (New York: Routledge, 2012).

40 Engin Isin, "Theorizing acts of citizenship," in *Acts of Citizenship*, eds. E. Isin and G. Nielsen (London, UK: Palgrave Macmillan, 2008), 15–43; Engin Isin, "Citizenship in flux: the figure of the activist citizen," *Subjectivity* 29 (2009): 367–88.
41 Isin, "Citizenship in flux: the figure of the activist citizen," 368.
42 Ibid., 371.
43 Ibid., 383.
44 Colectivo vírico Introducción. La letra pequeña en Rastros de Dixan. Islamofobia y construcción del enemigo en la era post 11-S. Virus editorial, 8–9.
45 Colectivo vírico Introducción. La letra pequeña, 9.
46 Colectivo vírico Introducción. La letra pequeña, 10–11.
47 Iker Barbero, "Historia contemporánea de la alteridad en el Derecho de extranjería," *Revista de estudios políticos* 164 (2014): 115–50.
48 Sandro Mezzadra, "The Right to Escape," *Ephemera. Theory & politics in organization theory of the multitude* 4, 3: 267–75.
49 Case 58438/00 Martinez Sala vs Spain, 2 November 2004 http://hudoc.echr.coe .int/sites/eng/pages/search.aspx#{%22dmdocnumber%22:[%22706631%22],%22 itemid%22:[%22001-67287%22]} Spain was condemned in 2004 by the European Court of Human Rights for failing to investigate the tortures and injuries to a group of detainees for terrorism after five days without communication.
50 The main argument of the prosecution was the possession of some kind of powder that was susbsequently shown to be Dixan, a detergent used in the laundry they worked in.
51 Iker Barbero, "When rights need to be (re)claimed. Austerity measures, neoliberal housing policies and anti-eviction activism in Spain," *Critical Social Policy* (in press, 2015).
52 Migreurop 2011. http://www.migreurop.org/IMG/pdf/Informe_CIE_Derechos _Vulnerados_2011.pdf; Ferrocarril Clandestino, SOS racismo and Médicos del mundo, 2009, http://cerremosloscies.files.wordpress.com/2011/12/ciesmaqueta-web.pdf

References Cited

Barbero, Iker. "El control selectivo de las fronteras y la transnacionalización de sus resistencias," *Arbor: Ciencia, pensamiento y cultura* 744 (2010): 689–703.
Barbero, Iker. "Expanding acts of citizenship: The struggles of Sinpapeles migrants," *Social & Legal Studies* 21, 4 (2012), 529–47.
Barbero, Iker. "Historia contemporánea de la alteridad en el Derecho de extranjería," *Revista de estudios políticos* 164 (2014): 115–50.
Barbero, Iker. "Orientalising citizenship: The legitimation of immigration regimes in the European Union," *Citizenship studies* 16, 5-6 (2012): 751–68.
Barbero, Iker. "When rights need to be (re)claimed. Austerity measures, neoliberal housing policies and anti-eviction activism in Spain," *Critical Social Policy* (2015).
Bayona, Jordi, and Fernando Gil, "Suburbanisation and international immigration: The case of the Barcelona metropolitan region (1998–2009)," *Tijdschrift voor econo-mische en sociale geografie* 103, 3 (2012): 312–29.
Bedoya, María Helena. "Mujer extranjera una doble exclusión: Influencia de la Ley de Extranjería sobre las mujeres inmigrantes," *Papers: revista de sociología* 60 (2000): 241–56.
Bigo, Didier. "Anastassia Tsoukala Terror," *Insecurity and Liberty: Illiberal Practices of Liberal Regimes after 9/11* (London: Taylor & Francis, 2008).

Bigo, Didier. "Sécurité, immigration et contrôle social. L'archipel des polices," *Le Monde Diplomatique* (Octobre 1996).

Calavita, Kitty. *Immigrants at the Margins: Law, Race, and Exclusion in Southern Europe* (New York: Cambridge University Press, 2005).

Colectivo vírico. "Introducción. La letra pequeña en Rastros de Dixan," *Islamofobia y construcción del enemigo en la era post 11-S*, Virus editorial: 8–9.

Coutin, Susan. "From Refugees to Immigrants: The Legalization Strategies of Salvadoran Immigrants and Activists," *International Migration Review* 32, 4 (1998): 901–25.

Coutin, Susan. "Subverting Discourses of Risk in the War on Terror," in *Risk and the War on Terror*, eds. Louise Amoore and Marieke de Goede (New York: Routledge, 2008), 218–32.

De Lucas, Javier. "Discursos de la invisible. Construir la presencia de los inmigrantes" in *Los otros entre nosotros: alteridad e inmigración* (Madrid: Círculo de Bellas Artes, 2003), 213–32.

de Sousa Santos, Boaventura. *Toward a New Legal Common Sense Law, Globalization, and Emancipation* (Cambridge: Cambridge University Press, 2002).

Delgado, Manuel. *La ciudad mentirosa: fraude y miseria del 'modelo Barcelona'* (Madrid: Los Libros de la Catarata, 2007), 166.

Emmanuel-Pierre, Guittet. "European Political Identity and Democratic Solidarity After 9/11: The Spanish Case," *Alternatives: Global, Local, Political* 29, 4 (2004): 441–64. http://www.hrw.org/reports/2005/spain0105/spain0105.pdf.

Fernández, Cristina, A. Manavella, and Jose Maria Ortuño. "The Effects of Exceptional Legislation on Criminalization of Immigrants and People Suspected of Terrorism," Challenge Report 9 (2009).

Fitzpatrick, Peter. *The Mythology of Modern Law* (London and New York: Routledge, 1992).

Fukuyama, Francis. "Identity, Immigration, and Liberal Democracy," *Journal of Democracy* 17, 2 (2006): 5–20.

Fullaondo, Arkaitz. "Inmigración y ciudad. El caso del área metropolitana de Barcelona" in *Pautas de asentamiento de la población inmigrante: implicaciones y retos sociojurídicos*, eds. Cristina Blanco Fernández de Valderrama and Iker Barbero González (Madrid: Dykinson, 2009).

Gregorio, Carmen. "Mujeres inmigrantes colonizando sus cuerpos mediante fronteras procreativas, étnico-culturales, sexuales y reproductivas," *Viento sur: Por una izquierda alternativa* 104 (2009): 42–54.

Huntington, Samuel. *The Clash of Civilizations and the Remaking of World Order* (New York: Simon & Schuster, 1998).

Isin, Engin. *Being Political: Genealogies of Citizenship* (Minneapolis: University of Minnesota Press, 2002).

Isin, Engin. "Citizenship in flux: The figure of the activist citizen," *Subjectivity* 29 (2009): 367–88.

Isin, Engin. "Theorizing acts of citizenship," in *Acts of Citizenship*, eds. E. Isin and G. Nielsen (London, UK: Palgrave Macmillan, 2008), 15–43.

Majid, Anouar. *We Are All Moors: Ending Centuries of Crusades against Muslims and Other Minorities* (Minneapolis, MN: University of Minnesota Press, 2009).

Martin, Miguel. "Pólvora mullada, del comando Dixan als onze del Raval," *La Directa* 374: 4.

Martín Corrales, Eloy. "El moro, decano de los enemigos exteriores de España: una larga enemistad (siglos VIII-XXI)," in *Los enemigos de España. Imagen del otro, conflictos bélicos y disputas nacionales (siglos XVI-XX)*, eds. Xoxe Muñez and Francisco Sevillano (Madrid: Centro de Estudios Políticos y Constitucionales, 2010), 165–82.

McNevin, Anne. *Contesting Citizenship: Irregular Migrants and New Frontiers of the Political* (New York: Columbia University Press, 2011).

Mestre i Mestre, Ruth. "Hilando fino: migraciones autóctonas de mujeres para trabajar en la industria del sexo," in *La condición inmigrante: exploraciones e investigaciones desde la Región de Murcia Manuel*, eds. Hernández Pedreño and Andrés Pedreño Cánovas (Murcia, Spain: Universidad de Murcia, 2005), 313–26.

Mezzadra, Sandro. "The Right to Escape," *Ephemera. Theory & politics in organization theory of the multitude* 4, 3: 267–75.

Moreras, Jordi. *Musulmanes en Barcelona: espacios y dinámicas comunitarias* (Barcelona: CIDOB, 1999).

Moreras, Jordi. "¿Ravalistán? Islam y configuración comunitaria entre los paquistaníes en Barcelona," *Revista CIDOB d'afers internacionals* 68 (2005).

Nyers, Peter. "In Solitary, In Solidarity: Detainees, Hostages, and Contesting the Anti-Policy of Detention," *European Journal of Cultural Studies* 11, 3 (2008): 333–49.

Nyers, Peter, and Kim Rygiel, *Citizenship, Migrant Activism and the Politics of Movement* (New York: Routledge, 2012).

Rygiel, Kim. "Bordering solidarities: migrant activism and the politics of movement and camps at Calais," *Citizenship Studies* 15, 1 (2011): 1–19.

Rygiel, Kim. *Globalizing citizenship* (Vancouver and Toronto: UBC Press, 2010), 178.

Salellas, Benet. "El Derecho contra la Justicia," in *Rastros de Dixan Islamofobia y construcción del enemigo en la era post 11-S*, eds. Abdennur Prado, Albert Martínez, Alberto López Bargados, Benet Salellas Vilar, David Fernàndez, Iñaki Rivera Beiras (Barcelona: Virus Editorial, 2009), 65–85.

Sartori, Giovanni. *Pluralismo, multiculturalismo e estranei: Saggio sulla società multietnica* (Milano: Rizzoli, 2000).

Squire, Vicki. "From Community Cohesion to Mobile Solidarities: The City of *Sanctuary* network and the *Strangers into Citizens* campaign," *Political Studies* 59, 2 (2011): 290–307.

Zapata-Barrero, Ricard, and Nynke De Witte, "Muslims in Spain: Blurring Past and Present Moors," in *Muslims in 21st century Europe: Structural and Cultural Perspectives*, dir. A. Triandafyllidou (London: Routledge, 2010), 181–98.

Zine, Jasmin. "Between orientalism and fundamentalism: The politics of Muslim women's feminist engagement," *Muslim World Journal of Human Rights* 3, 1 (2006).

8
Multicultural Society Must Be Defended?

Zaki Nahaboo

Abstract

This chapter investigates how orientalist citizenship is reinvented through attempts to define and defend multicultural society in Britain. I begin by describing how the normalizing function of 'state racism' charted in Michel Foucault's *Society Must Be Defended* has been partially recast through the 'post-racial', 'multiculturalist', and 'multiculture' conceptions of multicultural society. In doing so, this chapter helps us to identify the parameters through which new expressions of orientalist citizenship emerge to sustain contemporary state racism. This is exemplified in the figures of citizenship that manifest through an ethnic minority wing of the United Kingdom Independence Party, calls in the British media for intercultural dialogue, and the Stop the War Coalition's response to the War on Terror in the 2000s. Each captures how attempts at subverting identitarian life scripts, dichotomous subject positions, and essentialist identities become a means of reinventing orientalist citizenship. I conclude that the co-option of anti-essentialist challenges to orientalist citizenship facilitates a new imperative to state racism: 'multicultural society must be defended'.

Introduction

From the mid-1960s onwards, Britain became increasingly characterized as a multicultural society.[1] Yet its referent escapes consensus. The phrase 'multicultural society' is used to denote a political community marked by diversity in faith, 'race', nationality, attire, music, cuisine, language, customs, values, and citizenship status. What politicians and media commentators across the mainstream political spectrum tacitly agree upon is the irreversibility of multicultural society.[2] As Stuart Hall observes, contemporary Britain 'can [still] have purges...it can enforce assimilation but it can't go back to being stable and steady on its own mono-cultural foundations'.[3] This chapter explores the governmental effects of the naturalization and normalization of multicultural society upon orientalist citizenship.

The figure of the citizen is dominantly understood as having a Western genesis. Engin Isin notes that in the 'occidental tradition' it is considered a sovereign figure 'capable of judgment and being judged, transcending his (and much later her) tribal, kinship, and other primordial loyalties and belongingness'.[4] The orientalist citizen emerges when this figure is co-constituted with, and hierarchically opposed to, 'oriental' others who are said to lack these faculties.[5] This chapter demonstrates how certain attempts to define and defend multicultural society enables seemingly antithetical racist and anti-racist discourses to become combined to facilitate novel expressions of orientalist citizenship. This is exemplified through unique ways of constituting 'just-in-time' citizens, intercultural citizens, and anti-civilizational citizens. Each figure reveals how state racism, as outlined by Michel Foucault in *Society Must be Defended*, continues through overlapping post-racial, multiculturalist and 'multiculture' conceptions of multicultural society.

To legitimate its anti-immigration policies, the 2013 and 2014 campaigning by the United Kingdom Independence Party (UKIP) emphasized its multiracial membership. While UKIP's hostility towards multicultural society is now more thoroughly embraced, I draw attention to the brief campaigning by UKIP's ethnic minorities to reveal a moment where 'just-in-time' citizens mobilize a post-racial conception of multicultural society. This is shown to facilitate the rejection of recent immigrants beyond traditional terms of a national 'us' and a racialized 'them'.

The orientalist possibilities of intercultural citizens are revealed through *Make Bradford British*. The Channel 4 'documentary', broadcasted in 2012, reveals how critiques of essentializing definitions of multicultural citizenship can be disassociated from a progressive anti-racist trajectory. The programme exemplifies how state racism can be reconstituted even through challenges to dichotomous notions of an 'us' and 'them'. Finally, the Stop the War Coalition's (StWC) deployment of anti-civilizational citizens is analysed. It illustrates how the deconstruction of civilizational hierarchies through multiculture can unintentionally realize state racism through anti-civilizational citizens' normalization of secular protest.

These three figures of the citizen are politically incongruent. Yet they respectively capture how attempts at subverting identitarian life scripts, dichotomous subject positions, and essentialist identities have become a means of constituting orientalist citizenship. This chapter concludes that anti-essentialist possibilities to overcome orientalist citizenship have partially been co-opted and foreclosed through state racism's new imperative: 'multicultural society must be defended'.

Towards an Account of State Racism in Multicultural Society

From the seventeenth century onwards, populations in Western Europe statistically emerged in tandem with governmental concerns about how to regulate health, movement, productivity, and the relationship between resources and inhabitants.[6] Populations became perceived as natural phenomena that have their own regularities and constitution, thereby resituating governmental focus from the 'juridical-political' to objects of management.[7] Creating populations as natural phenomena to be steered, vitiated, and made productive meant that the scale of governmental address shifted onto facilitating life itself.[8] Foucault argued that during the nineteenth century this expression of 'biopolitics' became interwoven with earlier disciplinary strategies of normalizing and regulating society.[9] One of the lynchpins that enabled biopolitics to discriminate between healthy and unhealthy populations was state racism. This posited that 'society must be defended' against other 'races', now considered as an intrinsic element of society that must be expelled.[10] Crucially, every act of expulsion was made correlative to the health and hygiene of a population deemed rightful and authentic.[11] In other words, state racism introduced a socially diffused economy of life and death that can organize, legitimate, and sustain the traditional function of the sovereign's right to kill.

If European state racism gained its most virulent expression through Nazism and certain variants of socialism, as Foucault described, this does not mean that state racism explicitly relies upon biological or culturalist notions of race and class for its sustenance.[12] One of the central (if not always present) mechanisms of contemporary state racism is orientalist citizenship. This is evident through the War on Terror as principles of democracy and citizenship have begun to gain value *through* overseas wars on so-called fundamentalists.[13] Orientalist citizenship is also present when Muslims become classed as 'anti-citizens' and defined against a liberal secular population.[14] Both instances reveal how orientalist citizenship constitutes an 'us' and 'them' as a zero-sum political relation. In addition, these examples illustrate orientalist citizenship's tacit role in shaping the 'capacities' and pathways for defining what counts as legitimate expressions of political subjectivity.[15]

What occurs when expressions of orientalist citizenship become recast in terms of a nationally framed multicultural society? In this section, the labels 'post-racial', 'multiculturalist', and 'multiculture' are used to highlight separate points of departure for how multicultural society has been defined and defended. By providing an overview of each conception, the terrain through which transformed expressions of orientalist citizenship can be identified, along with their function for revitalizing state racism.

Multicultural society is sometimes used as a symbolic marker for a post-racial society. This conception utilizes the signifier of the multicultural to claim that racism has either been overcome or cannot be discussed without perpetually reaffirming its existence. However, the post-racial conception of multicultural society has enabled racism to thrive under the guise of cultural incommensurability and 'too much diversity'.[16] It is against this backdrop that statistically assessing whether racialized Muslims 'feel' loyalty to Britain becomes a gauge of inclusive citizenship.[17] After the 2005 bombings in London, the growth in polls by think-tanks and media outlets can be interpreted as one of the sites which made allegiance a central variable for constructing and discerning the health of multicultural society.[18] This enables state racism to operate in a bifurcated manner. Through a post-racial conception of defining and defending multicultural society, Muslims can be written into the national narrative as Britons who mostly belong. Yet the commonplace phrase 'most Muslims are not extremists' is qualified by Muslims being made answerable (although not responsible) for extremism.[19] Subsequently a 'good' and 'bad' Muslim is categorized to deflect the racializing process that ultimately structures Muslims as problem subjects.[20]

The multiculturalist conception of multicultural society has been more pessimistic about racism being overcome. While certainly varied in their construction of minorities, multiculturalist conceptions of society are united by their explicit prescription for dealing with racism as an issue of community relations. Multicultural toleration has become the dominant medium for realizing this objective. On the one hand, the valourization of (or aspiration for) a tolerant multicultural society that is free from racism becomes testimony to an inclusive national imaginary.[21] On the other hand, defending multicultural society in these terms has also fuelled the War on Terror through creating orientalized subjects as those who constitutively exceed the parameters of liberal tolerance.[22] These two possibilities of the multiculturalist conception do not exist in a dichotomous relation. As Alana Lentin and Gavin Titley argue, the division of populations according to 'good' and 'bad' forms of diversity shares the same concern around setting the 'acceptable limits of adversarial politics'.[23]

Positing multicultural society as a situation or 'experience' of multiculture illustrates a third conception of multicultural society.[24] According to this conception, multicultural society is not defined by its supposed communities. Instead, it is understood as a floating signifier of unsettled differences prior to statist attempts that 'manage the problems of diversity and multiplicity'.[25] Identities and racism do not cease to exist according to this conception of multicultural society. The setting of identities, both in racist terms, and banal presence with uncertain boundaries, is taken as an everyday feature of urban life. Multicultural society becomes viewed as a terrain where cultural racisms and the ethnic transformation of notions of belonging can coexist without conflict.[26] More specifically, adapting William Connolly's characterization of identity politics, attempts to 'pluralize' identities become symbiotic with attempts to 'fundamentalize' identities.[27] This does not always denote a political deadlock. Ash Amin, for instance, highlights how instances of multiculture which are orientated towards shared civic projects (not necessarily anti-racism) can indirectly untether culture from its presumed racialized bodies and undo racism.[28]

The post-racial and multiculturalist conceptions are points of departure for defining and defending multicultural society which necessarily involve a formula akin to 'us + others = multicultural we ≠ them'.[29] In other words, the post-racial and multiculturalist conceptions can facilitate a virtuous and legitimate population as multicultural. This population is simultaneously on the cusp of being divided into a 'them' by those who still retain their status as a demographic 'us'. In contrast, it would appear that the multiculture conception problematizes (rather than promulgates) a conjoined definition and defence of multicultural society. The anti-essentialist possibilities of 'multiculture' appear intrinsically less susceptible to state racism.

The post-racial, multiculturalist, and multiculture conceptions illustrate an unsettled dynamic of creating, governing, and contesting population differentiation. It is against this backdrop that state racism in Britain is beginning to adopt more nuanced dividing practices through new expressions of orientalist citizenship, which depend upon blurring these three conceptions. The remainder of this chapter illustrates this through attempts by just-in-time citizens, intercultural citizens, and anti-civilizational citizens at defining and defending multicultural society.

Just-in-Time Citizens: UKIP's Minorities

The biological underpinnings of nineteenth-century state racism contrasted with an earlier 'race struggle'.[30] This made race (understood as linguistic, cultural, national, or religious bonds) a counter-hegemonic discourse to undermine the rightfulness and virtue bestowed upon the dominant. Race struggle involved formulating a 'counterhistory' that undermined the tethering of a monumentalized history to sovereignty as a means of establishing the rightfulness and legality of rulers.[31] Put differently, just as state racism introduced historical narrative as a political device that legitimized a segmented population as the rightful inhabitants, race struggle drew attention to subjugated histories to constitute the marginalized as rights claimants.[32]

In 2000, a group of esteemed scholars, politicians, journalists, and race-equality experts were assembled to produce a report on the inequalities and challenges facing multicultural Britain. The ensuing report, *The Commission on Multi-Ethnic Britain: The Parekh Report*, can be viewed as one fleeting instance of race struggle. According to that report, creating a multicultural society free from racialized hierarchies necessitates rewriting national history and pluralizing ethnic representation in public life. The report stated that an obstacle to this goal was the 'unspoken racial connotations' that mired British identity.[33] The commissioners considered that this image of Britishness was suffused by traces of imperialism, which legitimated the advantageous position of the dominant ethnicities in Britain. Mounting a critique of imperialist amnesia through educational and media spheres would, in their view, require incorporating postcolonial history into the national narrative.[34]

This project of challenging the authorized narratives of Britain's history and undifferentiated rights regime depended upon reconceptualizing Britain as a 'community of communities and a community of citizens'.[35] The usage of citizens in this phrase denotes more than the regulative function civil rights discourse serves in communitarian visions of multicultural society. When taken in the context of the report's postcolonial critique, the citizen is transformed from its liberal non-racial positioning into what might be termed just-in-time citizens.

By this term I mean citizens who have firstly constituted themselves as having caught up with the national imaginary, and only through doing so position themselves as indistinguishable in status from the historically dominant non-racialized population. They are also subjects produced to inject the national narrative, occupational culture, and education with differences that both reflect and instill the ever-changing requirements for how a harmonious multicultural society is envisaged.

From the time of its publication, the media largely ignored the recommendations of the authors and instead wrongly perceived it as denouncing Britishness.[36] Over a decade has passed since postcolonial critique was rejected as a guide for British multicultural society to become non-racial. Just-in-time citizens failed to emerge as a postcolonial intervention for shaping anti-racist notions of belonging. They instead surfaced through what Paul Gilroy notes as the niche market of 'diversity and equality consultants': an outsourcing of anti-racism into the equal opportunity agendas of public bodies.[37] As the dominant image of the just-in-time citizen shifts from a subject who introduces difference to an agent of diversity management, this figure gained a new trajectory that further eroded its anti-racist potential. This can be explored through the United Kingdom Independence Party (UKIP).

Since its founding in 1993, UKIP has mostly remained on the margins of mainstream politics. The anti-immigrant party's major breakthrough came in 2014 when it beat both Labour and the Conservatives in the European elections.[38] What distinguishes it from other far-right groups is that UKIP supposedly runs on a non-racist platform of addressing nationally ungovernable immigration.[39] However, we know the party's leader, Nigel Farage, showed racialized hostility towards Romanians in general.[40] When this is viewed in conjunction with UKIP's support for wealthy commonwealth members, it reveals what was termed in the Balkan context: 'nesting orientalisms' (a hierarchy of orientalized subjects which need not correspond to dominant geo-historical manifestation of racialized difference).[41] Furthermore, Farage's comments about a supposed Muslim 'fifth column' existing in Britain, due to 'multiculturalism', illustrates the well-established tradition of using 'multiculturalism' as a proxy for orientalist notions of cultural incompatibility and inferiority.[42]

How UKIP defends multicultural society as a means of recasting state racism can be found elsewhere. As the contours of racialization encompass new (white) migrants, a post-racial discourse on immigration surfaces that enables racialized British citizens to become agents of anti-immigration politics. Racialized ethnic minority Britons have long perceived a complicity between stringent immigration laws and racism.[43] Yet in recent years this has been confounded by support for hard-line anti-immigration policies amongst a sizable minority of British Asians comparable to the white British population.[44] In 2013 and 2014, this development was politically expressed by British nationals from the new commonwealth (or those labelled as *n*th generation immigrants such as former UKIP member Sanya-Jeet Thandi) through constituting themselves as advocates of UKIP's anti-immigration.[45]

This development was termed UKIP's 'Clause IV' moment – a reference to the moment Labour formally abandoned its socialist objectives of worker ownership.[46] If we simply dismiss the inclusion of minority anti-immigrant sentiment as mere tokenism aimed at keeping old supporters while gaining new ones, rather than the identitarian sea-change the analogy implies, we miss an important development in how just-in-time citizens have come to express state racism. It marks an unprecedented shift in how racialized British citizens are able to constitute themselves for the first time as generators of state racism, rather than primary recipients.

Consider the UKIP 'carnival' held in Croydon during the run-up to the 2014 European and local elections. The UKIP candidate Winston McKenzie campaigned in front of a steel band, some of whom were initially unaware that they had been hired for a UKIP event.[47] The choice of music suggested a patronizing representation of ethnic diversity that has been used from 1980s onwards as a symbol of an inclusive multicultural society. However, as anti-UKIP protesters arrived, the black candidate was confronted by charges of racism from those who claimed to be Romanian.[48] This illustrates a complex situation of multiculture where the institutional racism of the prevailing migration regime, which Derek McGhee argues is supposedly partial to 'more EU (European, White, Christian) entrants', does not always correspond to the bodies that are traditionally associated with enacting or receiving state racism.[49] This is further exemplified with UKIP's response in 2013 to charges of racism by Lord Heseltine, a Conservative peer and former minister. Amjad Bashir, a UKIP MEP, stated he was more competent than the Conservative peer in using the term since, because of his Pakistani origin, he had experienced racism. Following from this, he called the charges by Heseltine counterproductive to a 'serious debate about immigration'.[50]

Just-in-time citizens' usage of racialized difference for justifying the parameters of citizenship, through its supposed insignificance for immigration debates, exemplifes an unforeseen twist in the politics of what Hall termed 'new ethnicities'.[51] The shift away from a black/white binary in identification and social ascription had previously been viewed as challenging essentialist assumptions of how racialized identities and anti-racist political agendas conjoin.[52] From the 1980s onwards, anti-racism became considered more effective if it took into account diverse practices of ethnic self-identification and non-equivalent 'modes of oppression'.[53] However, UKIP's minorities illustrate McGhee's observation that the host society, which is traditionally equivalent to a white population, has been partially severed through incorporating 'settled communities' as hosts.[54] Through this seemingly inclusive process, 'contingent insiders' emerge as subject to hierarchies of belonging that can in turn dispense new ways of excluding new arrivals.[55] Imporantly, UKIP's just-in-time citizens demonstrate how these new agents of state racism were produced on the spur of the moment when charges of racism were levelled at UKIP during 2013–14 from across the political spectrum.

Just-in-time citizens' enactment of state racism depends on a novel expression of orientalist citizenship. If, as Bryan Turner notes, orientalist citizenship traditionally operated through a 'system of absences – absent cities, the missing middle class, missing autonomous urban institutions and missing property' which prevented citizenship's emergence, then it follows that the other is considered to have a more fundamental lack.[56] This remains unstated in orientalist citizenship, but this lack involves the capacity to institute equality by virtue of excluding others. It is through the emergence of racialized just-in-time citizens that we find its articulation transformed to constitute and exclude new immigrants in a post-racial manner.

Hanif Kureishi argues new migrants are constituted as 'the undead, who will invade, colonize and contaminate'.[57] The contemporary immigrant can be deprived of citizenship without explicit recourse to orientalized and racialized difference. We should not misconstrue this development as another instance of the dominant anti-immigrant crisis of multiculturalism discourse.[58] Racialized otherness is no longer positioned, in this context, as a mark of citizenship's alterity. The dynamic between just-in-time citizens and zombie immigrants depends on the latter being stripped of all identity except that of an infringement on a 'post-racial' multicultural society.

The trajectory of just-in-time citizens reveals how the role of orientalist citizenship in sustaining state racism is becoming articulated in less traditional terms. The example of UKIP's just-in-time citizens shows that the capacity and ability to exclude others from rights emanates from an anti-essentialist enactment of minority identity politics. Orientalist citizenship was dispensed through inappropriate bodies (e.g., UKIP's minority candidates), as opposed to having permission and exclusion in multicultural society spring from what Ghassan Hage calls the 'white national manager'.[59]

Intercultural Citizens: *Make Bradford British*

Aside from recent immigrants being juxtaposed with a 'post-racial' multicultural society, those cast as desirable subjects of multicultural society have become defined as intercultural. This involves a 'descending individualism': establishing divergences from a 'norm' through scientific and disciplinary practices rather than identifying individuals through histories of exceptional ancestry.[60] The normal and calculable subject of multicultural society was first shaped during the pioneering Canadian experiment in multiculturalism in 1971.[61] This depended upon joining the 'multicultural assumption', which argued that developing 'self-esteem' in one's previously marginalized identity fosters acceptance by other groups, with the contact hypothesis.[62] The latter was derived from Gordon Allport's (1954) *The Nature of Prejudice,* which supposed that the more contact one had with different cultural

groups, accounting for variables in power, the more likely inter-group tolerance would surface.[63] While such practices once solely resided under the term
'multiculturalism', they have also come to be understood as interculturalism.

Theoretical differences between multiculturalism and interculturalism
are mostly imperceptible.[64] However, the 'inter' emphasizes one aspect of
a predominantly multiculturalist conception of society where the health
of society is determined through the quality of interactions that take place
across (and within) cultural communities. It is against this backdrop that
intercultural citizens emerge as subjects that normalize the terms of cultural
relations. This section demonstrates how this transforms expressions of orientalist citizenship to facilitate state racism.

Through envisaging multicultural society as comprised of multiplicity
rather than simply majorities and minorities, conditions for a shared dialogic
space become ostensibly possible. Bhikhu Parekh argues that intercultural
dialogue is essential to permit individuals to 'step outside of their culture...
[and] tease out its strengths and weaknesses'.[65] This correspondingly enables
them to realize the 'contingency of their culture and relate to it freely...
rather than as a fate'.[66] These dispositions are condensed into the figure of
the intercultural citizen.

The Council of Europe's *White Paper on Intercultural Dialogue: Living Together
as Equals in Dignity* published in 2008 stated that an intercultural approach,
involving the 'capacity to listen' and 'respectful exchange of views between
individuals and groups with different ethnic...backgrounds', is central to a
harmonious society.[67] While the intercultural citizen has enough curiosity
and ability to learn about others' 'habits and beliefs', this can lead to a position where one speaks for a culture, thereby petrifying its content, meaning,
and borders.[68] This sensitivity towards the otherness of the other is at odds
with the traditional figure of the spoken-for orientalized subject. As Ted Cantle argues, emphasizing the intercultural means recognizing how identities
are 'chosen and developmental', overlapping, and resistant to ascription.[69]

Yet orientalism is being transformed, rather than overcome, through the
intercultural citizen. It is a figure which largely corresponds to a multiculturalist conception of society and can be illustrated through the Channel 4
reality programme *Make Bradford British* aired in 2012. Like numerous media
representations of multicultural society, the documentary caused a brief
media frenzy and was later forgotten. It is, however, distinguishable through
its promotion of intercultural citizens. The programme mostly concurred
with many of the Labour Party's guidelines for community activism such as
'developing resilience' through sharing futures and notions of belongings,
while dispelling 'myths' and 'promoting interaction'.[70] Yet there was one
crucial difference. The narrator tacitly participated in the crisis of multiculturalism discourse by stating the programme was in response to Conservative Prime Minister David Cameron's suggestion that 'state multiculturalism'

promoted 'passive tolerance'.[71] The programme aimed to 'break away' from tolerance and cohesion discourse.[72] Instead, it explicitly assumed the mantle of enacting a decentralized, locally envisioned idea of what form desirable multicultural coexistence should assume by finding out how it 'really works' on the ground.[73]

Make Bradford British placed eight people from different classes, ethnicities, and postcodes under the same roof. What the individuals had in common was their labelling as 'failed citizens'. This was defined as those who had failed the Life in the UK citizenship test. The choice of locations within Bradford, predominantly white, Asian, and affluent or deprived areas, supposed that their 'failure' as citizens was related to their lack of everyday contact with different ethnicities. The figure of the failed British citizen created as a common starting line for all participants, regardless of class or ethnicity. This was possible since Britishness became a quantifiable attainment through the citizenship test, which enabled individuals to be collectively judged against a norm. In addition, as participants were said to share a common 'failure' and atypical segregated lifestyle, we were to assume some of the participants' racism was idiosyncratic and exceptional to Britain. Although the common starting point was derived from results of the citizenship test, over the course of the programme, the state that judges their collective failure receded from view. In its place the capacity for non-conflicting social interaction became a measure of citizenship.

An initial viewing of the programme reveals simply a renewed advocacy for contact theory, which makes 'acculturation' and 'adaptation' central for peaceably negotiated cultural difference.[74] In our context, this became a new way of instilling power relations. As *Make Bradford British* reached its conclusion, the majority of participants strove for an intercultural position. Even though racist and tolerant beliefs were maintained, participants who held these views were no longer marked as failed citizens. This became evident in the conclusion to the programme when they were brought back to the question of Britishness. This time, however, they were presented as British by virtue of being asked to define their cultural citizenship in subjective terms. Their various narratives were presented to the audience as representative of the plurality of the British national imaginary. The only participant who remained implicitly a failed citizen was the 'South Asian' 'taxi driver'. This was due to his premature departure from the show after his refusal to discuss his patriarchal beliefs. His absence at the end meant that he missed the opportunity given to his fellow participants, now intercultural citizens, to express their Britishness. The unplanned narrative of the programme is symbolic of how intercultural citizens opened spaces for challenging orientalist assumptions. At the same time, intercultural citizens emerged as disciplining subjects who discerned those who qualify as equal citizens.

Through this particular multiculturalist framing of multicultural society, orientalist citizenship is transformed. A split was created between those who can be normalized as competent for cultural dialogue and individuals perceived as trapped within cultural silos: the 'failed' citizens. However, this did not wholly depend on a crude state racism whereby an 'us' and 'them' are viewed as having mutually exclusive origins. Intercultural citizens constituted, and sought to undermine, the existence of failed citizens through a non-dichotomous understanding of 'us' and 'them'. Intercultural citizens were positioned as virtuous subjects in their claim to eradicate a failed citizen from within their own 'identity' and that of others. The unique relation between intercultural and failed citizens may appear to provide an opening for challenges to orientalism. However, intercultural citizens in the context of *Make Bradford British* reintroduced orientalist citizenship through the normalization of an intercultural position defined against orientalized others who are disbarred from (or refuse to) make this transition.

Anti-civilizational Citizens: Protest through the StWC

Multicultural society is not only expressed through shaping the legal and cultural conceptions of citizenship. It has also been characterized as the lived experience of multiculture. This can be understood as the diasporic, syncretic, hybrid, and processual performances of difference that can potentially arise to undermine the framing of culture through ethnic absolutisms.[75] As I previously argued, the multiculture conception of society places greater emphasis on how individuals can be located apart from statist categorizations of ethnicity and singularly quantifiable identities. Logically, it is impossible for multiculture to reinvent orientalist citizenship. When it exceeds being presented as a neutral descriptor of multicultural society, valourizing multiculture intrinsically undermines the genealogies that hold cultures as corresponding to discrete boundaries, bodies, and geographical origins. A brief discussion of the debate between Samuel Huntington and Edward Said reveals how this brand of multiculture can undermine orientalism. This debate provides a starting point from which to highlight changes in orientalist citizenship that incorporate, rather than oppose, progressive articulations of multiculture.

Samuel Huntington argued that humanity is organized into historically durable, hermetically sealed, and culturally incompatible civilizational blocs whose existence becomes threatened when transgression to their fault lines occurs.[76] Unlike Huntington, who, according to David Cannadine, 'urged accommodation rather than confrontation' between civilizations, Edward Said rejected engaging with the issue of accommodation.[77] This was due to an initial dispute around civilizational categorization. Said's response to Huntington can be summed up as follows: we live in 'a disorderly reality that won't be pigeonholed or strapped down'.[78] This view derives from the argument that the contemporary sectioning of humanity into 'distinct breeds or essences' should be exposed as both a false representation and an effect of power relations.[79] Instead, he posited culture as necessarily overlapping and appropriating in ways that resist its confinement to identitarian shorthand.[80] To discern inequity in power relations that transpires through multiculture, Said argued for humanism: 'the agency of human individuality and subjective intuition, rather than [reliance] on received ideas and approved authority'.[81]

Said's refusal to challenge orientalist discourse on its own terms, for example by reversing orientalism or promoting tolerance, is a vital means for contesting expressions of orientalism that pervade British media and political discourse. However, orientalism has not remained static in its post-9/11 'Islamophobic' and civilizational articulation. The orientalist War on Terror is partially sustained without relying upon (ideologically obscured) constructs of an 'us' and 'them'. In effect, it sidestepped the symbolic role the Huntington and Said debate has for illustrating our political conjuncture. To illustrate this we can turn to the Stop the War Coalition (StWC) protests. This reveals how an explicit refusal of orientalist terms, through casting oneself as a citizen against notions of civilizational difference, can in fact testify to a transformation in orientalist citizenship.

The StWC protest in 2003 helped organize the largest protest in UK history against the then impending Iraq war.[82] The StWC prided itself on the diversity of beliefs, nationalities, ethnicities, and ages involved in mobilization.[83] This diversity extended from the motivation of activism to the differing agendas of the Socialist Workers Party, Campaign for Nuclear Disarmament, and Muslim Association of Britain who were formative of StWC. The diversity of the act – Islamists marching alongside Quakers – embodied the shared demand for human dignity denied through the nascent War on Terror.

Emphasis on a common humanity was vital for contesting the terms of a War on Terror meted out on spectral subjects devoid of humanity, an undead presence that can be repeatedly killed because they are inexhaustible and unindividuated.[84] StWC resisted this form of orientalism by deconstructing the situation of humanity in the West. For example, in response to the disproportionate media coverage of the deaths of British soldiers overseas in relation to civilian fatalities, StWC sought to render the latter visible by reading out civilian names in public.[85] Bringing anonymous others into the sphere of nameable humanity, like the fallen British soldiers, defied the fused national and cultural boundaries of contemporary orientalist citizenship. The unintended function of this critique should also be scrutinized.

Aspects of the worldviews exemplified by Huntington (claiming mastery over an other which can be categorized and governed) and Said (the inability to categorize and govern through orientalism without perpetuating violence) have come to be selectively blended in a War on Terror that governs through risk. The effects of orientalism persist through what could be described as 'precautionary risk management'.[86] This 'displays an insatiable quest for knowledge: profiling populations, surveillance, intelligence, knowledge about catastrophe management, prevention, etc.'.[87] The pre-emptive forms of securitization appear to have legitimated the War on Terror, in particular the 2003 justification for the invasion of Iraq.[88] Less observed is how certain ways of refusing orientalist discourse can in themselves become part of the diffused securitizing strategies of governing in times of risk.

Despite the unplanned multicultural diversity and pluralism lauded in the StWC 2003 mobilization, attempts to politicize ethno-religious difference were heavily constrained. This absence was not conspicuous. Some members of the Muslim Association of Britain and the Islamist organization Al-Muhajiroun wanted to emphasize the war as a Muslim plight by excluding non-whites from the mainstream protest.[89] These individuals were marginalized.[90] Yet in so far as barring non-secular protesters prevented a specious claim of a war on Muslims, and prevented an inverted clash of civilizations discourse, this sustained practices of state racism. Through protesters being positioned beyond identitarian terms via their shared grievance, the protest assumed a function of vigilance, regulation, and disciplining of public space in case a potential legitimacy for religious protest emerged. According to Salma Yaqoob, the secular nature of the official protest also meant that 'moderate' protesters who offered anti-war rationales on religious grounds could not articulate their grievances as such.[91]

The StWC protests exemplified how an organic expression of multiculture, underpinned by a common political objective, potentially offers an avenue beyond the territorial and population-managerial underpinnings of state racism. At the same time as sustaining anti-civilizational citizens and multiculture, the protests became a site that marked the diffusion of risk-based anti-terrorism. As certain anti-civilizational citizens came to regulate the terms of protest, an unintended expression of orientalist citizenship hardened dividing practices in less perceptible ways than the traditional 'clash of civilizations' discourse.

Conclusion

Claiming 'society must be defended' is a task undertaken by those who have positioned themselves as part of a legitimate population who can dictate terms for excluding others. This move no longer involves a 'race struggle' where historical discontinuity is introduced into the prevailing notions of the rightful and authentic inhabitants. Instead, state racism emerges to preserve society as irrevocably tethered to the institutions of the state (and thereby constitute society as already 'ours').[92] This chapter has explored the ways state racism is expressed through attempts to define and defend multicultural society. I uncovered various ways orientalist citizenship has been transformed to enable state racism persistence through post-racial, multiculturalist, and multiculture conceptions of society.

The first exploration of orientalist citizenship focused on how it reinforced a conception of multicultural society as post-racial and anti-immigrant. By drawing attention to UKIP's just-in-time citizens, I argued that an anti-essentialist severing of a fused racialized identity and support for immigration partially occurred as racialized citizens assumed an orientalist position of excluding others. Second, I showed how *Make Bradford British* illustrated one way intercultural citizens have defined and defended a multiculturalist conception of society. Of significance was how normalized intercultural citizens were demarcated from failed citizens in non-dichotomous terms to facilitate a more inclusive notion of cultural citizenship. Yet it was precisely this attempt at creating intercultural citizens and failed citizens as occupying dynamic subject positions, rather than mutually exclusive identities, that the intercultural citizen became a disciplining position from which orientalist citizenship could gain a new expression. In a similar vein to UKIP's just-in-time citizens, the normalization of intercultural citizens revealed how transformations in orientalist citizenship enable state racism to persist in situations where biological and culturally defined hierarchies become untenable. Just-in-time and intercultural citizens illustrate positions from which racialized citizens can constitute the legitimate occupants of society and terms of exclusion.

Lastly, I investigated how anti-civilizational citizens emerged through (and depended upon) multiculture. A more thoroughgoing critique of state racism becomes possible through this figure. This is the case since multiculture can potentially erode a genealogy of identity as bearing pure inheritances and valourized statuses, which state racism has historically defined against those who can be killed with impunity. This anti-essentialist challenge to identity was illustrated through StWC protests. However, I demonstrated how this specific instance of deconstructing positions of 'us' and 'them' in the War on Terror also served as an orientalist disciplinary mechanism for normalizing protest as secular and circulating risk-based anti-terrorism.

According to Slavoj Žižek, when individuals become confined to politically acting under the label of cultural difference, heterogeneous struggles for equality become condensed and repressed into a 'post-political' discourse of managing cultural diversity.[93] The conceptions of multicultural society discussed, and the expressions of citizenship which loosely correspond to each conception, should not be interpreted as yet another general indictment of the 'culturalization of politics'.[94] This chapter instead analysed orientalist instances of just-in-time, intercultural, and anti-civilizational citizens to illustrate a distinctive issue: how state racism materializes through the co-option of anti-essentialist critique. State racism was shown to depend on these expressions of orientalist citizenship to fulfill its new imperative: multicultural society must be defended.

Notes

1   B. Parekh, "Integrating Minorities," in *Race Relations: A Developing Agenda*, eds. T. Blackstone, B. Parekh and P. Sanders (London: Routledge, 1998), 14.
2   D. Cameron, PM's speech at Munich Security Conference [online]. *Number10.gov* 2011. http://www.number10.gov.uk/news/speeches-and-transcripts/2011/02/pms -speech-at-munich-security-conference-60293 (accessed 5 June 2011); N. Clegg, "An Open, Confident Society," *The Liberal Democrats* 2011. http://www.libdems .org.uk/nick_clegg_speech_an_open_confident_society (accessed 18 July 2015); K. Livingstone, "Text of statement by Mayor Ken Livingstone," *Financial Times*, 2005.   http://www.ft.com/cms/s/2/dcdfe116-ef08-11d9-8b10-00000e2511c8.html - axzz3FDu9JDAb. (accessed 3 October 2014).
3   L. Back, S. Sinha, and C. Bryan, "New Hierarchies of Belonging," *European Journal of Cultural Studies* 15, 2 (2012): 679–80.
4   E. F. Isin "Citizenship after Orientalism: Ottoman Citizenship," in *Challenges to Citizenship in a Globalizing World: European Questions and Turkish Experiences*, eds. F. Keyman and A. Icduygu (London: Routledge, 2005), 31.
5   Ibid.
6   M. Foucault, "Governmentality," in *Power: The Essential Works of Foucault 1954-1984*, ed. James D. Faubion (New York: New Press, 2001), 216–17.
7   M. Foucault, *Security, Territory, Population: Lectures at the Collège De France 1977–1978* (Basingstoke: Palgrave Macmillan, 2009), 70.
8   M. Foucault, *Society Must Be Defended* (London: Penguin, 2003), 242–3.
9   Ibid., 256.
10   Ibid., 61.
11   Foucault, *Security, Territory, Population*, 257.
12   Foucault, *Society Must Be Defended*, 259–63.
13   L. Irigaray and M. Marder, "Is 'Democracy' Nothing More Than a Slogan Now?" *The New Statesman* 2014 (accessed 28 November 2014).
14   G. Sartori, cited in I. Barbero, "Orientalising Citizenship: The Legitimation of Immigration Regimes in the European Union," *Citizenship Studies* 16, 5-6 (2012): 759.
15   E. Isin, "Citizenship after Orientalism: An Unfinished Project," *Citizenship Studies* 16, 5-6 (2012): 568.
16   A. Lentin, "Post-Race, Post Politics: The Paradoxical Rise of Culture after Multiculturalism," *Ethnic and Racial Studies* 5–9 (2012).
17   V. Uberoi and T. Modood, "Who Doesn't Feel British? Divisions over Muslims," *Parliamentary Affairs* 63, 2 (2010): 304.
18   M. Sobolewska, "Religious Extremism in Britain and British Muslims: Threatened Citizenship and the Role of Religion," in *The New Extremism in the 21st Century*, ed. R. Eatwell and M. J. Goodwin (New York: Routledge, 2010), 29.
19   B. Parekh, "Muslim Alienation and the Obligations of Citizenship," *The Times*, 7 July 2006.
20   M. Mamdani, *Good Muslim, Bad Muslim: America, the Cold War, and the Roots of Terror* (New York: Pantheon, 2004).
21   Commission on the Future of Multi-Ethnic Britain (CMEB). *The Future of Multi-Ethnic Britain: The Parekh Report* (London: Profile Books).
22   W. Brown, *Regulating Aversion: Tolerance in an Age of Diversity* (Princeton, NJ: Princeton University Press, 2006), 183–4.

23 A. Lentin and G. Titley, *The Crisis of Multiculturalism: Racism in a Neoliberal Age* (London: Zed Books, 2011), 187.

24 S. Neal et al., "Living Multiculture: Understanding the New Spatial and Social Relations of Ethnicity and Multiculture in England," *Environment and Planning C: Government and Policy* 31, 2 (2013): 309.

25 S. Hall, "Conclusion: The Multi-Cultural Question," in *Un/Settled Multicultural-isms*, ed. B. Hesse (London: Zed Books, 2000), 209.

26 S. Hall, *The Multicultural Question* (Milton Keyenes: Pavis Centre for Social and Cultural Research, The Open University, 2000), 14.

27 W. E. Connolly, "Pluralism, Multiculturalism and the Nation-State: Rethinking the Connections," *Journal of Political Ideologies* 1, 1 (1996): 60.

28 A. Amin, "Ethnicity and the Multicultural City: Living with Diversity," *Environment and Planning A* 34, 6 (2002): 269–70.

29 E. Winter, *Us, Them, and Others* (Toronto: University of Toronto Press, 2011), 111.

30 M. Foucault, *Society Must be Defended*, 66–7.

31 Ibid.

32 A. Stoler, *Race and the Education of Desire* (London: Duke University Press, 1995), 62.

33 CMEB, *The Future of Multi-Ethnic Britain: The Parekh Report*, 38.

34 Ibid.

35 Ibid.

36 Ibid., 56.

37 P. Gilroy, "'My Britain Is Fuck All' Zombie Multiculturalism and the Race Politics of Citizenship," *Identities* 19, 4 (2012): 386.

38 P. Wintour and N. Watt, "Ukip Wins European Elections with Ease to Set Off Political Earthquake," *The Guardian* 2014 http://www.theguardian.com/politics/2014/may/26/ukip-european-elections-political-earthquake (accessed 2 January 2015).

39 N. Farage, Interview with Nigel Farage, Leader of the U.K. Independence Party 2014 http://www.washingtonpost.com/world/interview-with-nigel-farage-leader-of-the-uk-independence-party/2014/05/14/3b2f8c72-f855-47be-b3f8-8e7f638ad3a6_story.html (accessed 30 May 2014).

40 BBC, Nigel Farage Defends Romanian Comments Amid Racism Claims. *BBC* 2014 http://www.bbc.co.uk/news/uk-politics-27474099 (accessed 29 May 2014).

41 M. Bakić-Hayden, "Nesting Orientalisms: The Case of Former Yugoslavia," *Slavic Review* 54, 4 (1995): 918.

42 Farage cited in M. Holehouse, "Nigel Farage Blames Paris Attack on 'Rather Gross Policy of Multi-Culturalism,'" *The Telegraph* 2015 http://www.telegraph.co.uk/news/politics/nick-clegg/11332461/Nigel-Farage-blames-Paris-attack-on-rather-gross-policy-of-multi-culturalism.html (accessed 9 January 2015).

43 S. Saggar, "Immigration and the Politics of Public Opinion," *The Political Quarterly* 74 (2003): 178–94.

44 N. Lowles and A. Painter, "Fear and Hope: The New Politics of Identity," *Searchlight Educational Trust* 2012 http://www.fearandhope.org.uk/project-report/themes (accessed 13 July 2013).

45 S. Manzoor, "The New Faces of Ukip," *The Times* 2013 http://www.thetimes.co.uk/tto/magazine/article3938636.ece (accessed 3 January 2014).

46 A. Singh, "Why Are Ethnic Minorities Supporting Ukip?" *Independent* 2014 http://www.independent.co.uk/voices/why-are-ethnic-minorities-supporting-ukip-9347369.html (accessed 19 May 2014).

47   G. Graham and C. Hope, "Nigel Farage Feels Too 'Unsafe' to Attend His Own 'Ukip Carnival,'" *The Telegraph* 2014 http://www.telegraph.co.uk/news/politics/ukip/10844087/Nigel-Farage-feels-too-unsafe-to-attend-his-own-Ukip-carnival.html (accessed 3 January 2015).

48   G. Davies, "Nigel Farage Fails to Show as Ukip 'Carnival' Ends with Winston Mckenzie Calling Croydon an 'Absolute Dump,'" *Crydon Advertiser* 2014 http://www.croydonadvertiser.co.uk/Nigel-Farage-fails-Ukip-carnival-ends-Winston/story-21115536-detail/story.html (accessed 12 June 2014).

49   D. McGhee, "The Paths to Citizenship: A Critical Examination of Immigration Policy in Britain since 2001," *Patterns of Prejudice* 43, 1 (2009): 53–54.

50   BBC, "Ukip Is Not a Racist Party, Lord Heseltine Told," *BBC* 2013 http://www.bbc.co.uk/news/uk-politics-24385139 (accessed 16 June 2014).

51   S. Hall, "New Ethnicities," in *'Race', Culture and Difference*, eds. J. Donald and A. Rattansi (London: Sage, 1992).

52   Ibid.

53   T. Modood, "Difference, 'Multi' and Equality," in *The Plural States of Recognition*, ed. Michel Seymour (Basingstoke, UK: Palgrave Macmillan, 2010), 155.

54   D. McGhee, "Getting 'Host' Communities on Board: Finding the Balance between 'Managed Migration' and 'Managed Settlement' in Community Cohesion Strategies," *Journal of Ethnic & Migration Studies* 32, 1 (2006): 122–3.

55   Back, Sinha and Bryan, "New Hierarchies of Belonging," *European Journal of Cultural Studies* 15, 2 (2012): 140.

56   B. S. Turner, *Orientalism, Postmodernism & Globalism* (London: Routledge, 1994).

57   H. Kureishi, "The Migrant Has No Face, Status or Story," *The Guardian* 2014 http://www.theguardian.com/books/2014/may/30/hanif-kureishi-migrant-immigration-1 (accessed 30 May 2014).

58   A. Lentin and G. Titley, *The Crisis of Multiculturalism*, 2.

59   G. Hage, *White Nation: Fantasies of White Supremacy in Multicultural Society* (London: Routledge, 2000), 132–3.

60   Foucault cited in J. O'Neill, "The Disciplinary Society: From Weber to Foucault," *The British Journal of Sociology* 37, 1 (1986): 53.

61   P. Trudeau, Announcement of Implementation of Policy of Multiculturalism within Bilingual Framework, *Heritage Community Foundation* 1971 http://www.abheritage.ca/albertans/speeches/trudeau.html (accessed 25 June 2011).

62   J. W. Berry, R. Kalin, and D. M. Taylor, *Multiculturalism and Ethnic Attitudes in Canada* (Ottawa: Minister of Supply and Services, 1977).

63   T. F. Pettigrew, "Intergroup Contact Theory," *Annual Review of Psychology* 49 (February 1998): 66–9.

64   N. Meer and T. Modood, "How Does Interculturalism Contrast with Multiculturalism?," *Journal of Intercultural Studies* 33, 2 (2012): 175–96.

65   B. Parekh, *Rethinking Multiculturalism: Cultural Diversity and Political Theory* (Basingstoke, UK: Palgrave Macmillan, 2000), 167.

66   Ibid.

67   Council of Europe, White Paper on Intercultural Dialogue "Living Together as Equals in Dignity," *Council of Europe* 2008 bit.ly/MRx6jshttp://www.coe.int/t/dg4/intercultural/source/white paper_final_revised_en.pdf, 17 (accessed 6 November 2013).

68   W. Kymlicka, "Multicultural States and Intercultural Citizens," *Theory and Research in Education* 1, 2 (2003): 158–60.

69 T. Cantle, "Interculturalism: For the Era of Globalisation, Cohesion and Diversity," *Political Insight* (December 2012): 40.

70 J. Broadwood and N. Sugden, *Building Cohesive Communities: What Frontline Staff and Community Activists Need to Know* (London: Department for Communities and Local Government, 2009), 6–12.

71 L. Trott, "Lessons to Learn," *Channel 4* 2012 http://www.channel4.com/programmes/make-bradford-british/articles/lessons-to-learn (accessed 2 March 2012).

72 Ibid.

73 Channel 4, *Make Bradford British* (2012).

74 J. W. Berry, "Immigration, Acculturation, and Adaptation," *Applied Pyschology: An International Review* 46, 1 (1997): 6–7.

75 P. Gilroy, *The Black Atlantic: Modernity and Double Conciousness* (London: Verso, 1992); J. N. Pieterse, *Ethnicities and Global Multiculture: Pants for an Octopus* (Plymouth: Rowman & Littlefield, 2007).

76 S. P. Huntington, *The Clash of Civilizations and the Remaking of the World Order* (New York: Simon & Schuster, 1996).

77 D. Cannadine, *The Undivided Past: History Beyond Our Differences* (London: Allen Lane, 2013), 253.

78 E. W. Said, "The Clash of Ignorance," *The Nation* 2001 http://www.unipa.it/~michele.cometa/Said_The Clash of Ignorance.pdf (accessed 7 August 2013).

79 E. W. Said, *Orientalism* (London: Penguin, 2003[1978]), 348–9.

80 Said, *Orientalism*, xxii.

81 Ibid.

82 BBC, "'Million' March against Iraq War,'" *BBC* 2003 http://news.bbc.co.uk/1/hi/uk/2765041.stm. (accessed 10 December 2011).

83 L. German, "War and Resistance: Moving on Up" *The Socialist Review* 2002 http://www.socialistreview.org.uk/article.php?articlenumber=8187 (accessed 5 August 2013).

84 J. Butler, *Precarious Life: The Powers of Mourning and Violence* (London: Verso, 2004), 33–4.

85 StWC, Tyneside Stop the War Coalition Reads the Names of the Dead at Newcastle Monument. *North East Stop the War* 2009 http://www.northeaststopwar.org.uk/archive/manch08/100death.htm (accessed 2 August 2013).

86 C. Aradau and R. Van Munster, "Governing Terrorism through Risk: Taking Precautions, (Un)Knowing the Future," *European Journal of International Relations* 13, 1 (2007): 104.

87 Ibid., 91.

88 Ibid., 109.

89 R. Phillips, "Standing Together: The Muslim Association of Britain and the Anti-War Movement," *Race & Class* 50, 2 (2008): 101–13.

90 A. Murray and L. German, *Stop the War: The Story of Britain's Biggest Mass Movement* (London: Bookmark Publications, 2005), 61.

91 Y. Birt, "Islamophobia in the Construction of British Muslim Identity Politics," in *Muslims in Britain: Race, Place and Identities*, ed. Peter Hopkins and Richard Gale (Edinburgh, UK: Edinburgh University Press, 2009).

92 Foucault, *Society Must be Defended.*

93 S. Žižek, "Tolerance as an Ideological Category," *Critical Inquiry* 34 (2008): 660.

94 Ibid.

References Cited

Amin, Ash. "Ethnicity and the Multicultural City: Living with Diversity," *Environment and Planning A* 34, 6 (2002): 959–80.

Aradau, Claudia, and Rens Van Munster. "Governing Terrorism through Risk: Taking Precautions, (Un)Knowing the Future," *European Journal of International Relations* 13, 1 (2007): 89–115.

Back, Les, and Shamser Sinha (with Charlynne Bryan). "New Hierarchies of Belonging," *European Journal of Cultural Studies* 15, 2 (2012): 139–54.

Bakić-Hayden, Milica. "Nesting Orientalisms: The Case of Former Yugoslavia," *Slavic Review* 54, 4 (1995): 917–31.

Barbero, Iker. "Orientalising Citizenship: The Legitimation of Immigration Regimes in the European Union," *Citizenship Studies* 16, 5-6 (2012): 751–68.

BBC. "'Million' March against Iraq War," *BBC* (2003), http://news.bbc.co.uk/1/hi/uk/2765041.stm (accessed 10 December 2011).

BBC. "Nigel Farage Defends Romanian Comments Amid Racism Claims," *BBC* (2014), http://www.bbc.co.uk/news/uk-politics-27474099 (accessed 29 May 2014).

BBC. "Ukip Is Not a Racist Party, Lord Heseltine Told," *BBC* (2013), http://www.bbc.co.uk/news/uk-politics-24385139 (accessed 16 June 2014).

Berry, John W. "Immigration, Acculturation, and Adaptation," *Applied Pyschology: An International Review* 46, 1 (1997): 5–68.

Berry, John W., Rudolf Kalin, and Donald M. Taylor. *Multiculturalism and Ethnic Attitudes in Canada* (Ottawa: Minister of Supply and Services, 1977).

Birt, Yahya. "Islamophobia in the Construction of British Muslim Identity Politics," in *Muslims in Britain: Race, Place and Identities*, ed. Peter Hopkins and Richard Gale (Edinburgh: Edinburgh University Press, 2009).

Broadwood, Jo, and Nicola Sugden. *Building Cohesive Communities: What Frontline Staff and Community Activists Need to Know* (London: Department for Communities and Local Government, 2009).

Brown, Wendy. *Regulating Aversion: Tolerance in an Age of Diversity* (Princeton: Princeton University Press, 2006).

Butler, Judith. *Precarious Life: The Powers of Mourning and Violence* (London: Verso, 2004).

Cameron, David. "PM's Speech at Munich Security Conference," *Number10.gov* (2011) http://www.number10.gov.uk/news/speeches-and-transcripts/2011/02/pms-speech-at-munich-security-conference-60293 (accessed 5 June 2011).

Cannadine, David. *The Undivided Past: History Beyond Our Differences* (London: Allen Lane, 2013).

Cantle, Ted. "Interculturalism: For the Era of Globalisation, Cohesion and Diversity," *Political Insight* (December 2012).

Channel 4. *Make Bradford British* (2012).

Clegg, Nick. "An Open, Confident Society," *The Liberal Democrats* (2011) http://www.libdems.org.uk/nick_clegg_speech_an_open_confident_society (accessed 18 July 2015).

CMEB. *The Future of Multi-Ethnic Britain: The Parekh Report* (London: Profile Books, 2000).

Connolly, William E. "Pluralism, Multiculturalism and the Nation-State: Rethinking the Connections," *Journal of Political Ideologies* 1, 1 (1996): 53–73.

Council of Europe. White Paper on Intercultural Dialogue "Living Together as Equals in Dignity" (2008) http://www.coe.int/t/dg4/intercultural/source/white paper_final_revised_en.pdf (accessed 6 November 2013).

Davies, Gareth. "Nigel Farage Fails to Show as Ukip 'Carnival' Ends with Winston Mckenzie Calling Croydon an 'Absolute Dump'," *Crydon Advertiser* (2014) http:// www.croydonadvertiser.co.uk/Nigel-Farage-fails-Ukip-carnival-ends-Winston/ story-21115536-detail/story.html (accessed 12 June 2014].

Farage, Nigel. "Interview with Nigel Farage, Leader of the U.K. Independence Party 2014" http://www.washingtonpost.com/world/interview-with-nigel-farage-leader -of-the-uk-independence-party/2014/05/14/3b2f8c72-f855-47be-b3f8 -8e7f638ad3a6_story.html (accessed 30 May 2014).

Foucault, Michel. "Governmentality," in *Power: The Essential Works of Foucault 1954-1984*, ed. James D. Faubion (New York: New Press, 2001).

Foucault, Michel. *Security, Territory, Population: Lectures at the Collège De France 1977-1978* (Basingstoke: Palgrave Macmillan, 2009).

Foucault, Michel. *Society Must Be Defended* (London: Penguin, 2003).

German, Lindsey. "War and Resistance: Moving on Up 2002" http://www.socialistreview .org.uk/article.php?articlenumber=8187 (accessed 5 August 2013).

Gilroy, Paul. *The Black Atlantic: Modernity and Double Conciousness* (London: Verso, 1992).

Gilroy, Paul. "'My Britain Is Fuck All' Zombie Multiculturalism and the Race Politics of Citizenship," *Identities* 19, 4 (2012): 380–97.

Graham, Georgia, and Christopher Hope. "Nigel Farage Feels Too 'Unsafe' to Attend His Own 'Ukip Carnival'," *The Telegraph* (2014) http://www.telegraph.co.uk/news/ politics/ukip/10844087/Nigel-Farage-feels-too-unsafe-to-attend-his-own-Ukip-car- nival.html (accessed 03 January 2015).

Hage, Ghassan. *White Nation: Fantasies of White Supremacy in Multicultural Society* (London: Routledge, 2000).

Hall, Stuart. "Conclusion: The Multi-Cultural Question," in *Un/Settled Multicultural- isms*, ed. Barnor Hesse (London: Zed Books, 2000).

Hall, Stuart, "Cultural Identity and Diaspora," *Identity: Community, culture, difference* 2 (1990): 222–37.

Hall, Stuart. "The Meaning of New Times," in *Stuart Hall: Critical Dialogues in Cultural Studies*, eds. David Morley and Kuan-Hsing Chen (London: Routledge, 1996[1989]).

Hall, Stuart. *The Multicultural Question* (Milton Keyenes: Pavis Centre for Social and Cultural Research, The Open University, 2000).

Hall, Stuart. "New Ethnicities," in *'Race', Culture and Difference*, eds. James Donald and Ali Rattansi (London: Sage, 1992).

Hall, Stuart, and Les Back, "At Home and Not at Home: Stuart Hall in Conversation with Les Back," *Cultural Studies* 23, 4 (2009): 657–88.

Hesse, Barnor. "Diasporicity: Black Britain's Post-Colonial Formations," in *Un/Settled Multiculturalisms*, ed. Barnor Hesse (London: Zed Books, 2000).

Holehouse, Matthew. "Nigel Farage Blames Paris Attack on 'Rather Gross Policy of Multi-Culturalism', " *The Telegraph* (2015) http://www.telegraph.co.uk/news/ politics/nick-clegg/11332461/Nigel-Farage-blames-Paris-attack-on-rather-gross -policy-of-multi-culturalism.html (accessed 9 January 2015).

Huntington, Samuel. *The Clash of Civilizations and the Remaking of the World Order* (New York: Simon & Schuster, 1996).

Irigaray, Luce, and Michael Marder. "Is 'Democracy' Nothing More Than a Slogan Now?," *The New Statesman* (2014) (accessed 28 November 2014).

Isin, Engin F. "Citizenship after Orientalism: Ottoman Citizenship," in *Challenges to Citizenship in a Globalizing World: European Questions and Turkish Experiences*, eds. F. Keyman and A. Icduygu (London: Routledge, 2005).

Isin, Engin F. "Citizenship after Orientalism: An Unfinished Project," *Citizenship Studies* 16, 5-6 (2012): 563–72.

Kureishi, Hanif. "The Migrant Has No Face, Status or Story," *The Guardian* (2014) http://www.theguardian.com/books/2014/may/30/hanif-kureishi-migrant-immigration-1 (accessed 30 May 2014).

Kymlicka, Will. "Multicultural States and Intercultural Citizens," *Theory and Research in Education* 1, 2 (2003): 147–69.

Lentin, Alana, and Gavin Titley. *The Crisis of Multiculturalism: Racism in a Neoliberal Age* (London: Zed Books, 2011).

Lentin, Alana. "Post-Race, Post Politics: The Paradoxical Rise of Culture after Multiculturalism," *Ethnic and Racial Studies* (2012): 1–19.

Livingstone, Ken. "Text of Statement by Mayor Ken Livingstone," *Financial Times* 2005 http://www.ft.com/cms/s/2/dcdfe116-ef08-11d9-8b10-00000e2511c8.html - axzz3FDu9JDAb (accessed 3 October 2014).

Lowles, Nick, and Anthony Painter. "Fear and Hope: The New Politics of Identity," *Searchlight Educational Trust* (2012) http://www.fearandhope.org.uk/project-report/themes (accessed 13 July 2013).

Mamdani, Mahmood. *Good Muslim, Bad Muslim: America, the Cold War, and the Roots of Terror* (New York: Pantheon, 2004).

Manzoor, Sarfraz. "The New Faces of Ukip," *The Times* (2013) http://www.thetimes.co.uk/tto/magazine/article3938636.ece (accessed 3 January 2014).

McGhee, Derek. "Getting 'Host' Communities on Board: Finding the Balance between 'Managed Migration' and 'Managed Settlement' in Community Cohesion Strategies," *Journal of Ethnic & Migration Studies* 32, 1 (2006): 111–27.

McGhee, Derek. "The Paths to Citizenship: A Critical Examination of Immigration Policy in Britain since 2001," *Patterns of Prejudice* 43, 1 (2009): 41–64.

Meer, Nasar, and Tariq Modood, "How Does Interculturalism Contrast with Multiculturalism?," *Journal of Intercultural Studies* 33, 2 (2012): 175–96.

Modood, Tariq. "Difference, 'Multi' and Equality," in *The Plural States of Recognition*, ed. Michel Seymour (Basingstoke: Palgrave Macmillan, 2010).

Murray, Andrew, and Lindsey German. *Stop the War: The Story of Britain's Biggest Mass Movement* (London: Bookmark Publications, 2005).

Neal, Sarah. "The Scarman Report, the Macpherson Report and the Media: How Newspapers Respond to Race-Centred Social Policy Interventions," *Journal of Social Policy* 32, 01 (2003): 55–74.

Neal, Sarah, Katie Bennett, Allan Cochrane, and Giles Mohan. "Living Multiculture: Understanding the New Spatial and Social Relations of Ethnicity and Multiculture in England," *Environment and Planning C: Government and Policy* 31, 2 (2013): 308–23.

O'Neill, John. "The Disciplinary Society: From Weber to Foucault," *The British Journal of Sociology* 37, 1 (1986): 42–60.

Parekh, Bhikhu. "Integrating Minorities," in *Race Relations: A Developing Agenda*, eds. Tessa Blackstone, Bhikhu Parekh, and Peter Sanders (London: Routledge, 1998).

Parekh, Bhikhu. "Muslim Alienation and the Obligations of Citizenship," *The Times*, 7 July 2006.

Parekh, Bhikhu. *Rethinking Multiculturalism: Cultural Diversity and Political Theory* (Basingstoke: Palgrave Macmillan, 2000).

Pettigrew, Thomas F. "Intergroup Contact Theory," *Annual Review of Psychology* 49, February (1998): 65–85.

Phillips, Richard. "Standing Together: The Muslim Association of Britain and the Anti-War Movement," *Race & Class* 50, 2 (2008): 101–13.

Pickerill, Jenny, and Frank Webster, "The Anti-War/Peace Movement in Britain and the Conditions of Information War," *International Relations* 20, 4 (2006).

Pieterse, Jan N. *Ethnicities and Global Multiculture: Pants for an Octopus* (Plymouth: Rowman & Littlefield, 2007).

Saeed, Amir. "Media, Racism and Islamophobia: The Representation of Islam and Muslims in the Media," *Sociology Compass* 1, 2 (2007): 443–62.

Saggar, Shamit. "Immigration and the Politics of Public Opinion," *The Political Quarterly* 74 (2003): 178–94.

Said, Edward W. "The Clash of Ignorance," *The Nation* (2001) http://www.unipa.it/~michele.cometa/Said_The Clash of Ignorance.pdf (accessed 7 August 2013).

Said, Edward W. *Orientalism* (London: Penguin, 2003[1978]).

Singh, Amit. "Why Are Ethnic Minorities Supporting Ukip?" *Independent* (2014) http://www.independent.co.uk/voices/why-are-ethnic-minorities-supporting-ukip-9347369.html (accessed 19 May 2014).

Sobolewska, Maria. "Religious Extremism in Britain and British Muslims: Threatened Citizenship and the Role of Religion," in *The New Extremism in the 21st Century*, eds. Roger Eatwell and Matthew J. Goodwin (New York: Routledge, 2010).

Stoler, Ann. *Race and the Education of Desire* (London: Duke University Press, 1995).

StWC. "Tyneside Stop the War Coalition Reads the Names of the Dead at Newcastle Monument," *North East Stop the War* (2009) http://www.northeaststopwar.org.uk/archive/manch08/100death.htm (accessed 2 August 2013].

Trott, Laurie "Lessons to Learn," *Channel 4* (2012) http://www.channel4.com/programmes/make-bradford-british/articles/lessons-to-learn (accessed 2 March 2012).

Trudeau, Pierre E. "Announcement of Implementation of Policy of Multiculturalism within Bilingual Framework," *Heritage Community Foundation* (1971) http://www.abheritage.ca/albertans/speeches/trudeau.html (accessed 25 June 2011).

Turner, Bryan S. *Orientalism, Postmodernism & Globalism* (London: Routledge, 1994).

Uberoi, Varun, and Tariq Modood, "Who Doesn't Feel British? Divisions over Muslims," *Parliamentary Affairs* 63, 2 (2010): 302–20.

Winter, Elke. *Us, Them, and Others* (Toronto: University of Toronto Press, 2011).

Wintour, Patrick, and Nicholas Watt. "Ukip Wins European Elections with Ease to Set Off Political Earthquake," *The Guardian* (2014) http://www.theguardian.com/politics/2014/may/26/ukip-european-elections-political-earthquake (accessed 2 January 2015).

Younge, Gary. "The Multiculturalism the European Right Fears So Much Is a Fiction – It Never Existed," *The Guardian* (2011) http://www.guardian.co.uk/commentisfree/2011/mar/14/multiculturalism-fears-fiction-europe-state (accessed 14 March 2011).

Žižek, Slavoj. "Tolerance as an Ideological Category," *Critical Inquiry* 34 Summer (2008): 660–82.

9

Law, Orientalism, and Citizenship: British-Muslim Family Law

Lisa Pilgram

Abstract

A new field of British-Muslim family law is arguably evolving from the practices of Muslims in the UK who creatively bring about effective – but by no means uncontested – solutions to everyday problems of arranging family matters (across Muslim and English law). This requires us to abandon certain conventional ideas about law, orientalism, and citizenship. The present chapter contributes to current debates on multiculturalism, secularism, and Islam in Europe by first challenging an orientalized image of Sharia law in past and present European encounters. It then questions legal orientalism for its inability to conceptualize law outside formal legal norms and processes. It also highlights the crucial role of practices of the legal subject in the creative construction of legal fields. The chapter essentially asks questions about the implications of British-Muslim family law for how we think about citizenship.

Introduction

The growing presence of Muslims has become a central issue in many European countries including the UK. Debates about multiculturalism, identity, secularism, and societal values more often than not raise the question of Islam or, rather, how Islam and Muslim law are being practised today.

While cultural and religious pluralism may be fairly easily applicable in the majority of government policies, Muslim law – or Sharia law – is now subjected to public scrutiny and media attention with legal pluralism appearing as a threat to modern European societies and their values. While there may not even be a concerted claim by Muslim people to formalize such legal pluralism and to apply Muslim law in the UK, the so-called 'Sharia debate' gains traction by fears of foreign, alien, and archaic laws putting an end to the rule of law.

This particular discourse is well expressed by Tariq Ramadan, who writes:

There is a fundamental relationship between "values" and "laws" on the one hand, and "culture" and "diversity" on the other... Can Europe remain consistent with its own values (democracy, equality, justice, respect, etc) and at the same time tolerate and accommodate new citizens from different backgrounds and religions?

This argument reveals many of the ambiguities of political theory in reconciling pluralism with citizenship. The notion that values of European citizenship – such as democracy, equality, justice – are fixed contradicts the prerequisites of genuine pluralism, which would consider them as fluid, just as we accept culture as a fluid concept. It is important to recognize that 'law' is a fluid institution and, more than ever, is undergoing big changes, notably in relation to gender and sexuality through equality legislation which relates to family law. Moreover, why are these values singled out as Europe's 'own'? What monopoly does Europe have on democracy, equality, and justice? Finally, why does Ramadan invoke the image of law as being non-negotiable while he regards culture as negotiable?

The main issue here is that much of the Sharia debate in the UK poses the problem as a question of incompatibility between 'two different forms of life'.[1] But if we conceive of the two, Muslim law and English law, as fixed and fundamentally different from each other, there can of course never be compatibility or interrelation.

In this chapter, rather than remaining at the level of abstract political theory and its ideas of law, I engage with Muslim legal practice in the UK as an emerging socio-legal field. Inspired by Pierre Bourdieu's approach, I aim to illustrate how practices of law can inform political theory of citizenship. The importance of my focus on legal practices of Muslims in the UK is borne out of their everyday and widespread character.

Today, people marry, divorce, bring up children, and arrange their inheritance drawing on their understanding of a variety of norms, such as Muslim law, English family law, customary law, and so on. Sharia Councils, the Muslim Arbitration Tribunal, as well as private law firms offer Islamic legal services which work within, and to a certain extent combine, Muslim and English law. These services may include the issuing of Muslim divorce certificates, the drafting of marriage contracts, or the drawing up of wills that satisfy Muslim as well as English legal requirements.

Similarly, in courts in England, judges engage with some Muslim legal norms such as those covering prenuptial agreements[2] or divorce cases involving Muslim parties.[3] Statutory law, too, responds in various ways to the diversification of the citizenry in Britain by amending statutes, granting exceptions or refusing to do so. Since 1753, marriage concessions have been made to Jews and Quakers who remain exempt from certain rules regarding marriage solemnization under the 1949 Marriage Act. Finally, although not in the area of family law, the Finance Act 2003 opened the way for Islamic finance.[4]

Drawing from fieldwork focusing on everyday practices, the chapter argues that a new field of British-Muslim family law is emerging as a field of law which solves everyday problems of Muslims living in the UK.[5] From this perspective, the question becomes one of interaction between Muslim law and English law and evolving forms of hybrid legal subjectivity. This interaction may also be transnational in certain instances as many sources of Muslim law are from outside the UK. Having recognized British-Muslim legal practice as an emerging field of law, this chapter seeks to challenge and transform certain conventional ideas about law, orientalism (or more precisely orientalized legal spaces), and citizenship.

First, it challenges an orientalized image of Muslim law, or Sharia, in past and present European encounters. It then questions legal centralism for its inability to conceptualize law outside formal legal norms and processes. It also highlights the crucial role of practices of the legal subject in the creative construction of legal fields. The chapter essentially asks questions about the implications of British-Muslim family law for how we think about citizenship.

The Field of British-Muslim Family Law

The chapter argues that practices of British Muslims in arranging their private lives may have come to establish a legal field in its own right. The field of 'British-Muslim family law' involves a range of actors, practices, discourses, and institutions including Sharia Councils, the Muslim Arbitration Tribunal, private law firms offering Islamic legal services, English courts dealing with questions of Muslim law, English statutory law, judges, experts, solicitors, clients, claimants, and many more. The field evolves around a set of socio-legal practices that are developing in response to time- and place-specific issues affecting Muslims in Britain today. It is a hybrid field of law constituted through an interplay between rules and regulations provided by the British legal system, norms of Muslim law coming from authorities in and outside the UK, ideas of a global Muslim Ummah, family and community structures, and so on.

When it came to defining such a field, I was faced with the choice between different terms such as 'Islamic law', 'Muslim law', or 'Sharia law', which are all used apparently interchangeably in the literature without any clear explanation.[6] Naming a field is a normative act and gives an insight into the politics underlying a particular research study. For the purposes of the present case, the term 'Muslim law' is preferable to 'Islamic' or 'Sharia law' because it corresponds better to an understanding of law as a social practice. It encourages the reader – and the writer – to put the emphasis on the individuals (both Muslim and non-Muslim people) involved in creating the legal field of British-Muslim family law. However, in the present chapter, I also at times intentionally use the term 'Islamic law' to signal a specific authority and corpus of rules that is being invoked as 'Islamic law' by the people practising in the field.[7]

The term 'Sharia law', on the other hand, is used in this chapter only in very limited instances when describing the current 'Sharia debate'. This is because the term 'Sharia law' carries a particular connotation in certain media contexts – of being opposed, alien, and a 'threat' to Western laws – that is important to consider in my analysis of legal orientalism. Using these three different terms allows me to distinguish between the different concepts discussed below in more detail. This distinction, however, serves analytical purposes only. For the individuals involved in the legal field, this distinction is not experienced as such in the sense that it is not necessarily relevant, or meaningful, in existing discourse and legal practice.

As an analytical category, the term 'Muslim law' serves different discursive purposes than the term 'Islamic law' as it focuses on the people practising, or enacting, the law and therefore puts the emphasis on a continuously developing but clearly distinguishable set of practices of Muslims living in the UK. It is law made through practice by Muslim and non-Muslim people implicated in the field of British-Muslim family law. On the other hand, the term 'Islamic law' serves in this article as a referent to the established body of law and jurisprudence which encompasses a whole set of normative sources of different character ranging from the Qur'an and *sunna* (prophetic traditions) to *fiqh* (Islamic jurisprudence). In the field of British-Muslim family law it is an important discursive tool, used by practitioners as well as clients, which functions as a legal postulate, representing a claim to authority. For example, when legal professionals call their portfolios 'Islamic legal services' rather than 'Muslim legal services', arguably they are making a claim to legal authority. The phrase 'Islamic legal services' emanates authority, expertise, certainty, and legitimacy because it invokes in the minds of its users an 'Islamic' origin, sanctioned by appeal to sacred texts, rather than a 'Muslim' origin which may carry with it the connotation of subjective law made by (everyday) Muslim people.

The present chapter focuses specifically, but not exclusively, on the area of Islamic legal services offered by solicitors registered in England and Wales. These services may include the issuing of Muslim divorce certificates, the drafting of marriage contracts, or the drawing up of wills that satisfy Muslim as well as English legal requirements. To cater for their clients' demands, solicitors provide hybridized strategies and technologies by offering both English family law and Islamic legal services, and to some extent a combination of them.

Speaking about Islamic divorce certificates, one solicitor said,

> as solicitors, what we can offer them is a way in which they can enjoy and fulfill their Muslim obligation within English law as well, if possible... It's almost as if, if we do it, it makes it legal, not technically legal because it's

not binding in law ... The reason they come to us is that we are Muslim and also that we are solicitors.[8]

One of the main activities in the field is the drafting of Islamic wills. These particular wills are English legal documents with the distribution element of the estate being Islamic.[9] An interesting case concerned a client who had converted to Islam but whose family did not and were therefore non-Muslim. To him, drafting an Islamic will was of personal importance. However, the solicitor informed him that in Islamic law as a Muslim he could not make bequests to non-Muslims that exceed one-third of his estate. Undeterred, the client asked for the flat he was sharing with his mother to be declared as a gift to her and also left a gift of £50,000 to his cat. He was told that this was not Islamic, but he requested this clause to be included regardless. The solicitor followed his request and explained:

> as some people are very strict, they'd only do fully Islamic wills .... As for me, I feel I advised them that this is the Islamic issue and then, even though they know it's wrong, they still want to go ahead with it, then that's their responsibility. It's not for me to judge if really what you're doing is Islamic or not. Because I think they are old enough to make their own decisions.[10]

The solicitor therefore drafted an Islamic will, fully valid under UK law, stating that a Muslim is making a bequest to a non-Muslim exceeding a third of his estate. This is hard to imagine under a jurisdiction applying Islamic law. The very fact that British-Muslim family law is a hybrid allows for this. Under English law, wills can be drafted fairly flexibly, enabling the distribution element to be Islamic. An Islamic will which does not entirely follow the Islamic distribution element would not be valid in a jurisdiction based on Islamic legal principles but can still be enforceable under English law. This gives considerable room to navigate personal needs between various legal demands when drafting a person's will. The British-Muslim legal field is fluid enough to accommodate legal subjects' requirements shaped by Muslim and English law.

It is important to note that specific gender dynamics underlie and frame the emergence of this legal field and its practices. Dependents or relatives are able to dispute provisions of a will before English courts but, so far, Islamic wills have not been challenged. However, the solicitor I interviewed concedes that there is a possibility of a successful challenge because women receive a smaller part than men according to Islamic legal rules, which sanction that a daughter's share is half that of a son. The solicitor's statement shows the tension in this area:

> If challenged it would be interesting because this is unequal isn't it? The court would look at it as an individual will, not as an Islamic will, and

the daughter could argue it's not justified for her to get less. This would engage in Islamic law, or affect the ruling under Islamic law.

Another example of the gendered nature of British-Muslim family law appears in connection with divorce procedures. The fact that women, unlike men, cannot initiate unilateral divorce in Islamic law explains the growing importance of Sharia Councils in Britain, the vast majority of their users being women. These Councils host a board of religious authorities who have the power to dissolve marriages on the request of women and without the consent of their husbands. This prevents them from having to enter into potentially disadvantageous marriage settlements (khul' divorce) and from possibly being 'trapped' in an Islamic marriage.[11] While literature on Islamic law and women's rights often focuses exclusively on the static and subordinate (subject) position of women in Islamic legal rules, Samia Bano insists that by drawing on empirical data of Sharia Council users in Britain, we begin to see a more complex and nuanced image as we 'explore how multiple spaces in law, community and identity both empower and restrict women at different times and in different contexts'.[12]

The field of British-Muslim family law provides hybridized strategies and technologies to cater for the demands of legal subjects. The fact that Muslim solicitors in particular gain added value (income as well as recognition as experts) by offering both English family law and Islamic legal services can be seen as a reflection of how British Muslims have to navigate between different legal fields, gendered spaces, and subjectivities when arranging their private lives. This is now developing into a viable service market in Britain, providing a living for Muslim solicitors and other professionals in the field.

In this emerging field of British-Muslim family law, people are buying and selling legal services online and through solicitors' offices. They seek advice from specialist professionals who are able to offer consultation in both English and Muslim law. On the one hand, due to the changing make-up of Britain's citizenry, there is increased demand for Islamic wills, Islamic marriage and divorce certificates, and other legal documents such as agreements on the upbringing of children in mixed marriages. On the other hand, those working in the legal field as professionals drive forward a process of 'legalization' of British-Muslim practices as they develop ever more market solutions to the everyday problems of citizens.

Having thus recognized British-Muslim legal practice as an emerging field of law, I now want to discuss how this challenges an orientalized image of Sharia law.

Legal Orientalism

What is at stake in recognizing and documenting British-Muslim legal practice as an emerging field? It is a challenge to an orientalized image of Muslim law, or Sharia law, which aims to show how orientalism operates specifically in the area of law as 'legal orientalism'. Teemu Ruskola defines 'legal orientalism' as 'the ways in which "the Orient" – as well as "the West" – have been produced through the rhetoric of law'.[13] He traces the history of engagement with Muslim law both in a contemporary setting and a colonial context and provides crucial insights into the extent to which an orientalist perspective, or prejudice, has an impact upon existing discussions, often dubbed the Sharia debate, around Muslim law in Britain.

In current debates, claims for the accommodation of, or even serious engagement with, Muslim law are often perceived as conservative at best, if not non-progressive or anti-citizenship. Therefore, they have the potential to spark fierce public debate. Just how charged the image of Muslim law in the UK has become is illustrated by the reactions to the speech by Rowan Williams, then Archbishop of Canterbury, on 'Civil and Religious Law in England' on 7 February 2008. It attracted considerable public and academic attention. To recall, Williams began his lecture reflecting popular concerns and said 'the title of this series of lectures signals the existence of what is very widely felt to be a growing challenge in our society – that is, the presence of communities which, while no less "law-abiding" than the rest of the population, relate to something other than the British legal system alone'.[14] Williams was clearly aware that any discussion of this issue would be linked to difficult and politically charged questions that go beyond personal matters. He continued 'among the manifold anxieties that haunt the discussion of the place of Muslims in British society, one of the strongest, reinforced from time to time by the sensational reporting of opinion polls, is that Muslim communities in this country seek the freedom to live under Sharia law'.[15]

This anxiety is linked to an idea of Muslim law, or Sharia law, as a threat or the ultimate 'other' to Western civilization. We often come across a portrayal of Muslim law as the 'other' in an essentialist understanding of both 'Sharia' and 'the West'.[16] The idea of Western law as rational, secular, and fair is produced and upheld especially in contrast to Muslim law, which is seen as less able to provide justice in a modern liberal democracy. In this juxtaposition, Muslim law comes to inhabit the position of the oriental other, which is fundamentally different from its occidental counterpart.

Moreover, issues of gender and sexuality play an important part in the current discourse around Muslim family law. The idea that Muslim law is non-progressive and anti-citizenship is also linked to an image of Muslim law as anti-gender-equality.[17] Bano emphasizes the importance of gender and orientalism in this discourse: 'Western women are often presented as "enlightened" and the bearers of liberal legal ideals such as equality and non-discrimination while Muslim women are presented as the "other", victims of cultural and religious practices in violation of their human rights'.[18]

At this point it is necessary to note that family law is a very specific, sensitive, and gendered domain of law. It plays a different role to, for example, finance law, where Islamic finance was introduced in 2003 without any controversy comparable to questions regarding family issues.[19] The stakes are high when it comes to amending family law in (multicultural) societies because it deals with the intimate relations of the individuals involved, which are also closely linked to questions of personal and national identity. The question of according to which conventions we marry, divorce, bring up children, and deal with inheritance is, therefore, more than a simple matter of applying the correct rules. Family law is arguably a mirror of present social values and mores while at the same time influencing and shaping gender roles in a normative way. It is crucial to the normalization of dominant gender and sexual relations and conducts. The discourse around Muslim family law therefore becomes a playing field within which collective identity, self-image, and normalized gender roles are being negotiated by subjects and institutions.

How then does orientalism function in the debate around Muslim family law? As with other social fields, the ontological categories of orient and occident structure our (dominant) understanding of law too. Legal orientalism represents a perspective, or ideology, in which the ideal of modern state law is founded on universal and secular principles and is superior to other forms of normativity. Especially in the area of family law, however, it is apparent that this imagined legal neutrality is questionable in practice. As Ann Laquer Estin states,

> in the liberal democracies of Europe and North America, the legal system is understood to be based on universal and secular principles, affording the same rights to all citizens and rejecting any formal differentiation on cultural or religious grounds. The rules of official family law are far from neutral, however, and define a culturally specific set of minimum requirements and expectations for family formation and behavior.[20]

Whether or not it is explicit in practice, legal orientalism not only imagines but also produces a divide between the occident and the orient along the lines of law. On the one hand, Western civilization is characterized by its ability to bring into being rational secular law as independent from culture, religion, family, and so on, and on the other hand, non-Western civilizations lack the indigenous ability to develop 'law' proper – implicitly equated with state law.

The effect of orientalism is that Muslim (family) law becomes understood as inferior to Western law, relegated to private matters, either too rigid or too fluid and unpredictable to dispense justice effectively. Looked at through an orientalist lens, Muslim law therefore always remains inferior to occidental law: on the one hand, it is too rigid, as it is based on religious principles that cannot be challenged by the individual and are therefore anti-democratic. On the other hand, it is too unpredictable, as it is not based on a secular positivist notion of law, something Weber called *Kadijustiz*.[21] As Jedidiah Kroncke puts it, the 'continued flexibility of Islamic legal Orientalism [simultaneously serves] different, yet equally derogatory representational needs'.[22]

While legal orientalism was certainly intensified in the early years of the twenty-first century, there is also relevance to the history of colonialism and its relation to Muslim law for contemporary debates. A look at the history of British engagement with oriental laws exemplifies how legal orientalism has not only structured a particular European gaze on, but also created Muslim law as a category in (European) legal discourse and scholarship.[23]

The way Muslim law was presented to the readers of colonial textbooks on law, and what was omitted, tells a story of how a certain orientalist viewpoint determined the understanding and construction of a conception of Muslim law in legal scholarship which is still ongoing in today's discourse. In many different editions, standard works on Muslim law, on the one hand, omitted rules regarding worship and ritual, as they were not within the established framework of what 'law' is and therefore were omitted for the purpose of a 'legal textbook'. On the other hand, public law aspects were excluded probably because they were deemed not appropriate in a colonial context where Muslim law could only exist as private law anyway since the main legal framework was colonial law.

In a way, these early works drew the boundaries of what was to become Muslim law in Western scholarship. In 1964, Joseph Schacht, one of the most widely read scholars in the area, wrote *An Introduction to Islamic Law* which followed closely the approach of British colonial textbooks in stating that 'worship and ritual, and other purely religious duties as well as constitutional, administrative and international law have been omitted'.[24]

For example, by not considering its public law elements as relevant to the study of Muslim law in Britain, we designate the position of Muslim law as one pertaining solely to governance of minority private law with no mandate to govern relations between individuals and the government. This is not to say that Muslim legal norms may be a preferred framework to govern public affairs, but I use this example to question the assumption that contemporary socio-legal scholarship of Muslim law has rid itself entirely of its colonial antecedents. But this is neither to say that we should discard any attempt to engage in Muslim law as a neo-colonial project nor that we need to recover 'original' Muslim law to give a 'genuine' representation of it (as all legal fields are social representations of some sort).

The scholarly and political task at hand is to challenge an orientalized image of Sharia law in past and present European encounters. To do so, we need to move to an empirically grounded socio-legal perspective on Muslim law. Bourdieu developed the idea of the legal field in which practices of law take centre stage and which conceptualizes law as an integral part of the social field. Adopting such an empirical perspective carries with it the potential to articulate novel conceptions of 'law' by understanding the experiences of people who practise it. Also, by offering a different understanding of British-Muslim law as hybrid practice drawing (amongst other sources) on Muslim as well as English law, we counter the orientalist paradigm of insurmountable incompatibility between these two (legal) worlds.

I will now discuss legal pluralism and specifically why I think that Bourdieu's theory of the legal field allows me to challenge certain ideas about British-Muslim family law by analysing it as an evolving field of practice with a corresponding market of legal services. Arguing that Bourdieu does not pay enough attention to 'subjectivity', I elaborate on this concept to demonstrate how this field produces hybrid forms of legal subjectivity that – this chapter concludes – have implications for how we think about citizenship.

Plural Legal Fields

The emergence of British-Muslim legal practice, which relates to something other than English law alone, raises a new set of challenging questions about law outside formal legal norms and processes. How do we think of law in a plural social context? Is a situation possible in which plural legal fields operate side by side and function together? To what extent do legal fields operate alongside the state? And (how) is law different from culture, tradition, religion, or other forms of normativity?

This chapter combines Bourdieu's work on the legal field with aspects of legal pluralism scholarship to challenge the normative stance of legal positivists who, while conceding that there are lesser *norms* systems other than law, maintain there cannot be *law* outside sovereign state law.

An interview with a solicitor this chapter draws on indicates that it is indeed important to investigate the *legal* characteristics of practices among British Muslim communities because they are understood by its users as a form of law, and not solely as culture, tradition, or religion. Combining legal pluralism scholarship with Bourdieu's theory of the field enables us to uncover and examine precisely this *legal* character of these practices.

When investigating law in a plural context, legal pluralism scholarship assists us, on the one hand, to understand that normativity is not limited to (formal) state law and its standard textbooks or the judicial reasoning of judges in courts.[25] Bourdieu's work, on the other hand, helps to make a clear distinction between the legal field and other normative spheres of life, such as religion.[26] Of course, religion can be equally influential, or normative, on how people conduct themselves. However, if we frame the question of Muslim family law in the UK as purely one of religion, there would be no challenge to the law-making monopoly of the sovereign state;[27] and I argue that this is precisely one of the most powerful and important contributions a study of contemporary British-Muslim law has to make in challenging and transforming conventional ideas about law.

John Griffiths (1986 [1981]) in 'What is legal pluralism?' describes it as 'the presence in a social field of *more than one legal order*'.[28] Griffiths' contribution challenged the dominance of what he calls 'legal centralism', an ideology which 'is shown to reflect the moral and political claims of the modern nation state'.[29] Legal centralism corresponds to the idea of an ideology of superiority of secular state law. Griffiths provides a more detailed definition of legal centralism in which

> law is and should be the law of the state, uniform for all persons, exclusive of all other law, and administered by a single set of state intuitions. To the extent that other, lesser normative orderings, such as the church, the family, the voluntary association and the economic organization exist, they ought to be and in fact are hierarchically subordinate to the law and institutions of the state.[30]

Prakash Shah (2008) offers a definition of legal pluralism as

> a factual state of affairs whereby *different norm systems* are coming into interplay with each other with complex results. Methodologically, this requires attention to be focused not only upon how courts and other official agencies navigate and negotiate inter-culturally within this hybridity, but also upon the situation "on the ground".[31]

Legal pluralist scholarship appears to implicitly conflate the concepts of law and other normative orderings. This makes it more complicated to highlight the legal characteristics of practices within, for example, what is conventionally understood as the church or the family and so on – or in our case British-Muslim practices.

Here Bourdieu's theory of the legal field sheds light on the legal aspects of current practice. However, we should be careful not to concern ourselves too much with identifying the same traits mirroring established forms of state-administered law within the British-Muslim legal field. This is not the purpose of the present analysis, as such a venture would inevitably fail. By scanning the British-Muslim legal field for exactly the same characteristics of legal centralist concepts of (necessarily state) law, we predetermine a negative result. We also foreclose any potentially interesting insights into alternative non-state legal practices. As Margaret Davies argues, 'traditional legal theory has traditionally marginalized types of law, which do not have an institutional appearance comparable to Western law, labelling such laws as defective, primitive or merely cultural practices'.[32]

Bourdieu details the general characteristics that, according to him, make up the legal field and distinguish it from other social fields. He describes the legal field as characterized by legal formalization, neutralization and universalization, and professionalization. I will briefly explain these below in respect to British-Muslim family law.

Broadly, a legal field consolidates a clearly recognizable set of practices and discourses as well as corpuses of text. It is characterized by legal formalization, which serves to establish the legal field and to distinguish itself from other fields of normativity. The legal field, however, remains intimately linked with material and 'symbolic power' existing in the social world. An example is the establishment of the Muslim Arbitration Tribunal (MAT) working within the English legal framework under the Arbitration Act 1996 and with predefined procedural rules accessible on their website and hierarchical structures in settling disputes.

Legal language is distinguishable because it is based on neutralization and universalization. Among other features, it uses passive sentences, impersonal style, and is formulated as impartial and objective. For example, Muslim solicitors combine the standard heading for English wills with a standard Islamic heading to create a template for Islamic wills starting with 'Bishmillah ir-Rahman ir-Rahim Last Will and Testament'. The legal field is also characterized by professionalization, which produces a division between professionals and lay people. Many professionals working in the field of British-Muslim family law hold degrees in Islamic as well as English law, in some cases from institutions outside the UK.

Crucially, the development of a legal field is also inseparable from the constitution of a corresponding market in and through which services are exchanged and different forms of capital are accumulated. Professionals create the need for their own services by redefining problems expressed in ordinary language as legal problems. This then leads to a 'legalization' of certain dimensions of (everyday) practice, which become part of the legal field.

Applying Bourdieu's analysis to Muslim law in Britain allows us to see that this field also has a corresponding market of professional legal services. Examples I gave earlier indicate that this service market and the field associated with it have their own logic – the logic of practice implicated in the interaction of Muslim and English family law. In fact, the logic of the British-Muslim legal field is such that its hybrid normativity is sensible (though by no means without contestation or conflict) to people who are either providing or buying services available on its market.

Legal pluralism and Bourdieu's work on the legal field question more conventional legal methodology that privileges the content of formal legal texts and judgements rendered in courts. Moving our focus to the 'situation on the ground' requires us to ask what happens to the people involved in the legal process and to the figures of subjects that are implicated in its constitution?

From a hypothetical point of view, there is no legal field without its subjects. There is no law without its subjects understanding it, following it, breaking it, or changing it – thus creating it. Conversely, there are no sub-jects without a field summoning and addressing them as subjects. It is dif-ficult to imagine law as a social construct existing without a social field.[33] Law constructs and constitutes the individual's legal subjectivity, yet it exists only as represented in the thoughts, beliefs, and actions of individuals. In this regard, Bourdieu's theory is limited to a certain extent when investi-gating the subjects and subject positions of the legal field because it offers a more structuralist approach rather than foregrounding the legal subject's creative capacity in constructing the legal field.

When we make that move, an empirically grounded socio-legal research raises the following questions: What are the characteristics of the legal sub-ject implicated in the British-Muslim legal field? How is the use of legal ser-vices producing and sustaining British-Muslim legal subjectivity? How do people actually take up or challenge subject positions and so construct the field in creative ways?

To investigate how people see themselves and navigate through the legal processes which form part of their daily life, we need to transform the theory of the legal field to include the concept of legal subjectivity in our analysis of Muslim family law in the UK.

Legal Subjectivity

'Concern with the legal subject is ... a concern with how our processes of understanding affect and help constitute the cultural objects [such as the law] we comprehend.'[34] Because the law and the legal subject are social con-structs, it is important to consider how social construction leads to the legal subject's understanding of the legal system. The aim is not to exclude the object of legal understanding, that is substantial law, but 'to see the subject and object of legal interpretation as equal partners in the constitution of the legal system'.[35]

A focus on legal subjectivity is an inquiry into different forms of legal understanding, the contributions that individuals make to these forms of understanding, and the effects that legal understanding has on them, which in turn will determine how they comprehend the law. Experience with the law, or engagement with the law, is an activity of subjectification; it is some-thing individuals do with and to the law, and through this activity, they themselves are changed.[36] Anthony Allott sees law in a similar manner, call-ing it a 'communications system'.[37]

The concept of legal subjectivity is, however, not to be equated simply with individuality and a person's individual beliefs, background, and so on. It is true that every individual brings something distinctive to how each experiences the social world. However, many individuals of a simi-lar context will share to a great extent their beliefs, attitudes, or forms of understanding.

Thus, 'subjectivity' involves an individual experience that results in part from internalization of cultural norms and shared frameworks of understanding. These cultural norms and frameworks are not simply superimposed on an individual's pre-existing beliefs; they constitute her and form part of what makes her an individual. Subjectivity is what the individual subject brings to the act of understanding; it is what allows her to construct the object of her interpretation so that she can understand it. Yet what she brings may be quite similar to what others bring because of a shared ideology.[38]

The legal subject is embodied in a larger legal and political culture or framework – although not necessarily limited to national boundaries – which shapes the actual forms of the subject's understanding and is in turn shaped by it. The concept of subjectivity allows us to inquire how people engage in creating the law and incorporates a sense of agency of the legal subject. It inquires about how people position themselves, drawing on various sources of normativity.

The interaction particularly with the field of British-Muslim family law contributes to the emergence of a hybrid British-Muslim subjectivity. Legal practice, sociocultural context, and individual experiences with the legal field produce and sustain legal subjectivity. It is British-Muslim family law's association with legal formalities, processes, documents, language, authorities, and so on that makes the citizen's interactions with these services productive sites of legal subjectivity. In a dual process, British-Muslim family law is itself constituted by the subjects implicated in it.

Practices of British-Muslim family law engage a new subjectivity of obligation to follow the laws set out therein. People are engaging in activities and conversations, seeking advice, and buying and selling services. This constitutes legal subjects who, on the one hand, are entitled to receive, indeed expect to receive these services and, on the other hand, now feel obligated and 'responsibilized' by the judgements that they render or the conditions created by the contracts solicitors draw up.

A brief note on 'responsibilization' of citizens is necessary at this point. Following Foucault, Graham Burchell introduces the concept 'responsibilization' to capture how citizens are encouraged to freely and rationally conduct themselves in suggested ways.[39] It is closely related to what Nikolas Rose describes as neoliberal governmentality or governance at a distance.[40] The subject of government is provided with new obligations and duties. Rather than being governed directly, people are appealed to as free and independent citizens to take responsibility for their own acts and choices.

Employing the concept of the responsibilized citizen in the field of British-Muslim family law draws our attention to two important issues. First, the (call to) practice of Muslim law is often perceived as 'traditionalist', as a longing for premodern ways of living – possibly in an imagined, orientalized foreign land. Contrary to this idea of British-Muslim family law being anti-modernity, understanding it in connection with the question of governmentality shows that the emergence of this field is in fact a modern phenomenon embedded in the context of contemporary neoliberal Britain with its particular struggles and challenges to navigate around. Here, rather than interpreting the emergence of British-Muslim family law as a result of Muslim rejection of British law, we ought to also see it as related to neoliberal privatization of family law issues, entrepreneurialism and the retreat of the state's responsibility for economic welfare of the population, and internationalization of services. In other words, the emergence of British-Muslim family law is less an expression of 'traditionalism' but is in fact related to modern developments of relations between states and citizens.

Second, while the idea of 'responsibilization' allows us to highlight the law-making capacity of the legal subject in the field of British-Muslim family law, we have to remain careful when theorizing about 'agency' and 'choice'. Their invocation in the debate around Muslim law plays a particular role in relation to gender. Muslim women are often portrayed as not able to choose, being either openly oppressed by men or being implicitly understood as more 'religious', with the effect of being more susceptible to making irrational judgements. They are juxtaposed against images of Western women who are complete and genuine agents, conscious of their situation and able to make rational decisions. The idea that Muslim women lack the ability to choose, Wendy Brown argues, ignores 'the extent to which all choice is conditioned by as well as imbricated with power, and the extent to which choice itself is an impoverished account of freedom, especially political freedom'.[41] Similarly, Lila Abu-Lughod adds that 'the fiction that any of us can "choose freely" is maintained by conjuring up those in distant lands who live in bondage with no rights, agency, or ability to refuse or escape sex or violence'.[42]

While choice is never free from power, the concept of legal subjectivity in British-Muslim family law leaves space to understand how individuals engage practically in creating the law. This is because it incorporates a sense of agency within this particular sociocultural context in which people draw on different normative sources to arrange their lives and legal family matters. The field of British-Muslim family law develops and flourishes precisely through an interaction of Muslim and English law (among other influences) and produces a hybrid legal subjectivity constituted in their interplay. This is the dual role British-Muslim family law plays in the formation of hybrid legal subjectivity: not only is the substance of the law hybrid but so too is the subject implicated in the legal field.

The term 'hybridity' serves three purposes. First, it challenges assumptions of mutually exclusive, static identities such as purely Muslim or British legal subjects and their incompatibility. It offers the insight that the subject of law – as imagined in its canon – cannot simply be transposed to the everyday and equated with individuals who faultlessly inhabit the spaces defined for them by law. Second, new forms of hybrid subjectivity are evolving through the legal process of British-Muslim family law and provide sense and meaning, rights and responsibilities for the individuals involved who navigate between different normative positions. What is more, they also feed back into the substance of the legal field they relate to. In this way, legal subjects are not merely law abiding but also makers of law, rights, and obligations. Third, hybrid subjectivity at work in British-Muslim family law, which draws on Muslim and English law as well as other sociocultural frameworks, potentially challenges existing subject positions in the legal field. An example of how subject positions can be contested is the case of the Muslim convert who broke out of the strict frame of his (legal) position as a Muslim by making a bequest to a non-Muslim exceeding one-third of his estate when he declared in his will that his flat would be a gift to his mother. This is particularly interesting in connection with deeply gendered subject positions operating in many instances of Muslim family law. There may be relatively fixed positioning of women subjects in certain Muslim legal practices, for example the fact that daughters receive half the share of sons in inheritance law. As described above, one of the solicitors providing Islamic legal services pointed out that this may well be challenged in the future.

To investigate how people see themselves and navigate through the legal processes which form part of their daily life, we need to transform the legal field's framework to highlight the crucial role of the legal subject in the creative construction of British-Muslim family law. By accommodating the legal subject in legal analysis, we are able to observe particular forms of subjectivity being constituted in the practices of British-Muslim family law. These hybrid, and often transnational, forms of subjectivity challenge orientalist ontologies of an incompatibility of 'British' and 'Muslim', 'occidental' and 'oriental' legal subjectivity. Moreover, these developments also have implications for how we think about citizenship (after orientalism).

How Should We Approach Political Theory of Citizenship?

To conclude, present understanding of the British-Muslim legal field and subjectivity may be influenced by a history of orientalism in the European encounter with Muslim law (legal orientalism), a difficulty to conceptualize law outside formal legal norms and processes governed by the state (plural legal fields), and a structuralist understanding of law which does not pay enough attention to the crucial role of the legal subject in the construction of legal fields (legal subjectivity).

A methodological perspective, which focuses on the practices that sustain the legal field, moves away from abstract ideas of law by asking questions about the interaction between Muslim law and English law as well as evolving forms of transnational, hybrid legal subjectivity. If citizens' interaction with law draws on transnational sources and is not limited to state law, several important questions arise in terms of our conception of citizenship as a settled legal institution. Is it possible to understand the development of British-Muslim family law as a new practice of citizenship that challenges (the effects of legal) orientalism? Can we empirically sustain the claim that citizenship is an exclusively national matter? To what extent is citizenship instituted in state law or in practice?

The emergence of British-Muslim family law challenges how we think about citizenship in the following ways. First, by establishing that hybrid subjectivity across and in between English and Muslim law (and various other sources) can thrive and provide a space within which individuals take up meaningful subject positions, we begin to unsettle orientalist presumptions of incompatibility between occidentalized and orientalized forms of political subjectivity. The former is seen as a superior form of civic citizenship which is juxtaposed to the latter forms of primitive belonging locked into relationships of religion, status, gender, and so on. The paradigm of ontological difference between the two appears less and less sustainable when we consider the emergence of a field of British-Muslim family law and its corresponding flourishing market. In this market, professionals successfully build careers and make a living out of exactly what has been conceived as impossible: the creative navigation between and merging of different legal orders.

Second, by practising British-Muslim family law, new subjectivities of citizens and of belonging are arguably being forged. Established conceptions of citizenship theorize membership in only one, clearly defined and often territorially limited, polity. These new forms of subjectivity, however, draw on more than one source for authority and reference, which may characterize them as hybrid, transnational, and as belonging to more than one polity.

Third, the fact that Muslim legal practices involve, to a large degree, authorities located outside, or only partly within, the established state legal framework indicates that citizenship, even in its legal aspect, cannot be the sole domain of the state. While Thomas Humphrey Marshall has highlighted the contribution of non-state actors to the constitution of 'social citizenship', there is no role for the legal subject in creatively constructing the legal field outside, or only partly within, state law and its formal processes in conventional ideas about citizenship. Western conceptions define the citizen as a member in the nation-state answerable to the rule of law governed by the state and its institutions. The proposition that in British-Muslim family law non-state legal authorities or actors enact themselves as citizens and contribute to the legal field, and even state law, thus questions the definition of the citizen as governed solely through the formal legal system of the nation-state.

The field of British-Muslim family law is rich in legal formalities, processes, documents, legalized language, authorities, and so on. This makes the citizens' interactions with these services particularly productive sites of legal subjectivity. Given that citizens have to navigate between different legal fields, it makes sense that British-Muslim family law produces a hybrid legal subjectivity constituted in the interplay of different norms and frameworks: rules and regulations provided by the British legal system, norms of Muslim law coming from authorities in and outside the UK, ideas of a global Muslim ummah, family and community structures, and so on. This is the dual role British-Muslim family law plays in the formation of hybrid legal subjectivity: not only is the substance of the law hybrid but so too is the subject implicated in the legal field.

Notes

1 Ahdar and Aroney, *Shari'a in the West*.
2 Radmacher v Granatino [2009] EWCA Civ 649, [2009] 2 FLR 1181.
3 Ali v Ali (2000, unreported) in Menski, "Immigration and multiculturalism in Britain: new issues in research and policy," 8.
4 Finance Act 2003, Family Law Act 1949.
5 The analysis in this article is limited to the law of England and Wales (in short 'English law'). However, I prefer to use the term 'British-Muslim family law' to describe the phenomenon I investigate as it is prevalent in England, Wales, Northern Ireland, and Scotland.
6 The fact that key literature in different areas of scholarship is using different terms to refer to Sharia indicates that scholars (consciously or unconsciously) indeed perceive them as different from each other, as two linked but still separate phenomena. Andrew March (2009), a political theorist, in his book *Islam and Liberal Citizenship* mentions without further comment in the introduction that 'the present study is ... a work of political theory that seeks to analyse Islamic (as opposed to Muslim) attitudes toward shared citizenship through a methodology of comparative political ethics'. Knut S. Vikør (2005), in legal scholarship, conducted his study on 'Islamic' legal theory and history. John L. Esposito (2001, xiv) writing on law and gender states, 'Muslim family law provides the primary example of Islamic reform in the twentieth century. Islamic law (the Shariah) constitutes the ideal blueprint for Muslim society'. Esposito does not explain the discrepancy between the use of Muslim family law and Islamic law. However, his writing seems to suggest that Islamic law, or advocating the introduction of Islamic law, is an important element in constructing an overarching Islamic identity, an abstract image or a blueprint of a subject position which a number of Muslims can see themselves as occupying. Baudoin Dupret (2007), a scholar of Islamic law, while not replacing Islamic law with a different term, critiques an essentialist conception of Islamic law and asserts that the question as to what Islamic law *is*, is flawed: 'There is no reason to assume that what people refer to as Islamic law is identical to, or different from, the set of technical provisions that form the idealized model of Islamic law. The question is not relevant, because it is totally disembodied from actual practices; and it fails to address the phenomenon itself, i.e., the practice of referring to Islamic law. For the question, "What is Islamic law?" we should substitute the question, "What do people do when referring to Islamic law?"' (p. 3).

7   It is important to note at this point that Islamic law encompasses various different schools of law with their own particular characteristics. Similarly, the Muslim population in Britain is made up of a variety of different Muslim communities based on ethnic or national origin, language, affiliation to a certain school, and so on.

8   Interview conducted with author on 30 January 2012.

9   Although qualified will writers can also draft wills, under English law only solicitors are allowed to give advice on tax planning too.

10 Interview conducted with author on 30 January 2012.

11 Khul' divorce requires the wife to give up her claim to her dowry.

12 Bano, *Muslim Women and Shari'ah Councils*, 5.

13 Ruskola, "Legal Orientalism," 193.

14 Williams, "Civil and religious law in England – a religious perspective," 262.

15 Ibid., 263.

16 See Barbero, "Orientalising citizenship: the legitimation of immigration regimes in the European Union."

17 See Sabsay, "The emergence of the other sexual citizen: orientalism and the modernisation of sexuality."

18 Bano, *Muslim Women and Shari'ah Councils*, 13–14.

19 The Finance Act 2003 opened the way for Islamic finance which is now on offer at many high street banks.

20 Laquer Estin, "Unofficial family law," 451–2.

21 See Weber, *Economy and Society: An Outline of Interpretive Sociology*.

22 Kroncke, "The Flexible Orientalism of Islamic Law," 42.

23 See Strawson, "Islamic Law and English Text"; Strawson, "Islamic Law and English Texts in Laws of the Postcolonial"; Strawson, "Revisiting Islamic Law. Marginal Notes from Colonial History."

24 Schacht, *An Introduction to Islamic Law*, 112.

25 See Griffith (1986), Engle (1988), Chiba (1989), Dalberg-Larsen (2000), Shah (2005), Grillo et al. (2009).

26 Bourdieu, "The force of law."

27 It is worth noting that this is further complicated by the existence of an established church in England and perhaps by the secular understanding of the relationship of church and state.

28 Griffiths, "What is legal pluralism?," 1.

29 Ibid., 1.

30 Ibid., 3.

31 Shah, "Religion in a Super-Diverse Legal Environment," 64.

32 Davies, "The Ethos of Pluralism," 107–8.

33 See also the concept of the semi-autonomous social field: S. F. Moore, "Law and social change: The semi-autonomous social field as an appropriate subject of study," *Law & Society Review* 7, 1 (1972): 719–46.

34 Balkin, "Understanding Legal Understanding," 1, footnote 1.

35 Ibid., 3.

36 For a related area of study, see the concept of 'legal consciousness' as developed by Ewick and Silbey (1998) who define law, or legality as they say, as 'a social structure actively and constantly produced in what people say and in what they do. Proceeding on the basis of that definition, we listened to people's stories of their everyday lives in order to discover the contours of legality in the world' (p. 223).

37 Allott, *The Limits of Law*, viii.

38 Balkin, "Understanding Legal Understanding," 4.

39 Burchell, "Liberal government and techniques of the self," 29.

40 See Rose, *The Politics of Life Itself.*
41 Brown, "Civilizational Delusions: Secularism, Tolerance, Equality."
42 Abu-Lughod, *Do Muslim women need saving?*, 111.

References Cited

Abu-Lughod, L. *Do Muslim women need saving?* (Cambridge: Harvard University Press, 2013).

Allott, A. *The Limits of Law* (London: Butterworths, 1980).

Ahdar, R., and N. Aroney, eds. *Shari'a in the West* (Oxford: Oxford University Press, 2010).

Balkin, M. "Understanding Legal Understanding: The Legal Subject and the Problem of Legal Coherence," *Yale Law Journal* 103, 105 (1993).

Bano, S. *Muslim Women and Shari'ah Councils. Transcending the Boundaries of Community and Law* (Basingstoke: Palgrave Macmillan, 2012).

Barbero, I. "Orientalising citizenship: The legitimation of immigration regimes in the European Union," *Citizenship studies* 16, 5–6 (2012): 751–68.

Bourdieu, P. "The force of law: Toward a sociology of the juridical field," trans. Richard Terdiman, *Hastings Law Journal* 38 (1987): 805–53.

Brown, W. "Civilizational Delusions: Secularism, Tolerance, Equality," *Theory & Event* 15, 2 (2012).

Burchell, G. "Liberal government and techniques of the self," in *Foucault and Political Reason: Liberalism, neo-liberalism and rationalities of government,* eds. A. Barry, T. Osborne, and N. Rose (London: UCL Press, 1996).

Chiba, M. *Legal pluralism: Toward a general theory through Japanese legal culture* (Tokyo: Tokai University Press, 1989).

Dalberg-Larsen, J. *The unity of law, an illusion? On the legal pluralism in theory and practice* (Berlin: Galda Wilch, 2000).

Davies, M. "The Ethos of Pluralism," *Sydney Law Review* 27, 1 (2005): 87–112.

Dupret, B. "What Is Islamic Law? A praxiological answer and an Egyptian case study," *Theory, Culture and Society* 24, 2 (2007).

Engle Merry, S. "Legal pluralism," *Law & society review* 22, 5 (1988): 869–96.

Esposito, J. L., and N. J. DeLong-Bas. *Women in Muslim Family Law,* 2nd edition (Syracuse: Syracuse University Press, 2001).

Ewick, P., and S. Silbey. *The Common Place of Law: Stories form Everyday Life* (Chicago: The University of Chicago Press, 1998).

Griffith, J. "What is legal pluralism?," *Journal of legal pluralism & unofficial law* 1, 1 (1986): 1–55.

Grillo, R., R. Ballard, A. Ferrari, A.J. Hoekema, M. Maussen, and P. Shah. *Legal practice and cultural diversity* (Aldershot: Ashgate, 2009).

Kroncke, J. "The Flexible Orientalism of Islamic Law," *UCLA Journal of Islamic and Near Eastern Law* 4 (2004–05): 41–73.

Laquer Estin, A. "Unofficial family law," *Iowa law review* 94, 2 (2009): 449–80.

March, A. F. *Islam and Liberal Citizenship: The Search for an Overlapping Consensus* (New York: Oxford University Press, 2009).

Marshall, T. H. "Citizenship and the Social Class," reprinted in *Class, Citizenship, and Social Development,* T. H. Marshall (Chicago: The University of Chicago Press, 1977 [1949]).

Menski, W. "Immigration and multiculturalism in Britain: New issues in research and policy," lecture delivered at Osaka University of Foreign Studies (2002) http://www .casas.org.uk/papers/pdfpapers/osakalecture.pdf (accessed 18 January 2011).

Rose, N. *The Politics of Life Itself* (Oxford: Blackwell Publishers, 2007).

Ruskola, T. "Legal orientalism," *Michigan law review* 101, 1 (2002): 179–234.

Sabsay, L. "The emergence of the other sexual citizen: orientalism and the modernisation of sexuality," *Citizenship Studies* 16, 5-6 (2012): 605–23.

Strawson, J. "Islamic Law and English Texts," *Law and Critique* 21, 21 (1995): 21–38.

Strawson, J. "Islamic Law and English Texts," in *Laws of the Postcolonial*, eds. E. Darian-Smith and P. Fitzpatrick (Ann Arbor: The University of Michigan Press, 1999).

Strawson, J. "Revisiting Islamic Law. Marginal Notes from Colonial History," *Griffith Law Review* 12, 2 (2003): 362–83.

Schacht, J. *An Introduction to Islamic Law* (Oxford: Clarendon Press, 1964).

Shah, P. "Religion in a Super-Diverse Legal Environment: Thoughts on the British Scene," in *Law and Religion in Multicultural Societies*, eds. R. Mehdi et al. (Copenhagen: DJØF Publishing, 2008).

Vikør, K.S. *Between God and the sultan: A history of Islamic law* (Oxford: Oxford University Press, 2005).

Weber, M. *Economy and Society: An Outline of Interpretive Sociology*, trans. Guenther Roth and Claus Wittich (Berkeley: University of California Press, 1978).

Williams, R. "Civil and religious law in England – a religious perspective," *Ecclesiastical law journal* 10, 3 (2008): 262–82.

Part III
Refiguring Citizenship

10
Performing Citizenship: Acts of Writing

Alessandra Marino

Abstract

This chapter examines the performative quality of writing by drawing upon speech act theory and literary criticism. Focusing on Arundhati Roy and Mahasweta Devi's acts of collecting people's stories and deeds, I explore the subject formation of activist writers as a result of the process of facilitating the passage from oral accounts to written texts. Marginalized subjects and their acts, disqualified from the domain of politics *proper*, find in literature a field of struggle. After addressing how Roy and Devi's literature promotes the visibility of 'unimagined communities', I turn to the performative quality of their writing, which shapes and supports citizenship struggles. 'Small dreams', 'small talks', and 'small gods' counteract the capitalist imperative to have 'big' revenues and 'big' development projects. Their transformation of the language of rights reveals how indigenous political subjectivity exceeds the capture of law.

Introduction

Investigating 'citizenship after orientalism' requires a multilayered project of historical reconstruction and exploration of political theory. It involves questioning the relation between the institution of citizenship, its origin in European political thought, and the colonial past of the old continent. The same belief that informed John Locke's vision of indigenous people in America, which linked nomadism to the lack of political subjectivity, justified the domination of 'tribal' groups in British India.[1] For the ostensible lack of private property and cash economy, Adivasis (indigenous people) were considered primitive and prone to illegal activities. In 1871, when the British Empire was expanding its domain in the subcontinent, The Criminal Tribes Act outlawed some of the nomadic tribes and introduced legal provisions, such as compulsory registrations and regular checks in police stations, in an attempt to control their movements. Further amendments of this law, following 1911, officially required fingerprinting for members

of the criminalized tribes (also called 'notified' tribes).[2] These colonial policies and contemporary discourses described indigenous people as both rebellious, hence in need of being tamed, and backward. These two elements, as
Edward Said's *Orientalism* famously highlighted, feature within an orientalist
repertoire of representation of colonial subjects that opposes them to the
advancing forces of Western modernization. This chapter concerns how the
legacy of this two-faceted stereotype, which sees tribals as naïve and dangerous, permeated contemporary Indian culture and law of citizenship not so
much as its legacy but as its history of the present.

In *Citizenship and Its Discontents: An Indian History*, Naraja Gopal Jayal provides to date the most comprehensive historical account of Indian citizenship
and its paradoxes. Her work points out that the orientalist charge of indigenous backwardness, produced during colonialism, infiltrated modern theories
of citizenship. British laws actively disseminated and supported this stereotype, from which the modern constitution did not break away. During the late
nineteenth century, a series of British Acts instituted tribal areas first as scheduled districts (India Act XIV of 1874), then as 'backward tracts'. Being under
the direct governance of the Governor General on behalf of the Parliament,
they were excluded from governance and representation. As the Government
of India Act of 1919 stated, these areas were inhabited by 'people [that] are
primitive, and there is as yet no material to found political institutions'.[3] In
brief, backwardness meant lack of political subjectivity, which derived from a
more general lack of adherence to modern rationality. This politically charged
vocabulary was redeployed by the creators of the legal apparatus of independent India. Perhaps surprisingly, the Constituent Assembly of India, in charge
of drafting the new constitution, retained the label of 'backward communities'
in the formation of a group-differentiated model of citizenship. According to
the constitution, tribes such as Mundas, Sabars, or Bhils belong to 'Scheduled
Castes' within the wider group of 'backward communities'. The fact that colonial nomenclature actively informs the legal and cultural aspects of citizenship reveals that the suffix 'post' defining postcolonial citizenship does not
refer to a past long gone. Rather, it acts as a reminder of the presence of colonialism, and orientalism, in workings of contemporary politics and society.

Citizenship and Orientalism

This historical background is important yet insufficient to address the question of tribal citizenship today. Merely looking at the continuity between
colonial policies and contemporary law leaves the voices of the tribals
unheard. In the analysis of the formal conditions of tribal domination, their
actions are only present in their interpretation by colonial agents. However,
the activities of tribals, sometimes violent and riotous, had attracted the
attention of colonial administrators. Mindful of this background and of Gayatri Spivak's famous remarks on the impossibility to recover a purely subaltern voice,[4] I look elsewhere for the representations of their current struggles.

Even though Adivasis rarely feature on the front pages of the national newspapers, there is no scarcity of journalistic accounts of grassroots tribal movements and ongoing struggles for water, land, and basic rights – once you look for them. In recent years, a literature has emerged as a precious reservoir of personal and collective tribal stories: in the case of Arundhati Roy's involvement in the protests against a mega-dam in the Narmada Valley and Mahasweta Devi's lifelong commitment to tribal rights, their writings are an asynchronous experiment of storytelling, turning the spotlight onto tribal acts, and making rights claims. In this chapter I argue that literature is a political agent supporting environmental and social struggles. To do so, I demonstrate that the performative feature of literature resignifies law and disrupts the nexus between legality and justice.

I read Roy's essay 'The Greater Common Good' and Devi's novel *Chotti Munda and His Arrow* in relation to the specific sites in which the experiences of grassroots activism inspired their writing. The Narmada Valley (Madhya Pradesh) is the area where the 25-year-long protest of the Narmada Bachao Andolan against the Sardar Sarovar dam still goes on. Purulia (West Bengal) is home for the association for the *Kheria Sabar* tribe, the *Paschim Banga Kheria Sabar Kalyan Samiti*, of which Devi is honourary president. The involvement of Roy and Devi in tribal activism takes place through their presence within fields of struggle and through their writings. With her essay, Roy managed to direct an international audience towards the efforts of the NBA in a moment in which public attention towards their *satyagrahas* was declining. Devi put Purulia on the map of contemporary India: by naming tribes and tribal borderlands, she brought them into existence in the national imagination. Spivak maintains that Devi's stories are an antidote against the concealing power of the notion of India, which often works like a 'lid on an immense and equally unacknowledged subaltern heterogeneity'.[5]

In Madhya Pradesh and West Bengal, my experience of meeting activists and engaging with people involved in protests, endless court cases, and unjust instances of dispossession gave me an insight into the writing of these works of fiction and non-fiction. In both cases, I realized that the writers' immersion in a field of struggle constituted part of what could be called, following Eve K. Sedgwick's reflections on literary language, the 'texture' of their artworks. Sedgwick uses the term 'texture' to describe the evident relation between the substance and the surface of writing.[6] Texture is the deep and yet superficial composition that determines literary aesthetics: experiencing it means looking at its 'sedimentation',[7] its history and the process through which language has been carved out of feelings and memories attached to the author's body.

Instead of seeing literature as a vehicle to transpose reality into a fictional dimension, I am interested in how writing is influenced and shaped by the contingency of its production; and in turn, how the material form of a text determines its literary character. I follow Derrida's idea that the literary character of a text is defined by its material, rhetorical, and noematic structure.[8] The structure of Roy and Devi's works incorporates conversations, interviews, and tribal tales; their forms, as well as their contents, demonstrate not only that subaltern subjects act in and by speaking through counter-hegemonic languages but that literature can be a platform where writers speak along-side, or *nearby*, less visible subjects, as writer Assia Djebar advocates in the 'Ouverture' of *Women of Algiers in Their Apartment*.[9] There is no pure subal-tern message to be recovered. Language and translation, as psychoanalysis reminds us, do not allow for purity or neutrality.[10] And yet, the intersubjec-tive and dialogic process that allows the emergence in literary texts of tribals as political agents is worth investigating. What is the process through which literature can perform the coming into being or the existence of a political subject? And what is the relation between literature and law?

Literature as a Supplement of Law

Here theoretical and political questions fold upon each other. Yet from the standpoint of dominant political theory, this often occurs well below the radar. But, as just suggested, I do not regard literature merely as a form of representation – or as a 'locutionary' act, as J. L. Austin calls the ensemble of the actual utterance, its ostensible meaning, and its phonetics. Assuming that literature is just an account of things does not explain the political and social conjuncture that pushes authors to write people's stories, nor does it clarify why tribal people interact with writers. Using the expression 'acts of writing', which recalls Austin's speech acts and the revisions of his thoughts carried out by his interlocutors, I suggest that the performative character of literature transforms political theory. The theoretical resources that inspire my own reflections on 'the materiality of language' and its active life range from Austin to Derrida, to Felman, Butler, and Sedgwick. In this chapter, I overlook the specific differences between some of these authors, for example between Butler and Felman's understandings of performativity, and confine myself to looking at the relation between the performativity of literature and the law. Then, I move back to the specific examples of Roy and Devi to explore how they challenge the normativity of law.

During the last 40 years, Austin's study of performative utterances has become a critical contribution to understanding the relation between speech, but also writing, and the real. In *The Scandal of the Speaking Body*, Shoshana Felman explains that performatives are 'expressions whose function is not to inform or describe, but to carry out a "performance", to accomplish an act through the very process of their enunciation'.[11] Establishing a relation between language and actions, between saying and doing, performatives challenge the idea that language merely represents the world. The referent cannot be accessed directly but can be approached through language, which is not a neutral medium of representation but a force of transformation. Fel-man's use of the image of the 'scandal' reminds of Derrida's reflections on speech acts first published in *Of Grammatology*. As Derrida puts it in 'That

Dangerous Supplement', performatives reveal the scandal of knowledge: 'the scandal is that the sign, the image or the representer become "forces" that make the world move'.[12] Since the theory of performative utterances maintains that the only possible way of being in the world is through the mediation of signs, it questions the very existence of a world outside the speaking subject that can be known through representation.

For Derrida and Felman, language has both a material existence and a creative power;[13] language does not substitute reality but generates a force that acts upon it. Felman affirms that, as a consequence of Austin's reflections, the referent appears 'no longer [as] a preexisting substance but an *act*, that is, a dynamic movement of modification of reality'.[14] In other words, referential knowledge 'is not knowledge about reality, but knowledge that has to do with reality'.[15] Highlighting that the effect of certain utterances is to perform an action that exceeds language and modifies the real, speech acts can undo the traditional separation between materialism and idealism. In Felman's words:

> It is precisely here that Austin's originality lies, for through the new concept of language act, he explodes both the opposition and the separation between matter (or body) and language: matter, like the act, without being reducible to language, is no longer entirely separable from it, either.[16]

The speech act here appears as the materialization of a performative force. This material aspect of language is the most threatening yet interesting feature of the performative, which undermines the faith in the objective existence of reality.

Recognizing this threatening potential, Derrida referred to the materiality of signs as 'dangerous'. 'That Dangerous Supplement' maintains that, whether oral or written, language implies the production of signs that supplement physical and sensorial experience. Writing, in particular, constitutes an attempt to substitute the absence of speech with a performance of presence. What is the danger? With interpretation becoming an inextricable part of knowledge and the world being constituted with and through language, the objectivity of the descriptive language of law becomes questionable. Because of the switch from interpretation to materiality, the textual and narrative aspects of politics become relevant to the analysis of law and of citizenship. 'The narrative "I" frightens the law',[17] for it creates a dangerous supplement that not only modifies reality but multiplies the dimensions that make up our idea of it.

This shift from interpretation to materiality provokes a move away from studying what literature is to analysing how it does politics. From this perspective, the performative force of literature and its relation with law come under the spotlight. Being constituted of and through language, literature and law both present a performative function: they reinforce their own authority through the reproduction and demarcation of a certain field of knowledge and conduct. But also, as Butler explains in her work *Excitable Speech*, their common performative character implies that they are fundamentally opened to rearticulation and resignification. The law, as Butler's reading of Althusser points out, is performative because it derives its authority from its own repetition and the accumulation of exemplary cases.[18] On the other hand, Derrida notes that the very foundation of the law, as the law of a particular state, takes place in a performative moment that is also a violent one: a body of written rules is instituted as a set of injunctions that citizens are required to comply with. Both Derrida and Butler, though, agree that the making of the law takes place in a textual network and requires an interpretative effort. This interpretative quality also determines the possibility of resignifying the law. The performative character of language blurs the divide between the fictional quality of literature and the presumed objectivity of law.

It is not by chance that several thinkers that explored the functions of speech used literary examples to investigate the complex relations between normative utterances, law, and its effects. Austin turned to novels (such as *Alice's Adventures in Wonderland* and *Don Quixote*),[19] Derrida to short stories (Kafka), and Felman to plays (*Don Juan*) in order to demonstrate that language does not merely describe reality but intervenes in it or even creates it. Derrida, in particular, approaches a fundamental discussion of law through a reading of Franz Kafka. Kafka's short story 'Before the Law' tells of a poor man who enters the gate of the Law and asks the doorkeeper to appear before it, but his numerous requests are continuously rejected. His failure is irrefutable, since the law never shows itself: the man ages and eventually dies without achieving his purpose. In Derrida's reading of Kafka's story, the countryman's failure is determined by his will to relate to the law by trying to touch it and 'enter' into physical contact with it. Law cannot be accessed; but it can be 'deciphered'.[20] Since law is not to be seen or accessed, its existence seems unquestionable: the ultimate law states the atemporal presence of the law. The story, though, exposes that despite the very existence of the law being left unquestioned, the fact that the law depends on interpretation makes its authority vulnerable.

For Derrida, it is possible to decipher the law (as *droit*) because it is founded in interpretable textual strata. This possibility, for poor and peripheral subjects, becomes an imperative to take up deconstruction as a political tool to counteract the fictitious universality of law. Contesting its role as an arm of justice can be the task of literature:

> Laws, constitutions, the declaration of the rights of man, grammar or the penal code are not 'natural realities' and they depend upon the same structural power that allows novelesque fictions or mendacious inventions and the like to take place. This is why literature and the study of literature have so much to teach us about right and law.[21]

In brief, Derrida highlights, literature and laws are made of the same textual structure. The performative force of literature permits the creation of a 'dangerous supplement': 'literature itself makes the law, emerging in that place where the law is made'.[22] Literature is 'a dangerous supplement' because it 'can *play the law*, repeating it while diverting it or circumventing it'.[23] Making use of the double meaning of the verb 'to play', Derrida highlights two points: first, literature can act like, or even impersonate the law by reproducing its formulae and imperative tone; second, in doing so and revealing their common fabric, literature subversively shows that law has no meaning without performance.

In the same vein, Hélène Cixous has provided an interesting reading of the aporetic position of the poor man in 'Before the Law' and showed that the scandalous secret of Kafka's story lies in exposing that the law is but a word. For Cixous, this is what literature irreverently teaches us about law.[24]

Devi and Roy's Acts of Writing

Derrida, Cixous, Felman, and Sedgwick have paid attention to deconstructing the imperative of law through referring to literary writing. The reason has to do with a deconstruction of normativity. If Austin upholds the normative function of law for creating accountable and respectable citizens, critical thinkers have uncovered the repetitive character and performative work that grants to law its authority. Derrida and Cixous are concerned with questioning the law of phallogocentrism; Felman tries to decentre the linguistic paradigm that has effaced the body from the production of knowledge; Butler exposes the performative openness of the law of gender; and Sedgwick focuses on the law of women's oppression, drawing a connection between homosociality and misogyny. If writing resignifies the law, exploiting the openness of its performativity, as these writers point out, literature can provide an insight into other ways of being political subjects before, beyond, and even against the law. From this perspective, the experiential and visceral dimension giving birth to writing as well as the scenes of literature may appear relevant for rethinking citizenship, law, and justice.

Derrida's references to performatives in 'Force of Law' and 'Before the Law' are important contributions challenging classical conceptions of the naturalness of law and its pivotal role in the pursuit of justice. As hinted before, Roy and Devi's activist literature directly interrogates this aspect, questioning the applicability of specific laws. But also, it attempts to unveil the colonial principles concealed in the fabric of the contemporary legal system. Devi denounces the heritage of British laws that criminalized the tribals. Roy exposes the dispossession of Adivasi land carried out by the government for big infrastructural projects and in the name of 'The Greater Common Good'. In the Narmada Valley, The Land Acquisition Act, another colonial law, became the tool for depriving indigenous citizens of their basic rights. In this section, I look closely at the form and content of Roy's 'The Greater

Common Good' and Devi's *Chotti Munda* to show how they challenge the legacy of colonial legislations, resignify the language of backwardness of the Indian constitution, and free the conception of political subjectivity from the limits imposed by a postcolonial legal framework.

'The Greater Common Good' maintains that the linear narrative of progress, on which the idea of development relies, posits Adivasis as expendable subjects. The title of the essay is sarcastic, questioning the dark side of a project aiming at the pursuit of the good for a whole nation. Despite the Nehruvian promises of a country 'united in diversity', the supposed 'ethnic otherness' of the tribals justified their obliteration from the political national scene: 'A huge percentage of the displaced are Adivasis (57.6 per cent in the case of the Sardar Sarovar dam). ... It's like having an expense account. Someone else pays the bills. People from another country. Another world.'[25] Roy believes that the language of national interest, like the ones of the global market and human rights, has colonized people's minds, inhibiting their ability to imagine a world devoid of the structures of the postcolonial nation-state and its discourse of progress. While the voices cheering for the rise of 'India shining' are clearly heard, the tragedy of the displaced and landless tribals remains unaccounted for in the public domain. Adivasis emerge as other citizens, backward because they remained behind in the race towards development and stayed away from the centre of civilization.

The evolutionary logic of progress rooted in colonial ideology informs the economic agenda of development, which underpins the thinking behind displacement plans. To equate modernity and industrialization creates a linear representation of the ladder of progress, where the West occupies the higher level. Dhar and Chakrabarti (2010) have called 'capitalocentric orientalism' the consequential hegemonic depiction of Southern, indigenous, and marginal economies as backward or lacking the fundamental premises leading to a fully developed economic market. Their book *Dislocation and Resettlement in Development* claims that the establishment of private property as the rationale for acknowledging the modernity of economic structures marginalizes alternative systems and institutes a form of orientalism. Incorporated into developmental schemes, Adivasis are the targets of both aggressive land acquisition and benevolent activities aimed at managing poverty. Their subjectivity, though, remains effaced from the realm of socio-political production: 'the "Adivasis" appear everywhere in the development register, in the thousand models drawn up in their name, but they are only present as a lacking other, as lifeless figures of pathology out of sync with the modern capitalist economy that the discourse of development has established as the norm(al).'[26] Economic and social aspects of Adivasi life are rewritten into contemporary orientalist narratives of development, which are influenced by colonial norms on land use.

In the context of the Sardar Sarovar, the construction of the dam, with its brutal evictions and repression of resistance, are inextricable from the forcible implementation of colonial laws. Strategically enforcing the Land Acquisition Act (1894) and the Forest Acts (1927–) to displace tribal groups, the postcolonial nation-state reiterates the othering of indigenous people in disputes over property and land use. Property and land ownership are among the essential values inscribed in modern citizenship and constitute the requirements of modernity that indigenous people implicitly defy. But the price that Adivasis pay for not being assimilated into mainstream society is their disappearance from the national imagination. Rob Nixon has labelled the crowds of the displaced 'unimagined communities' because they get written from the history and imagination of the nation.[27]

Roy restores the existence of tribals within mainstream society through describing in detail the meetings with some of the people affected by the displacement. Her encounter with Bhaiji Bhai, one of the Adivasis who lost his land with the submergence of the valley, becomes paradigmatic:

> I'd seen him in an old documentary film, shot more than ten years ago, in the valley. He was frailer now, his beard softened with age. But his story hadn't aged. It was still young and full of passion. It broke my heart, the patience with which he told it. … Bhaiji Bhai, Bhaiji Bhai, when will you get angry? When will you stop waiting? When will you say 'That's enough!' and reach for your weapons, whatever they may be?[28]

Roy appeals to anger as a motivation for more forceful actions of resistance, but her solidarity with Bhaji Bhai seems to be ignited by the stories of dispossession and stark poverty that the writer collected across the valley during her trips.

Re-narrating people's stories, Roy contrasts the 'imaginative displacement' of local communities 'from the idea of the developing nation-state'.[29] She also denounces the estrangement of indigenous people from the language of law and official documents. The framework of legality (on which citizens ought to be able to rely to obtain justice) does not seem to guarantee any help to the oustees (those who have been dispossessed of their land). On the contrary, instituting an imposed foreign language on the customary management of land, law creates a yoke of violence on Adivasis deprived of their livelihood. Elsewhere, Roy reflects:

> The Fifth Schedule of the Constitution provides protection to Adivasi people and disallows the alienation of their land. But it doesn't seem to matter at all. It looks as though the clause is there only to make the constitution look good – a bit of window-dressing, a slash of make-up. Scores of corporation, from relatively unknown ones to the biggest mining companies and steel manufacturers in the world, are in the fray to appropriate Adivasi homelands – the Mittals, Jindals, Tata, Essar, Posco, Rio Tinto, BHP Billion and, of course, Vedanta.[30]

The principle of equality and the promise of protection of indigenous minorities written in the constitution do not offer to tribal subjects adequate weapons to resist displacement. The depredation of tribal land is one of the ways in which a neoliberal war against the poor takes place. She says: 'an undeclared civil war is being waged on its citizens in the name of "development"'.[31] This war, fought in the name of growth, implies a redefinition of national inclusion and of the image of citizenship.

In the much-debated essay 'Walking with the Comrades', written during three weeks spent in the jungle with a Naxalite guerrilla group, Roy disputed the government's description of these indigenous Maoist combatants as a threat to national security and to the image of a thriving Indian nation. These allegedly violent rulers of the forests are, in Roy's words, 'desperately poor tribal people living in conditions of chronic hunger'.[32] She adds:

> They are people who, even after sixty years of India's so-called Independence, have not had access to education, health care or legal redress. They are people who have been mercilessly exploited for decades, consistently cheated by small businessmen and moneylenders, the women raped as a matter of right by police and forest department personnel.[33]

Roy is aware of the historical factors that, during and after colonialism, contributed to keeping Adivasis and untouchables in a state of indigent poverty. In *The Cost of Living*, the author had already pointed out that the exclusion of tribal voices from the mediascape takes place hand in hand with their displacement from ancestral land, the abuse of their labour force, and the institution of a regime of terror in rural villages, where the police carries out theft and rape. In this battle of world-views, literature resonates with people's acts aimed at gaining visibility in the public sphere: it popularizes their point of view and supports both their peaceful and violent remonstrations against detrimental environmental and social policies. 'The Greater Common Good' was, first and foremost, a public appeal for people to join the struggle of the Narmada Bachao Andolan movement through physically taking part in 'Rally for the Valley', a march expressing public dissent.

Mahasweta Devi and Roy differ in age, style, and public reception, yet Devi's writing is similar to Roy's, insofar as her literature bears the mark of her involvement in court cases and legal battles in support of the poor. Having worked with indigenous communities all her life, Devi became increasingly involved in the activism of associations and movements advocating basic rights of land, water, and labour. Like Roy, Devi highlights the estrangement of the poor from the spaces of decision-making and asks how can progressive laws really help people's life if they remain unimplemented. The persistence of bonded labour despite its formal abolition and the lack of enforcement of minimum wage are just two examples of how the acquisition of citizenship by tribals, which was ratified with the constitution, did not fulfill its promise of equality. As Arya affirms, tribal areas remain 'islands of slavery' in the 'vast ocean of independence' where questions related to land, water, education, and health care continue to remain unanswered.[34]

Devi's novel *Chotti Munda* presents a revolt against the persistence of tribal exploitation, enforced through 'bad laws and worse implementation'.[35] Almost a *summa* of Devi's work, *Chotti Munda* deals with a wide range of themes, from the criminalization of poverty to the contemporary fear of Naxalite uprisings. The novel covers a time frame of over 70 years, from the turn of the twentieth century to Independence and the Emergency, and follows Chotti's life and his gradual ascent to tribal leadership.

Chotti is a young and bright Munda boy who soon becomes 'a famous archer in a community of archers' winning fair after fair.[36] His talent in archery is such that his bow is considered spellbound and able to reach any target. Stories proliferate around Chotti, while he is trained in archery by the old Dhani Munda. Dhani had been banned from archery after participating in the revolt against the British led by the historical leader Birsa Munda. The reference to the series of rebellions led by the freedom fighter Birsa Munda is significant. Between 1895–1900, in a period known as the Great Tumult, tribal groups targeted the British system of control and privatization of tribal land. Police stations, officials, and missionaries were regularly attacked. Even though the revolts were eventually suppressed, and Birsa Munda died in mysterious circumstances at only 25, his memory fills both history and legend.

Taking Mundas as a paradigmatic example of the simultaneous inscription and marginalization of tribals in modern India, the novel reveals the national aspiration of transforming Adivasis from rebellious subjects of a foreign rule into good citizens. While portraying endless social injustice and exploitation during colonialism and after independence, what arises is a sense of suspense for another revolution to come.[37] The next rebellion will be guided by Chotti Munda, who has the authority to challenge government officers and lead bond slaves as well as starving Adivasis against the contractors who exploit their work and their ignorance.[38] If the truest and most brutal aspect of India is visible in its villages, its administration and wealth appear to be elsewhere. In a dialogue between Chotti and the academic Shankar, the latter affirms: 'the law is not bad, Chotti, but nothing works by the law. For the law is never applied'.[39] Just like Bashai Tudu, Chotti brings up the gap existing between the spaces of decision-making and the reality of the poor. He asks Shankar:

Who makes this law?Government.Where does this Gormen live?In Delhi. It's far away, nah?Yes.

Makes t' law, does good, stays afar. But if Adivasi or untouchable dies in t' forest, they don' know.[40]

Does this statement refer to the law of citizenship as well? Chotti is denouncing formal inclusion without substantial rights. By doing so, he resignifies an ideal of civilization borrowed from the West. The question that follows this dialogue is: 'Can this go on in a civilized country?'. The burning realization for the reader is that the ideal of civilization borrowed from the West, which defines modernity, could not give an account of the complexity of Indian social and political scenes. Also, it could not simply be contrasted with the allegedly backward or primitive state of the tribals that remains written in the constitution. Reacting against this attribution of backwardness, literature opens up a space of freedom from this ascriptive label. *Chotti Munda* implicitly poses an urgent question: given that the colonial mark of backwardness remained attached to Adivasis' national status, how could rebellious archers, like the Mundas, become straight-arrow, law-abiding citizens?

Devi rebels against social categories such as 'denotified tribes' that retain the colonial history of notification (or criminalization) of tribal communities as well as the colonial ideology. She maintains that the existing disregard for tribal communities, still considered to be backward, and the failure in the implementation of welfare actions in their support have worsened their conditions of social marginalization. The joint reading of Devi's literature and Jayal's socio-legal study of citizenship highlights two issues that have to do with the performativity of law: first, constitutionally crafted group tags have become prescriptive, rather than descriptive, markers of identity and have the effect of keeping people in separate social groups. Backwardness has become a marker of Adivasis' identity, not only a colonial prejudice dying hard. Second, inequality has to be fought at a formal and material level, because affirmative laws are meaningless if they are not implemented.

But even as Devi identifies the yoke that law imposed on tribal subjectivity, she does not portray Adivasis as passive recipients of colonial law or of the neglect of government actions. Through literature, she collects acts that testify to how tribals fall outside the categories of primitive subjects of the empire, or citizens belonging to constitutionally prescribed groups. For this reason Chotti replaces images of tribal savagery with accounts of actual exploitation. He questions how civilization can coexist with bonded labour and asks: 'we are savage jungle folk, what is our crime that so many police have descended upon our area? So sir, if you say that the state wants the house, who am I to say no?'[41] The interrogative style of Chotti's discourse vis-à-vis the authority is far from being submissive. It preludes to the final scene of revolt, in which Chotti is under the threat of being killed by a sub-divisional officer (SDO). Almost representing decades of subjugation, the tribal and the officer stand on opposite grounds. Chotti 'on one side. SDO on the other, and in between a thousand bows upraised in space. And a warning announced in many upraised hands'.[42] Stubborn bows and raised hands perform a gesture of subaltern solidarity in resistance that contradicts the narrative of Adivasis' helplessness. Through his subversive act, Chotti's performance of savagery within the novel resignifies the attribute of backwardness that defines indigenous citizenship.

Conclusion

Roy and Devi's stories illustrate how the rigid boundaries of law and institutional citizenship have to be rewritten for indigenous political subjects to count as equal citizens. Their major contribution has been bringing Adivasis into being as political agents rather than framing them as political abjects needing discipline or aid. Without denying the risks of objectification involved in the praxis of writing subaltern stories, these writers courageously exploit the performative power of literature to intervene into political debates over who counts as a citizen of modern India.

To summarize, Roy and Devi's literary works make four interventions. First, collecting the tribals' acts of protest, they promote the visibility of what Rob Nixon calls 'unimagined communities',[43] left out of nationalist narrations. Second, texts participate in the articulation of movements' struggles, since the creativity of the literary language formulates slogans, demands, and legal analyses. The third movement is that literature deconstructs the objectivity of law, questioning the contentious history of its making. Finally, and more radically, literature transforms the language of rights and reveals how Adivasis' political subjectivity exceeds the capture of law. Since literature is performative, its creative intervention is crucial for mapping the limits of citizenship and questioning the division between humanities and social sciences.

Roy and Devi's acts of writing are not only similar because they emerged in sites of urgent political demonstrations, their aesthetics stretch and bend the language of law beyond its limits. Devi has claimed that the constitution merely guaranteed to the poor the right to poverty: 'the Indian constitution respected every citizen's fundamental right to become whatever he could by dint of his guts. The poor therefore had the right to become poorer still'.[44] Roy reacted against the Indian nuclear policy and its violence against the poor by declaring her right to secede and become an independent republic. She wrote: 'if protesting against having a nuclear bomb implanted in my brain is anti-Hindu and anti-national, then I secede. I hereby declare myself an independent, mobile republic. I am a citizen of the earth. I own no territory. I have no flag'.[45] The universal language of rights is here scaled down to the specific necessities of people living in destitution.

The move is clear: opposing the capitalist imperative to achieve 'big' revenues through 'big' development projects, Roy obsessively reiterates the importance of listening to 'small' talks and welcoming 'small gods', often unseen, into the political arena. Expressing the same sensibility, Devi says:

> All my life I have seen small people with small dreams. It looked like they wanted to put them all in a box and keep them locked up... but somewhere, some of them escaped, as if there has been a jailbreak of dreams. Like the Naxalites. Their crime is that they dared to dream. And why shouldn't they?[46]

In the mainstream political theory, the Naxalites are anti-citizens; they are a criminal guerrilla army against which the government has waged a war. For Devi, though, they are small people, whose small dreams of escaping poverty and oppression have fuelled armed actions. Their dreams represent a right. So how does the image of citizenship change if we consider, as Devi suggested, the right to dream small dreams as a fundamental right?

The transformation of Naxalites from anti-citizens into citizens provides us a renovated political theory. Rewriting the stigma of backwardness, literature makes unruly subjects, like the tribals, heroes of stories of justified resistance. Showing the social values of tribal communities and their struggles for forests and land, texts reinscribe Adivasis in the domain of politics. In this light, Devi and Roy's acts of writing counteract the legal erasure of indigenous political subjectivity and resignify the nationalist fiction of a democratic India. Concretely contributing to indigenous fights against exploitation and invisibility, through and beyond representation, these works are literary forms of social activism. These acts of writing, in specific times and places, change mainstream perception of indigenous groups. They initiate, as Felman puts it, 'a dynamic movement of modification of reality' and show that literary aesthetics and the poetics of 'dreaming' can carry a disruptive political force for both transforming theory and what it performs.

Notes

1 I will use here the term 'tribals' and 'Adivasi' to refer to the indigenous people that were classified and categorized as distinct social groups during the British colonial period. 'Adivasi' literally means 'original inhabitant', and it refers to heterogeneous tribal groups living all over the subcontinent.
2 Simon A. Cole, "Native Prints," in *Suspect Identities: A History of Fingerprinting and Criminal Identification* (Cambridge, Mass.; London: Harvard University Press, 2001).
3 Crispin Bates, "Lost Innocents and the Loss of Innocence: Interpreting Adivasi Movements in South Asia," in *Indigenous Peoples of Asia*, eds. R.H. Barnes, Andrew Gray, and Benedict Kingsbury (Michigan: Association of Asian Studies, 1995); Alessandra Marino, "'The Cost of Dams': Acts of Writing as Resistance in Postcolonial India," *Citizenship Studies* 16, 5-6 (2012).
4 Gayatri Chakravorty Spivak, "Can the Subaltern Speak?," in *Marxism and the Interpretation of Culture*, eds. Cary Nelson and Lawrence Grossberg (Urbana: Illinois University Press, 1988).

5   See Gayatri Chakravorty Spivak, *Outside in the Teaching Machine* (New York; London: Routledge, 1993), 88.
6   Eve Kosofsky Sedgwick, *Touching Feeling: Affect, Pedagogy, Performativity* (Durham: Duke University Press, 2002), 13.
7   Ibid., 4.
8   See Jacques Derrida, *Acts of Literature*, ed. Derek Attridge (New York; London: Routledge, 1992), 44. In *Without Alibi*, Derrida refers to de Man's discussions on Rousseau's *Reveries* and *Confessions* to highlight the interconnection between the formal and the material aspect of his texts. If rhetorical language supplements referential illusion, Derrida claims that the formal and material aspects of a text are inseparable from each other and dependent on (although irreducible to) the textual event of their production. See Jacques Derrida, *Without Alibi*, ed. Peggy Kamuf (Stanford: Stanford University Press, 2002), 152.
9   Assia Djebar, *Women of Algiers in Their Apartment* (Charlottesville; London: University Press of Virginia, 1999), 2.
10   See Diane Elam, "Speak for Yourself," in *Who Can Speak? Authority and Critical Identity*, eds. Judith Roof and Robyn Wiegman (Urbana: University of Illinois Press, 1995).
11   Shoshana Felman, *The Scandal of the Speaking Body: Don Juan with J.L. Austin, or Seduction in Two Languages* (Stanford: Stanford University Press, 2003), 6.
12   Derrida, *Acts of Literature*, 85.
13   I am aware that, at this point, I seem to propose an equation between speech and language. However, while acknowledging that speech does not exhaust all possibilities of language, I uphold Cixous and Derrida's readings of the performativity of speech as the most threatening political feature of language.
14   Felman, *The Scandal of the Speaking Body: Don Juan with J.L. Austin, or Seduction in Two Languages*, 51.
15   Idem.
16   Ibid., 108–9.
17   Derrida, *Acts of Literature*, 206.
18   See Judith Butler, *The Psychic Life of Power: Theories in Subjection* (Stanford, Calif.: Stanford University Press, 1997).
19   *How to Do Things with Words: The William James Lectures Delivered at Harvard University in 1955* (Clarendon Press, 1962), 90. Ibid., 27.
20   Derrida, *Acts of Literature*, 206.
21   Jacques Derrida, *Limited Inc*, trans. G. Graff (Evanston, Illinois: Northwestern University Press, 1988), 134.
22   Derrida, *Acts of Literature*, 216.
23   Idem.
24   In the first chapter of *Readings*, entitled 'Writing and the Law', Cixous notes that the strength and literary appeal of some texts come from their way of exposing the originary gesture of their creation. In an initial and programmatic statement, she says: 'I want to work on texts that are as close as possible to an inscription – conscious or unconscious – of the origin of the gesture of writing and not of writing itself', Helene Cixous, *Readings: The Poetics of Blanchot, Joyce, Kafka, Kleist, Lispector, and Tsvetayeva* (Minneapolis: University of Minnesota Press, 1991), 1. Cixous and Derrida, who share an interest in Kafka's literary reflections on the law, both point out how, in writing, the materiality of language conveys a creative force that overcomes the contingency of the writing act and makes itself tangible even in absentia of the speaker. But far from transferring the intention of the subject, the act of writing necessarily involves frustration and dispossession. As Derrida stresses through a quote of de Man: 'writing always includes the moment of

dispossession in favour of the arbitrary power of the play of the signifier', Derrida, *Without Alibi*, 159. Disregarding the intention of the writer, texts obey the unpredictable laws of playfulness and arbitrariness. These terms of Austinian derivation are used here in an anti-Austinian spirit. Rather than rejected as aberrations of communicative language, playfulness and arbitrariness are incorporated as integral features of texts having to do with law.

25   Arundhati Roy, *The Cost of Living* (New York: Modern Library, 1999), 19.

26   Anjan Chakrabarti and Anup Kumar Dhar, *Dislocation and Resettlement in Development: From Third World to the World of the Third* (London: Routledge, 2010), 44.

27   Rob Nixon, *Slow Violence and the Environmentalism of the Poor* (Cambridge, Mass.; London: Harvard University Press, 2011), 150.

28   Roy, *The Cost of Living*, 77–9.

29   Nixon, *Slow Violence and the Environmentalism of the Poor*, 150.

30   Arundhati Roy, *Broken Republic: Three Essays* (New Delhi: Hamish Hamilton, 2011), 25.

31   Arundhati Roy, *An Ordinary Person's Guide to Empire* (London: Penguin, 2005), 169.

32   Roy, *Broken Republic: Three Essays*, 7.

33   Idem.

34   Shachi Arya, *Tribal Activism: Voices of Protest: With Special Reference to Works of Mahasveta Devi* (Jaipur: Rawat Publications, 1998), 102.

35   Ibid., 173.

36   Mahasweta Devi, *Chotti Munda and His Arrow*, trans. Gayatri Chakravorty Spivak (Malden, MA: Blackwell, 2003), 46. Munda people are Adivasis based in central and Eastern India and in Bangladesh. Their language is Mundari.

37   Devi's novel pays particular attention to the continuity that remains tangible during Emergency: 'the hollers like "eliminate poverty", "bond labour's illegal", "now moneylenders' loan for agriculture is illegal" become posters and get stuck on trees and stations and bus-bodies in the remotest parts of the country. But in reality people like Chotti and Chhagan continue to get ground down. These five reigning years are dedicated to the task of making the rich richer, keeping the lower castes and the Adivasis crushed underfoot, and, above all, turning those designated hoodlums without portfolios into cannibal gods with police support', Ibid., 238.

38   The songs collected in the novel express the point of view of the Mundas and provide an impression of their broken Bengali language. One of the first songs the reader encounters contains the prophecy of a rebellion that will be guided by Chotti Munda. Chotti is a leader because his bow can scare the police and his pleas can reach the 'Gormen': 'Ye raise the bow, ye hit t'target/Makes the Daroga [police officer] mighty afraid, mate –/Ye go to Gormen and tell'em our pleas/ Makes Daroga mighty afraid, mate –/So they didn' let ya play yer arrer…Which Munda knows t' bowspell?/Only ye, mate–/Which Munda is Gormen's buddy?/ Only ye, mate –/So they didn' let ya play yer arrer', Ibid., 190.

39   Ibid., 239.

40   Idem.

41   Ibid., 226.

42   Ibid., 288.

43   Nixon, *Slow Violence and the Environmentalism of the Poor*, 159.

44   Mahasweta Devi, *Bashai Tudu* (Calcutta: Thema, 1990), 87.

45   Roy, *The Cost of Living*, 109.

46   See http://www.dnaindia.com/node/1792445

References Cited

Arya, Shachi. *Tribal Activism: Voices of Protest, With Special Reference to Works of Mahasveta Devi* (Jaipur: Rawat Publications, 1998).

Austin, J.L. *How to Do Things with Words: The William James Lectures Delivered at Harvard University in 1955* (London: Clarendon Press, 1962).

Bates, Crispin. "Lost Innocents and the Loss of Innocence: Interpreting Adivasi Movements in South Asia," in *Indigenous Peoples of Asia*, eds. R.H. Barnes, Andrew Gray, and Benedict Kingsbury (Ann Arbor, MI: Association of Asian Studies, 1995), 109–19.

Butler, Judith. *Excitable Speech: A Politics of the Performative* (New York and London: Routledge, 1997).

Butler, Judith. *The Psychic Life of Power: Theories in Subjection* (Stanford, CA: Stanford University Press, 1997).

Chakrabarti, Anjan, and Anup Kumar Dhar. *Dislocation and Resettlement in Development: From Third World to the World of the Third* (London: Routledge, 2010).

Cixous, Helene. *Readings: The Poetics of Blanchot, Joyce, Kafka, Kleist, Lispector, and Tsvetayeva* (Minneapolis, MN: University of Minnesota Press, 1991).

Cole, Simon A. "Native Prints," in *Suspect Identities: A History of Fingerprinting and Criminal Identification* (Cambridge, MA: Harvard University Press, 2001), 60–96.

Derrida, Jacques. *Acts of Literature*, ed. Derek Attridge (New York: Routledge, 1992).

Derrida, Jacques. "Force of Law," *Cardozo Law Review* 11, 919 (1990): 921–1045.

Derrida, Jacques. *Limited Inc.*, trans. G. Graff (Evanston, IL: Northwestern University Press, 1988).

Derrida, Jacques. *Without Alibi*, ed. Peggy Kamuf (Stanford, CT: Stanford University Press, 2002).

Derrida, Jacques, and Gayatri Chakravorty Spivak. *Of Grammatology* (Baltimore, MD: Johns Hopkins University Press, 1976).

Devi, Mahasweta. *Bashai Tudu* (Calcutta: Thema, 1990).

Devi, Mahasweta. *Chotti Munda and His Arrow*, trans. Gayatri Chakravorty Spivak (Malden, MA: Blackwell, 2003).

Djebar, Assia. *Women of Algiers in Their Apartment* (Charlottesville, VA: University Press of Virginia, 1999).

Elam, Diane. "Speak for Yourself," in *Who Can Speak? Authority and Critical Identity*, eds. Judith Roof and Robyn Wiegman (Urbana, IL: University of Illinois Press, 1995), 231–8.

Felman, Shoshana. *The Scandal of the Speaking Body: Don Juan with J.L. Austin, or Seduction in Two Languages* (Stanford, CT: Stanford University Press, 2003).

Jayal, Niraja Gopal. *Citizenship and Its Discontents: An Indian History* (Cambridge, MA: Harvard University Press, 2013).

Marino, Alessandra. "'The Cost of Dams': Acts of Writing as Resistance in Postcolonial India," *Citizenship Studies* 16, 5-6 (2012): 705–19.

Nixon, Rob. *Slow Violence and the Environmentalism of the Poor* (Cambridge, MA: Harvard University Press, 2011).

Roy, Arundhati. *Broken Republic: Three Essays* (New Delhi: Hamish Hamilton, 2011).

Roy, Arundhati. *The Cost of Living* (New York: Modern Library, 1999).

Roy, Arundhati. *An Ordinary Person's Guide to Empire* (London: Penguin, 2005).

Said, Edward W. *Orientalism* (London: Routledge and Kegan Paul, 1978).

Sedgwick, Eve Kosofsky. *Touching Feeling: Affect, Pedagogy, Performativity* (Durham, NC: Duke University Press, 2002).

Spivak, Gayatri Chakravorty. "Can the Subaltern Speak?" in *Marxism and the Interpretation of Culture*, eds. Cary Nelson and Lawrence Grossberg (Urbana, IL: Illinois University Press, 1988), 66–111.

Spivak, Gayatri Chakravorty. *Outside in the Teaching Machine* (New York: Routledge, 1993).

11
Haunted Citizens: Of Ghosts, Gang Rapes, and Āzādī

Tara Atluri

Abstract

At times, 'citizenship' erupts as a mode of political subjectivity by refusing to follow the rules. In this chapter, I discuss the 2012 Delhi[1] gang rape protests and the 2013 decision made by the Supreme Court of India to uphold Section 377, India's sodomy bill. Citizenship after orientalism is best expressed by the refrain of protesters, heard in the streets at that time: 'Āzādī' a Persian word meaning freedom, liberty, and independence. This is an account of how subaltern subjects recover symbolic and resonant names not only to cite and iterate but also to resignify their political subjectivity.

Introduction

We are all governed by and reproduce political theories of otherness that demand investigation. One can utilize philosophy to question how those who are constructed by dominant discourses that imagine them to be politically docile invent new modes of citizenship. Subaltern bodies can and do reinvent the polis and modes of political subjectivity that exist outside of orientalist ideology. While the 'oriental woman' is imagined by colonial and nationalist powers as a submissive and docile body, this chapter discusses new inventions of citizenship and the remapping of the polis that feminists and queers within the Indian subcontinent enact. This chapter suggests that understandings of citizenship rooted in occidentalist understandings of governance are constantly challenged through the subversive actions of subaltern bodies. These forms of citizenship after orientalism are often unintelligible to those who only understand the citizen in reference to colonial ideology and Eurocentric, patriarchal understandings of politics.

There are moments in which 'citizenship' erupts as a mode of political subjectivity that ironically enacts the utmost political gestures by refusing to follow the rules.

207

A woman is gang raped, tortured, and murdered on a bus in the capital city of a 'postcolonial' nation. The buses of the world carry haunting histories of violence and struggle. On 16 December 2012 in Delhi, India, a woman named Jyoti was gang raped, tortured, and inflicted with such bodily harm that she died two weeks later.[2] Her male companion Awindra was also severely beaten by the assailants. All of this remarkable madness happened in the mundane space of a bus. The bus was hijacked by a group of men and was not representative of any laws regarding public transport in Delhi or national laws pertaining to gender violence. The sheer brutality of the case perhaps stood outside of all laws of human morality. As one young woman I spoke with at an anniversary protest in 2013 remarked, the case perhaps expressed '....the limit of humanity itself...'[3]

Unprecedented levels of protest began in Delhi and spread throughout India, leading to a transnational media spectacle, changes in national law, and an ongoing debate regarding gender in the region. The story of the Delhi gang rape case of 2012 is as much a story of 'citizenship' as one of postcolonial history.[4]

On 16 December 2012, Jyoti was gang raped to death on a bus in Delhi, India. Six men were legally implicated in her tragic and gruesome murder, one of whom committed suicide while awaiting trial, one of whom was given a lesser sentence as he was tried as a minor, and the remainder of whom were sentenced to death. Perhaps it was the sheer brutality of the bodily violence enacted against this woman that caused the Indian public and the international press to take notice. Jyoti was penetrated with a metal rod that was pulled out of her body with such force that her intestines unraveled. Medical experts and physicians commented that the level of violence that she underwent was chilling, and many repeatedly referred to the trauma that she underwent as torture.[5] Less than two weeks after the attack, Jyoti was later moved to a Singapore hospital where she died. Her male companion was also severely beaten. Massive and unprecedented levels of protest spread throughout the Indian subcontinent, with the case generating international media attention leading to a transnational debate regarding gender justice, public safety for women in India, and rape culture. Five days before the anniversary of the Delhi gang rape case of 2012, the Supreme Court of India made the decision to recriminalize same-sex desire, upholding Section 377, India's sodomy bill. Protests also erupted throughout India and transnationally.

This is a story of resilience. It is a story that begins with the authorial madness of misogyny and the authorial madness of the state, one that moves into the streets and has at its centre the incredible will of people to resist against all odds. This is a story of the resilience of a word and perhaps an idea – Āzādī – carried across borders and resurrected at the most unlikely times, binding disparate struggles for human dignity and freedom, timelessly.

While a neoliberal discourse of 'India shining'[6] posits the 'new urban Indian woman' as 'free' owing to market vitality, arguably, meaningful freedom from orientalist evocations of 'citizenship' is best expressed by the inspiring refrain of protesters heard in the streets: 'Āzādī', a Persian word meaning freedom, liberty, liberation, and independence. Āzādī is now of common use in Farsi, Kurdish, Pashto, Urdu, and Hindi. Interestingly, the word as a protest chant was popular in anti-colonial rebellions in South Asia.[7] The cry of 'Āzādī' could also be heard in Delhi when just one year after the Delhi gang rape case, the Supreme Court of India made the decision to uphold Section 377, criminalizing India's sodomy bill despite a decision by the Delhi High Court to overturn this old colonial law in 2009. In 2001, the Naz Foundation, a Delhi–based queer and feminist advocacy organization, filed a petition in the Delhi High Court against Section 377 as an unconstitutional piece of legislation. As The Lawyers Collective states,

> In 2001, The Lawyers Collective, on behalf of *Naz Foundation (India) Trust*, filed a writ petition in Delhi High Court challenging the constitutionality of Section 377 on grounds of violation of right to privacy, dignity and health under Article 21, equal protection of law and non-discrimination under Articles 14 and 15 and freedom of expression under Article 19 of the Constitution.[8]

They further discuss the 2009 ruling stating, 'On 02.07.2009, the Delhi High Court passed a landmark judgment holding Section 377 to be violative of Articles 21, 14 and 15 of the Constitution, insofar as it criminalised consensual sexual acts of adults in private.'[9] The decision effectively criminalizes same-sex desire and queer people in the region.[10]

This is a story of Āzādī. This is a story of how an idea and refrain heard throughout history is translated in the contemporary moment through the defiant tongues and spirits of gendered bodies. How and why does 'Āzādī' articulate itself in gendered terms? Rather than offering an exhaustive history of Āzādī, I focus on its contemporary usage by outlining a genealogy of the limits of gendered citizenship in India. I trace the archetypal Indian woman, first constituted within colonial discourse and law, into the nationalist period where she is reimagined to support fantasies of cultural 'purity' and violently marked by histories of partition. I then follow her into the streets of contemporary urban India, where she embodies the new incarnation of Āzādī. Finally, I trace the gendered eruption of 'Āzādī' through Internet counter-publics that rematerialize 'citizenship' against the material gendered body. 'Āzādī' resonates with political acts that exist outside of colonialism and Hindu nationalism. However, contemporary 'Āzādī' finds new grammars of articulation. Contemporary feminist and queer, largely urban enactments of citizenship engage with technology, media spectacle, and global queer and feminist discourse. Indian life-worlds cut across Internet wires and through lines of transnational labour structured by oppressive workings of capital.

In *Violence*, Žižek discusses Internet tycoon Bill Gates, a figure whom he refers to as an icon of 'frictionless capitalism'.[11] The utopian promises made on behalf of technology should perhaps not be sealed in stone. One need only recall the unfortunate and undeniable truths regarding who owns the means of production, who attains the most profits from cyber technologies, and the nameless masses who often construct these technologies. Žižek states that there is a fantasmatic dimension to Gates' popularity as we imagine that he is '...a subversive, marginal hooligan who has taken over and dressed himself up as a respectable chairman'.[12] The idea of Gates as a subversive capitalist overshadows the dark sides of technological production, which often involve the exploitation of workers in the Global South. One can consider the mass attention that was given to the death of cyber capitalist Steve Jobs in comparison to the almost complete inattention to the multiple and repeated suicides of Chinese workers in Jobs' Foxconn factories in 2010.[13] Žižek states that

> [w]hat we have here is an ideological short-circuit between the two versions of the gap between reality and virtuality: the gap between real production and the virtual/spectral domain of Capital, and the gap between experiential reality and the virtual reality of cyberspace.[14]

And yet, I suggest that the skewed space and time of a technologically driven urban India, not running according to the workings of succinct calendars and clocks of a single nation, where voices and labour cut across Internet wires from Bangalore to Boston, might enable new grammars of gendered citizenship after orientalism.

Raped Nations and Unrapeable Wives: The Colonized Woman as 'Anti-citizen'

In 'Citizenship after orientalism', Engin Isin discusses the making of the modernist 'citizen' as a project tied to colonialism and orientalism. Isin states,

> ... the occidental tradition has constituted the Orient as those times and places where people have been unable to constitute themselves as political precisely because they have been unable to invent that identity the occident named as the citizen. The figure of the citizen that dominated the occidental tradition is the figure of that sovereign man (and much later woman) who is capable of judgment and being judged, transcending his (and much later her) tribal, kinship, and other primordial loyalties and belongingness.[15]

The making of 'the citizen' had implications for the simultaneous construction of the imagined 'Indian woman' as anti-citizen. If, as Isin suggests, the constitution of the occidental woman as citizen came 'much later', the temporal mappings of the so-called 'oriental woman' as citizen may never have arrived. One can ask how the colonial constitution of the orientalist body as unfree and unable to achieve full citizenship had and continues to have lasting implications for the making of the Indian woman as an object rather than a subject. As many postcolonial feminist writers suggest, if colonized men were unable to attain full countenance as subjects, colonized women were often constituted as visible to the state only to the extent that they could be counted as the property of elite men.[16] The construction of the Indian woman as property has its roots in colonial law and continues to have an impact upon normative forms of sexual violence in the Indian subcontinent.

One can consider that following the Delhi gang rape protests of 2012, the government of India made the decision to legally sanction marital rape despite recommendations from the Verma Committee, a judiciary review board appointed to review rape law in the subcontinent. The committee was comprised of

> ...retired Justice J.S. Verma, retired Justice Leila Seth and Solicitor General Gopal Subramanian, was constituted on December 23, 2012, to look into the possible amendments in the criminal laws related to sexual violence against women.[17]

The decision was justified on the basis that criminalizing marital rape would '...threaten the Indian family.'[18] A recent 2014 court ruling only further confirmed the legal sanction of rape. The judiciary ruled that a man who allegedly drugged a woman, forced her to marry him, and raped her was not legally culpable of any crime. The presiding judge stated that owing to their wedded union, '...the sexual intercourse between the two, even if forcible, is not rape and no culpability can be fastened upon the accused'.[19] There is a parallel between owning women's bodies as property of husbands and owning land that turns rape into a legally sanctioned act imbued with nationalist power. In counting the 'Indian woman' as the property of men, her rights of citizenship as bodily integrity are not only violated, they are nonexistent. The invisibility of the 'Indian woman' as gendered/sexual subject rather than object has its roots in occidentalist strategies of governance and the legal countenance of woman as property.

In *Codes of Misconduct: Regulating Prostitution in Late Colonial Bombay*, Ashwini Tambe discusses how the East India Company, which ruled India on behalf of the British Crown up to the Uprising of 1857, turned the rights of women into the rights of men who were thought to own them. Tambe writes that

> [t]he East India Company upheld the right of husbands to buy wives and parents to sell children, and it targeted the 'enticing' of children and women into prostitution as an infringement on these property rights of husbands and parents. The law thus largely enshrined male private property rights to women and children...[20]

The colonial construction of women as property informs the legal sanction of marital rape, despite opposition from progressive thinkers. Ongoing activist campaigns not limited to the 2012 Delhi gang rape protests are attempting to challenge these colonial laws and ideologies. One can ask how the narrative of 'protection' that emerged following the Delhi gang rape case of 2012 echoed colonial ideas that posit Indian women as victims of barbaric culture and also nationalist ideas that construct the Indian woman as the valued property of elite men.

Narratives of victimization and global sympathy that followed the Delhi gang rape case of 2012 can be seen as being tied to a genealogy of colonial desire, in which a missionary ethos also informs the feigning of care for the body of the colonized woman. While the global media covered this case and there was an outpouring of attention regarding it, one can question the writings of Western affluent neoliberal feminists who often constructed 'India' through an orientalist imaginary. Within certain narratives, the 'brown woman' in India was seen as a consummate victim of gendered violence in ways that supported a civilizational ideology of Western 'progress'.[21] Roy Chowdhury discusses how Awindra, Jyoti's male companion disappeared from the case, with many mainstream media narratives being scripted as what Spivak terms an old colonial tale of 'white men saving brown women from brown men.'[22] Narratives of 'poor brown women' emerge out of colonial history and its simultaneous construction of the cultural and political immaturity of colonized people. For example, Partha Chatterjee suggests that the sympathy that was lent to 'the Indian woman' can and should be thought of in relation to a deeper desire to govern and rule. Chatterjee writes,

> By assuming a position of sympathy with the unfree and oppressed womanhood of India, the colonial mind was able to transform this figure of the Indian woman into a sign of the inherently oppressive and unfree nature of the entire cultural tradition of a country.[23]

Chatterjee further discusses how Indian nationalists promoted a reverse orientalism to glorify 'Indian womanhood' and to construct a specific ideal of upper-caste Hindu womanhood. As Sangeeta Ray states, '...the discursive construction of the Indian nation by nationalists and imperialists was often inseparable from their idealisation of a Hindu India epitomised in a particular Hindu female figure.'[24] The constitution of the 'Indian woman' as a symbol of national 'culture' has been used throughout narratives of the Delhi gang rape case of 2012 and debates regarding the criminalization of queer desire, to frame sexual violence within an existing paradigm of heteronormative familial normalcy. For example, the construction of Jyoti as 'India's daughter' clearly functioned throughout mainstream narratives of the case to divide 'deserving' from 'undeserving victims'.

Discussing the use of names within narratives of the Delhi gang rape case of 2012 with feminist and queer activists, it was clear that conservative politicians and mainstream journalists constructed Jyoti as an idealized biopolitical subject against the bodies of those 'daughters' whose lives are not marked with the vitality of the nation. For example, the rape and murder of queer women, Dalit women, Muslim women, and 'Other' women often does not garner national empathy as these women's bodies are not marked with the stamp of 'Mother India', of those who will reproduce 'pure' bodies to serve nationalist visions of a pure nation. This approach to sexual violence uses rape cases to support conservative interests, law, and public policy including the criminalization of same-sex desire using Section 377 of the Indian Penal Code, India's colonial sodomy law.

Colonial Baggage Claims: From Partition to Contemporary Politics

The relationship between the Delhi gang rape case of 2012 and 'citizenship' in India gestures to histories of partition that mark the making of postcolonial India with blood. Kavita Daiya suggests that '…if there is a singular moment in the history of South Asia and Britain that had a profound and lasting effect on the politics and societies of many of the nations that make up contemporary South Asia, it is the 1947 Partition'.[25] The feminist and queer 'Āzādī' speaks to how freeing 'postcolonial' nations from British rule did not involve freeing 'the citizen' from gendered norms, shaped by British colonial law and moralities. The cry of 'Āzādī!' that echoes in the ears of all who bear witness to emerging feminist and queer movements is a cry for 'freedom' that may not fully translate into text, a freedom from colonial baggage that drags at the heels and souls of the nation. There is a long history of marking colonized people as 'non-citizens', one signalling the ambivalence of Empire. Bhabha quotes Lord Macaulay, a colonial officer who drafted Section 377 of the Indian Penal Code, India's sodomy law. In his essay on the East India Company, Macaulay wrote,

> It is probable that writing 15,000 miles from the place where their orders were to be carried into effect, the Directors of the East India never perceived the gross inconsistency of which they were guilty…Whoever examines their letters written at that time, will find there many just and humane sentiments…an admirable code of political ethics…Now these instructions, being interpreted, mean simply, 'Be the father and the oppressor of the people; be just and unjust, moderate and rapacious.'[26]

Bhabha reads these moments for their signs of inherent ambivalence, for their psychic and social anxiety. He suggests that,

> 'Be the father and the oppressor...just and unjust' is a mode of contra-dictory utterance that ambivalently reinscribes, across differential power relations, both coloniser and colonised. For it reveals an agonistic uncer-tainty contained in the incompatibility of empire and nation; it puts on trial the very discourse of civility within which representative govern-ment claims its liberty and empire its ethics...[27]

The utterance 'Be the father and the oppressor' speaks to the duplicity of colonial rule as the duplicity of patriarchal power. Years after Lord Macaulay wrote these words, his originary laws are upheld by the Supreme Court of India to criminalize queer desire. 'Sly civility' emerges not only through pro-test but everyday acts of deviance that ironically enact political 'citizenship' by laughing in the face of law. In the smallest gestures of queer people loving one another, of women occupying public space, of working people reclaim-ing the commons, the inability of the bureaucratic word to contain the body is expressed.

Āzādī: A New Genealogy of the Gendered 'Citizen'

Rather than seeing feminist and queer movements as being at odds with 'Indian culture', one can ask how these movements express the best parts of 'Indian culture', as political culture. While there were many who tried to turn the 2012 Delhi gang rape case into a chance to assert protectionist narratives regarding women 'in danger', the Āzādī moments that erupted gesture to how the South Asian subcontinent is haunted by histories of revolt. What is perhaps interesting about the Āzādī of 2012 in Delhi lies in how this moment of political revolt arose without warning, gesturing to a chronic and everyday problem of sexual violence in Delhi and through-out India. While the magnitude of torture inflicted onto Jyoti's body was beyond human comprehension, the moment of protest challenged constant and silently accepted acts of rape, sexual harassment, and deeply ingrained cultures of masculinist violence.

The spontaneous eruption of protest and revolt in the streets of Delhi, which spread throughout India and caused the whole world to, if only for a moment, take notice, was perhaps a contemporary illustration of Walter Benjamin's writings regarding states of emergency. For Benjamin, the state of emergency is not a suspended state or crisis point, but an everyday emer-gency that might also function as a point of political emergence.[28] One com-ment uttered over and over again in Delhi and throughout India was that this was just 'such a normal day'. This was 'just a bus ride'. This was just 'two people returning from seeing a movie after work'.[29] While as mentioned, the narrative of 'India's daughter' was used to divide normative bodies of women from the abjected, it was perhaps the violence of just another day in India that spoke to a moment of emergence born out of the state of emergency. This incident was not an exception but an expression of what can happen on 'just another day', not to 'certain' women but to all those who navigate public space in burgeoning urban centres such as Delhi, India. For a woman on the Delhi metro, for a maid raped in a middle-class suburban Delhi home, for a schoolgirl touched by her teacher, this was what Kannibaran calls 'the violence of normal times',[30] which is met perhaps by the miracle of the political event.[31] This is a common refrain from many I speak to who are active in social justice movements. At a protest following the decision to reinstitute Section 377 in 2013, I meet an activist who discusses the politically charged space of Delhi, stating,

> Every place has its pros and cons. But the pros of Delhi – in the entire country, this is the place that is most political. So if you belong to a marginal community, Delhi provides a space to voice your opinions and concerns. It's also the capital of the country, so there are a lot of people coming in, a lot of cultural intermingling. So, I live Delhi for that reason. I know there are a lot of problems with Delhi in that it's not safe for women. But I wouldn't leave Delhi for that, I would like to change Delhi. That's more important. Rather than just quit Delhi, change Delhi.[32]

Frantz Fanon once wrote, 'decolonisation is a violent process'.[33] Fanon is perhaps an important figure to consider in relation to contemporary feminist and queer struggles in India. Despite Fanon's obvious sexism and homophobia,[34] it was perhaps his centring of the dignity of minoritarian bodies that serves to make his ideas important in relation to contemporary feminist and queer struggles.

Contemporary neoliberal feminism, often aligned with the 'NGO-ization' of sexual politics, turns 'gender justice' into bureaucratic exercise. However, in the violence of street spectacle and the epistemic, psychological, and cultural struggle to alter normative understandings of gender that enable violence, anti-colonial political movements of today resonate with the Āzādī of anti-colonial histories. A founding member of the Forum to Engage Men, a nationwide non-governmental agency (NGO) that engages men against gendered violence, gestures to Delhi as a place of paradox. He states,

> ...we have to understand that Delhi has become a capital of protest against violence against women. So all of the issues about violence against women are being highlighted. So, some people are saying that Delhi is the global rape capital. But we are saying that you could also see this the other way, that Delhi has become the global protest capital against rape.[35]

The making of Delhi as the site of both sexual violence and protest is tied to the history of the subcontinent, the erection of borders, narratives of religious violence, and anxieties regarding cultural 'purity'. The will to contain the 'citizen' in regards to markings of religious, racial, 'cultural', and national 'purity' is tied to constructions of a 'pure' gendered body. And yet, this also produces what Isin terms 'activist citizens', as those that defy countenance by stable national categories. The emergence of foreign populations and stateless people corresponds to emerging activist movements that also create new vocabularies of political subjectivity and expand categories of national belonging. Within the context of India, one might see a cyclical pattern of partially failed efforts to contain bodies that defy colonial categorization. As Isin writes,

> We have categories to describe this figure: foreigner, migrant, irregular migrant, illegal alien, immigrant wanderer, refugee, émigré, exile, nomad, sojourner and many more that attempt to fix it. But so far this figure resists these categories not because it has an agency as such but because it unsettles the very attempt to fix it.[36]

The inability to fix categories of emergent political subjectivity gives way to new vocabularies of 'citizenship'. Perhaps emergent forms of gendered protest gesture to enactments of sexual politics that challenge the narrow countenance of bodies by the state, often rooted in patriarchal Hindu models of the family. Isin suggests that throughout the twentieth century we have seen political acts that defy categorization, both of bodies and the spaces they occupy as political subjects. And yet, the 'newness' of sexual politics can be questioned by examining how bodies that defy categorization might point to novel genealogies of political subjectivity in the subcontinent. Contemporary sexual politics are part of a longer genealogy that moves outside teleological ideas of 'progress'.

Hauntings: Sexy and Unsexy Ghosts

Political movements of today cannot be divorced from what authors discuss as foundational political histories that are endemic to India. Viswanath and Malik cite the work of Mushirul Husan who states that

> [n]o other country in the twentieth century has seen two such contrary movements taking place at the same time. If one was a popular nationalist movement, unique in the annals of world history for ousting the colonisers through non-violent means, the other, in its underbelly, was the counter movement of Partition, marked by violence, cruelty, blood- shed, displacement and massacres....[37]

While anti-colonial struggle produced alternative images of masculinity as evinced in figures such as Gandhi, partition involved expressions of violent masculinities deeply tied to modernist nations. The communal assault of women marked as 'other' during partition served as a symbolic power that expressed nationalist superiority through masculinist sexual violence. Women's bodies, both Hindu and Muslim, were used as objects to express a war between men and nations. The Delhi gang rape case, an act of group sexual violence committed by men in a vehicle moving through the streets of Delhi resonates with this history of communal uses of rape as a tool of power. While those accused of committing the crime were Hindu, as were their victims, they were marked as bearing lesser entitlements to masculinist power owing to class position and displacement within the urban sphere. In marking the woman, who perhaps exemplified the emerging middle-class urban face of India, there was a violent use of her body to claim patriarchal ownership not only over her life, but urban and national space. Isin notes that the ancient Greek city constructed the citizen as associated with masculinity, warriorship, and property. He states,

> At that moment, it seems that a new actor entered onto the stage of history, which was male, warrior, and owned property (not the least of which was the means of warfare)... Those who were not male and did not own property such as women, slaves, peasants, merchants, craftsmen, sailors increasingly found themselves as the others of the citizen – namely as subjects and abject...[38]

The warring, property-owning, male urban subject constituted the ideal political subject upon which the modern nation was built. What is specific to the history of India is the moment of the 1947 partition as one in which the making of the modern Indian nation involved enacting occidentalist 'citizenship' against the bodies of others. The citizen became a man and the man became a citizen often through asserting warriorship, masculinity, and entitlement to land against his distant and anxiously guarded-against cousins of Pakistan.[39] The brutality of sexual violence in India, its often group and communal nature, cannot be divorced from the making of India itself. There is a resonance to histories of trauma that defy ideas of linear time. One can consider the evocations of narratives of partition during the Gujarat riots of 2002. Avery Gordan uses the term 'haunting'

> ... to describe those singular and yet repetitive instances when home becomes unfamiliar, when your bearings on the world lose direction, when the over and done comes alive, when what's been in your blind field comes into view.[40]

The experience of gendered violence that enacts crimes against humanity within liminal space gestures to the uncomfortable place of women's bodies within nations, one that gives way to a loss of bearing. And yet, what might be endemic to the ritualistic enactment of gendered violence is perhaps the historical haunting of partition. It was through making women 'unhomely', through women's displacement, kidnapping, and violent sexual marking, that men express a masculinist and nationalist idea of 'home'.[41] Furthermore, the experience of warring men claiming entitlement to women's bodies also resonates with colonial narratives in which men became 'citizens' by using women's flesh to mark territory. Reading Isin's 'activist citizen' alongside Gordan gestures to the haunting resonance of anti-colonial struggle in India. Gordan suggests that haunting can be used to refer to a,

> socio-political-psychological state when something else, or something different from before, feels like it must be done, and prompts something to be done.[42]

The 'to be done' of 'Āzādī' speaks to something that haunts in the form of colonial markings of bodies as less than 'citizen', as less than human. Yet, the 'to be done' also lies in a sexual politics in which women and queers occupy city spaces in ways that enact a new political intelligibility. The urgency of what is 'to be done' was expressed in my conversations with a new generation of feminist and queer activists in India. One queer activist discusses the decision to reinstitute colonial sodomy laws as a moment of haunting futurity, a moment haunted by colonial rule and yet propelling something 'to be done'. He states,

> Before this judgment I was very proud about my sexuality or whatever but I was not someone who was going to do anything about it. But now, suddenly your country shuns you, you suddenly feel this need to go out and say something against it. And I think that is something, the activism that has come out since 2013. And before 2013, of course there was a lot of activism. But since 2013 I think people have started realising that we can't keep fighting amongst each other because the bigger aim is something else. And I see this now. There used to be protests held by one organisation and the other organisation would not attend but I see this going away. I see people coming forward and saying, okay, let's just attend it anyway. And it's beautiful to see.[43]

The 'unhomely' hauntings of gendered/sexual bodies that are marred through violence and colonial law can be left without bearing, giving way to finding one's bearings, in the streets and in the histories of anti-colonial rebellion that also haunt the subcontinent. The unsexy ghosts of Lord Macaulay meet the historical resonances of passion that haunt the political subject in inspiring ways. Gordan suggests that haunting involves a 'core contest over the future, over what's to come next or later'.[44] The futurity of colonial and partition haunting that surround the eerie workings of gendered violence and colonial laws in India are expressed in the work of contemporary activists, who wage a struggle over the future.

Untouchable Dignity: Ambedkar and Bodily Integrity

Many activists whom I speak to in regards to Section 377 of the Indian Penal Code and the Delhi gang rape of 2012 continually make reference to the concept of 'dignity'. The enshrinement of dignity within the Indian constitution and perhaps the Indian psyche can be traced back to revolutionary figures such as B. R. Ambedkar (1891–1956), anti-caste activist, barrister, political leader, and Dalit rights activist. Ambedkar once suggested that '[t] he individual is an end in itself'.[45] He perhaps believed that individuals are granted certain inalienable rights under the Indian constitution that cannot be interfered with or curtailed.[46] One can ask how the words and ethos of Ambedkar can exist alongside communal and colonial understandings of gender and sexuality that threaten the gendered body's ability to express itself outside of familial, communal, and nationalist norms? The Delhi gang rape case of 2012 expressed a lingering haunting of communally enacted sexual violence against women in public space. Similarly, Section 377 expressed the usage of colonial law in ways that gestured to the haunting resonance of the contemporary political moment. These moments, both violent episodes in a history of colonial violence and moments of potential revolt that can open up alternative political genealogies, speak to how haunting exists in the violence of the state as much as the work of Ambedkar and others might haunt the futurity of sexual politics. The notion of the individual body as carrying an inalienable dignity within and not in spite of its marked skin, gestures to histories of anti-caste activism in which the 'touchability' of untouchables might inform sexual and feminist politics in the region. The body as contagion, as toxic object of fear in regards to criminalized queers and women marked as 'bad' or 'tainted' is also perhaps tied to a genealogy of the body of the untouchable, gesturing to how anxieties of bio-political 'purity' in Hindustan are tied to a broader colonial and nationalist history.

While the case of Jyoti was clearly narrated by mainstream media as one of 'respectable' womanhood and believable victimization of an idealized Hindu woman, there was perhaps something about how the violence enacted against her body moved so many to political action that gestured to a resonance of ideas of bodily integrity across time. Again and again, in the streets of Delhi, protesters make reference to bodily violence enacted in the Delhi gang rape case, gesturing to a lack of humanity that breaks from archetypal feminist scripts regarding gendered violence to a larger questioning of bodily dignity beyond gender. One woman whom I speak to at an anniversary protest of the Delhi gang rape case states, 'I don't know what has happened. How have people lost all sense of morality, all sense of dignity?'[47] Such a questioning and return to concepts of bodily integrity resonates with Ambedkar's writings used to champion the entitlements of Dalits. The Delhi gang rape protests cannot be divorced from the hauntings of colonial rule and partition and the return to bodily integrity central to anti-colonial struggles throughout the history of the Indian subcontinent.

No Space Called Home: Unhomely Bodies, Estranged Desires

While there was an understandable shock regarding the magnitude of torture within the Delhi gang rape of 2012, and an outrage regarding the Supreme Court decision to uphold Section 377, bodies exist in space. What emerges as a constant refrain in conversations regarding gender justice within urban India is the often-uncomfortable spaces that gendered bodies occupy. While the body may have a dignity counted as constitutional right, the body does not live in constitutions. In the real time of the streets, the feminist and queer body is often violently haunted by colonial rule and narratives of partition in the everyday acts of trying to live a life. I speak with a young migrant man from UP who works at the multinational coffee chain Café Coffee Day. He discusses feeling 'disgusted' by the 2012 Delhi gang rape case and states that there is a problem regarding who feels entitled to occupy public spaces in cities. He states quite clearly, 'Long, long time the problem has been in India, that the space, all the space belongs to men.'[48] Against the will of affluent political elites to pathologize young migrant men as the enemies of women, he sees himself in solidarity with women. 'The city does not belong to me either. But it is even less belonging to women.'[49] Roy Chowdhury states that the mainstream media constructed Jyoti as a Hindu middle class urban woman who was attacked by impoverished migrant men. The author states however, that Jyoti was also a migrant to Delhi and her "family was part of the Kurmi community, a lower caste group with agricultural origins; her attackers, it turns out, also belong to lower caste groups..."[50] What migrant workers and women perhaps have in common in cities such as Delhi lies in their inability to be seen as the rightful owners of the city. If, as Isin suggests, the figure of the occidentalist citizen is seen as a property-owning, warring male subject, the body of the feminized impoverished migrant worker in Delhi as well as the feminized body trying to navigate city streets are both constituted as lesser citizens. As I will develop further, given the deep inequalities in the occupation of public space in the city, technology and cyber activism has increasingly emerged as a way that young workers, women, and other disenfranchised bodies can assert political opinion.

The use of the Internet as a means of not only localized but transnational activism was clearly expressed following the 2013 decision by the Supreme Court of India to criminalize same-sex desire using a colonial law dating back to the height of British rule. Cyber activism is one means through which global days of solidarity were held around the world, and also a means through which many people who feared harassment, abuse, and murder in the streets could express themselves and seek solidarity. One queer activist whom I speak with in India discusses the spatialized fears of queer people following the institution of Section 377. He discusses queer couples who express fear following the 2013 Supreme Court ruling. He makes reference to the case of a couple who have been together for three years, during which the Delhi High Court judgement of 2009 offered them some protection. He states,

> They've been living together for three years now, but now, they think what if they tell the neighbours to not park their car there and they get pissed off and call the police. And the maid who works here, might say, oh I've seen them sleeping together in the bed. And then, before you know it, the police might stop them and say we are stopping them from doing an offense against 377. And this is how 377 works.[51]

The occidentalist constitution of 'the citizen' as a warring, masculine, and property-owning subject continues to inform who is imagined as entitled to spaces of pleasure, desire, and mobility within city space. Shilpa Phadke has written extensively about the relationship between gender and public space in India. I speak with her in Mumbai where she teaches at the Tata Institute of Social Sciences. She states,

> Often in India the understanding of public space is very much structured around safety. And I think now, because it is out there in the public and there is a discussion happening there is a space for *Back-off Āzādī*.[52] There is an idea for fun and loitering which my colleagues and I have tried to advance. I think what the last year has done is to create little spaces for *Back-Off Āzādī* and to talk about what we have been doing, which is to speak about fun and loitering. The idea of a right to public space.[53]

Yet, while she is optimistic and suggests that her enduring hope comes from the continued tenacity of women to occupy public space, she also acknowledged the continued policing and erasure of gendered bodies in city spaces. She makes the astute observation that the Delhi gang rape protests have generated a dialogue regarding public space, while not necessarily altering the ways that bodies continue to move within public space. She observes,

> ...in many ways it's changed the ways we talk about public space. I don't know if it's changed how we inhabit public space, if you know what I mean. At least public space is an actor in this conversation....[54]

Rather than seeing cyber activism as a substitute for street-based action, or as a default position within hostile spaces, the counter-publics of Internet time might gesture to the haunted temporalities of urban India. The Indian city is one housed somewhere between a digital divide that prevents the majority of the public from access to basic electricity, water, and housing, while newly criminal queers and women can take refuge online. The class privilege of being able to access the Internet, to communicate and understand often English-centric writings, meets spaces of haunted streets. In a panel discussion regarding cyber feminism in India, one cyber feminist points out that Internet activism often appeals to women and queer people due to its ability to level the material power of bodies. 'You have women saying that they are free online, because no man is bigger than them online, no man can crowd them out of the space.'[55] While she went on to discuss cyber harassment, she remains adamant that many women see the Internet as liberation from the bodily bullying of streets. She writes over email, 'Online I am as big as any man, and I can SHOUT JUST AS LOUD.'[56]

Narrow Paths and Broadband Connections: Āzādī.com?

Through the dim light of a computer screen, flickering like candles sheltered from the wind at protests held one year ago, after a woman, yet another woman, was raped and murdered in 'the world's largest democracy', I receive a message. It reads only, 'My country sucks!' The attached PDF document is marked by all the terms of legality, of bureaucracy, of the forked tongues of civility imposed in a viciously cold Queen's English. The Supreme Court of India has struck down all petitions made regarding Section 377 of the Indian Penal Code, India's sodomy bill. Petitions filed by scholars, feminists, activists, lawyers, petitions filed by 'citizens', petitions filed by criminals. Since Lord Macaulay first wrote those old colonial laws, the Indian body has been pushed, pulled, and prodded by text. And yet, how might the Internet world open up the possibility for new worlds and words? While there are ongoing debates regarding the digital divide in India, Rosi Braidotti, Donna Haraway, and South Asian cyber feminists such as Radhika Gajjala discuss the role the Internet plays in feminist and queer movements in India.[57] One can consider the key role that the Internet played in organizing demonstrations following the Delhi gang rape case of 2012 and in disseminating information regarding the actions globally.[58] One can also consider the role of the Internet in generating global support for queer people following the decision to reinstitute Section 377 of the Indian Penal Code, with 'Days of Rage' being held worldwide.[59] It is perhaps important to read uses of the Āzādī of the Internet within contemporary political struggles in India in a transnational framework. The Arab Spring protests of 2011 gave way to an inspiring moment of resistance, largely witnessed by much of the world outside of Egypt through the Internet. Antonio Negri discussed the use of the

'Internet commons' in these protests as a means through which an intelligent population could self-organize for radical political aims. Negri wrote,

> ...social network tools, such as Facebook, Youtube, and Twitter are the modes of expression of an intelligent population capable of using the at hand to organize autonomously.[60]

Ravinder Barn also discusses uses of social media and Internet-based technologies used in the Delhi gang rape protests in relation to the Arab Spring. Barn suggests that the use of Internet technologies was a means through which urban middle classes were able to stage a protest and create a discourse of new feminist politics that reached beyond its own gaze. Barn states,

> What has been striking about the Indian protests is that while they were led by both young men and women, who were educated, urban and middle class, they reached out and connected with others from a diverse range of backgrounds throughout Indian society.[61]

While the digital divide still operates within India, largely dividing urban publics from rural areas where the Internet is often not available, the space of urban India is increasingly one in which many people have access to mobile phones and Internet mediums across class. Speaking with NGO activists who work with youth in the slums of Delhi, they are adamant that young men and women in slums have access to mobile phones and Internet technologies, often accessed through large cultures of digital piracy that make such tools increasingly accessible.[62] The rise of neoliberal models of business and the outsourcing of call centres has also led to the proliferation of Internet-driven industries and forms of labour, in which increasingly, young workers are becoming literate in Internet mediums. However, as mentioned previously in regards to the exploitation of workers in the IT industry, there are obvious downfalls to the supposed 'technological revolution'. While cyber feminism has been heralded by some as being part of a fourth wave of the feminist movement, particularly giving rise to new transnational activist networks, the virulent misogyny of cyberspace cannot be denied. While the Internet is a means for dissent, it is also a means through which many women and queer people are stalked, harassed, abused, and made vulnerable to violence. For example, the Internet can be used to stalk women from the screen to the street, creating cyber environments that harm women psychologically and emotionally and lead to rape, physical violence, and murder.[63]

The Delhi gang rape protests and protests regarding Section 377 of the Indian Penal Code, India's sodomy bill, are indicative of a constant contest in cyberspace between feminist and activist voices and those that espouse the vitriol of misogyny, whether it be from political leaders, state forces, or everyday patriarchs. Ravinder Barn charts the emergence of new feminist movements in India as being tied to the large number of Internet and social media users in India. Barn suggests that

> [i]t is evident that India as a country is witnessing a significant technolog-ical revolution. It is estimated that the number of broadband connections in India is more than twice the size of the British general population. And there are 65 million Facebook users and an estimated 35 million Twitter accounts.[64]

The use of the Internet to articulate dissent perhaps expresses the haunting fear of the truth of gendered power that disciplines bodies in public spaces, to the point of death. The cries of 'Āzādī' that were tweeted and 'shouted' online bore witness to the real lack of freedoms of the body within the city street while also using Internet space and time to move bodies into streets. The subsequent use of water cannons against protesters in December of 2012 by the Delhi police, and closing of the Delhi metro which enclosed protest-ers at India Gate,[65] preventing the acts from growing and challenging consti-tutional rights of freedom of mobility and assembly, expressed the violence of state power. The Internet, however, offered a means through which these abuses of power could be recorded and broadcast throughout the world, shaming the state in its flagrant abuse of power.

One can perhaps see the Internet as a means through which what Fou-cault terms a 'regime of truth' is challenged. In a 1977 interview, 'The politi-cal function of the intellectual', Foucault suggests that 'truth isn't outside power, or deprived of power: on the contrary, truth is produced by virtue of multiple constraints [a]nd it induces regulated effects of power'.[66] Foucault discusses a 'regime of truth' in relation to the acts of power that are used to separate 'truth' from 'error'. The 'truths' of state power within the Delhi gang rape protests of December 2012 were produced through an existing regime of colonial governmentality and neoliberal models of governance in which the dissent of people could be managed to support an 'India shining' model, while gesturing to a patriarchal imperialist power that rules through force, against constitutional rights and basic principles of justice. The unruly body of the protester could be physically assaulted and immobilized by state power in ways that speak to the ironies of a patriarchal state that disciplines and violates bodies of protesters, feminized by the masculine power of the state in similar ways as gendered bodies are feminized in acts of street-based violence.

The protection of 'our daughters' produced a truth of the idealized 'vic-tim' of gendered violence as a Hindu middle-class woman, fighting against a lower-class man. This rewriting of the truth through nationalist and familial tropes erases the violence of the police and state in using water cannons and excessive force against many of 'India's daughters', namely protesters who moved quickly from 'perfect victims' to abject citizens in their acts of protest. James Baldwin once commented, 'A victim who can articulate their victimization, ceases to become a victim and becomes a threat.'[67] The 'victimization' of the Indian woman can be thought of in relation to longer discourses of orientalist images of Indian women that inform the current regime of postcolonial governance. The Indian woman as a consummate victim, in need of patriarchal and state governance, has a long history that can be traced back to colonialism. The 'truth' told by the Indian state functions within this regime of imperialist power and governance. However, Foucault also makes clear that if the truth is contextual and contingent, the task one is presented with is to create alternative truths. Foucault suggests that the task of the leftist thinker is to consider alternative spaces outside of regimes of bureaucratically sanctioned truth.[68] Within India, the Internet functions as a means through which counter-discourse enters the public sphere in ways that make other truth claims possible. However, it is important to draw a distinction between 'social media' and uses of the Internet by the state for the purposes of governance. And yet, what is deeply interesting about the Delhi gang rape protests of 2012 and Section 377 of the Indian Penal Code, the Indian sodomy bill, lies in how the protest movements that originated in December of 2012 and December of 2013 might have gestured to how protesters and transnational witnesses to gendered violence could use the Internet to pressure and shame political leaders. Still, from my fieldwork in India it is also clear that the Internet might create the illusion of people power without any meaningful and lasting changes at the level of governance.

One can also consider how the transnational flows of information and access to bodies of women and children in the Indian subcontinent through the Internet can also support human trafficking, medical experiments on impoverished feminized bodies, organ trafficking, and questionable practices of international adoption and surrogacy. However, as I suggest throughout this chapter, the Internet and new forms of technological communication can also enable women and queer people to not only challenge sexual and physical violence but also to interrupt the ongoing epistemic violence of colonial history. As I suggest, the Internet offers an intertext to the authorial claims of the state in ways that may not affect governance but may help to build new communities of political subjects, across and in spite of borders.

One year after the Delhi gang rape of 2012, I returned again to India. Shortly before the anniversary of this case, the streets again felt haunted. The old ghost of Lord Macaulay was back, as the Supreme Court of India made the shocking decision to uphold Section 377 of the Indian Penal Code, India's sodomy bill. Most protests I have attended regarding Section 377 of the Indian Penal Code and the Delhi gang rape case were organized online, through listservs, social media, emails, and text messages. The Internet functions as the medium that enables bodily assembly, movements, and the creation of political events as much as it speaks to the ironies of 'postco-lonial' cities that resonate with the repressive gestures of imperial history. Interviews with feminists and particularly with newly 'criminal' queers are often organized online. The question of safety and freedom in public space is a haunting one that perhaps gestures to how the litany of press cover-age regarding sexual violence in India as well as the historical memory of women, queers, feminists, and activists carries traces of the deeply imbri-cated worlds of personal and political violence in the subcontinent.

Avery Gordan discusses the complex terrains that people navigate, ones that belie easy narratives of acute victimization or triumphant will. While global media often narrate cases such as the Delhi gang rape case and Sec-tion 377 as simplistic tales of persecuted women and queers, or spectacles of protest, she suggests that human subjectivity and political subjectivity are complex. Gordan states that

> even those who live in the most dire circumstances possess a complex and oftentimes contradictory humanity and subjectivity that is never adequately glimpsed by viewing them as victims or, on the other hand, as super human agents.[69]

She goes on to discuss complex personhood as an acceptance that 'stories people tell about themselves, about their troubles, about their social worlds, and about their society's problems are entangled and weave between what is immediately available as a story and what their imaginations are reach-ing toward'.[70] In my conversations in India regarding gender violence, there is an entanglement that Gordan discusses regarding immediate narratives of sexual violence coupled with imagining a future that inspires political action.

On the day before the anniversary of the Delhi gang rape, I am walking past a local park. A man is following me, at a close enough distance that I am aware of his gaze and body at every turn. I wait for him to pass. He is gone, lost to the darkness of a street with faulty lighting and narrow paths women navigate, his menacing stare another ghostly matter that chills to the bone. I hear someone cry out, an unintelligible muttering. He is there again, masturbating in full view, looking me dead in the eye. This is 'India shining', one of broadband connections and narrow paths, one of women gang raped, tortured, and murdered on public buses and memorialized the world over through flickering screens of computers, shining like candles at another vigil, for another woman, on just another day in 'the world's largest democracy'.[71]

I awake the next day and the day after to attend demonstrations, meet-ings, events, and discussions regarding the Delhi gang rape protests of 2012 and Section 377, India's sodomy bill. When speaking to people not affili-ated with feminist, queer, or activist movements, I mention the story of the man masturbating. The first reaction often involves a questioning of what time of night it was, what I was wearing, if I was alone or if I had been 'partying'. The other reaction is one of a moralistic outrage tied to both a Hindu nationalist and class-based ethos of 'cleanliness' and a colonial script of bodily 'purity'.[72] The incident is 'dirty' and speaks to a 'certain type of person', one from a 'bad community'. These reactions concur with Shilpa Phadke's research regarding popular perceptions of gender violence in India, which often aim at protecting 'respectable', meaning upper-class Hindu Indian women not only from 'bad men' but also in ways that excuse the abuse of 'Other' women and even see these women as a threat to the 'respectable' image of the good Hindu woman/wife.[73] In the gap between the experiences of the body, apprehended in the city street through disciplinary gendered power that justifies and informs violence and the colonial texts of history's shame and anxiety is a dream of translation. It is the dream of translating bodily shame and violation outside of categorizations that order people's pain in ways that make them objects of selective empathy and chilling contempt. While the masturbating man might be read as a threat to women's modesty, the legal sanction of rape speaks to a naturalization of heteronormative male sexual desire and right against the 'unnatural' and invisible desires of women and queers. One can consider that Section 377 of the Indian Penal Code criminalizes 'unnatural' sexual acts, including masturbation. One year before the masturbating man entered the scene as an object of scholarly inquiry, the Delhi police set off a litany of water cannons onto protesters, wasting water in a country in which many still die of dehydration. The Delhi police used resources garnered from labour of 'citizens' to blatantly attack protesters. I could not help but think of the similitude between images of men masturbating all over the streets of India, all over the days of women in India, and the Delhi police spraying an impotent power into crowds. A year after displays of state-led masturbatory power were captured and disseminated through Internet wires, I ventured into the streets to find a space of protest, of translation. In conducting fieldwork in Delhi, at a commemorative protest held on the anniversary of the Delhi gang rape of 2012, I meet Pavel, a Delhi-based queer and feminist activist. Pavel states,

> I think things have changed. Now when you speak to your friends, your colleagues, your classmates, things like gender are being spoken about. That to me is what the protests were about. Not just about this case but about raising awareness about how gender comes to act upon all our lives. And to talk about it. Gender is a controlling aspect. Whether man or woman, everyone has felt the controlling aspects of gender. And this was a time for everyone to come together and say we won't go through this control forever. But it also has to come in your everyday engagement with life, in your everyday cognizance of life.[74]

Pavel suggests that the Delhi gang rape case protests and queer rights are connected:

> The anti-rape protests are very much connected to the queer rights movement. Whether it's a fight for gender equality, sexuality, caste, it's about basic dignity. To be able to live with dignity, to have the liberty to be who you are. On another level, it's also against a certain harassment and a certain suppression you go through. So really it's about protecting the integrity of the person, whether that individual be Dalit, be queer, working class. It's about a struggle for dignity for everyone.[75]

The countenance of 'citizenship' through colonial classification makes individuals intelligible to the nation in gendered terms. Homi Bhabha writes,

> If hybridity is heresy, then to blaspheme is to dream. To dream not of the past or present, nor the continuous present; it is not the nostalgic dream of tradition, nor the Utopian dream of modern progress; it is the dream of translation as 'survival' as Derrida translates the 'time' of Benjamin's concept of the afterlife of translation, as sir-vivre, the act of living on borderlines...[76]

Making desire translatable through cyber networks enables the survival of political movements and the psychic and social survival of those alienated in their 'home'. And yet, translation is a two-way street that traffics in multiple mythologies. In translating sexual politics into the language of 'Āzādī', traces of anti-colonial resistance also survive. The significance of 'Āzādī' lies in its ability to speak in a grammar outside of teleological ideas of 'progress', in which feminism and queerness are associated with Western secular capitalist modernity. The use of a language spoken across borders of India, Pakistan, and beyond challenges Jasbir Puar's 'homonationalist' body, a queer and feminist subject aligned with succinct nationalist interests. A gendered Āzādī lives on borderlines, defying the nation's investments in the imagined 'purity' of 'culture' and of people. While we labour and dream of spaces not haunted by the violent histories of colonial rule, we gather strength and solidarity, sharing new words for old desires: *Āzādī*.[77]

Notes

1   'Delhi' refers to both New Delhi and Old Delhi. The city of Delhi is the capital of the Indian subcontinent and encompasses both the New and Old districts of the urban metropolis.

2 See: Esha Shah, "Understanding the Structure of Violence," 1 February 2013. Kafila. Online edition. http://kafila.org/2013/02/01/delhi-gang-rape-understanding-the-structure-of-violence/ (accessed 7 September 2014). In this piece, Shah discusses the Delhi gang rape case in relation to the obsessive agency on the part of those who engage in crimes against humanity. Shah draws parallels between the obscene and incomprehensible brutalities enacted against Jyoti's body and those of Nazi soldiers. Shah draws on the work of Elaine Scarry and her understanding of the body in pain and the role it plays in regards to the forming of subjectivity. Shah's work also gestures to the writings of Slavoj Žižek, who discusses the obscene underbelly of the official scripts of law and order. One can consider that the 2012 Delhi gang rape happened within a time in which the Indian subcontinent is branding itself as a neoliberal success story, living in an 'India shining' of technological progress and a growing urban middle class. The obscene underbelly perhaps lies in the lived material violence enacted against the bodies of women and queers. One can also consider laws that are discussed throughout this work that make 'marital rape' legal. The obscene underbelly of the official law which allows men as husbands to rape women as wives is perhaps expressed in these extreme spectacles of street-based assaults, while normative abuse and rape is hidden from public view in the Hindu middle-class family home and supported by law. See Slavoj Žižek, *Violence: Six Sideways Reflections* (London: Picador, 2006).

3 Anonymous street interview, Jurrat memorial protest 16 December 2013. Interview by Tara Atluri 16 December 2013. The interviews that are referenced in this chapter are taken from fieldwork done in the Indian subcontinent at different intervals between December 2012 and June 2014. The interviews involve several participants, some of whom were interviewed during ongoing protests regarding the brutal gang rape and murder of Jyoti Singh Pandhey in Delhi, India, and the 2013 decision to criminalize same-sex desire in India using Section 377, India's colonial sodomy law. Interviews were also conducted with those who participated in panel discussions, meetings, colloquiams, and conferences regarding these two historic moments, changes to national rape and sexual harassment law, and debates regarding gender, sexuality, and urban space. Further interviews were done with non-governmental organizations in Delhi and throughout India, such as Jagori, Crea, the Forum to Engage Men(Fem), the JNU Jawaharlal Nehru University students' association, students from Delhi University, Tata Institute of Social Sciences, Indira Gandhi National Open University, and other institutions in Delhi and throughout India. Street interviews were also conducted in Delhi with many people, primarily young women and men who participated in the Delhi gang rape protests and the protests regarding Section 377, India's sodomy bill. Finally, in-depth interviews were done with young women and men who consented to discuss sexual violence, homophobia, and queer politics in India through professional and personal contacts. These interviews were done due to agreements of confidentiality between myself and those I spoke with. The number of people interviewed during two years of ongoing protests, which often took place on the street and informally, is hard to gauge. Ten in-depth personal interviews regarding rape, homophobic hate crime, and gender-based violence were done.

4 The archival and qualitative research utilized in this chapter is part of a forthcoming full-length monograph regarding the 2012 Delhi gang rape protests

and protests regarding the criminalization of same-sex desire in India by the 2013 Supreme Court decision to uphold Section 377, India's sodomy law. This research would not have been possible without the generous support of the Social Sciences and Humanities Research Council of Canada, through which I received two years of post-doctoral funding to conduct this work. I would like to extend my sincere gratitude to the Social Sciences and Humanities Research Council of Canada and all those who support my applications for grant funding.

 5 See Esha Shah, "Understanding the Structure of Violence" 1 February 2013. Kafila. Online edition. http://kafila.org/2013/02/01/delhi-gang-rape-understand-ing-the-structure-of-violence/ (accessed 7 September 2014). In this piece, Shah discusses the Delhi gang rape case in relation to the obsessive agency on the part of those who engage in crimes against humanity. Shah draws parallels between the obscene and incomprehensible brutalities enacted against Jyoti's body and those of Nazi soldiers. Shah draws on the work of Elaine Scarry and her under-standing of the body in pain and the role it plays in regards to the forming of sub-jectivity. Shah's work also gestures to the writings of Slavoj Žižek, who discusses the obscene underbelly of the official scripts of law and order. One can consider that the 2012 Delhi gang rape happened within a time in which the Indian sub-continent is branding itself as a neoliberal success story, living in an 'India shin-ing' of technological progress and a growing urban middle class. The obscene underbelly perhaps lies in the lived material violence enacted against the bodies of women and queers. One can also consider laws that are discussed throughout this work that make 'marital rape' legal. The obscene underbelly of the official law which allows men as husbands to rape women as wives is perhaps expressed in these extreme spectacles of street-based assaults, while normative abuse and rape is hidden from public view in the Hindu middle-class family home, and sup-ported by law. See Slavoj Žižek, *Violence: Six Sideways Reflections* (London: Picador, 2006).

 6 As Vinay Sitapti has discussed in relation to the 'India shining' election campaign launched by the BJP and the rise of neoliberal economies and political governance in New Delhi and throughout urban India, The Bharatiya Janata Party's catch-phrase may have misfired in the 2004 general elections, but 'India shining' cap-tures a mood and a class that is undeniably true. The birth of 'India shining' as a middle-class movement is closely linked to the opening of the Indian economy, first in the early 1980s when foreign capital was allowed to enter India (41).

 7 See Saurabh, 124.

 8 Lawyers Collective, "LGBT Section 377" (2015).

 9 Ibid.

10 Journalist Samyukta Maindarkar cites queer activists in the region, writing that upholding Section 377 denies basic human rights to sexual minorities in the country. Further, they say, it will inhibit discussion on an issue already considered controversial and taboo, especially as discussion on sex and sexuality in any form is rare (Maindarkar 2013). Feminists, activists, and queer people I speak with in India suggest that often despite the technical criminalization of all non-penile and vaginal sex, Section 377 is largely used to target same-sex desire and queer people.

11 Žižek (2015).

12 Žižek, *Violence*, 17.

13 Branigan, *The Guardian Online* (2010).

14 Žižek, *The Universal Exception*, 228.
15 Isin, "Citizenship After Orientalism," 32.
16 McClintock (1995); Chatterjee (1989); Sreenivas (2008).
17 *The Hindu* (2013).
18 Menon, *Kafila* (2013).
19 Zimmerman, *Globalpost* (2014).
20 Tambe, 28.
21 Dordi and Walton Roberts further write,

   Many consider the lifestyle of the diaspora to be a model that can overcome societal and civil woes 'back home'. Unlike 'back home' where women are expected to be submissive, obedient, and meek, Canadian culture is supposed to allow them to be strong, independent, and liberated. Consequently, when South Asian-Canadian women are intimidated, assaulted, raped, or even killed, there is a very uncomfortable debate about whether these events represent the 'west's' or the 'east's' version of rape culture [2].

22 Roy Chowdhury, Poulami. "The Delhi Gang Rape: The Making of International Causes." *Feminist Studies*. Vol. 39, No. 1 (2013), 283.
23 Chatterjee, 622.
24 Daiya, 4.
25 Ibid., 5.
26 Bhabha, 135.
27 Ibid., 136.
28 Benjamin (2009).
29 Atluri, fieldwork notes (2013).
30 Kannibaran (2005).
31 Badiou (2007).
32 Atluri, fieldwork notes (2014).
33 Muñoz (1999). In *Disidentifications: Queers of Colour and the Politics of Resistance*, José Esteban Muñoz suggests that through processes of disidentification, women and queer people can both identify with Fanon's revolutionary ethos while also questioning his explicit and implicit sexism and homophobia. Munoz discusses the monocausal protocols that stop subjects from accessing different identities. For example, he suggests that female and queer subjects of colour are implicitly barred from accessing revolutionary subject positions within the texts of canonical postcolonial scholars in which there is an implicit assumption that the black body is male and the white body is female.
34 See Bergner (1995).
35 Atluri, fieldwork notes (2014).
36 Isin, "The Activist Citizen," 367.
37 Viswanath and Malik, 61.
38 Isin, "The Activist Citizen," 367.
39 Daiya (2008).
40 Gordan, 2.
41 Daiya (2008).
42 Gordan, 3.
43 Atluri, fieldwork notes (2014).
44 Gordan, 3.
45 Mishra, 172.

46 Ray and Ray, 7. In the article, 'B.R. Ambedkar and His Philosophy on Indian Democracy: An Appraisal," the authors outline the principles of Ambedkar's thought. They write:

The dignity of the individual, political liberty, social progress and human rights are necessary constitutional safeguards which form Ambedkar's basic decent democratic ideals in the political democracy. To him, the ground plan means the social structure of a community to which the political plan is sought to be applied. Political democracy and liberty are nothing if not beaked and bucked up by equal social patterns, because the political structure rests on the social structure...It is, therefore, essential that before passing any Judgment on any scheme of political relationship even making plans for economic reforms, the people must consider the ground plan that means social relations. Democracy should be regarded as both a social and a political method.

47 Atluri, fieldwork notes (2014).
48 Ibid.
49 Ibid.
50 Roy Chowdhury, 284.
51 Atluri, fieldwork notes (2014).
52 Krishnan (2013). Kavita Krishnan (Secretary of the All-India Progressive Women's Association) delivered a speech following the Delhi gang rape protests in which she used the phrase 'Back Off: Azadi'. This slogan was utilized by protestors following the Delhi gang rape case to launch a campaign for freedom for women in public spaces, against Hindu nationalist arguments that reframe gendered violence as a justification for protectionism. http://freedomwithoutfearplatformuk. blogspot.ca/2013/12/indias-anti-rape-movement-experiences.html
53 Atluri, fieldwork notes (2013).
54 Ibid.
55 Atluri, fieldwork notes (2014).
56 Ibid.
57 Braidotti (1996); Haraway (1991); Gaijala (2005).
58 Atluri, fieldwork notes (2014).
59 Pain, occupy.com (2014).
60 Hardt and Negri (2011). It should be noted that Hardt and Negri's reference to Arab protesters as 'the new pioneers' is perhaps contentious as it speaks to an effort to place them within a genealogy of Western enlightenment, speaking perhaps to the lingering orientalist ethos that haunts one's language and political appraisals of protests in the Arab world. However, their general arguments regarding the exemplary uses of technology by intelligent, passionate activist is still deeply important and offers a meaningful appraisal of contemporary cyberspace as a tool for political dissent. For a discussion from the Oecumene: Citizenship After Orientalism research group that involved discussing the question 'Were the Arabs awakened?' from a perspective that critiqued orientalist approaches to political theory see 'Who Decides?' Open Forum Questions. Oecumene: Citizenship After Orientalism, 25 March 2011. http://www.oecumene.eu/forum/ open-questions/were-the-arabs-awakened/who-decides Online edition (accessed 7 September 2014).
61 Barn (2013).

62 Vishnu (2013). Vishnu notes,

> New media has made its way into slums – 72.7 per cent households have phones, of which 63.5 per cent have only mobile phones and 10.4 per cent slum households have computers. Also, 94.1 per cent slum households have a kitchen inside their homes and 51.3 per cent use either LPG or piped gas to cook. However, a high percentage of slum households (47.4 per cent) still use polluting fuels such as wood, cow dung cakes and kerosene to cook.

63 Saha and Srivastava (2014).
64 Barn (2013).
65 India Gate is a popular site for protest in New Delhi and a nationalist monument.
66 Foucault (1977).
67 Baldwin, 115.
68 Foucault (1977).
69 Gordan, 4.
70 Ibid.
71 Far from being endemic to Delhi, feminists have documented the ways in which public masturbation occurs in urban centres throughout India and globally. In particular, Indian scholars document the occurrence of masturbation as a tool of sexual violence against women on public transport in major Indian cities. This research serves to document the street as a site of violence, politicizing women and queer people's right to occupy public space and the everyday crimes they face for doing so. It should, however, be noted that this violence should not obscure the larger problems of normalized levels of abuse, harassment, coercion, rape, and misogyny that are safely guarded within the Hindu middle-class home and other idealized domestic and familial structures. See K. Chockalingam and Annie Vijaya, "Sexual Harassment of Women in Public Transport In Chennai City: A Victimological Perspective," *Editorial DM Mitra 165 Criminology* (2008), 167.
72 McClintock (1995). In *Imperial Leather,* Ann McClintock discusses the relationship between cleanliness, bodily conceptions of 'purity' and imperialist ideologies of 'race', class, and sexuality.
73 See Shilpa Phadke, "Unfriendly Bodies, Hostile Cities: Reflections on Loitering and Gendered Public Space," *Economic and Political Weekly* 68, 39 (28 September 2013). Phadke states that 'respectable', meaning affluent Hindu women were perceived as

> ...unsafe due to the presence of two categories of people first, that of a certain kind of man, usually lower class, mostly migrant, often unemployed and sometimes uncomfortably Muslim; second, that of the un-respectable woman: the street walker, the bar dancer. The first group was perceived to be a threat to women's physical safety, the second and by no means less important group was perceived to produce a threat to the reputation of even 'respectable' women (51).

74 Atluri, fieldwork notes (2013).
75 Atluri, fieldwork notes (2013).
76 Bhabha, 321.
77 This chapter would not have been possible without the collegial engagement and thoughtful ideas of those whom I worked with as part of *Oecumene: Citizenship After*

Orientalism. I am deeply grateful for the scholarly support, guidance, and friendship that I received in working with *Oecumene.* I would like to especially thank Dana Rubin, who read a draft of this paper in my absence at the final *Oecumene: Citizenship After Orientalism* conference in the UK, while I was in India conducting fieldwork and participating in feminist enactments of the political. *āzādī.*

References Cited

Atluri, Tara. Fieldwork notes (New Delhi: 2013, 2014) unpublished.

Badiou, Alan. *Being and Event* (London: Continuum, 2007).

Baldwin, James. *The Devil Finds Work* (New York: Vintage Books, 1976).

Bhabha, Homi. *The Location of Culture* (London: Routledge, 1995).

Benjamin, Walter. *On the concept of history* (New York: Classic Books America, 2009).

Bergner, Gwen. "Who is that masked woman? Or, the role of gender in Fanon's Black skin, white masks," *Publications of the Modern Language Association of America* (1995): 75–88.

Braidotti, Rosi. *Nomadic Theory: The Portable Rosi Braidotti* (New York: Columbia University Press, 2008).

Branigan, Tania. "Latest Foxconn suicide raises concern over factory life in China," *The Guardian Online,* 17 May 2010. Online edition (accessed 9 September 2014).

Chatterjee, Partha. "Colonialism, Nationalism, and Colonialized Women: The Contest in India," *American Ethnologist* 16, 4 (Nov. 1989): 622–33.

Daiya, Kavita. *Violent Belongings: Partition, Gender, and National Culture in Postcolonial India* (Philadelphia: Temple University Press, 2011).

Dordi, Huzan and Margaret Walton-Robarts. "The Delhi gang rape and the South Asian diaspora: apathy or empathy," 7 February 2013 https://www.cigionline.org/blogs/outside/delhi-gang-rape-and-south-asian-diaspora-apathy-or-empathy (accessed 3 January 3 2015).

Foucault, Michel. *Radical Philosophy* 17, 13 (1977): 126–33.

"Freedom Without Fear Platform," 7 December 2013. http://freedomwithoutfear-platformuk.blogspot.ca/2013/12/indias-anti-rape-movement-experiences.html (accessed 6 January 2015).

Gaijala, R. *Cyber Selves: Feminist Ethnographies of South Asian Women* (Oxford: AltaMira Press, 2004).

Gordon, Avery. "Some thoughts on haunting and futurity," *Borderlands* 10, 2 (2011): 1–21.

Isin, Engin F. "Citizenship after orientalism," *Citizenship in a global world: European questions and Turkish experiences* 3 (2005): 31.

Isin, Engin F. "Citizenship in flux: The figure of the activist citizen," *Subjectivity* 29, 1 (2009): 367–88.

Kannabirān, Kalpana. *The violence of normal times: Essays on women's lived realities.* Women Unlimited, an associate of Kali for Women, 2005.

Maindarkar, Samyukta. "Section 377 and LGBT Rights: Here's What You Need to Know," 11 December 2013 http://www.samachar.com/section-377-and-lgbt-rights-here-s-what-you-need-to-know-nmlsKOebahf.html (accessed 22 May 2014).

McClintock, Anne. *Imperial Leather: Race, Gender, and Sexuality in the Colonial Contest* (New York: Routledge, 1995).

Menon, Nivideta. "'The impunity of every citadel is intact' – The Taming of the Protests Across the Globe Against Indian Supreme Court Judgment on Section 377."

3 February 2013, Kafila. http://kafila.org/2013/02/03/the-impunity-of-every-citadel
-is-intact-the-taming-of-the-verma-committee-report-and-some-troubling-doubts/
(accessed 9 September 2014).

Galaxy Magazine: Empowering Expressions. Online blog. http://www.gaylaxymag
.com/latest-news/protests-across-the-globe-against-indian-supreme-court
-judgement-on-section-377/ (accessed 16 February 2014).

Lawyers Collective. "LGBT Section 377." http://www.lawyerscollective.org/vulnerable
-communities/lgbt/section-377.html (accessed 3 January 2015).

Mishra, S.N., ed. *Socio-economic and Political Visions of B.R. Ambedkar* (New Delhi: Concept Publishing, 2010).

Muñoz, José Esteban. *Disidentifications: Queers of Colour and the Politics of Resistance* (Minnesota: University of Minnesota Press, 1999).

Pain, Paromita. "How Global Day of Rage Fueled Solidarity Protests," 2 January 2014, Occupy.com. http://www.occupy.com/article/how-global-day-rage-fueled-solidarity
-protests-indias-lgbt-community (accessed 7 September 2014).

Puar, Jasbir. *Terrorist Assemblages: Homonationalism in Queer Times*
(Durham, NC: Duke University Press, 2007).

Ray, Ishita Aditya, and Sarbapriya Ray. "BR Ambedkar and his Philosophy on Indian Democracy: An Appraisal," *Journal of Education and Practice* 2, 5 (2011): 74–82.

Roy Chowdhury, Poulami. "The Delhi Gang Rape: The Making of International Causes." *Feminist Studies*. Vol. 39, No. 1 (2013), p. 283.

Saha, Tanaya, and Akancha Srivastava. "Indian Women at Risk in the Cyber Space: A Conceptual Model of Reasons of Victimization," *International Journal of Cyber Criminology* 8, 1 (2014).

Saurabh, Sumit. "Revisiting Partition, 1947: Gender, Community and Violence," *Social Action* 64 (2014).

Sitapati, Vinay. "What Anna Hazare's movement and India's new middle classes say about each other," *Economic & Political Weekly* 66, 30 (2011): 39–44.

Sreenivas, Mytheli. *Wives, widows, and concubines: The conjugal family ideal in colonial India* (Bloomington, IN: Indiana University Press, 2008).

Su Kyi, Aung San. "Liberty" Lecture One. BBC Reith Lecture Series: Securing Freedom. 28 June 2011. Online transcript. http://downloads.bbc.co.uk/rmhttp/radio4/
transcripts/2011_reith1.pdf (accessed 16 February 2014).

The Hindu. "Full text of Justice Verma's Report (PDF)," 24 January 2013 http://www
.thehindu.com/news/resources/full-text-of-justice-vermas-report-pdf/
article4339457.ece (accessed 3 January 2015).

"Verma Committee Report, and some troubling doubts." Kafila, 3 February 2013 http://
kafila.org/2013/02/03/the-impunity-of-every-citadel-is-intact-the-taming-of-the
-verma-committee-report-and-some-troubling-doubts/ (accessed 16 February 2014).

Vijaya, Annie. "Sexual Harassment of Women in Public Transport in Chennai City: A Victimological Perspective," *The Indian Journal of Criminology and Criminalistics* 39, 3 (2008).

Vishnu, Uma. "34% in slums have no toilet, but 63% own mobile phone," *The Indian Express*, 22 March 2013 http://archive.indianexpress.com/news/34--in-slums-have
-no-toilet-but-63--own-mobile-phone/1091573/ (accessed 6 January 2015).

Viswanath, Gita, and Salma Malik. "Revisiting 1947 Through Popular Cinema," *Economic & Political Weekly* 10, 3 (5 September 2009).

"Who Decides?" Open Forum Questions. Oecumene: Citizenship After Orientalism. 25 March 2011 http://www.oecumene.eu/forum/open-questions/were-the-arabs
-awakened/who-decides. (accessed 7 September 2014).

Zimmerman, Jess. "Marital Rape Is Officially Legal in India," *Globalpost,* 13 May 2014. Online edition (accessed 21 May 2014).

Žižek, Slavoj. "Nobody has to be vile," 28, 7 (6 April 2006). Online resource (accessed 3 January 2015).

Žižek, Slavoj. *The Universal Exception* (London: Continuum, 2006).

Žižek, Slavoj. *Violence: Six Sideways Reflections* (London: Picador, 2008).

2012 Delhi Gang Rape. Wikipedia. http://en.wikipedia.org/wiki/2012_Delhi_gang _rape (accessed 16 February 2014).

12
Foolish Citizens

Deena Dajani

Abstract

This chapter provides a history of reason told through the figure of the fool. Drawing on the work of Michel Foucault and the naturalization of madness as mental illness, the chapter brings to light the role folly has played in this process. The argument is that folly has been implicated in establishing the 'mimicry of madness' as a configuration to be analysed separately to madness. This is traced in humanist literature (the chapter focuses on Erasmus's *Praise of Folly* 1511/1514) and in social and cultural histories of fools where a distinction was invented between 'natural' and 'artificial' folly. In the renaissance, madness as folly became useful and desirable, but madness otherwise disappeared from within courts (as an incoherent knowledge of the 'beyond'). In these ways, folly emerged as a structure that would come to stand 'in between' madness and reason, marking the border that distinguished them. Such imagined binaries are also shown to play into spatial and geographical configurations. This is illustrated through drawing on a tenth-century monograph by the scholar al-Nisabūri whose little book *'Uqalā' al-Majjanīn* (in translation: The Wise Madmen) has never been translated from Arabic in its entirety and yet reveals the extraordinary breadth and incoherence of traditions of madness at the time, providing glimpses into experiences of madness that have largely disappeared today.

Introduction

There is a considerable amount of literature on humour as critique. Within this literature, the figure of the fool holds special significance. Some argue the fool is symbolic of a historical relationship between humour and critique, based on the fool's license to speak truth to power. Others disagree, pointing out that the proximity of the fool to the court represents the limits of humour as critique; then, as now, those romanticizing an image of an outspoken fool overlook how ridicule and humour maintain, rather than question, the status quo. The genealogy of the fool proposed here does not enter into these debates over humour as critique but attempts something altogether different, and possibly even absurd: it constructs a possible history of reason (more particularly, the separation of reason from madness) told, for the first time, through the figure of the fool.

The grand narratives of reason attribute to it an ever-progressive trajectory that began with the enlightenment and has continued to the present day.[1] As a result, reason has become synonymous with progress. To write a history of reason, then, that documents its route not as an unfolding and self-evident 'truth' but through a series of contingent accidents, is an interesting (and formidable) challenge.[2] The fool illustrates one such contingent history of reason.

The chapter has five sections. The first section provides a brief discussion of the 'figure of man' central to liberal political theory and explores how this figure's claim to an objective and transcendental 'reason' reduces the scope of what is understood as political action. The second section follows from this first by considering 'reason' alongside what became symbolically associated as its 'other': madness. For this purpose the section offers a discussion of Foucault's thesis in *History of Madness*. To Foucault, the 'Classical Age' saw the resignification of madness: once a form of moral transgression, it became increasingly viewed as a natural phenomenon that can be objectively examined, and even cured, by the medical establishment.

The third section further attends to the separation between madness and reason described by Foucault by discussing the role of humanist writing. It pays particular attention to Erasmus's *Moria Encomium*, widely referred to as *Moria*, or *[The] Praise of Folly* in translation. The exact date of the manuscript is unknown, though it is believed the Christian reformist theologian and reformist Desiderius Erasmus (1466-1536) wrote it while recovering from a bout of sickness in England while staying at the home of his close friend and fellow theologian and reformist Thomas More some time between 1509 and 1511. Several different manuscripts exist, with slight variations. Most translations are based on the 1514 manuscript.[3]

This section argues that the discrepancy Erasmus created between what the manuscript's lead character and narrator, Stultitia, claimed she was (a fool) and what she really seemed to be (a sharp wit), constitutes the emergence or introduction of the theatrical metaphor into debates of the time. As far as I can ascertain, this is not something that has been discussed in the literature on Erasmus's *Moria*. The section shows that Erasmus effectively invoked a 'pretend madness' to symbolize the 'pretend reason' of those he opposed, effectively giving rise to configurations of 'authentic reason' (his own, superior, Christian reason) and 'authentic madness' (what is now recognizable as mental illness).

The fourth section traces this same distinction in historic figurations of fools, which at various time reproduced their own versions of the 'authentic/ pretend' classification, more commonly referred to in the literature as the 'natural/artificial' distinction. The persistence of various attempts to affirm this distinction, from the court to the church, all represent a vested interest in making a clear distinction between the 'mimicry of madness' and 'madness proper'. In so doing, they were effectively creating a structure through which something would come to stand 'in between' madness and reason, marking the boundary that distinguished them. Folly as 'pretend madness' came to personify this structure, and the ambiguity of its figure (drawing as the fool did on both madness and reason) was decisive for this separation.

Following these sections, the chapter turns to a tenth-century Islamic scholar by the name of Abu al-Qasem al-Hasan al-Nisabūri and tries to trace what other possible traditions of 'pretend madness' existed beyond those constituting the Western tradition of folly – traditions that did not rely on or reproduce the 'natural/artificial' distinction.

Reason's Man

It has been widely argued that liberal political theory relies on the 'figure of man' – that 'autonomous, self-directing subject of its own representations and behaviour' – as the locus of reason, agency, and will.[4] Feminists have furthermore argued that liberal and socialist political theory alike – although offering different interpretations of freedom and equality – both propagate a notion of the individual that is remarkably similar: one that claims to inhabit a universal, undifferentiated place but is nonetheless sexually particular, 'constructed on the basis of male attributes, capacities and modes of activity'.[5]

While the 'figure of man' can no longer escape identification as exclusionary, political theory's reliance on it continues through the invention of mechanisms such as 'inclusion', which promise the opening up of the subject position citizen to subjects previously unrecognized in its fashioned (and fashionable) guise – that is, subjects marked by race, gender, sexuality, and class. Through inclusion, the 'figure of man' is retained as benevolent and tolerant, allowing, even inviting in, those 'others'. It is important to acknowledge that any such transition in legal status – to a voting, participating, property-owning member of the public – remains to a large extent theoretical; in practice, experiences of marginality, inequality, and unfairness linger after nominal inclusion has been achieved.

For all its professed goodwill, inclusion is yet to develop a critical consciousness that recognizes how exclusion acted (and acts) to render invisible both the presence as well as the contributions of 'others' to the values of politics and justice. Instead, the invitation of inclusion is always restricted to being recognized from now on, forwards. A good example is Janet Radcliffe Richard's attempt to incorporate feminism into individualist liberalism, to bring it into and keep it within the boundaries of John Rawls's influential theory of justice.[6] Richard applies Rawls's theory to illustrate how women systematically suffer from forms of injustice and to argue that these systematic injustices must be eliminated. Yet, her stated aim in doing so is to emerge with a feminism that breaks with the 'inadequate reasoning' and 'moral confusion' she believes blights 'radical' and 'dogmatic' feminists. Richard sets out to prove that women can in fact be reasonable and unemotional, thereby contributing to a feminism with 'more general acceptability than it has at present' – a task for which Rawls is very useful.[7] As Carole Pateman recognizes, this approach does not consider how Rawls's theory, influential as it is, is inherently patriarchal.[8] Moreover, Pateman insists that this amounts to a domestication of feminism, neutralizing its radical intervention and thus making it safe for academic theory. In other words, the gesture to include feminism within existing and influential theories of justice amounts to an act of disarmament: it promises only to recognize women from now on, forwards.[9] There is no place, in inclusion, for considering how the very construction of the values held, assumed to be universal, taken to represent the good, are themselves constitutive of exclusions marked by difference.

This is just one example of how the claim to an objective and transcendental 'reason', one that excuses the silencing of some voices because of their 'irrationality', continues to surface, effectively affirming the imagined limits of what should – and should not – be considered 'political'.

Though inclusion is often championed as a contribution of liberal political theory, Richard Bellamy demonstrates how the extension of suffrage to all adult men and women in the late nineteenth and early twentieth century was deeply contested by political theorists in Western Europe and North America. Bellamy shows that scholars feared 'mass democracy' as a contradiction of the very ideals of rationality and individual agency their concept of democracy relied on. This produced a process of rethinking democracy that he traces in the works of Gaetano Mosca, Robert Michels, and Max Weber. It is Weber who culminates this process of rethinking and emerges with a conception of democracy not as a means by which the ruled control their rulers but as a 'mechanism for legitimating and improving the quality of control exercised by rulers over the ruled'. Rational democracy was best preserved, Weber found, by a political space whereby elite groups compete for the representation of a plurality of electoral groups.[10]

What of attempts to organize the world differently to these imagined limits and prescriptions of liberal political theory? We can name these attempts politics as political subjectivity, and they survive in various ways. Some, including social movements such as feminisms, civil rights movements, and environmental movements, mount challenges to institutionalized forms of politics through mass mobilization. This chapter, however, is concerned with attempts at organizing the world differently that are less researched than social movements, attempts that are captured by Hannah Arendt's description of the 'inarticulate political' and Michel Foucault's 'subjugated knowledges'. To both theorists, these attempts to organize the world differently were easily erasable because they were rendered illegible. Yet, they continue to survive, as Dwight Conquergood writes, as 'active bodies of meaning... eluding the forces of inscription that would make them legible, and thereby legitimate'.[11]

Foucault outlines two such knowledges. First, erudite knowledges that 'have been buried or disguised in a functionalist coherence or formal system-atisation'.[12] These are the historical contents that, once uncovered, reveal the struggles and contentions masked by the single, progressively unfolding narratives of systematizing thought. Second are what he refers to as popu-lar or naïve knowledges that are unqualified or even directly disqualified, 'located low down on the hierarchy, beneath the required level of cognition of scientific knowledges'.[13] These are parallel and marginal knowledges, such as that of the psychiatric person, the nurse, the doctor – but they are not common-sense knowledge; they are particular, incapable of unanimity or of producing unitary theories or claims to transcendental 'truth'.

Arendt's 'inarticulate political' is also concerned with how common sense came to dominate knowledge production and prescribe the limits of pol-itics. She marks as a 'foundational moment' the Roman commitment to extract common sense and save it from the past in the form of tradition, that is, the insistence on imposing *permanent* rules to govern the *changing* circumstances of acting citizens. As this became the highest criterion for the management of public affairs, traditions that did not fit into this prescrip-tive category and standard fell into constant danger of oblivion. The endan-gered subject that concerned Arendt was that of Greek drama and poetry which offered a different way of understanding human nature and organ-izing the world. The political possibilities of this endangered subject lie in its acting and doing, and in its uncertainty and unintentionality of action. That is, the open-endedness of possibilities. This put it at complete odds with the common-sense understanding of political action: one reduced to means-end calculus and extraction from the past as a means to governing self and others.[14]

This tradition Arendt traces to Plato. From Plato onwards, she writes, the category of the political offered by Greek drama and poetry (of subjects act-ing with uncertainty) is replaced by the 'figure of man' as governor of the self and others. She therefore attributes this to Plato's constitution of ideas as superior to action.[15]

Yet, could there be another way of understanding the division? One prem-ised on the very 'theatricality' of the subject of drama and poetry, consti-tuted not just as inferior to ideas but also on the basis of its 'inauthentic' representations. It could be argued that from Plato and extending to Rous-seau there exists a tradition of defining what politics is by an ardent rejection of *mimesis* (imitation) through poetry (in the case of Plato) and theatre (in the case of Rousseau). The former would banish poets from his ideal repub-lic, while the latter actively wrote against the establishment of theatres in Geneva because of how detrimental he perceived theatre to be towards the aim of establishing an ideal political state. What this suggests is that at the limits of understandings of politics is a commitment to 'authenticity' and a fear of 'artificiality'.

If like Foucault and Arendt we think of these subjugated knowledges as the 'inarticulate political', then the commitment that arises is towards uncovering them and writing their genealogies as historical sites of struggle, harbouring within their folds the memories and possibilities of a world differently organized. In this vein, this chapter attempts to uncover how one particular way of organizing the world (once) existed along the margins of reason. The subject of this story is the fool. The fool, in many ways, is always present. In the historic imaginary it is present in the midst of court – at the very centre – through the figure of the court-fool: witty and subversive, inseparable from the king, able to voice aloud and close to the centre of power criticism exchanged only in whispers outside. This is also a story of how this particular way of organizing the world was accommodated – brought into and maintained – within the premises of rationality. Today, the dual figures of court-fool and king sometimes collapse into each other, so that only a short while ago we easily described George W. Bush as a fool as means of dismissing him, perhaps at the expense of naming with grave seriousness the effects of the decisions and actions he took in his position as a powerful and dangerous 'king'.

Undifferentiated Reason

Feminists have long made the argument that culturally valued rationality was developed by a shedding of values symbolically associated with femaleness.[16] By claiming that reason is male, Genevieve Lloyd insisted that this does not mean that women have their own truth or that there are distinctively female criteria for reasonable belief. Rather, it is to say that from the beginnings of philosophical thought, femaleness was constructed to signify what reason 'left behind': the dark powers of the earth goddesses, of forces mysterious and unknown. She began with early Greek literature to outline the centrality of the theme of rational gods and goddesses displacing the fertility and earth goddesses. In Euripides's version, she writes,

> [T]he infant Apollo slays the Python which guards the old Earth oracle, thereby breaking the power of the Earth Goddess. She takes revenge by sending up dream oracles to cloud the minds of men with a 'dark dream truth'. But these voices of the night are stilled through the intervention of Zeus, leaving the forces of Reason installed at Delphi.[17]

This transition, she writes, is presented as a triumph of the voices of reason over earlier earth mysteries. And from these early beginnings, Lloyd traces this process of the displacement of dark 'truths', or their shedding, through Plato and onwards in the Western philosophical tradition.

If all attempts at domination are but ones of occultation, these dark and mysterious powers, their relationship with forces unknown and their heralding of truths unclear and indeterminate, labelled female and left behind, can be seen reconfigured in the early renaissance in depictions of madness. In painting, art, and iconography, the passion and intensity with which artists have explored the dark secrets parallels the feverishness the cults of earth goddesses once provoked.[18] And yet, before these mysterious forces, once symbolically associated with femaleness and now finding expression through madness, could mount a possible challenge to reason, they were subjugated, this time through a long process that – as Foucault has shown us – constitutes our present history, where madness is confined as disease, as mental illness.[19]

Foucault argued in *History of Madness* that understandings of madness today are confined to mental illness.[20] This has been the case since the eighteenth century, when madness became the object of a medical establishment that explains madness as disease and aims to cure it. 'The language of psychiatry', he writes, 'is a monologue by reason about madness'.[21] It is a language that could have only come into existence where silence has taken over dialogue, giving the impression that a separation is there, has always been there, is nature itself. Such silence 'expels from the memory all those imperfect words, of no fixed syntax, spoken falteringly, in which the exchange between madness and reason was carried out'.[22] He thus describes his work as an archaeology of this silence.

Foucault identifies two shifts. The first occurred in the renaissance (that he identifies as the fifteenth and sixteenth centuries) and the second in what he calls the classical age (the seventeenth and early eighteenth centuries). Foucault describes the early renaissance as characterized by a proliferation of images relating to madness, where madness is depicted as a way of understanding the world – a knowledge – that relates to its tragic experiences, its intrinsic chaos, and the frailty of its human institutions.

The point here is that madness in the early renaissance constituted an undifferentiated experience of reason, one heavily associated with images of the apocalypse and death, of unknown and uncontrollable forces, and offering a different way of understanding how the world is organized (that is, one that is intrinsically chaotic). By the classical age, madness was given a concise and finite form as mental illness. Within this transformation another one occurs. The initial confinement of the mad in the early classical age was a moral – not medical – issue. Madmen were locked up with others considered 'deviant': prostitutes, the blasphemous, beggars, the unruly, and the unemployed.[23] Their rejection of reason was considered a rejection of nature, a moral and ethical transgression. Among those they were locked up with, they alone would come to be seen as natural objects, classified as such by the medical profession, while the others who once shared their spaces of exclusion continue to be confined for 'moral' reasons.

This process – which he refers to as the naturalization of madness – is then a dual process of differentiation. It operated, firstly, through classifying madness as a morally reprehensible rejection of nature, and then through its reclassification as natural object. And through this dual process of differentiation reason was established as superior, able to explain madness, to contain it, thus effectively suppressing knowledge of the tragic, of death, that madness alone could provide. Within this transformation in the relationship between reason and madness, the role played by folly is of particular interest.

Foucault writes that the beginning of the differentiation of experiences of madness occurred by means of two processes: first, madness became a form related to reason; and second, madness then became a form *of* reason. The first process he attributes to writings such as those of Erasmus, where reason and madness were clumped together, existing only in relation to each other, caught up in a circle of affirming and denying the other's 'truth', but both kept at bay by Christian thought that maintained itself as distant from both reason and madness, speaking about them from across an unbridgeable gap of irony.

The second process therefore emerges from this first. It begins, Foucault tells us, with Erasmus, is distilled through Montaigne and Charron, and comes full circle in Pascal, and it produces madness not as related to reason but as a part of it, a moment that exists within reason's wider and transcendental truth. Madness is even celebrated as a form of inspiration for reason, a resource to be utilized. In effect, however, madness ceases to be a driving force in itself; it exists within reason and is therefore containable within it. Here we have the emergence of reason that recognizes its own madness and is thus a reason in control, more powerful than ever:

> Now the truth of madness is at one with the victory of reason and its definitive mastery, for the truth of madness is to be interior to reason, to be one of its figures, a strength and a momentary need to be sure of its own powers.[24]

What Foucault does not make explicit is how the above two processes were enabled through the figuration of the fool and the different madmen of differing sanities that came to occupy that figure.

It has been argued that Foucault's readers have conflated or confused the understandings of madness ascribed to the medieval and renaissance eras. For example, Stephen Harper suggests that what many scholars refer to as 'the medieval conception of madness' belongs in fact to a later period. He therefore attempts to distinguish between definitions of 'madness' and 'folly', arguing that in languages besides French, 'madness' was used to refer to medical conditions, and 'folly' was used to refer to professional satirists.[25] While Harper is correct in assessing a conflation between the medieval and renaissance understandings of madness, his proposed 'clarification' of madness as distinct from folly compounds the problem. It attempts to create coherent and neat arrangements but fails to ask critical questions about how this came to be. Rather than accept distinctions as given representations of things, we should ask ourselves why a distinction was made at all, what social, economic, and political transformations the distinction was respond-ing to and what acts and experiences it was trying to curtail and limit. Only by engaging with the how of how folly was defined can we gain an under-standing of the eventual confinement of madness as mental illness, and the common-sense emergence of reason as superior, universal, and transcenden-tal – still held today as a value intrinsic to the 'figure of man' and the liberal political theories it sustains.[26]

Why did that conflation continue? The remainder of this chapter commits to illustrating how this conflation is itself significant. The preoccupation with distinguishing folly from madness masks the more interesting process: how folly emerged as a structure through which madness was separated from reason. This has given rise to four possible configurations: 'pretend madness', 'pretend reason', and, by implication, 'authentic reason' and 'authentic mad-ness'. Folly was central to the invention of these configurations that came to displace the spaces of undifferentiated reason; it was central to the ways they were conflated and have overlapped, as it was to the ways they diverged and transformed, with some further delineated and others disappearing.

Reconfiguring Reason

The following two sections illustrate how folly played a central part in recon-figuring the experiences that once constituted the spaces of undifferentiated reason. This section, following Foucault, traces this through the humanist literary tradition of the late renaissance but focuses particularly on Erasmus whose *Moria* is widely considered instrumental in the transformation of folly into a literary tradition. The next section traces how this happened through the historical figuration of the fool that had a genuine existence outside humanist writing.

To begin with the first of these two tasks then, by the late renaissance (roughly the turn of the sixteenth century) a literary tradition had taken hold (through Erasmus as well as the writings of Montaigne and Rabelais) where madness was no longer tragic but critical. The great theme of this humanist writing, notes Jean Khalfa, is to indicate – through symbolically invoking madness – the discrepancy between what men are and what they *pretend* to be.[27] This reaches its most expressive form in Erasmus, where an attachment to oneself becomes the first sign of madness. Effectively, mad-ness is no longer linked to the world (to death, chaos, and experiences of the tragic), but 'slips into man', becomes a personal relationship between man and himself: in place of madness come human follies.

Erasmus's influence and popularity cannot be underestimated.[28] To Walter Kaiser, it was Erasmus's thesis on folly that has '*given* Europe the paradox of the wise fool'.[29] The oxymoronic fool is argued to have first emerged in its modern and influential form in the figure of Stultitia in Erasmus's *Moria*. Stultitia's sustained irony, writes Kaiser, became the prototype of fools to follow.

Up and until this moment, folly and madness were interchangeable. In fact, most of the references Foucault makes to medieval madness in his thesis are in fact references to folly and fools. For example, in order to underline the liminal situation of the mad in medieval society he evokes the theme of the 'Ship of Fools', a growing literary commonplace that he controversially claims had a genuine existence.[30] The exact meaning of the practice is not clear, he writes, but Foucault is interested in its symbolic associations: in the way different kinds of madmen (together called fools) were banished from city walls, left to wander between one city and the other, or in the countryside, and sometimes (he claimed) on boats that carried them to places of pilgrimage, indicating that they may have been thought of as senseless pilgrims in search of their reason. In Foucault's words,

> This enforced navigation is both rigorous division and absolute Passage, serving to underline in real and imaginary terms the liminal situation of the mad in medieval society. It was a highly symbolic role, made clear by the mental geography involved, where the madman was confined at the gates of cities. His exclusion was his confinement, and if he had no prison other than the threshold itself he was still detained at this place of passage. In a highly symbolic position he is placed on the inside of the outside, or vice versa. A posture that is still his today, if we admit that what was once the visible fortress of social order is now the castle of our own consciousness. [31]

This circulation of the mad places them beyond the confines of cities, or rather, as constantly displaced and in flux subjects between cities.

The distinction between madness and folly made by humanist writers did not (yet) exist at the time medieval writers such as Sebastian Brant, among many others, wrote of ships and the many different fools aboard them.[32] Humanist writers such as Erasmus would substitute the many fools aboard for a single fool closer to home. Unlike wandering madmen caught up in-between borders (and symbolically representing the rupture at the moment those borders were instilled), the humanist fool constitutes a different tradition, one that focuses on the state of affairs within the gates of cities, even internal to individual citizens. In other words, it breaks its previous relationship to what is beyond the border.

It is important to remember that Erasmus wrote as a reformer, and so he employed folly as a critical tool through which he could denounce peers whom he saw as lacking reflective capacities: philosophers, theologians, and statesmen blinded by their excessive use of reason. This Erasmus pursued not by rejecting their ideas or behaviour but by implying that their reason was a 'pretence', and therefore not 'real'.

Erasmus is widely interpreted as a pacifist and has been criticized for his apparent refusal to commit to either side of the reformation struggle.[33] Some, like Kathleen Williams, present this stance differently, arguing instead for his commitment to mediating between the two positions. She reads the *Moria* in this light as symbolically representing the inseparability of 'good' and 'bad', in relation to the arguments of both sides of the reform debate, as well as in relation to human reason itself. Rhetorically drawing on Erasmus's meaning, she asks,

> May not worldly wisdom be called folly, and is not the truly Christian life folly when regarded from the point of view of such wisdom?[34]

This important literature on Erasmus's ideas fails to recognize the subtle ways in which Erasmus did take a strong position in the *Moria*. To consider that 'folly' in the *Moria* represented the inseparability of the 'good' from the 'bad' and 'wise' from 'foolish' fails to take into account the changing nature of these concepts themselves. Madness and reason were undergoing processes of change at the time Erasmus wrote the *Moria*, and rather than folly being understood as symbolic of their 'inseparability', it should be analysed for its contribution to transforming and redefining this relationship.

Erasmus's *Moria* played a pivotal part in this transformation, and this has not been recognized nor discussed in relation to his political ideas. Erasmus in fact introduces into the debates of his time what can be referred to as the 'theatrical metaphor', that is, the denouncement of political debate on the basis of its 'theatricality'. The heritage of this (unfortunate) metaphor can also be traced to Rousseau, as mentioned earlier, and to Plato before him. Erasmus – as far as I can ascertain – has never been considered as contributing to defining the relationship between theatre and politics.

In the opening line of the *Moria*, Erasmus clearly states that it is Goddess Folly (Stultitia) and not himself who speaks henceforth, but he follows this claim with a sharpness of wit and intelligent irony that is sustained throughout. This creates a discrepancy between what Stultitia claimed she was (a fool) and what she really seemed to be (a sharp wit). This 'pretend madness' ascribed Stultutia becomes more pronounced as her criticisms become sharper and she takes on the learned men of theology. As she skillfully unravels their actions, and shows them to be in contradiction to the teachings of Christ, the discrepancy between what these men claim they are (reasonable and devout) and how they actually act (self-serving) becomes clear. Stultitia's 'pretend madness' enables the reader to recognize the 'pretend reason' of the clergy. This is effectively the invocation and application of the theatrical metaphor into the debates of the time.

The fool thus took on monumental symbolic significance. He was no longer the blabbering madman, whose many impenetrable utterances were thought of as expressing the logics of transcendental tragic truths non-interpretable to man (with only a few sharp and critical utterances in between). In Erasmus and later humanist writings, the fool's *every* utterance is witty, intelligent, and purposeful: the discrepancy between his given title and his utterances suggesting an inverted state of affairs: a need to examine oneself more closely.

In other words, by utilizing a witty and ironic fool ('pretend madness') to question the claims to reason by some of his contemporaries (whom he indirectly ascribed a 'pretend reason'), Erasmus was in fact claiming an 'authentic reason' – his own Christian reason – without having to make an argument for it at all. Thus, by giving rise (without naming them) to configurations such as 'pretend madness' and 'pretend reason' in order to argue for 'authentic reason' without actually arguing for it, what emerges (if by implication or silence) is the assumed existence of an 'authentic madness' as well. In fact, in the *Moria,* discussions of madness are relatively scarce. The issue is raised and passed, enabling folly to define itself as a 'special kind of madness' – a desirable madness – that is able to pursue and share pleasure and amusement, a path to freedom from worry and anxiety, a personification of jest, laughter, and humour.[35] Erasmus's personification of folly in the *Moria* proved very popular and established a new literary tradition of its own.[36] And in this particular way, what folly in the *Moria* enabled – as a critical trope – was the setting up of a confrontation between the dominant reason of the court and church and Erasmus's own superior reason (a race between the 'good' and the 'better', if you will). Madness, in this equation, is redundant – the use of one of its figures merely a stunt.

By considering the relationship of Erasmus's 'fool' to madness as well as reason, we can emerge with a conception of the *Moria* not as symbolically representing the 'inseparability' of wise and foolish but as an important contribution to changing and redefining this very relationship. Therefore we can claim that Erasmus tames madness *by* praising folly; that is, by creating a separation where none existed before, he created a structure – folly – through which madness *as folly* became useful and desirable, but madness otherwise disappeared from the hierarchy of recognized knowledge.

This story, though, is incomplete. I now argue in the following section that the separation between madness and folly that came to occupy the spaces of undifferentiated experiences of reason was produced not only through humanist writings but alongside them, informing them and responding to them, in and through historic figurations that at different times assumed the role of fool. What these historic figures illustrate are the tensions surrounding the configurations of madness and reason ('pretend/authentic') that folly gave rise to. This led to the invention of a distinction between 'natural' folly and 'artificial' folly that found its way into law as the following section will present. The crux of the argument is this: while folly's ambiguity at times assumed critical and subversive possibilities, its continued reliance, vis-à-vis Erasmus, on the trope of a folly that is not 'really' mad led to the privileging of madness only when that madness is a pretence, an illusion, a madness that is 'unreal'. Among the many figures of madness, the one that most closely approximates the 'figure of man' – the witty court-fool – is the one that would survive.

Genealogy of the Fool

The second process through which the separation between madness and reason was enacted existed alongside the literary tradition, informing it and reconfiguring it, through the fool's genuine existence in medieval and renaissance society. The word 'fool' itself evokes a powerful historic imaginary: a figure costumed to some extent, wearing an elaborate hat on his head, certainly entertaining but also potentially scathing and randomly so, making him somewhat troublesome because of this unpredictability.[37]

The story of the fool who became the court-fool of this historic imaginary begins in the medieval times with the lunatics and the 'grotesques' (dwarfs and hunchbacked men – and they were, in most instances, men) who were scouted for and then adopted into royal and elite households for varied reasons, from entertainment to charity to superstition. Many were ridiculed and mocked for their physical and intellectual infirmities, indicating that they may have played a role similar to the mock-kings of early fertility festivals.[38] Most would enter the service of the court willingly.[39] It must be that even the 'mad' recognized the value of being housed, clothed, fed, and paid monthly wages.

Foucault's focus on the liminal position of the mad along the border of cities, as subjects continuously in flux and in between borders, meant that he neglected to consider the symbolic significance of the mad that were 'let in'. The structure established *within* kingship for the mad (the fool that stands at the side of the king, speaking of things reasonable and unreasonable), only affirms Foucault's thesis on the liminal position of madness vis-à-vis the borders. At the founding of the kingdom, writes William Willeford, the drawing of boundaries (a necessary process to indicate the effective power of the centre) resulted in the exclusion of what lay beyond, a beyond where the magical field is still alive. The fool, to Willeford, is one prototype of the relationship to these numinous powers sacrificed at the founding of the kingdom.[40]

Most interestingly for the purposes of the argument here, court-fools were considered unaccountable for their actions (speech being considered an action), and were therefore granted impunity from punishment.[41] But the fool was on the cusp of gaining monumental recognition through the art and writings of the renaissance. In what remains the most expansive social and cultural history of the fool, Enid Welsford notes that '[w]hereas during the Dark Ages and the first part of the medieval period the fool makes but fitful appearances, by the beginning of the Renaissance he has become a fashion in society'.[42] When really successful in the practice of his art, she continues, he could acquire something of the notoriety of a modern music artist or film star. She mentions 'the infamous Gonella' who worked in the court of Marquis of Ferrara in return for a 'handsome salary'. Significantly, Welsford insists that it was commonly accepted that Gonella's folly was not of '… poverty of mind, but sprang from his vivacity, his acuteness and his sublime genius'.[43] And he was no exception. A few centuries into the renaissance, sixteenth and seventeenth century German court records reveal that court-fools (at least 14 of them) were employed as entertainers *because* they were 'clever, observant men, deeply engaged in the religious controversies of the time'.[44]

Through this transformation (if that is how the displacement of the mad and grotesque men at the hands of professional entertainers is to be called) the court-fool acquired a lineage as the antithesis of the supposed conformism and dogmatism of the medieval period. As is often the case, the fool's significance was attributed backwards, so that the medieval fool was ascribed renaissance values prior to them being identified as such. Anton Zijderveld insists the medieval fool represented the radical individualism the renaissance espoused, effectively teasing 'medievalness' with a tantalizing glimpse of what was to follow. The fool, he writes, held up a looking glass, like a mirror, that turned the norms of (medieval) reality upside-down: all of a sudden, albeit only momentarily, the foolish appeared wise and the wise foolish.[45] It was only a figure completely unrestrained by the norms of the times – like the fool – that could do this.

Significantly, then, the fool became the subject through which the transition into a new modern age was communicated. In other words, it is through historicizing folly by placing it in the transition from medieval times towards the enlightenment that the fool becomes a political figure. That is, a figure that communicates a social, economic, and political transformation.

Before the institutionalization of the renaissance fool as a 'type' was celebrated as radical individuality's surpassing medieval dogmatism, we now know that the ambiguity of the fool was a cause of concern. Beginning in the fifteenth century, a distinction was invented between what became referred to as 'artificial' folly and 'natural' folly. To Kaiser, the fact that the adjective 'natural' was considered necessary implies that 'artificial fools', from whom 'natural fools' had to be distinguished, had come into existence. 'Natural fools', it was believed, could not comprehend the conventions of society, religion, or state. It therefore followed that they could not be expected to obey a code incomprehensible to their minds and so their transgressions were tolerated, even laughed at. The new emerging category of 'artificial fools', however, could not be similarly tolerated because their transgressions were intentional: they turned nonconformity into iconoclasm and frankness into satire, they criticized the accepted order of things and voiced daring indictments of church or throne or law or society.[46] Thus was born the historic figure of the court-fool as critical – at around the same time Erasmus wrote the *Moria* – through a distinction between 'natural' madness and 'artificial' madness.

This distinction became institutionalized through law. In 1449, Scotland passed *The Act for the Putting Away of Feynet Fools,* meting out punishments like ear pinning, ear amputating, or even hanging to any court-fools discovered to be 'artificial', that is, actually sane.[47] The act is addressed to beggars and sorners (i.e., spongers, those living off others).[48] Importantly, it is only fools considered 'artificial' that were condemnable and therefore threatening. The 'natural' fools – those whose madness was considered 'authentic' – were presented as harmless to the institution of court.

Of major significance is that this tradition of thinking of folly as a disguise is a trope inherited directly from the medieval period the renaissance was trying hard to distinguish itself from. In medieval theatre folly was always a figure in disguise, not to be trusted because while appearing to be harmlessly playful, when unrobed it would be revealed that folly was vice attempting to conceal itself, to disguise its essence. Therefore, using this same trope, and entering through the distinction invented between 'artificial' folly and 'natural' folly, the renaissance came to produce folly again as disguised, but this time as disguised wisdom.

This trope of disguise can be traced back further to the thirteenth century French theologian Geuilelmus Peraldus to whom Sandra Billington attributes the earliest known explicit association between folly and the devil. Of interest here is how and why Peraldus came to make this association; Bellington writes,

> Whereas the church continued its protection of the witless man, an awareness developed of the need to distinguish such men from their mimics who were beginning to profit from the idiot's immunity from work in the houses of the great. As a discouragement, the church excommunicated all who earned their living in this blasphemous way.[49]

The distinction between 'real' madness and its imitation, variously emerging through the church in the thirteenth century and the court in the fifteenth century, reveals not the legitimacy or driving force of the economic interests informing the classification but a profound fear of madness that expresses itself through economic and political terms. This deep fear manifests itself through attempts to confine the mad, to control the possibilities of madness, and to punish those that do not adhere to this clear and neat arrangement. I suggest that it was not the fool's political or economic leverage that was the cause of concern, even when these are cited as his culpable transgressions. Within descriptions of these transgressions we find a pattern that establishes the mimicry of madness as a configuration to be analysed separately from madness itself.

Let us think of this in tandem with the previous section. The dispersed historic evidence suggests that the mimicry of madness (or 'pretend madness') was produced as a separate configuration, to be treated differently from 'authentic madness'. This separate configuration was initially seen as criminal and dangerous. This, as has been suggested, happened at the time that Erasmus wrote the *Moria* where, it has been argued, he introduced the idea that folly as 'pretend madness' has something to say about the state of affairs as 'pretend reason'. And yet, this transformation of madness into critical moral satire – through folly – if initially subversive, was quickly replaced by the emergence of 'pretend madness' as a form of professional entertainment, an avenue for celebrity and material gain. And in this process, 'authentic madness' – and by that I mean not to endorse the idea that such a thing as 'authentic madness' exists but rather to recall other figures of madness also once called fools – now disappeared, both within courts, as possessors of knowledge from 'beyond', and from prisons, as immoral (and therefore) dangerous subjects.

It is relevant to consider this with the thesis put forth by R. Houston in *Madness and Society in Eighteenth-Century Scotland*, which examines civil court inquests into the ability of individuals to manage their own affairs based on their mental capacity and insanity defences in criminal trials between 1700 and 1820.[50] One of the striking themes that emerge from Houston's book is how discriminating nineteenth-century witnesses were in describing madness as mental illness. He goes to great lengths to demonstrate how madness was distinguished from what could be mistaken for it, such as bad behaviour (brought about by the effects of drinking or gambling) as well as depression (by relating changes in behaviour to recent emotional and economic circumstances). Yet, while Houston takes this evidence to critique the idea that mental illness is a modern invention, his evidence can also be read differently. The complex and highly discriminate ways in which eighteenth-century Scots distinguished madness from all that could be mistaken for it (bad behaviour, depression, or those using the insanity defence to receive reduced sentences for crimes committed) are not reducible to Houston's presumption that madness is in fact a natural disorder – mental illness.[51] The evidence can also be taken to illustrate how the ability to distinguish between 'authentic madness' and 'pretend madness' (both inventions of the previous century, as I have demonstrated) was itself a defining feature of what it meant to be reasonable in the eighteenth century. In other words, the lengths to which witnesses went to argue for or against an individual's madness reflected how a rational disposition was related to the ability to clearly identify what was not part of reason: madness. If we rephrase this in the terms guiding this chapter, an ability to distinguish 'authentic madness' from 'pretend madness' made one reasonable and of a judgement and mental capacity admissible in court.

The conclusion of this section is that the recognizable court-fool is an ideologically saturated figure as he came to mark the transition between medieval conformity and renaissance individualism. To this end, the court-fool had to be invented in a particular guise, one that emulated the values the renaissance espoused. This was possible by adopting the criteria used by different authorities – theological, economic, and political – to distinguish between 'natural' and 'artificial' folly, the 'witless idiot' and his 'mimic'. Adopting these distinctions through the trope of disguise ensured the continued political impotency of madness.

The Travelling Folly

This invention of a distinction between 'natural' and 'artificial' folly, part literary and part historic, is the dominant framework through which the fool's critical possibilities are understood. In this sense we can say that understandings of madness are further limited in an important way: this tradition of folly, by separating folly from madness, rendered the fool political only if he was 'artificially foolish', if his folly was a disguise, if he was in court on the license of the 'natural fool' while not actually being one himself. It follows that the birth of the court-fool as a political figure turns out to also be the moment of the subjugation of other fools occupying the peripheries of rationality as widely conceived. This process described so far is not a naturalization of madness per se as much as it is a naturalization of the imagined binary between madness and reason, a binary that defined madness as reason's 'other'; a condition contained and represented by reason.

What is at stake is how such imagined binaries play into spatial and geographical configurations that also naturalize similarly imagined binaries. I am referring here to Edward Said's *Orientalism* and his insistence that the image of the European as 'rational, virtuous, mature, "normal"' corresponded to an 'Orient' conceived as 'irrational, depraved (fallen), childlike, "different"'.[52] Indeed there is great need to consider in detail the many ways in which the processes of the separation between reason and madness, and 'Occident' and 'Orient', speak to each other (and indeed the ways that they don't). Consider, for example, the coupling of 'irrational' and 'childlike' to describe (separately) madness and the 'East'. It reveals the double-sided impulse to dismiss but romanticize, to insist on the inferiority of the 'other' while at once relating to it a form of greater purity and innocence. This requires analytic work, as do other not so congruent forms of the two arguments each detailing how an imaginary binary came to be naturalized and take form as an inert 'fact of nature'. To Foucault, this can only be the result of contingency.[53] To Said, such distinctions are decades in the making; he writes, 'To say simply that Orientalism was a rationalization of colonial rule is to ignore the extent to which colonial rule was justified in advance by Orientalism, rather than after the fact.'[54] There is need for further research in this regard.

This chapter, which has committed to uncovering the role folly played in the processes of naturalizing imagined distinctions, will now further consider this in relation to the imagined distinction of 'East' and 'West'.

In this section I will therefore consider other relationships between madness and reason that existed beyond the borders of where the 'Western tradition' of folly (and the separation between madness and reason it enacted) is often discussed. More particularly, I seek to uncover traditions of folly that did not rest on the renaissance distinction between 'natural' and 'artificial' folly. In what ways could folly be politically transgressive without it reproducing itself as 'pretend madness' or reason in disguise?

To these ends I draw on a tenth-century monograph by the scholar al-Nisabūri (from Nishapur in modern-day Iran) who died in 1016 C.E. (406 Hijrī). Al-Nisabūri's little book is titled *'Uqalā' al-Majanīn* (in translation: The Wise Madmen) and has never been translated from Arabic in its entirety, and yet it reveals the extraordinary breadth and incoherence of traditions of madness at the time, providing glimpses into madnesses (that is, experiences and understandings of madness) that are no longer familiar to us.[55]

Al-Nisabūri's book includes an introduction that serves as the theoretical part of his book. In this introduction he makes an argument for madness *as* discourse, drawing on verses of the Qur'an alongside historical citations to demonstrate how 'madness' was used as a framework to interpret anyone whose values differed from the dominant. Al-Nisabūri uses his evidence to demonstrate how all prophets, from Noah to Abraham to Jesus to Mohammad, were accused of madness, especially during the early days of their prophecy, because of the aberration of the values and truths they spoke of from the norms of the time. He takes this to mean that madness then is not so much a condition as it is an interpretative framework used by those whose minds have been habituated to thinking a certain way.[56]

Following this theoretical introduction is a large number of short chapters comprising stories passed down to him, each relating to madness and folly.[57] Some chapters group stories according to a central theme (examples include 'He whose madness came from knowing and fearing Allah' and 'He who enacted madness and folly and sanity'), while others group stories relating to a particular infamous fool (examples include 'Bahlūl the fool' or 'Madman in Damascus'). Of interest for the purposes of our chapter here are four chapters that each group together a distinct tradition of what we may call 'pretend madness' that does not necessarily produce or rely on a 'natural/artificial' distinction. These chapters are titled 'He who enacted madness and folly and sanity', 'He who enacted folly for material gain', 'He who enacted folly to live a blissful life', and 'He who enacted folly to escape sin and crime'. Each of these chapters comprises several stories, but for purposes of demonstration, I will translate the first story of each of these chapters.[58] These translations have never been attempted before. Some types of folly will seem familiar, such as enacting folly for material again, as they survived (as we know) through the renaissance and became central to the historic imaginary of fool as we know him. But others offer examples of traditions of madness that, as described above, are no longer familiar.

He who enacted madness and folly and sanity

There are several types of such self-inflicted folly. Among them are those who choose madness as a way of getting to know themselves whilst also protecting themselves from others. I heard through Abu Mūsa 'Imran bin Muhamad bin al-Haṣīn who said ... I saw in al-Muṣīṣa a sheikh who wore around his neck a chain, and children were stoning him while he chanted,

> There are those who appear in the image of humans,
> But upon closer examination they turn out no humans to be.

I approached him and I said, 'Are you mad?' He said, 'I have madness of the limbs not of the heart', then he continued to chant,

> And I dissimulated my being with madness in order to avoid self-obsession,
> To those who are surprised by this logic, what can I say except: my logic is unknown.

He who enacted folly for material gain

I heard Aba Naṣr Muhamad bin Mazaḥim al-Badkhshī, who came to us a pilgrim, say ... There was among us a sane man, a laureate possessing the understanding of a poet who was called 'Āmer, and he was with his art a transgressor of what is permissible. A friend of mine told me that my friend 'Āmer had gone mad, so I asked after him until I found him in some villages with a group of youngsters around him laughing. And I said, 'Oh, 'Āmer, how long have you been in this state?' and he said,

> I have made myself mad in order to gain materially,
> for a brain in these days is forbidden.
> Oh, friend, do not blame a foolish brother, or laugh at him,
> for folly is many colours.

He who enacted folly to live a blissful life

The story was told by 'Abū 'Abdallāh Muhamad bin Saleḥ al-'Andalusī al-Ma'arfī who said ... I asked Zayd Ibn Sa'yd al-'Abdī, 'why have you let yourself and your appearance go so?' He said: 'I lived seriously and it drained me, so I took on folly and brought amusement to those around me, and a loss of anxiety to myself.'

He who enacted folly to escape sin and crime

We were told by 'Abū 'Aḥmad bin Quraysh bin Suleiman in the year 38 in Marū al-Rūdh that ... When *fitna* befell the reign of 'Uthman (may Allah be pleased with him) a man said to his family, 'Please chain me so I may be prevented from hurting you, for I am mad'.[59] So they restrained him. But after 'Uthman (may Allah be pleased with him) was killed the man said, 'Release me, I have awoken from madness with the grace of Allah who cured me from wanting to murder 'Uthman.'

Of the four stories, the second resembles the renaissance court-fool the most. First, 'Āmer is introduced as a very intelligent man. Second, he tells us he turned to folly for material gain. Third, he implies a second ulterior and subversive reason: that the intellectual environment of the time did not value thought (we already know his art was deemed transgressive). Finally, through his claim to madness he invites reflection on the foolishness of men around him ('Oh, friend, do not blame a foolish brother, or laugh at him, for folly is many colours.'). Nearly five centuries later, many of these characteristics of 'pretend madness' would emerge in Erasmus's Stultitia.

Though the three other stories can be themed under a notion of 'pretend' or 'enacted' madness, none of them produce this enactment as a theatrical or 'artificial' trope. Indeed, it is humanity that is theatrical, not madness ('There are those who appear in the image of humans, But upon closer examination they turn out no humans to be'). Interestingly, in all three stories, madness is associated with what is visible and material – the body: in the first story, madness is described as affecting the limbs not the heart, it is a falling out of the habituated ways of living in the world; in the third story, madness is associated with not taking care of one's appearance, that is, dropping out of the norms of civility; and in the fourth story, madness is related to a request to restrain the body and to live in proximity to but distant from one's own family. In the three other stories, then, madness is symbolic of a forsaking of the norms of the time in a visible way that is articulated through the body. This can be through neglecting to care for one's appearance as is expected of a civil man (as in the third story), withdrawing from civil life either through requesting to be put in chains (as in the fourth story) or roaming on one's own (as in the first story) which entailed choosing to be without the support of a family or tribe, without a city one belonged to, and thus to be at the mercy of cruelty and aggression (stone-throwing children). And yet, and this is what is truly fascinating, this focus on the body in no way gives way to an understanding of madness that is objective or natural. There is no 'natural' madness nor an 'artificial' one. The body seems symbolic of interaction with the world in which one lives. Therefore to forsake that world – as a form of protest – is to forsake the body, the medium through which that interaction happens.

The above stories in Al-Nisabūri's little book suggest this: that although the titles imply the fools in question 'pretended' to be mad, the stories actually describe people who practised withdrawal from the norms of society for various ethical reasons, whether as protest against a self-interested and individualistic culture or a means of living separately from a government perceived as corrupt, unjust, and immoral. No 'natural' state of madness is mentioned nor any such thing as 'artificial madness'. Pretend madness offered in real and material terms a different way of living in the world that was sometimes temporary and other times more permanent.

Conclusion

Today, folly as 'pretend madness' can be traced in traditions of the stand-up and satirical comedians, their (licensed) folly lasting the duration of the show or the episode; afterwards, they go back to families, they negotiate contracts with agents, they book holidays and pay tax. For to 'pretend to be mad' in the tradition of the renaissance is exactly to continue living in the world, or rather, in civility. There is no confusion, none whatsoever, with regards to their sanity. The criticism their enactment produces is licensed criticism that is protected under the right to 'freedom of speech and expression' and symbolically plays into claims of liberal democracy as healthy and tolerant.

Madness, today reduced to mental illness, is also implicated with various performances of civility. As symbolic of the 'figure of man's' benevolence, more and more attention is given to the treatment of those classified as mentally ill. Today, more privileges, such as voting, are extended to the mentally ill to mark their 'inclusion' as citizens.[60] The 'naturally' mad, the view seems to be, can be trained to enact reason as a testament to civility and liberal democracy. Correspondingly, the 'artificially' foolish (in their modern-day guises as satirists) can voice criticism freely, also as a testament to civility and liberal democracy. If this argument has any merit at all, then it is the fool, rather than the 'figure of man', that best explains the hegemony of reason in its liberal form today.

Notes

1 See for example, Peter Gay, *The Enlightenment: An Interpretation: The Rise of Modern Paganism* (New York: Alfred A. Knopf Inc., 1966).
2 See Walter Mignolo, *The Darker Side of the Renaissance: Literacy, Territoriality, and Colonization* (Ann Arbor, MI: The University of Michigan Press, 1995).
3 For a detailed discussion of the differences between the various manuscripts, particularly the exclusions of later publications, see Michael Andrew Screech, *Ecstasy and 'The Praise of Folly'* (London: Gerlad Duckworth & Co., 1980).
4 Christine Helliwell and Barry Hindess, "Political Theory and Social Theory," in *The Oxford Handbook of Political Theory*, eds. John Dryzek, Bonnie Honig, and Anne Phillips (Oxford: Oxford University Press, 2006), 816.

5 Carole Pateman, "Introduction: The Theoretical Subversiveness of Feminism," in *Feminist Challenges: Social and Political Theory*, eds. Carole Pateman and Elizabeth Gross (Lebanon, NH: Northeastern University Press, 1986).

6 Janet Radcliffe Richards, *The Sceptical Feminist: A Philosophical Enquiry* (Harmondsworth, UK: Penguin, 1982).

7 Richards, *The Sceptical Feminist*, see "Introduction" and "The Fruits of Unreason."

8 See Kearns, "A Theory of Justice and Love: Rawls on the Family," *Politics* 18, 2 (1983): 36–44.

9 Carole Pateman, "Introduction," x.

10 Richard Bellamy, "The Advent of the Masses and the Making of a Modern Theory of Democracy," in *The Cambridge History of Twentieth Century Political Thought*, eds. Terence Ball and Richard Bellamy (Cambridge, UK: Cambridge University Press), 70–103.

11 Dwight Conquergood, "Performance Studies: Interventions and Radical Research," *TDR (The Drama Review)* 46, 2 (2002): 146.

12 Michel Foucault, "Two Lectures," in *Culture/Power/History*, eds. Nicholas Dirks, Geoff Eley, and Sherry Ortner (Princeton, NJ: Princeton University Press, 1994), 202.

13 Ibid., 203.

14 Hannah Arendt, *The Promise of Politics*, Kindle edition (New York: Schocken Books, 2009), L970, 981, 1131.

15 Ibid., L1402.

16 Genevieive Lloyd, *The Man of Reason: 'Male' and 'Female' in Western Philosophy* (Minneapolis: University of Minnesota Press, 1984).

17 Lloyd, *The Man of Reason*, 3 – my emphasis.

18 See for example, Pinson Yona, *The Fools' Journey: A Myth of Obsession in Northern Renaissance Art* (Ann Arbor: The University of Michigan, 2008) on the iconography and visual representation of folly and its associations with death in the early renaissance.

19 Yannick Rippa inverts this reconfiguration of madness and femaleness; she considers that the confinement of women in the nineteenth century emerged from this earlier practice of the confinement of the mad as bearers of truths. *Women and Madness: The Incarceration of Women in Nineteenth-Century France* (Paris: Polity Press, 1990).

20 Michel Foucault, *History of Madness* (Abingdon, UK: Routledge, 2009).

21 Foucault, *History of Madness*, xxiii.

22 Ibid.

23 Ibid., xvii.

24 Foucault, *History of Madness*, 34–5. Many critiques of Foucault read this process as a favourable one; in other words, they seem to suggest that Foucault was advocating the recognition of the 'relationality' between madness and reason. Rather than idealize this process, I read Foucault as illustrating how this newly invented relationality was critical for the eventual naturalization of madness as mental illness. See for example Erik Midelfort's frequently cited chapter, "Madness and Civilization in Early Modern Europe: A Reappraisal of Michel Foucault" in *After the Reformation, Essays in Honour of J. H. Hexter*, ed. Barbara C. Malament (Manchester, UK: Manchester University Press, 1980).

25 Stephen Harper, *Insanity, Individuals, and Society in Late-Medieval English Literature: The Subject of Madness* (Lewiston, NY: Edwin Mellen Press, 2003), 11–17.

26 I would further argue that it is based on a misunderstanding of Foucault's reading of medieval madness, which Harper seems to interpret as a tradition of

permissiveness towards madness (see pages 13–21). Foucault, as I read him, does not make this claim. Indeed, he shows medieval madness to be a liminal position, ascribed spaces 'beyond' those of the city, indicative of moral transgressions. The epistemological break Foucault identifies relates to the change from understanding madness as a moral transgression towards classifying it as a phenomenon of nature that can be objectively treated with medicine. The epistemological break is not – as Harper seems to interpret it – a claim about 'free' madmen being (later) confined.

27 Jean Khalfa, "Introduction," in Michel Foucault, *History of Madness*, xvi–xvii.

28 Various scholars have discussed his influence on Rabelais; see for example chapters by Preserved Smith, Hoyt H. Hudson, and Kathleen Smith in Kathleen Williams, ed., *Twentieth Century Interpretations of the Praise of Folly: A Collection of Critical Essays* (New Jersey: Prentice-Hall, 1969).

29 Walter Kaiser, *Praisers of Folly: Erasmus, Rabelais, Shakespeare* (London: Victor Gollancz Ltd, 1964), 21 – my emphasis.

30 See Winifred Maher and Brendan Maher, "The Ship of Fools: Stultifera Navis or Ignis Fatuus?" *American Psychologist* 37, 7 (1982), 756–61.

31 Foucault, *History of Madness*, 11.

32 See Hoyt H. Hudson, "The Folly of Erasmus," in *Twentieth Century Interpretations of the Praise of Folly: A Collection of Critical Essays*, ed. Kathleen Williams (Oakland, CA: University of California Press, 2007), 24.

33 For a discussion, see Kathleen Williams' contribution in *Interpretations of the Praise of Folly: A Collection of Critical Essays*, ed. Kathleen Williams (Oakland, CA: University of California Press, 2007).

34 Ibid., 6.

35 Desiderius Erasmus, *Praise of Folly*, trans. Roger Clarke (Surrey, UK: Oneworld Classics Limited, 2008), 44–60.

36 Michael Andrew Screech convincingly argues that Erasmus's view on madness was more nuanced. Screech considers Erasmus's descriptions of Christian ecstasy a testament to the ethical value of being 'outside oneself' – that is, mad. And yet, Screech's argument reads this more nuanced understanding of madness into the *Moria* through Erasmus's other later works, notably his translation into Latin of the New Testament. Thus, regardless of what Erasmus 'really' thought or intended (the author, after all, is [metaphorically] dead), the discussion of madness in the *Moria* itself is too passing to mark a significant position. See Michael Andrew Screech, *Ecstasy and 'The Praise of Folly'* (London: Gerlad Duckworth & Co., 1980).

37 See Beatrice K. Otto, *Fools Are Everywhere: The Court Jester around the World*, (Chicago: The University of Chicago Press, 2007).

38 William Willeford, *The Fool and His Sceptre: A Study in Clowns and Jesters and Their Audiences* (London: Edward Arnold Publishers, 1969).

39 Enid Welsford, *The Fool: His Social and Literary History* (London: Faber and Faber Limited, 1968), 160.

40 Willeford, *The Fool and His Sceptre*, 156–7.

41 Otto, *Fools Are Everywhere*.

42 Enid Welsford, *The Fool: His Social and Literary History*, 139.

43 Welsford, *The Fool*, 128.

44 Ibid., 139.

45 Anton C. Zijderveld, *Reality in a Looking-Glass: Rationality through an Analysis of Traditional Folly* (London: Routledge & Kegan Paul, 1982).

46 Kaiser, *Praisers of Folly*, 7.

47 The act is named as such by Otto (2007, 36). On *The Records of the Parliament of Scotland* the act is titled 1450/1/20 'sonners and beggers' and is the ninth act among those issued by James II on 19 January 1449 AD [1450]. The act is available via the RPS Archives online: www.rps.ac.uk/trans/1450/1/11.

48 The translation of the act, as provided by the Scottish Archives above, reads: 'Item, it is ordained for the putting away of sorners, overliers, masterful beggars with hors, hounds and other goods, that all officers, both sheriffs, barons, aldermen and bailies, both within and outeith burghs, take enquiry at each court that they hold of the foresaid things, and, if any such are found, that their horses, hounds and other goods be escheat to the king, and his person put in the king's ward until the king has said his will to them. And also that the said sheriff, bailies and officers inquire at each court whether there are any that make themselves fools that are not bards, or such runners about. And if any such be found, that they be put in the king's ward, or in his irons, for their trespass, as long as they have any goods to live upon. And from the time that they have nothing to live upon, then their ears shall are to be nailed to the tron, or to another tree, and their ears shall be cut off and [they shall be] banished from the country. And if thereafter are found again, that they be hanged.'

49 See Sandra Billington, *A Social History of the Fool* (Sussex, UK: The Harvester Press Limited, 1984), 20.

50 Robert Allen Houston, *Madness and Society in Eighteenth-Century Scotland* (Oxford: Oxford University Press, 2000).

51 Indeed, it seems redundant to critique Foucault by trying to establish that madness as mental illness did in fact exist. Foucault's thesis, at least as I read it, is not an attempt to define what madness was and was not, it is instead an attempt to examine how the many possible interpretations of madness, and the many different figures of madmen, become reducible to the one: the mentally ill and confined patient.

52 Edward Said, *Orientalism* (New York: Random House, 1978), 40.

53 See for example, Michel Foucault, "Nietsche, Genealogy, History," *The Foucault Reader*, ed. Paul Rainbow (New York: Pantheon Books, 1984), 76–100.

54 Said, *Orientalism*, 39.

55 Shereen el Ezabi has attempted a translation of this introduction; see "Al-Naysaburi's Wise Madmen: Introduction," *Alif: Journal of Comparative Poetics* 14 (1994), 192–205.

56 Abi al-Qassem al-Hassan Ibn Muhammad Bin Habib al-Nissabouri, *Uqalā' al-Majjanīn* (Lebanon: Dar al-Kotob al-Ilmiyah, 2003).

57 In the Islamic tradition of *isnad,* he relates the process of narration through which the story was transmitted over the years. That is, he provides a genealogy of the narrators through which each individual story was preserved.

58 The translations are all my own, and they are based on the Arabic text of the manuscript as published by Dar al-Kotob al-Ilmiyah in 2003 (see note 56 above for full reference). This edited text is based on a handwritten manuscript that dates back to 300–400 hijrī (equivalent to the tenth and early eleventh centuries). The text is also available online. In the original text, each story begins with the *isnad* (see note 57 above) followed by the story itself, told through a mixture of prose and verse. In the translations I have provided, I have tried to replicate the fluidity of the language, as it traverses conventional genres, moving easily from prose to verse. I have, however, omitted the *isnad* that precedes each story, leaving only the most recent narrator that al-Nisabūri cites.

59 *Fitna* in this context can be defined as a period of affliction, strife, and corruption.
60 See Amelie Perron, Trudy Rudge, and Dave Holmes, "Citizen Minds, Citizen Bodies: The Citizenship Experience and the Government of Mentally Ill Persons," *Nursing Philosophy* 11, 2 (2010): 100–11.

References Cited

Arendt, Hannah. *The Promise of Politics*, Kindle Edition (New York: Schocken Books, 2009), L970, 981, 1131.

Bellamy, Richard. "The Advent of the Masses and the Making of a Modern Theory of Democracy," in *The Cambridge History of Twentieth Century Political Thought*, eds. Terence Ball and Richard Bellamy (Cambridge, UK: Cambridge University Press), 70–103.

Billington, Sandra. *A Social History of the Fool* (Sussex, UK: The Harvester Press Limited, 1984).

Conquergood, Dwight. "Performance Studies: Interventions and Radical Research," *TDR (The Drama Review)* 46, 2 (2002): 146.

Duncan, Andrew. *A letter [to His] Majesty's Sheriffs-Depute in Scotland, recommending the establishment of four national asylums for the reception of criminal and pauper lunatics* (Edinburgh, UK: Patrick Neill, 1818).

Erasmus, Desiderius. *Praise of Folly*, trans. Roger Clarke (Surrey, British Columbia, Canada: Oneworld Classics Limited, 2008).

el Ezabi, Shereen. "Al-Naysaburi's Wise Madmen: Introduction," *Alif: Journal of Comparative Poetics* 14 (1994): 192–205.

Foucault, Michel. "Two Lectures," in *Culture/Power/History*, eds. Nicholas Dirks, Geoff Eley, and Sherry Ortner (Princeton, NJ: Princeton University Press, 1994), 202–3.

Foucault, Michel. *History of Madness* (Abingdon: Routledge, 2009).

Gay, Peter. *The Enlightenment: An Interpretation: The Rise of Modern Paganism* (New York: Alfred A. Knopf Inc., 1966).

Harper, Stephen. *Insanity, Individuals, and Society in Late-Medieval English Literature: The Subject of Madness* (Lewiston, ME: Edwin Mellen Press, 2003).

Helliwell, Christine, and Barry Hindess, "Political Theory and Social Theory," in *The Oxford Handbook of Political Theory*, eds. John Dryzek, Bonnie Honig, and Anne Phillips (Oxford, UK: Oxford University Press, 2006), 816.

Houston, Robert Allen. *Madness and Society in Eighteenth-Century Scotland* (Oxford, UK: Oxford University Press, 2000).

Hudson, Hoyt H. "The Folly of Erasmus," in *Twentieth Century Interpretations of the Praise of Folly: A Collection of Critical Essays*, ed. Kathleen Williams (Oakland, CA: University of California Press, 2007).

Kaiser, Walter. *Praisers of Folly: Erasmus, Rabelais, Shakespeare* (London: Victor Gollancz Ltd, 1964).

Kearns, Deborah. "A Theory of Justice and Love: Rawls on the Family," *Politics* 18 (1983): 36–44.

Lloyd, Genevieive. *The Man of Reason: 'Male' and 'Female' in Western Philosophy* (Minneapolis, MN: University of Minnesota Press, 1984).

Maher, Winifred, and Brendan Maher, "The Ship of Fools: Stultifera Navis or Ignis Fatuus?" *American Psychologist* 37, 7 (1982): 756–61.

Midelfort, Erik. "Madness and Civilization in Early Modern Europe: A Reappraisal of Michel Foucault," in *After the Reformation, Essays in Honour of J.H. Hexter*, ed. Barbara C. Malament (Manchester, UK: Manchester University Press, 1980).

Mignolo, Walter. *The Darker Side of the Renaissance: Literacy, Territoriality, and Colonization* (Ann Arbor, MI: The University of Michigan Press, 1995).

al-Nisabūri, 'Abu al-Qasem al-Ḥasan Ibn Muḥammad Bin Ḥabib. *Uqalā' al-Majjanīn* (Lebanon: Dar al-Kotob al-Ilmiyah, 2003).

Otto, Beatrice K. *Fools Are Everywhere: The Court Jester around the World* (Chicago: The University of Chicago Press, 2007).

Pateman, Carole. "Introduction: The Theoretical Subversiveness of Feminism," in *Feminist Challenges: Social and Political Theory*, eds. Carole Pateman and Elizabeth Gross (Lebanon, NH: Northeastern University Press, 1986).

Perron, Amelie, Trudy Rudge, and Dave Holmes. "Citizen Minds, Citizen Bodies: The Citizenship Experience and the Government of Mentally Ill Persons," *Nursing Philosophy* 11, 2 (2010): 100–11.

Richards, Janet Radcliffe. *The Sceptical Feminist: A Philosophical Enquiry* (Harmondsworth: Penguin, 1982).

Rippa, Yannick. *Women and Madness: The Incarceration of Women in Nineteenth-Century France* (Paris: Polity Press, 1990).

Said, Edward. *Orientalism* (New York: Random House, 1978).

Screech, Michael Andrew. *Ecstasy and 'The Praise of Folly'* (London: Gerald Duckworth & Co., 1980).

Spragens, Thomas A. *Reason and Democracy* (Durham: Duke University Press, 1990).

Willeford, William. *The Fool and His Sceptre: A Study in Clowns and Jesters and Their Audiences* (London: Edward Arnold Publishers, 1969).

Williams, Kathleen. "Introduction," in *Twentieth Century Interpretations of the Praise of Folly: A Collection of Critical Essays*, ed. Kathleen Williams (Oakland, CA: University of California Press, 2007).

Yona, Pinson. *The Fools' Journey: A Myth of Obsession in Northern Renaissance Art* (Ann Arbor, MI: The University of Michigan Press, 2008)

Zijderveld, Anton C. *Reality in a Looking-Glass: Rationality through an Analysis of Traditional Folly* (London: Routledge & Kegan Paul, 1982).

13
Citizenship's Empire

Engin F. Isin

Abstract

However it may have originated, during the nineteenth and twentieth centuries, modern citizenship became an institution deployed for colonial and imperial campaigns to create governable (rather than merely subject) peoples. Many postcolonial nations and states inherited and then effectively instituted citizenship for governing – dividing, classifying, disciplining, regulating – peoples. We observe this development in previously colonized territories and frontiers carved up by colonial powers such as in the Americas, Africa, and Asia as well as those that were ostensibly never colonized and yet were subject to imperial interventions, such as the Ottoman and Chinese empires. Today, many seemingly intractable questions about territory, people, sovereignty, and political subjectivity that are played out in postcolonial, postoriental, or even ostensibly decolonized societies, inherit this empire and willingly or unwittingly serve its ends, unable to break the hold of its allure and seduction, if not domination. Working with this premise, this chapter draws on studies of extraterritoriality as a technology of government that enabled empires to literally make up people in both domestic and foreign territories. These studies are intended to illustrate the origins of the contemporary workings of citizenship and develop a thesis for further research.

Introduction

The birth of the nation-state and the age of nationalism are often traced back to a long century from the age of revolutions in the late eighteenth century until the beginning of the twentieth century. It is in this period that the world became increasingly divided into nation-states, each with its claims to a people, control over a territory, and sovereignty over that territory by its people.[1] Whatever transnational or international arrangements and institutions may have come into being since then, such as the United Nations or the European Union, they have been based on the people, territory, and sovereignty principle of the nation-state.[2] Even a regime such as human rights is based on the recognition of this principle with its affirmation of the right to nationality as a human right.[3] The overall assumption is that the era of the nation-state has now displaced the era of empires.[4] In fact, nation-states are often seen as emerging out of crumbling and dissolving empires. The irony is, however, it has also been in this era of the nation-state that new forms of imperialism have emerged and persisted into the present. Since the late nineteenth century, it is not only that the old empires such as the British and French have assumed new forms but also new empires such as the American and Chinese have appeared on the global stage.[5] So it is rather difficult to describe modern history as an age of nation-states displacing if not replacing an age of empires as, arguably, not only is there an overlap between these two ages but also a mutual dependence between empires and nation-states, and by extension, between imperialism and nationalism. To put it differently, the overlapping border regimes of dividing people into citizens, strangers, outsiders, and aliens describes our world much better than an image of the world as an order of contiguous nation-states.

This is increasingly the emerging view in more recent studies on empires and imperialism.[6] In their impressive survey *Empires in World History*, Burbank and Cooper provide an example of this approach.[7] They explicitly reject a narrative of 'replacement' or 'displacement' of empires by that of 'nation-states' and illustrate how various repertoires of rule were taken up and deployed to govern both subject peoples and citizens. Similarly, Kumar recently questions whether empires and nation-states should be seen as opposite developments rather than as forms of rule that overlap and co-exist.[8] The importance of this relationship between empire and nation-state, between imperialism and nationalism, can shed some light on the puzzling relationship between nationality and citizenship. What, if any, relationship can we establish between nationality as membership in a people and citizenship as membership in a state? I have this question in mind as I reconsider the relationship between imperialism and nationalism in this chapter.

My point of departure is *The Origins of Totalitarianism* published more than 60 years ago, where Hannah Arendt provided more than a hint when she suggested that 'in theory, there is an abyss between nationalism and imperialism; in practice, it can and has been bridged by tribal nationalism and outright racism'.[9] How did Arendt see a relationship between nationalism and imperialism mediated through tribalism and racism? There is enough evidence in *Origins* that Arendt thought that imperialism, especially of the kind that emerges in the late nineteenth century (she often uses 1874 as the marker year), and nationalism had more than a spurious relationship.[10] In fact, it is so crucial that it is possible to interpret her argument about the origins of totalitarianism as residing in this very relationship: that European empires did not simply transform into competing nation-states; rather nationalism was a new form of rule that enhanced, facilitated, and transformed imperialism. A proposition then can be formulated as follows. Empires, or perhaps more precisely, empire-states such as Britain, France, and Germany actively encouraged nationalism both at home and abroad (though, as we shall see, differently) as a strategy of governing peoples with graded and differentiated statuses and actively encouraged the formation of postcolonial yet imperial nations – imperial in the sense that these newly formed nations remained within the orbit of imperial control and influence yet each aspiring to the people, territory, and sovereignty principle.

This is clearly an ambitious proposition, and it must be said that I am more teasing it out of *Origins* than suggesting that Arendt pursued it with any determination. My hope is that the more recent studies of empire and imperialism can be used to develop this proposition not only for a better understanding of her political insights but also to shed light on the relationship between nationalism and imperialism and nationality and citizenship. This chapter explores how nationalism may have functioned as a strategy of governing peoples through imperialism and the profound consequences this has for understanding modern citizenship as a technology of government. I elaborate further on this proposition in the section that follows, provide an empirical illustration from extraterritoriality laws in the subsequent section, and propose a thesis for further investigation in the concluding section.

Imperialism and Nationalism: Territory, People, Sovereignty

There are many variations of the nevertheless dominant thesis of the nation-state. But the common narrative that binds its threads together is – whether we choose 1648, 1776, or 1789 as its origins – that the nation-state gradually comes into being and eventually supplants if not displaces an age of empires by 1914. An extended yet contested version of this narrative would see 1989 as the definitive end of an age of empires and the triumph of the nation-state, especially the version presented as the Western type with the rule of law, democracy, and human rights as its linchpin.[11] The other skein that conjoins this narrative is two opposing movements: nationalism and imperialism. Out of the ruins of empires, first in Europe and America throughout the nineteenth century, and then across the world throughout the twentieth century, nationalism conquers imperialism, and the world is transformed into a world of about 200 nation-states.[12] This narrative prevails not only amongst the scholars of nations and nationalism but also amongst the most influential and astute scholars of empires and imperialism. Perhaps the most influential interpreter of imperialism, J. A. Hobson, for example, thought that 'nationalism is a plain highway to internationalism, and if it manifests divergence we may well suspect a perversion of its nature and its purpose. Such a perversion is imperialism'.[13] Hobson thought imperialism was a diversion if not a perversion from nationalism. For Schumpeter too, '[imperialism] does not coincide with nationalism and militarism, though it fuses with them by supporting them as it is supported by them'.[14] Both Hobson and Schumpeter argued that nationalism, though it may have found its sources in imperialism, heralded the disintegration of empires, the formation of territorially bounded states, and the formation of peoples in each of them. For both, imperialism is a perversion of nationalism proper.

As I have already suggested, more recent scholarship has shown some weariness about a unidirectional and comprehensive transition from a world of empires to a world of nation-states. Even Eric Hobsbawm and Charles Tilly, who are otherwise proponents of such a narrative, showed some restraint in expressing it. Hobsbawm, for example, thought that 'in the twentieth century more empires have ended than in any other; we know this, even though it is by no means clear what we mean by this statement'.[15] For Hobsbawm, although we may think that the empires have disintegrated, their legacy lives on through institutions that postcolonial and postimperial nation-states have inherited. Tilly too thought that 'only during the last two centuries have consolidated states – coercion-wielding organizations governing directly and rather uniformly in a series of heterogeneous and clearly bounded territories – become the dominant state form, first in the European world, and then, by conquest and emulation, in the world as a whole'.[16] Yet, Tilly also warned that '[f]rom Herodotus to Montesquieu and beyond, poets, historians, and philosophers have recurrently produced one of our culture's standard literary forms: the dirge for a fallen empire. Reflection on imperial decline has world-historical resonance because it records for all to see the fallibility of seemingly unshakeable human enterprises'.[17] So this variation of the thesis of the triumph of nationalism is that empires, although ruined and disintegrated, continue to live on in their traces or legacies. Edward Said in *Culture and Imperialism* argued that imperialism is a legacy rather than a living present. After agreeing with the prominent interpreters of imperialism – he notes Luxemburg, Hobson, Lenin, Schumpeter, and Arendt amongst them – Said staked his contribution as 'the privileged role of culture in the modern imperial experience'.[18] He thought in terms of the shadow that classical imperialism casts in our age rather than of imperialism as a living presence, let alone something that has perhaps given rise to nationalism. Said accepted that the age of empire ended but wanted to draw attention to the 'cultural influence' that it has continued to exert.

Arendt was amongst the first and perhaps the only scholar of her generation who explicitly rejected a transition from imperialism to nationalism and saw the two connected with each other. Moreover, she saw this connection not as a contingent but rather a necessary one. As she put it, 'imperialism must be considered as the first stage of political rule of the bourgeoisie rather than as the last stage of capitalism'.[19] Her claims have scarcely been discussed seriously and require further, albeit brief, consideration here.[20]

Written several years before the publication of the *Origins*, Arendt published a series of articles in which she made the argument that rather than being opposites, imperialism is an instigator of the kind of nationalism that emerged in the late nineteenth and early twentieth centuries.[21] Clearly distinguishing 'empire' from 'imperialism' and 'expansion' from 'conquest',

Arendt argues that despite well-known differences between French and British imperialism – the former attempting to create an integrated empire with colonies and the latter attempting to rule at a distance – both forms came to more or less resemble each other.[22] Older empires (before the nineteenth century) conquered and ruled colonies, but the nineteenth-century imperialism was based on expansionism and, surprisingly, nationalism. The new concept of nation that emerged from the French Revolution at the end of the eighteenth century constituted the principle of the sovereignty of the people and by its active consent the legitimacy of its government. But with its expansionism it became rapidly and increasingly difficult to maintain the narrative of sovereignty with fledgling and sprawling territories and peoples. For Arendt, it was important to understand the logic of this expansionism before understanding the response to it. What was the origin of this expansionism? For Arendt, it was capitalism in the sense that it was the new surplus people and capital that the rapid growth of industrial production had engendered. Although Arendt does not use the phrase, it was over-accumulation of capital *and* of people (in the sense Marx used it) that led to imperialist expansionism. But, unlike Marx, Arendt did not think that this was an inevitable consequence of an inherent development in capitalism.[23] Rather, it was a consequence of a series of events and rationalities – often accidental and contingent – that resulted in a new logic of imperialism. To give an account of this logic, Arendt tracks back to the late eighteenth century and suggests that the bourgeoisie, as the class that resignified private property, became the driving force in the development of the nation. For Arendt, the bourgeoisie was not originally interested in politics as long as the state protected private property. But its gradual political emancipation from both aristocracy and royalty arose from its need to invest both surplus capital and 'surplus' people in overseas adventures. (Arendt names these as superfluous capital and superfluous people.) This need arose from an over-accumulation of capital that could no longer create markets for investment and the surplus people it created because of its unequal distribution of ownership. The crucial insight here is that, for Arendt, the bourgeoisie invested in the idea of the nation to protect its interests as it expanded beyond the borders that contained it.[24] Meanwhile, people also began emigrating outside Europe. Arendt says, 'the new fact of the imperialist era is that these two superfluous groups, the owners of superfluous capital and the owners of superfluous working power, joined hands and left the country together'.[25] The argument that Arendt considers original is that the political emancipation of the bourgeoisie coincided with its entry into politics, and this transformed the relationship between nationalism and imperialism from one of opposition to protection.

It is worth then dwelling a bit longer on what Arendt herself thought was an original argument. The emergence of nationalism was not only contemporary with imperialism: nationalism engendered imperialism with the entry of bourgeoisie into the political scene. Empire in the historical sense of the term of creating an integrated government of subject peoples was almost impossible with this expansion since nationalism increasingly focused upon a sovereignty of people that could not be extended to subject peoples. Arendt emphatically says that providing citizenship to subject peoples was out of the question for both British and French imperial authorities, though the latter briefly experimented with it in Haiti. The question for imperialism was how to rationalize the essence of emerging citizenship in the nation with the status of subject peoples? It was this question that led to the invention of two new devices of imperialism: racism and bureaucracy, which, Arendt says, solved the inner contradiction between the body politic of the nation and its sprawling and fledgling territories. Calling both the owners of surplus capital and of labour alienated, Arendt says that in the colony both found themselves as new agents of nationalism. Having escaped the class struggle at home, they developed a new class consciousness as the bearers of their nations outside its borders. It was through them that 'expansion gave nationalism a new lease on life and therefore was accepted as an instrument of national politics'.[26] But what transpired in the colony at a distance from the centre was chauvinism, and it was this that bridged imperialism and nationalism. Arendt uses chauvinism to describe a heightened missionary nationalism in 'Imperialism, Nationalism, Chauvinism' but in the *Origins* she calls it 'tribal nationalism'.[27] Whether it is chauvinistic or tribal, the kind of nationalism that supported imperialism, or to put it differently, the kind of imperialism that needed nationalism, was rife with both race-thinking and bureaucracy. Between 1874 and 1914, rather than imperialism receding into history and nationalism triumphing, Arendt sees the emergence of a new form of rule that is neither nationalism nor imperialism and for which she does not have a name. Nevertheless, what is decisive for Arendt is that it is this form of rule that provides the logic of both the authoritarianism and totalitarianism that savaged the twentieth century.

I have provided here a condensed version of the argument where Arendt attempts to relate imperialism and nationalism especially at the turn of the twentieth century, and particularly between 1874 and 1914. The key point here is that her insistence on the emergence of race or the problem of governing subject races as a special problem and the rise of a new cadre of officers, what she calls bureaucracy, of imperial administration is a crucial insight that needs following through. Arendt's proposition that the political emancipation of the bourgeoisie and its territorial expansion gave rise to race and bureaucracy and this led to the development of a kind of nationalism – tribal nationalism or chauvinism – has profound and wide-ranging implications.[28] Here, I would rather leave the consequences that she draws from this logic aside and explore instead the effects of this argument on citizenship as a technology of government. Clearly, by using 'tribalism' and 'chauvinism' for describing the kind of nationalism that imperialism engendered, Arendt was closer to the prevailing view expressed by Hobson and Schumpeter, who saw imperialism as a perversion of nationalism proper.[29] But an empirical illustration of how the invention of race and bureaucracy were precipitated by the political emancipation of bourgeoisie, which in turn resulted in what Burbank and Cooper call empire-state, highlights the relevance of her insights for understanding modern citizenship.[30] The form of rule that Arendt did not – and perhaps could not – name may well be best described as 'empire-state'.

Governing Subject Peoples: Extraterritoriality as a Technology of Government

The problem of governing subject peoples was articulated anew during the course of the nineteenth century in colonial political thought. As Said observed, imperial bureaucrats such as Balfour, Curzon, Cromer, and Rhodes '... could say what they said, in the way they did, because a still earlier tradition of Orientalism than the nineteenth-century one provided them with a vocabulary, imagery, rhetoric, and figures with which to say it. Yet Orientalism reinforced, and was reinforced by, the certain knowledge that Europe or the West literally commanded the vastly greater part of the earth's surface'.[31] By the early twentieth century, especially British and French imperial officers had become convinced that military imperialism had exhausted the possibilities of governing subject peoples at a distance; new legal and political 'methods' had to be invented to govern subject peoples, which practically meant disciplining colonial peoples to govern themselves. How it is that colonial political thought reached this moment is too complex to discuss here, but Lord Cromer's 1908 piece on 'the government of subject races' is still a poignant testament to the incipient logic of the empire-state.[32] As Jack Harrington has illustrated, such thoughts were already emerging decades earlier.[33] Yet, Cromer clearly illustrated this logic by separating imperial power that carried its force with violence (he calls this 'the sword') from governing subject peoples through disciplinary techniques. He expressed doubt as to whether colonial peoples under British imperial rule could be solely governed through violence and obedience. The time was coming when subject peoples or colonial peoples would gradually be introduced to methods of governing themselves through discipline, civility, and liberty. He was certain that '[t]he main justification of Imperialism is to be found in the use which is made of the Imperial power. If we make a good use of our power, we may face the future without fear that we shall be overtaken by the Nemesis which attended Roman misrule'.[34] But such power was applicable only if the subject races were disciplined enough to subject themselves to it. For Cromer, imperial power was '...a method which is thoroughly uncongenial to Oriental habits of thought. ... Before Orientals can attain anything approaching to the British ideal of self-government they will have to undergo very numerous transmigrations of political thought'.[35] How were these transmigrations of political thought to be accomplished? For Cromer, the principle was that '... whilst the sword should be always ready for use, it should be kept in reserve for great emergencies, and that we should endeavour to find, in the contentment of the subject race, a more worthy and, it may be hoped, a stronger bond of union between the rulers and the ruled'.[36] These methods included fiscal, commercial, and administrative monitoring, oversight, and the negotiating of concessions and privileges. They applied not only to subject peoples in colonized territories, such as India, Egypt, or Sudan, but also to previously not colonized territories such as Ottoman, Japanese, and Chinese empires. In other words, the new techniques of governing subject peoples – enabled by racial categorization and expansion of the scope of bureaucratic management – also expanded the number of people who could be put under imperial influence. To effect imperialism did not require colonialism or even militarism; populations could be subjected to imperial rule at a distance through new imperial technologies of governing subject peoples.

Amongst such technologies of government for achieving imperialism without colonialism was extraterritoriality, which began as the privileges of imperial sojourners, travellers, merchants, and settlers in foreign polities and then turned into an intricate set of complex legal arrangements by which rights were organized for imperial subjects coming into contact with foreign territories. Western empires such as the British, French, and Dutch, but also the Russian and later the American, secured considerable rights for their own 'subjects', protecting them from the local laws in the foreign territories in which they found themselves. As empires previously not colonized, the Chinese, Ottoman, and Japanese empires were the most prominent polities that encountered extraterritoriality. Legal and social historians have studied these cases.[37] But more recently, extraterritoriality has been studied in the context of broader movements of imperialism and orientalism.[38] In her study on extraterritoriality in Uruguay in the nineteenth century, Laura Benton observes that 'the formal nature of extraterritoriality and its longer history (and later demise) in the Ottoman Empire and China may suggest that it was an altogether different phenomenon from the informal influences in Latin America and the collective legal strategies of foreigners there'.[39] Benton does suggest that the comparative legal status of foreigners in political discourse is important as it provides an insight into the making of the state in both Asian and American experiences of colonialism. Yet, Benton does not draw out possible consequences for this for the relation between empire and nation. I would like to suggest that the legal status of foreigners could shed light on the relationship between imperialism and nationalism that Arendt had observed. In other words, extraterritoriality as a technology of governing subjects connects imperialism and nationalism.

To elaborate this idea, I will illustrate how extraterritoriality was used by various European empires to influence both Ottoman and Chinese populations resident within their territories. There are instructive parallels as well as differences between how Ottoman and Chinese populations were subjected to imperial rule through extraterritoriality. But before that, let me attempt a preliminary definition of extraterritoriality. It is a technology of government that was extensively used by European empires from the eighteenth to twentieth centuries with increasing sophistication, whereby they put their own subjects living in other places under their own jurisdiction. This is an inadequate description since it does not do justice to its complexity. While extraterritoriality began with protecting merchants, diplomats, and other travellers, it increasingly became a governing technology whereby subjects living under different jurisdictions were claimed to 'belong' to European empires by language, religion, ethnicity, and culture and thus placed under their protection. So what began as mercantile and diplomatic protection gradually evolved into a technology of governing subject peoples that can be described with Ian Hacking's phrase 'making up people'.[40] European empires literally began making up subject peoples in other territories and jurisdictions by claiming them as their own as a way of expanding their spheres of influence. Of course, these claims were never one way, as they involved subject peoples in other territories responding to this interpellation by performing a subjectivity of belonging to European empires and enacting new forms of nationalism. It is this latter development of extraterritoriality that is of interest for shedding light on the relationship between nationalism and imperialism and the birth of the empire-state.

For the Ottoman Empire, the earliest extraterritorial privileges are known under the term 'capitulations' since most of these privileges were originally considered as concessions won by European imperial powers for their merchants and sojourners residing or travelling within Ottoman territories.[41] But the term 'capitulation' also conceals a more complicated history and imposes a later perspective on these privileges from the late nineteenth century when many thought that these capitulations were amongst the causes of the decline of the empire. However, these privileges go back to the mid-sixteenth century, and their granting could not at the time have been considered merely as capitulations. Privileges to foreigners under imperial jurisdiction were first granted to French subjects and then extended to British, Dutch, and eventually American and German subjects. As Quataert says, a capitulation meant that all subjects of a foreign king or subjects of republics would remain under the laws of their government once the privilege had been granted.[42] Throughout the sixteenth and seventeen centuries, Ottoman authorities granted such privileges with charters known as *ahdnames*.[43] Such charters set out the privileges granted, their scope, and limits and implementation. As Boogert shows, these charters created a network of legal documents which all together constituted an overall framework of privileges as governing subject peoples.[44] Such charters also created a category of persons known as *müste'min* – privileged sojourners and residents of the Ottoman empire. Such privileges became quite extensive and, in addition to French subjects, British and Dutch also acquired privileges. What started as mercantile and tax privileges increasingly became a more complicated system of claiming subjects at a distance or making up people.[45] Moreover, and more importantly, during the eighteenth century, *müste'min* privileges became intertwined with the privileges of *zimmis*, non-Muslim subjects of empire. Through legal certificates known as *berats*, non-Muslim subjects of empire began acquiring *müste'min* privileges, thus blurring privileges and rights. Such rights for *zimmis* included tax exemptions from the state and jurisdiction exemption from Ottoman courts, practically creating a new category of legal persons who were Ottoman subjects yet enjoyed British, French, or Dutch rights within Ottoman Empire.[46] The so-called *millet*, according to which various 'religious' groups were given privileges within the empire, originates from these *ahdname* privileges, especially with the emergence of the new legal category of persons that crossed between *müste'min* and *zimmis*. The concept of *millet*, which means 'nation' was a nineteenth-century invention to describe the relationship between religious groups, Jews and Christians, and Ottoman law. By the nineteenth century imperial authorities – European as well as American and Russian – increasingly created these categories of subjects with rights within the Ottoman Empire. This effectively generated 'communities of loyalty' and 'spheres of influence' on the one hand and on the other a pressure on Ottoman authorities to define subjecthood increasingly along religious grounds to distinguish the new category of persons with rights from other categories of Ottoman subjects. Arguably, the rise of nationalism within the empire in the nineteenth century had to do less with so-called inherent stirrings and more with the creation of this legal category of persons with rights as protection under British, French, and Russian imperialism. European, American, and Russian imperial authorities certainly played a major role in creating nationalism by interpellating subjects as their own: on the one hand, secessionist movements were encouraged by enabling the creation of a new person with rights and, on the other hand, pressure was created on Ottoman authorities to define Ottoman sovereignty and nationalism.[47]

The technology of governing subject peoples through extraterritoriality unfolded rather differently in China, though with remarkably similar consequences. First, European empires began deploying extraterritoriality in China much later than in the Ottoman Empire. It was essentially a nineteenth- and twentieth-century development. We cannot observe a similar transformation of a privileges system from mercantile, taxation, and jurisdiction privileges into a religious protection of groups. Second, most extraterritorial privileges were negotiated through treaties rather than a complex system of charters as in the Ottoman Empire. But the consequences were comparable in that 'conflict over extraterritoriality was also central to the formation of Chinese nationalism and demands for full state sovereignty'.[48] Similarly, extraterritoriality in China involved producing and protecting rights for foreigners and laws and courts associated with them. As Scully observes, 'between 1844 and 1900, over eighteen countries acquired extraterritorial privileges in China; in addition, Britain, France, and the U.S., extended these legal immunities to protégés or subjects from their respective colonies and protectorates'.[49] Clearly, more than a few empire-states found extraterritoriality a useful technology of government to claim subjects at a distance.

What is exactly at stake with extraterritoriality as it gradually evolved into a technology of making up people? I discern two significant processes that require empirical investigations to substantiate. First, what I called making up people at a distance (by drawing on Hacking) interpellated subjects whose loyalties, affinities, and interests became aligned with the empire-state. This process was much more complex than Arendt's observation about surplus people and capital migrating from the incipient empire-states and settling in colonies. It certainly included that. But it also involved governing previously never colonized societies such as the Ottoman and Chinese and creating subject peoples in them. This resulted in the invention of minorities in these polities – people who had not been subjectified as minorities and whose differences from dominant governing peoples were lived through various other arrangements. The appropriation or interpellation of peoples in other societies as their 'own' – British, French, German, or Dutch – transformed them into minorities whose rights empire-states undertook to protect. The technology of governing subject peoples through extraterritoriality meant making them up in this quite literal sense of creating people who identified with empire-states. It also meant extending the sovereignty of the empire-state across other territories and societies without colonizing them in the historical sense of that development.

The second consequence of making up people at a distance or in other societies is the creation of majorities and minorities as antagonistic social groups. If we consider the first consequence of making up people as creating a set of minorities, the obverse effect was the increasing pressure on previously dominant social groups – often quite heterogeneous and permeable, such as 'Ottomans' or 'Chinese' – in societies subjected to empire-state influence that began organizing themselves along homogenous and impermeable forms to coalesce into a nationality. The invention of 'Turk' or 'Han' as homogenous majorities and the inscribing of them with national characteristics such as a specific religion, culture, and even physical characteristics is the obverse effect of creating minorities.

What needs to be explored is whether the combined effects of these two processes was the recoding of citizenship as nationality. In both empire-states and their subject-states, with their division of peoples into majorities and minorities, citizenship – understood as membership in an empire-state or subject-state – became densely coded with the characteristics of the dominant majority, or its 'nationality'.

Citizenship's Empire

> To the memory of the British Empire in India which conferred subject-hood on us but withheld citizenship; to which yet every one of us threw out the challenge: '*Civis Britannicus Sum*' because all that was good and living within us was made, shaped, and quickened by the same British Rule.[50]

The dedication by Nirad Chaudhuri in his *Autobiography* four years after India achieved its independence as a sovereign nation-state captures the brilliant ambiguity of citizenship's empire. Whether this dedication was misunderstood is perhaps beside the point.[51] Its ambiguity points to my argument in this chapter: while empire's rule may have ended, citizenship's empire persists since that rule had already produced the citizen capable of ruling itself. This was in many ways also the point of liberal imperialism: the point was not to rule but to govern subjects insofar as they become capable of governing themselves. How that rule was established differed depending on whether it was deterritorialized (as was the case in postcolonial nation-states), reterritorialized (as was the case in numerous Euro-American colonies that remained dependent), or extraterritorialized (as was the case in the Chinese and Ottoman empires). What Ottoman and Chinese experiences with extraterritoriality illustrate is that governing subject peoples did not only involve subjugating indigenous peoples in colonized territories such as India but also creating categories of people subject to citizenship laws at a distance. The more recent studies on 'imperial citizens' as those who have been constituted as subjects of empire (especially the French and British empires) have shed some light on 'imperial subjects'.[52] These have focused on how people became imperial citizens once European empires occupied and colonized a territory.[53] Harrington, for example, illustrates how, as a result of French invasion and conquest, British subjects in Algeria lost the privileges they enjoyed under Ottoman rule and were bound by the law as it pertained among European nations.[54] But there has been scarcely any discussion of the creation of subjects of imperial government at a distance and its consequences for the invention of modern citizenship since the end of the Second World War – the ostensible end point of imperialism. We can legitimately ask what role did extraterritoriality play in the creation of modern citizenship? It was Barry Hindess who argued that governing internal subjects ought to be linked to governing distant subjects.[55] He said: '[A]lthough citizenship is most commonly regarded as a matter of relations between individuals and the state to which they belong – that is, of relations that are internal to the state in question – it is also one of the markers used by states in their attempts to regulate the movement of people across borders. These two aspects of citizenship are usually treated separately but there is much to be said for bringing them together.'[56] For Hindess, 'the imperialism of Western states and the development of citizenship within them had the effect of dividing the world into distinct kinds of populations: the citizen populations of Western states; noncitizen populations governed by these states; and populations of states that were neither subject to direct rule nor recognized as full members of the states' system'.[57] Although we now believe that this system of imperial citizenship has come to an end, Hindess argues, 'for all the striking differences between the order of European imperialism and our contemporary global order, there is an equally striking continuity between them'.[58] Yet, rather than seeing a continuity between empires and states, the thesis I would like to propose for further investigation is a different break than that which we have come to expect: rather than seeing the emergence of nation-states, we can discern the transformation of empires into empire-states that extended their sovereignties by making up people in other territories and societies. Postcolonial independence in previously colonized states and societies was perhaps entirely consistent with the formation of the empire-state. Perhaps even the postcolonial state as a subject state was an effect of the empire-state. It is in this sense that I believe the origins of the relationship between imperialism and nationalism and technologies of government such as extraterritoriality can shed considerable light on the formation of the modern empire-state and subject-state relations. The complex border regimes of dividing people into citizens, subjects, and aliens regardless of where they reside describes our contemporary situation much better than an image of the world as contiguous and symmetrical order of nation-states, each with its own people, territory, and sovereignty. It is also in this sense that I believe citizenship's empire persists through governing these relations between empire-states and subject-states.

That I reached this conclusion at the end of a project on citizenship after orientalism is both obvious and surprising at once. It is obvious because I originally followed the steps of Max Weber who, more consistently and explicitly than any scholar, not only thought that citizenship was a unique Western institution but that it was also the linchpin of modernity and capitalism. For Weber, citizenship enabled the performance of a 'pure and simple' identity that was above and beyond any other affiliation or belonging.[59] Citizenship meant to conduct oneself as a rights-bearing subject with no obligations other than those that are connected to those rights that one bears as an abstract (pure and simple) subject. Was Weber right in thinking that citizenship was a uniquely occidental (as he termed it) institution? This question appears at first rather a benign if not a banal question. But the more I dwelt on the question and tried to understand what Weber may have meant by this distinction and what importance he may have attached to it in the context of his broader comparative historical sociology, the more I became concerned with a latent assumption of his thought. We can call this assumption orientalism in the sense of assuming that there was indeed a fundamental distinction between occidental (European) and oriental (Chinese, Indian, and Islamic) political subjectivities and identities. As the chapters of this book attest, citizenship after orientalism means to interrogate the assumption that the West or Euro-American societies can usurp the image of rights-claiming or rights-bearing subjects as citizens. That Weber's orientalism was unfolding at the height of a new era of Euro-American empire was quite obvious to Edward Said if not in *Orientalism* (1979) at least in *Culture and Imperialism* (1994).[60] To establish the links between the workings of the complex institution of citizenship by which people are divided, disciplined, and governed and how empire-states and nation-states have been formed in our present is an obvious task of political theory.

Yet, what is less obvious, and hence perhaps more surprising, is to observe how political theory continues to consider citizenship as a phenomenon of the nation-state rather than the empire-state and provides contained and isolated images of its workings. Perhaps this is why struggles over citizenship are still understood in contained and isolated political forms rather than across comparative or cross-sectional transpositions that better articulate how they are experienced.

Notes

1   W. Brown, *Walled States, Waning Sovereignty* (New York: Zone, 2010).
2   A. Linklater, *Critical Theory and World Politics: Citizenship, Sovereignty and Humanity* (London: Routledge, 2007).
3   K. Nash, "Dangerous Rights: Of Citizens and Humans," in *Rights in Context: Law and Justice in Late Modern Society*, ed. R. Banakar (Farnham, UK: Ashgate, 2010).
4   There is, of course, a massive literature on the periods of empires and nation-states, but the two books by E.J. Hobsbawm illustrate the problem well where he ends the age of empires in 1914 yet he begins the age of nation-states in 1780. E.J. Hobsbawm, *The Age of Empire, 1875–1914* (New York: Vintage, 1987); E.J. Hobsbawm, *Nations and Nationalism since 1780: Programme, Myth, Reality*, 2nd ed. (Cambridge, UK: Cambridge University Press, 1990).
5   J. Burbank and F. Cooper, *Empires in World History: Power and the Politics of Difference* (Princeton, N.J.: Princeton University Press, 2010); J. Darwin, *Unfinished Empire: The Global Expansion of Britain* (London: Allen Lane, 2012); C. Douzinas, *Human Rights and Empire: The Political Philosophy of Cosmopolitanism* (London: Routledge-Cavendish, 2007).
6   The interest in empires and imperialism has been called variously as the 'imperial turn' or the 'turn to empire'. See A. M. Burton, ed., *After the Imperial Turn: Thinking with and through the Nation* (Durham, NJ: Duke University Press, 2003); J. Pitts, *A Turn to Empire: The Rise of Imperial Liberalism in Britain and France* (Princeton, NJ: Princeton University Press, 2005).
7   Burbank and Cooper, *Empires in World History: Power and the Politics of Difference.*

8 K. Kumar, "Nation-States as Empires, Empires as Nation-States: Two Principles, One Practice?," *Theory and Society* 39, 2 (2010).

9 H. Arendt, *The Origins of Totalitarianism*, 2nd ed. (New York: Harcourt Brace Jovanovich, 1973), 153.

10 E.F. Isin, "Citizens without Nations," *Environment and Planning D: Society and Space* 30, 1 (2012).

11 Hobsbawm, *Nations and Nationalism since 1780: Programme, Myth, Reality*; F. Fukuyama, *The End of History and the Last Man* (New York: Free Press, 1992); Hobsbawm, *The Age of Empire, 1875–1914*; M. Mann, *The Sources of Social Power: Rise of Classes and Nation States, 1760–1914* (Cambridge, UK: Cambridge University Press, 1993).

12 In fact, the phrase 'from the ruins of empires' is amongst the most commonly used phrases to describe this transformation from empires to nation-states. P. Mishra, *From the Ruins of Empire: The Revolt against the West and the Remaking of Asia* (London: Allen Lane, 2012).

13 J.A. Hobson, *Imperialism: A Study*, 3rd ed. (London: Allen & Unwin, 1938), 9.

14 J.A. Schumpeter, *Imperialism: Social Classes (Two Essays)*, trans. H. Norden (Cleveland: Meridian, 1951), 97.

15 E.J. Hobsbawm, "The End of Empires," in *After Empire: Multiethnic Societies and Nation-Building: The Soviet Union and Russian, Ottoman, and Habsburg Empires*, eds. K. Barkey and M. Von Hagen (Boulder, CO: Westview Press, 1997), 12.

16 C. Tilly, "How Empires End," ibid., eds. K. Barkey and M. Von Hagen (Boulder, CO: Westview Press, 1997), 1.

17 Ibid.

18 E.W. Said, *Culture and Imperialism* (New York: Vintage, 1994), 5.

19 H. Arendt, "Expansion and the Philosophy of Power," *The Sewanee Review* 54, 4 (1946): 608.

20 Arendt, *The Origins of Totalitarianism*, 153.

21 H. Arendt, "Imperialism, Nationalism, Chauvinism," *The Review of Politics* 7, 4 (1945); H. Arendt, "The Imperialist Character," *The Review of Politics* 12, 3 (1950); H. Arendt, "Totalitarian Imperialism: Reflections on the Hungarian Revolution," *The Journal of Politics* 20, 1 (1958); Arendt, "Expansion and the Philosophy of Power."

22 My summary of Arendt's argument here is based on the following: Arendt, "The Imperialist Character"; Arendt, "Totalitarian Imperialism: Reflections on the Hungarian Revolution"; Arendt, "Expansion and the Philosophy of Power."

23 M. Canovan, *Hannah Arendt: A Reinterpretation of Her Political Thought* (Cambridge, UK: Cambridge University Press, 1992), 75–9.

24 Three decades later, Michel Foucault practically developed the same argument but especially illustrated how the bourgeoisie, rather than constituting itself as a class in fact constituted itself as *the* nation. I examine the resonances between Arendt and Foucault on the emergence of the bourgeoisie as the nation in Isin, "Citizens without Nations."

25 Arendt, "Imperialism, Nationalism, Chauvinism," 452–3.

26 Ibid., 457.

27 Arendt, *The Origins of Totalitarianism*, 153.

28 As some commentators on Arendt have remarked, many of her assertions in the *Origins* are rather opaque, or perhaps she did not bother either to develop them further or took them for granted. Margaret Canovan, for example, remarks that 'Arendt did not make great efforts to communicate her ideas. As she once

explained in an interview, the motive behind her work was her own desire to understand, and writing was part of the process of understanding. ... This unusual sense of detachment from her readers was part of her more general detachment from academic debate, that "majestic indifference" to the standard academic literature on her subject on which Sheldon Wolin commented when reviewing her last book.' M. Canovan, *Hannah Arendt: A Reinterpretation of Her Political Thought* (Cambridge, UK: Cambridge University Press, 1992), 12–13.

29 It is true that *Origins* is practically considered a relic from the past rather than a contribution to political theory, political sociology, or historical sociology with a genealogical approach. But I agree with King and Stone's suggestion that Arendt's empirical work in *Origins* is too stimulating and original to dismiss or to read from the point of view of her later work. See R. King and D. Stone, eds., *Hannah Arendt and the Uses of History: Imperialism, Nation, Race, and Genocide* (New York: Berghahn Books, 2007).

30 Burbank and Cooper, *Empires in World History: Power and the Politics of Difference.*

31 E.W. Said, *Orientalism* (New York: Vintage, 1979), 41.

32 Lord Cromer, "The Government of Subject Races," *The Edinburgh Review* 207, 423 (1908): 1–27. See a similar argument, L. de Saussure, "Psychologie De La Colonisation Française Dans Ses Rapports Avec Les Sociétés Indigènes," in *Imperialism*, ed. P. D. Curtin (New York: Harper & Row, 1972).

33 J. Harrington, *Sir John Malcolm and the Creation of British India* (Basingstoke: Palgrave Macmillan, 2010). Referring to the early nineteenth century, he argues that 'Sir Henry Lawrence ... presented the strategic problem of governing British India in language that could easily have been drawn from' an even an earlier era, Malcolm's *Political History* or his *Government of India*. He quotes Lawrence saying, 'The land . . . has for nearly a thousand years been held by the sword' and that 'the time may yet come when we shall find our best safeguard in the hearts of a grateful people – but that time has not yet come, nor is there a near prospect of its advent. The sword, whether in the hand or in the scabbard, has yet some work to do' (169).

34 Lord Cromer, "The Government of Subject Races," 2.

35 Ibid., 13–14.

36 Ibid., 27.

37 M.H.B. van den, *The Capitulations and the Ottoman Legal System: Qadis, Consuls and Beraths in the 18th Century* (Leiden: Brill, 2005); P. K. Cassel, *Grounds of Judgment: Extraterritoriality and Imperial Power in Nineteenth-Century China and Japan* (Oxford: Oxford University Press, 2012); T. Kayaoğlu, *Legal Imperialism: Sovereignty and Extraterritoriality in Japan, the Ottoman Empire, and China* (Cambridge, UK: Cambridge University Press, 2010); G. W. Keeton, *The Development of Extraterritoriality in China* (London: Longmans & Co., 1928); S. S. Liu, *Extraterritoriality: Its Rise and Its Decline* (New York: Columbia University Press, 1925).

38 T. Ruskola, *Legal Orientalism: China, the United States, and Modern Law* (Cambridge, MA: Harvard University Press, 2013); E.P. Scully, *Bargaining with the State from Afar: American Citizenship in Treaty Port China, 1844–1942* (New York: Columbia University Press, 2001); L. A. Benton, *Law and Colonial Cultures: Legal Regimes in World History, 1400–1900* (Cambridge, UK: Cambridge University Press, 2002).

39 Benton, *Law and Colonial Cultures: Legal Regimes in World History, 1400–1900*, 251.

40 I. Hacking, "Making up People," in *Reconstructing Individualism*, eds. T.C. Heller, M. Sosna, and D. E. Wellberg (Stanford, CT: Stanford University Press, 1986).

41 J.B. Angell, "The Turkish Capitulations," *The American Historical Review* 6, 2 (1901); V.L. Menage, "The English Capitulation of 1580: A Review Article," *International Journal of Middle East Studies* 12, 3 (1980).

42 D. Quataert, *The Ottoman Empire, 1700–1922*, 2nd ed. (Cambridge, UK: Cambridge University Press, 2005), 79.

43 M. H. van den Boogert, *Capitulations and the Ottoman Legal System*, 27–9.

44 Ibid., 29.

45 Quataert says, 'In the sixteenth century, only small numbers of merchants obtained these legal and tax immunities. By the eighteenth century, however, large numbers of foreigners within the empire advantageously did business thanks to these tax exempting privileges', Quataert, *The Ottoman Empire, 1700–1922*, 79.

46 Ibid., 78–9; van den Boogert, *Capitulations and the Ottoman Legal System*, 54–5.

47 This is how Benton outlines the process: 'One of the most interesting elements of this complex political manoeuvring involved the alliances between Western powers and non-Muslim Ottoman subjects. France claimed a special relationship with Roman Catholics within the empire, and Russia with the much more numerous Orthodox Christians. Britain experimented with sponsorship and protection of Ottoman Jews, even viewing favourably the settlement of Jews in Palestine. The interventions encompassed support for political revolts (of the Serbs and Greeks, for example) and pressures on the courts in individual legal cases' Benton, *Law and Colonial Cultures: Legal Regimes in World History, 1400–1900*, 245.

48 Ibid., 249.

49 Scully, *Bargaining with the State from Afar: American Citizenship in Treaty Port China, 1844–1942*, 6.

50 N.C. Chaudhuri, *The Autobiography of an Unknown Indian* (London: Macmillan, 1951), vi.

51 See T. Koditschek, *Liberalism, Imperialism and the Historical Imagination: Nineteenth Century Visions of Great Britain* (Cambridge, UK: Cambridge University Press, 2011), 341–5.

52 S. Banerjee, *Becoming Imperial Citizens: Indians in the Late-Victorian Empire* (Durham, NC: Duke University Press, 2010); D. Gorman, *Imperial Citizenship: Empire and the Question of Belonging* (Manchester, UK: Manchester University Press, 2006).

53 J. Harrington, "Orientalism, Political Subjectivity and the Birth of Citizenship between 1780 and 1830," *Citizenship Studies* 16 (2012).

54 Harrington develops this argument in his contribution to this volume.

55 B. Hindess, "Citizenship and Empire," in *Sovereign Bodies: Citizens, Migrants, and States in the Postcolonial World*, eds. T.B. Hansen and F. Stepputat (Princeton, NJ: Princeton University Press, 2005); B. Hindess, "Divide and Rule: The International Character of Modern Citizenship," *European Journal of Social Theory* 1, 1 (1998).

56 Hindess, "Citizenship and Empire," 243.

57 Ibid., 246.

58 Ibid., 256.

59 M. Weber, *The Religion of India*, eds. H.H. Gerth and D. Martindale (New York: Free Press, 1917), 103.

60 Said, *Culture and Imperialism*, 154; Said, *Orientalism*, 259.

References Cited

Angell, James B. "The Turkish Capitulations," *The American Historical Review* 6, 2 (1901): 254–9.

Arendt, Hannah. "Expansion and the Philosophy of Power," *The Sewanee Review* 54, 4 (1946): 601–16.

Arendt, Hannah. "Imperialism, Nationalism, Chauvinism," *The Review of Politics* 7, 4 (1945): 441–63.

Arendt, Hannah. "The Imperialist Character," *The Review of Politics* 12, 3 (1950): 303–20.

Arendt, Hannah. *The Origins of Totalitarianism* (1951), 2nd ed. (New York: Harcourt Brace Jovanovich, 1973).

Arendt, Hannah. "Totalitarian Imperialism: Reflections on the Hungarian Revolution," *The Journal of Politics* 20, 1 (1958): 5–43.

Banerjee, Sukanya. *Becoming Imperial Citizens: Indians in the Late-Victorian Empire* (Durham, NC: Duke University Press, 2010).

Benton, Lauren A. *Law and Colonial Cultures: Legal Regimes in World History, 1400–1900* (Cambridge, UK: Cambridge University Press, 2002).

Brown, Wendy. *Walled States, Waning Sovereignty* (New York: Zone, 2010).

Burbank, Jane, and Frederick Cooper. *Empires in World History: Power and the Politics of Difference* (Princeton, NJ: Princeton University Press, 2010).

Burton, Antoinette M., ed. *After the Imperial Turn: Thinking with and through the Nation* (Durham, NC: Duke University Press, 2003).

Canovan, Margaret. *Hannah Arendt: A Reinterpretation of Her Political Thought* (Cambridge, UK: Cambridge University Press, 1992).

Cassel, Pär Kristoffer. *Grounds of Judgment: Extraterritoriality and Imperial Power in Nineteenth-Century China and Japan* (Oxford, UK: Oxford University Press, 2012).

Chaudhuri, Nirad Chandra. *The Autobiography of an Unknown Indian* (London: Macmillan, 1951).

Darwin, John. *Unfinished Empire: The Global Expansion of Britain* (London: Allen Lane, 2012).

de Saussure, Léopold. "Psychologie De La Colonisation Française Dans Ses Rapports Avec Les Sociétés Indigènes," in *Imperialism*, ed. Philip D. Curtin (New York: Harper & Row, 1972), 85–92.

Douzinas, Costas. *Human Rights and Empire: The Political Philosophy of Cosmopolitanism* (London: Routledge-Cavendish, 2007).

Fukuyama, Francis. *The End of History and the Last Man* (New York: Free Press, 1992).

Gorman, Daniel. *Imperial Citizenship: Empire and the Question of Belonging* (Manchester, UK: Manchester University Press, 2006).

Hacking, Ian. "Making up People," in *Reconstructing Individualism*, eds. T.C Heller, M. Sosna and D.E. Wellberg (Stanford, CT: Stanford University Press, 1986).

Harrington, Jack. "Orientalism, Political Subjectivity and the Birth of Citizenship between 1780 and 1830," *Citizenship Studies* 16 (2012): 573–86.

Harrington, Jack. *Sir John Malcolm and the Creation of British India* (Basingstoke, UK: Palgrave Macmillan, 2010).

Hindess, Barry. "Citizenship and Empire," in *Sovereign Bodies: Citizens, Migrants, and States in the Postcolonial World*, eds. Thomas Blom Hansen and Finn Stepputat (Princeton, NJ: Princeton University Press, 2005), 241–56.

Hindess, Barry. "Divide and Rule: The International Character of Modern Citizenship," *European Journal of Social Theory* 1, 1 (1998): 57–70.

Hobsbawm, E.J. *The Age of Empire, 1875–1914* (New York: Vintage, 1987).

Hobsbawm, E.J. "The End of Empires," in *After Empire: Multiethnic Societies and Nation-Building: The Soviet Union and Russian, Ottoman, and Habsburg Empires*, eds. Karen Barkey and Mark Von Hagen (Boulder, CO: Westview Press, 1997), 12–16.

Hobsbawm, E.J. *Nations and Nationalism since 1780: Programme, Myth, Reality* (1990), 2nd ed. (Cambridge, UK: Cambridge University Press, 1990).

Hobson, J.A. *Imperialism: A Study* (1902), 3rd ed. (London: Allen & Unwin, 1938).

Isin, Engin F. "Citizens without Nations," *Environment and Planning D: Society and Space* 30, 1 (2012): 450–67.

Kayaoğlu, Turan. *Legal Imperialism: Sovereignty and Extraterritoriality in Japan, the Ottoman Empire, and China* (Cambridge, UK: Cambridge University Press, 2010).

Keeton, George Williams. *The Development of Extraterritoriality in China* (London: Longmans & Co., 1928).

King, Richard, and Dan Stone, eds., *Hannah Arendt and the Uses of History: Imperialism, Nation, Race, and Genocide* (New York: Berghahn Books, 2007).

Koditschek, Theodore. *Liberalism, Imperialism and the Historical Imagination: Nineteenth Century Visions of Great Britain* (Cambridge, UK: Cambridge University Press, 2011).

Kumar, Krishan. "Nation-States as Empires, Empires as Nation-States: Two Principles, One Practice?," *Theory and Society* 39, 2 (2010): 119–43.

Linklater, Andrew. *Critical Theory and World Politics: Citizenship, Sovereignty and Humanity* (London: Routledge, 2007).

Liu, Shih Shun. *Extraterritoriality: Its Rise and Its Decline* (New York: Columbia University Press, 1925).

Lord Cromer. "The Government of Subject Races," *The Edinburgh Review* 207, 423 (1908): 1–27.

Mann, Michael. *The Sources of Social Power: Rise of Classes and Nation States, 1760–1914* (Cambridge, UK: Cambridge University Press, 1993).

Menage, V.L. "The English Capitulation of 1580: A Review Article," *International Journal of Middle East Studies* 12, 3 (1980): 373–83.

Mishra, Pankaj. *From the Ruins of Empire: The Revolt against the West and the Remaking of Asia* (London: Allen Lane, 2012).

Nash, Kate. "Dangerous Rights: Of Citizens and Humans," in *Rights in Context: Law and Justice in Late Modern Society*, ed. Reza Banakar (Farnham, UK: Ashgate, 2010), 71–82.

Pitts, Jennifer. *A Turn to Empire: The Rise of Imperial Liberalism in Britain and France* (Princeton, NJ: Princeton University Press, 2005).

Quataert, Donald. *The Ottoman Empire, 1700–1922*, 2nd ed. (Cambridge, UK: Cambridge University Press, 2005).

Ruskola, Teemu. *Legal Orientalism: China, the United States, and Modern Law* (Cambridge, MA: Harvard University Press, 2013).

Said, Edward W. *Culture and Imperialism* (New York: Vintage, 1994).

Said, Edward W. *Orientalism* (New York: Vintage, 1979).

Schumpeter, Joseph Alois. *Imperialism: Social Classes (Two Essays)*, trans. Heinz Norden (Cleveland, OH: Meridian, 1951).

Scully, Eileen P. *Bargaining with the State from Afar: American Citizenship in Treaty Port China, 1844–1942* (New York: Columbia University Press, 2001).

Tilly, Charles. "How Empires End," in *After Empire: Multiethnic Societies and Nation-Building: The Soviet Union and Russian, Ottoman, and Habsburg Empires*, eds. Karen Barkey and Mark Von Hagen (Boulder, CO: Westview Press, 1997), 1–11.

van den, Maurits H. Boogert. *The Capitulations and the Ottoman Legal System: Qadis, Consuls and Beraths in the 18th Century* (Leiden, the Netherlands: Brill, 2005).

Weber, Max. *The Religion of India,* eds. Hans H. Gerth and Don Martindale (New York: Free Press, 1917).

Index

Printed and bound by CPI Group (UK) Ltd, Croydon, CR0 4YY